LOGIC FOR PHILOSOPHY

Logic for Philosophy

Theodore Sider

OXFORD
UNIVERSITY PRESS

Great Clarendon Street, Oxford OX2 6DP

Oxford University Press is a department of the University of Oxford.
It furthers the University's objective of excellence in research, scholarship,
and education by publishing worldwide in

Oxford New York

Auckland   Cape Town   Dar es Salaam   Hong Kong   Karachi
Kuala Lumpur   Madrid   Melbourne   Mexico City   Nairobi
New Delhi   Shanghai   Taipei   Toronto

With offices in

Argentina   Austria   Brazil   Chile   Czech Republic   France   Greece
Guatemala   Hungary   Italy   Japan   Poland   Portugal   Singapore
South Korea   Switzerland   Thailand   Turkey   Ukraine   Vietnam

Oxford is a registered trade mark of Oxford University Press
in the UK and in certain other countries

Published in the United States
by Oxford University Press Inc., New York

© Theodore Sider 2010

British Library Cataloguing in Publication Data
Data available

Library of Congress Cataloging in Publication Data
Data available

Printed in Great Britain
on acid-free paper
by MPG Books Group,
Bodmin and Kings Lynn

ISBN 978–0–19–957559–6 (Hbk.)
ISBN 978–0–19–957558–9 (Pbk.)

For Ed Gettier

PREFACE

This book is an introduction to logic for students of contemporary philosophy. It covers (i) basic approaches to logic, including proof theory and especially model theory, (ii) extensions of standard logic (such as modal logic) that are important in philosophy, and (iii) some elementary philosophy of logic. It prepares students to read the logically sophisticated articles in today's philosophy journals, and helps them resist bullying by symbol-mongers. In short, it teaches the logic you need to know in order to be a contemporary philosopher.

For better or for worse (I think better), during the last century or so, philosophy has become infused with logic. Logic informs nearly every area of philosophy; it is part of our shared language and knowledge base. The standard philosophy curriculum therefore includes a healthy dose of logic. This is a good thing. But in many cases only a single advanced logic course is required; and the material taught in that course becomes the only advanced logic that many undergraduate philosophy majors and beginning graduate students ever learn. And this one course is often an intensive survey of metalogic (for example, one based on the excellent Boolos et al. (2007)). I do believe in the value of such a course, especially for students who take multiple logic courses or specialize in "technical" areas of philosophy. But for students taking only a single course, that course should not, I think, be a course in metalogic. The standard metalogic course is too mathematically demanding for the average philosophy student, and omits material that the average student ought to know. If there can be only one, let it be a crash course in logic literacy.

"Logic literacy" includes knowing what metalogic is all about. And you can't really learn about anything in logic without getting your hands dirty and doing it. So this book does contain some metalogic (for instance, soundness and completeness proofs in propositional logic and propositional modal logic). But it doesn't cover the central metalogical results one normally covers in a mathematical logic course: soundness and completeness in predicate logic, computability, Gödel's incompleteness theorems, and so on.

I have decided to be very sloppy about use and mention. When such issues matter I draw attention to them; but where they do not I do not.

A range of exercises are included. Some are routine calculation; others require more creativity. The ones that involve metalogic fall into the second category, are generally more difficult, and could be skipped in a more elementary course. Solutions to exercises marked with a single asterisk (*) are included in Appendix A. Exercises marked with a double asterisk (**) tend to be more difficult, and have hints in Appendix A.

I drew heavily from the following sources, which would be good for supplemental reading: Bencivenga (1986) (free logic); Boolos *et al.* (2007, chapter 18) (metalogic, second-order logic); Cresswell (1990) (two-dimensional modal logic); Davies and

Humberstone (1980) (two-dimensional modal logic); Gamut (1991*a*; *b*) (descriptions, λ-abstraction, multi-valued, modal, and tense logic); Hilpinen (2001) (deontic logic); Hughes and Cresswell (1996) (modal logic—I borrowed particularly heavily here—and tense logic); Kripke (1965) (intuitionistic logic); Lemmon (1965) (sequents in propositional logic); Lewis (1973*a*) (counterfactuals); Mendelson (1987) (propositional and predicate logic, metalogic); Meyer (2001) (epistemic logic); Priest (2001) (intuitionistic and paraconsistent logic); Stalnaker (1977) (λ-abstraction); Westerståhl (1989) (generalized quantifiers).

Another important source, particularly for Chapters 6 and 8, was Ed Gettier's 1988 modal logic class at the University of Massachusetts. The first incarnation of this work grew out of my notes from this course. I am grateful to Ed for his wonderful class, and for getting me interested in logic.

I am also deeply grateful for feedback from many students, colleagues, and referees. In particular, Marcello Antosh, Josh Armstrong, Elizabeth Barnes, Dean Chapman, Tony Dardis, Justin Clarke-Doane, Mihailis Diamantis, Mike Fara, Gabe Greenberg, Angela Harper, John Hawthorne, Paul Hovda, Phil Kremer, Sami Laine, Gregory Lavers, Brandon Look, Stephen McLeod, Kevin Moore, Alex Morgan, Tore Fjetland Øgaard, Nick Riggle, Jeff Russell, Brock Sides, Jason Turner, Crystal Tychonievich, Jennifer Wang, Brian Weatherson, Evan Williams, Xing Taotao, Seth Yalcin, Zanja Yudell, Richard Zach, and especially Agustín Rayo: thank you.

CONTENTS

1

WHAT IS LOGIC?

S INCE YOU ARE READING this book, you probably know some logic already. You
probably know how to translate English sentences into symbolic notation, into
propositional logic:

English	*Propositional logic*
Either violets are blue or I need glasses	$V \lor N$
If snow is white, then grass is not green	$S \rightarrow {\sim} G$

and into predicate logic:

English	*Predicate logic*
If Grant is male, then someone is male	$Mg \rightarrow \exists x Mx$
Any friend of Barry is either insane or friends with everyone	$\forall x [Fxb \rightarrow (Ix \lor \forall y Fxy)]$

You are probably also familiar with some techniques for evaluating arguments written
out in symbolic notation. You have probably encountered truth tables, and some
form of proof theory (perhaps a "natural deduction" system, perhaps "truth trees").
You may have even encountered some elementary model theory. In short: you have
taken an introductory course in symbolic logic.

What you already possess is: literacy in elementary logic. What you will get out
of this book is: literacy in the rest of logic that philosophers tend to presuppose, plus
a deeper grasp of what logic is all about.

So what *is* logic all about?

1.1 Logical consequence and logical truth

Logic is about many things, but most centrally it is about *logical consequence*. The
statement "someone is male" is a logical consequence of the statement "Grant is
male". If Grant is male, then it *logically follows* that someone is male. Put another
way: the statement "Grant is male" *logically implies* the statement "someone is male".
Likewise, the statement "Grant is male" is a logical consequence of the statements
"It's not the case that Leisel is male" and "Either Leisel is male or Grant is male"
(taken together). The first statement *follows from* the latter two statements; they
logically imply it. Put another way: the argument whose premises are the latter two
statements, and whose conclusion is the former statement, is a *logically correct* one.[1]

---

[1] The word 'valid' is sometimes used for logically correct arguments, but I will reserve that word for a
different concept: that of a logical truth, under the semantic conception.

So far we've just given synonyms. The following slogan advances us a bit further: logical consequence is *truth-preservation by virtue of form*. To say that an argument "preserves truth" is to say that *if* its premises are all true, *then* its conclusion is also true. "By virtue of form" requires that the truth-preservation be due solely to the form, not the content, of the argument. For example, if you drop an apple it will fall; so in a sense, the inference from "you drop the apple" to "the apple falls" is truth-preserving. But the former does not logically imply the latter because the truth-preservation relies on the content of the argument, in particular the fact that the premise is about dropping and the conclusion is about falling. By contrast, the fact that the argument from "Grant is male" to "Someone is male" preserves truth has nothing to do with the fact that its content concerns Grant and maleness; *any* argument of the form "α is F; therefore someone is F" preserves truth. "By virtue of form" is also usually thought to require that the argument preserve truth of necessity. If an argument's mere form guarantees that it preserves truth, then the fact that it's truth-preserving can't depend on the vicissitudes of the world. Thus the argument from "the apple was dropped" to "the apple fell" is again disqualified, since it would be *possible* for a dropped apple not to fall. By contrast, it's necessarily true that if Grant is male, then someone is male. As we'll see shortly, there are many open philosophical questions in this vicinity, but perhaps we have enough of an intuitive fix on the concept of logical consequence to go on with, at least for the moment.

A related concept is that of a *logical truth*. Just as logical consequence is truth-preservation by virtue of form, logical truth is *truth by virtue of form*. Examples might include: "It's not the case that snow is white and also not white", "All fish are fish", and "If Grant is male then someone is male". As with logical consequence, logical truth is thought to require necessity and to hold by virtue of form, not content. It is plausible that logical truth and logical consequence are related thus: a logical truth is a sentence that is a logical consequence of the empty set of premises. One can infer a logical truth by using logic alone, without the help of any premises.

A central goal of logic, then, is to study logical truth and logical consequence. But the contemporary method for doing so is somewhat indirect. As we will see in the next section, instead of formulating claims about logical consequence and logical truth themselves, modern logicians develop formal models of how those concepts behave.

1.2 Formalization

Modern logic is called "mathematical" or "symbolic" logic, because its method is the mathematical study of formal languages. Modern logicians use the tools of mathematics (especially the tools of very abstract mathematics, such as set theory) to treat sentences and other parts of language as mathematical objects. They define up formal languages, define up sentences of the languages, define up properties of the sentences, and study those properties. Mathematical logic was originally developed to study mathematical reasoning, but its techniques are now applied to reasoning of all kinds.

Take propositional logic, the topic of Chapter 2. Here our goal is to shed light on the logical behavior of 'and', 'or', and so on. But rather than studying those words directly, we will develop a certain formal language, the language of propositional logic. The sentences of this language look like this:

$$P$$
$$(Q{\to}R) \vee (Q{\to}{\sim}S)$$
$$P \leftrightarrow (P {\wedge} Q)$$

Symbols such as $\wedge$ and $\vee$ represent natural-language logical words like 'and' and 'or'; and the sentence letters $P, Q, \ldots$ represent declarative natural language sentences. We will then go on to define (as always, in a mathematically rigorous way) various concepts that apply to the sentences in this formal language. We will define the notion of a *tautology* ("all Trues in the truth table"), for example, and the notion of a *provable formula* (here we will do this using a system of deduction with rules of inference; but other methods, such as truth trees, are available). These defined concepts are "formalized versions" of the concepts of logical consequence and logical truth.

Formalized logical consequence and logical truth should be distinguished from the real things. The formal sentence $P{\to}P$ is a tautology, but since it is uninterpreted, we probably shouldn't call it a logical truth. Rather, it *represents* logical truths like "If snow is white, then snow is white". A logical truth ought at least to be *true*, after all, and $P{\to}P$ isn't true, since it doesn't even have a meaning—what's the meaning of P? (Caveat: one might *give* meanings to formal sentences—by translation into natural language ("let P mean that snow is white; let $\wedge$ mean *and*..."), or perhaps by some direct method if no natural-language translation is available. And we may indeed speak of logical truth and logical consequence for *interpreted* formal sentences.)

Why are formal languages called "formal"? (They're also sometimes called "artificial" languages.) Because their properties are mathematically stipulated, rather than being pre-existent in flesh-and-blood linguistic populations. We stipulatively define a formal language's grammar. (Natural languages like English also have grammars, which can be studied using mathematical techniques. But these grammars are much more complicated, and are discovered rather than stipulated.) And we must stipulatively define any properties of the symbolic sentences that we want to study, for example, the property of being a tautology. (Sentences of natural languages already have meanings, truth values, and so on; we don't get to stipulate these.) Further, formal languages often contain abstractions, like the sentence letters $P, Q, \ldots$ of propositional logic. A given formal language is designed to represent the logical behavior of a select few natural-language words; when we use it we abstract away from all other features of natural-language sentences. Propositional logic, for example, represents the logical behavior of 'and', 'or', and a few other words. When a sentence contains none of these words of interest, we represent it with one of the sentence letters $P, Q, \ldots$, indicating that we are ignoring its internal structure.

1.3 Metalogic

There are many reasons to formalize—to clarify meaning, to speak more concisely, and so on. But one of the most powerful reasons is to do *metalogic*.

In introductory logic one learns to *use* certain logical systems—how to construct truth tables, derivations, truth trees, and so on. But logicians do not develop systems only to sit around all day using them. As soon as a logician develops a new system, she begins to ask questions *about* that system. For an analogy, imagine people who make up new games for a living. If they invent a new version of chess, they may spend some time actually playing it. But if they are like logicians, they will quickly tire of this and start asking questions *about* the game. "Is the average length of this new game longer than the average length of a game of standard chess?" "Is there any strategy that guarantees victory?" Analogously, logicians ask questions about logical systems. "What formulas can be proven in such and such a system?" "Can you prove the same formulas in this system as in system X?" "Can a computer program be written to determine whether a given formula is provable in this system?" The study of such questions *about* formal systems is called "metalogic".

The best way to definitively answer metalogical questions is to use the methods of mathematics. And to use the methods of mathematics, we need to have rigorous definitions of the crucial terms that are in play. For example, in Chapter 2 we will mathematically demonstrate that "every formula that is provable (in a certain formal system) is a tautology". But doing so requires carefully defining the crucial terms: 'formula', 'provable', and 'tautology'; and the best way to do this is to formalize. We treat the languages of logic as mathematical objects so that we can mathematically demonstrate facts about them.

Metalogic is a fascinating and complex subject; and other things being equal, it's good to know as much about it as you can. Now, other things are rarely equal; and the premise of this book is that if push sadly comes to shove, limited classroom time should be devoted to achieving logic literacy, rather than to a full study of metalogic in all its glory. But still, logic literacy *does* require understanding metalogic: understanding what it is, what it accomplishes, and how one goes about doing it. So we will be doing a decent amount of metalogic in this book. But not too much, and not the harder bits.

Much of metalogic consists of proving things about formal systems. And sometimes, those formal systems themselves concern proof. For example, as I said a moment ago, we will prove in Chapter 2 that every provable formula is a tautology. If this seems dizzying, keep in mind that 'proof' here is being used in two different senses. There are *metalogic proofs*, and there are *proofs in formal systems*. Metalogic proofs are phrased in natural language (perhaps augmented with mathematical vocabulary), and employ informal (though rigorous!) reasoning of the sort one would encounter in a mathematics book. The Chapter 2 argument that "every provable formula is a tautology" will be a metalogic proof. Proofs in formal systems, on the other hand, are phrased using sentences of formal languages, and proceed according to prescribed formal rules. 'Provable' in the statement 'every provable formula is a tautology' signifies proof in a certain formal system (one that we will introduce in

Chapter 2), not metalogic proof.

Logicians often distinguish the "object language" from the "metalanguage". The object language is the language that's being studied. One example is the language of propositional logic. Its sentences look like this:

$$P \wedge Q$$
$$\sim(P \vee Q) \leftrightarrow R$$

The metalanguage is the language we use to talk about the object language. In the case of the present book, the metalanguage is English. Here are some example sentences of the metalanguage:

'$P \wedge Q$' is a formula with three symbols

Every formula has the same number of left parentheses as right parentheses

Every provable formula is a tautology

Thus we formulate metalogical claims about an object language in the metalanguage, and prove such claims by reasoning in the metalanguage.

Using the metalanguage to make statements about words can sometimes be tricky to do properly. In an effort to make a statement about the name of the United States's most excellent city, suppose I say:

(1) Philadelphia is made up of twelve letters

Sentence (1) does not at all capture my intention. It says that a certain *city* is made up of twelve letters. But cities aren't made up of letters; they're made up of things like buildings, streets, and people. The problem with sentence (1) is that its subject is the word 'Philadelphia'. The word 'Philadelphia' refers to the city, Philadelphia; thus sentence (1) says something about that city. But I intended to say something about the *word* that names that city, not about the city itself. What I should have said is this:

(2) 'Philadelphia' is made up of twelve letters

The subject of sentence (2) is the following expression:

'Philadelphia'

That is, the subject of sentence (2) is the result of enclosing the word 'Philadelphia' in quotation marks; the subject is not the word 'Philadelphia' itself. So (2) says something about the word 'Philadelphia', not the city Philadelphia, which is what I intended.

The moral is that if we want to talk about a word or other linguistic item, we need to refer to it correctly. We cannot just *use* that word (as in (1)), for then that word refers to its referent (a city, in the case of (1)). We must instead *mention* the word—we must instead use some expression that refers to the word itself, not an expression that refers to the word's referent. And the most common device for doing this is to enclose the word in quotation marks (as in (2)).

However: having made such a big deal about this issue, I propose henceforth to ignore it. Zealous care about use and mention would result in an ugly proliferation of quotation marks. So, instead of writing things strictly correctly:

The formula '$P{\to}P$' is a tautology

I will mostly write somewhat naughty things instead:

The formula $P{\to}P$ is a tautology

Now that you're clued into the distinction between use and mention, you'll be able to detect where I've been sloppy in this way.[2]

> **Exercise 1.1** For each of the following, (i) is it a sentence of the object language or the metalanguage? (ii) is it true?
>
> (a)* '$P{\vee}{\sim}P$' is a logical truth.
>
> (b)* $(P{\vee}Q){\to}(Q{\vee}P)$
>
> (c)* 'Frank and Joe are brothers' logically implies 'Frank and Joe are siblings'.
>
> **Exercise 1.2** Each of the following sentences confuses use and mention. In each case, fill in quotation marks to fix the problem.
>
> (a)* Attorney and lawyer are synonyms.
>
> (b)* If S_1 is an English sentence and S_2 is another English sentence, then the string S_1 and S_2 is also an English sentence.

1.4 Application

The modern method for studying logical consequence, then, is to construct formalized versions of the concepts of logical consequence and logical truth—concepts applying to sentences in formal languages—and to mathematically study how those concepts behave. But what does the construction of such formalized concepts establish? After all, *some* formalized constructions shed no light at all on logical consequence. Imagine defining up a formal proof system that includes a rule of inference allowing one to infer ${\sim}P$ from P. One could define the rules of such a system in a perfectly precise way and investigate its mathematical properties, but doing so wouldn't shed light on the intuitive notion of logical consequence that was introduced in section 1.1—on "genuine" logical consequence, as I will call it, to distinguish it from the various formalized notions we could stipulatively define. It would be ridiculous to claim, for example, that the existence of this system shows that 'Snow is not white' *follows from* 'Snow is white'.

Thus the mathematical existence and coherence of a formal system must be distinguished from its value in representing genuine logical consequence and logical

---

[2]Cartwright (1987, appendix) has interesting exercises for learning more about use and mention.

truth. To be sure, logicians use formal systems of various sorts for many purposes that have nothing to do with reasoning at all: for studying syntax, computer programming, electric circuits, and many other phenomena. But one central goal of logic is indeed to study genuine logical consequence.

What, exactly, might it mean to say that a formal system "represents" or "models" or "sheds light on" genuine logical consequence? How are formal systems to be *applied*? Here's an oversimplified account of one such claim. Suppose we have developed a certain formal system for constructing proofs of symbolic sentences of propositional logic. And suppose we have specified some translation scheme from English into the language of propositional logic. This translation scheme would translate the English word 'and' into the logical expression '∧', 'or' into '∨', and so on. We might then say that the formal system accurately represents the logical behavior of 'and', 'or', and the rest in the following sense: one English sentence is a logical consequence of some other English sentences in virtue of 'and', 'or', etc., if and only if one can prove the translation of the former English sentence from the translations of the latter English sentences in the formal system.

The question of whether a given formal system represents genuine logical consequence is a philosophical one, because the question of what is a genuine logical consequence of what is a philosophical question. This book won't spend much time on such questions. My main goal is to introduce the formalisms that are ubiquitous in philosophy, so that you will have the tools to address the philosophical questions yourself. Still, we'll dip into such questions from time to time, since they affect our choices of which logical systems to study.

1.5 The nature of logical consequence

I have distinguished genuine logical consequence from the formal notions we use to represent it. But what *is* genuine logical consequence? What is its nature? The vague slogan "truth-preservation by virtue of form" was intended only to provide an initial fix on the notion; surely we can do better.

The question here is analogous to questions like "What is knowledge?" and "What is the good life?" It's a philosophical question, to be answered using the methods of philosophy. (This is not to deny that formal results from mathematical logic bear on the question.) Like any philosophical question, it is debatable how we should go about answering it. Do we use conceptual analysis to explore the nuances of our ordinary concept? Do we seek rational insight into the nature of objective reality behind our ordinary concept? Do we jettison ambiguous and vague ordinary concepts in favor of shiny new replacements? All this is up for grabs.

It's important to see that there really is an open philosophical question here. This is sometimes obscured by the fact that terms like 'logical consequence' and 'logical truth' are often stipulatively defined in logic books. The open question does not concern such stipulated notions, of course; it concerns the notion of logical consequence that the stipulative definitions are trying to represent. The question is also obscured by the fact that one conception of the nature of logical consequence—the model-theoretic one—is so dominant that one can forget that there are alternatives.[3]

This is not a book on the philosophy of logic, so after this section we won't spend more time on the question of the nature of genuine logical consequence. But perhaps a quick survey of some competing philosophical answers to the question, just to convey their flavor, is in order.

The most popular answer is the *semantic*, or *model-theoretic* one. What's most familiar here is its implementation for formal languages. On this approach, one chooses a formal language, defines a notion of model (or interpretation) for the chosen language, defines a notion of truth-in-a-model for sentences of the language, and then finally represents logical consequence for the chosen language as truth-preservation in all models (ϕ is represented as being a logical consequence of $\psi_1, \psi_2, \ldots$ if and only if ϕ is true in any model in which each of $\psi_1, \psi_2, \ldots$ is true).

Now, as stated, this isn't a theory of genuine logical consequence. It's only a way of representing logical consequence using formal languages. What theory of genuine logical consequence lies behind it? Perhaps one like this: "ϕ is a logical consequence of $\psi_1, \psi_2 \ldots$ if and only if the meanings of the logical expressions in ϕ and $\psi_1, \psi_2 \ldots$ guarantee that ϕ is true whenever $\psi_1, \psi_2 \ldots$ are all true." (Logical expressions are expressions like 'and', 'or', 'not', 'some', and so on; more on this below.) This theory of genuine consequence does seem to mesh with the model-theoretic formal method for representing consequence; for since (as we'll see in section 2.2) everything other than the meanings of the logical expressions is allowed to vary between models, truth-preservation in all models seems to indicate that the meanings of the logical expressions "guarantee" truth-preservation. But on the other hand, what does that mean exactly? What does it mean to say that meanings "guarantee" a certain outcome? The "theory" is unclear. Perhaps, instead, there isn't really a semantic/model-theoretic *theory* of the nature of logical consequence at all, but rather a preference for a certain approach to formalizing or representing logical consequence.

A second answer to the question about the nature of logical consequence is a *proof-theoretic* one, according to which logical consequence is more a matter of provability than of truth-preservation. As with the semantic account, there is a question of whether we have here a proper theory about the nature of logical consequence (in which case we must ask: what is provability? by which rules? and in which language?) or whether we have merely a preference for a certain approach to formalizing logical consequence. In the latter case, the approach to formalization is one in which we define up a relation of provability between sentences of formal languages. We do this, roughly speaking, by defining certain acceptable "transitions" between sentences of formal languages, and then saying that a sentence ϕ is provable from sentences $\psi_1, \psi_2, \ldots$ iff (i.e. if and only if) there is some way of moving by a series of acceptable transitions from $\psi_1, \psi_2, \ldots$ to ϕ.

The semantic and proof-theoretic approaches are the main two sources of inspiration for formal logic, and certainly for the systems we will discuss in this book.

---

[3] See Etchemendy (1990, chapter 1).

But there are alternate philosophical conceptions of logical consequence that are worth briefly mentioning. There is the view of W. V. O. Quine: ϕ is a logical consequence of $\psi_1, \psi_2 \dots$ iff there is no way to (uniformly) substitute expressions for nonlogical expressions in ϕ and $\psi_1, \psi_2 \dots$ so that $\psi_1, \psi_2 \dots$ all become true but ϕ does not.[4] There is a modal account: ϕ is a logical consequence of $\psi_1, \psi_2 \dots$ iff it is not possible for $\psi_1, \psi_2 \dots$ to all be true without ϕ being true (under some suitable notion of possibility).[5] And there is a primitivist account, according to which logical consequence is a primitive notion.

> **Exercise 1.3*** Let sentence S_1 be 'There exists an x such that x and x are identical', and let S_2 be 'There exists an x such that there exists a y such that x and y are not identical'. Does S_1 logically imply S_2 according to the modal criterion? According to Quine's criterion?

1.6 Logical constants

It's natural to think of logic as having something to do with "form". (Recall the slogans of section 1.1.) The idea can be illustrated by seeing how it clashes with the modal conception of logical consequence from the previous section. Since it is impossible to be a bachelor without being unmarried, the modal account says that 'Grant is a bachelor' logically implies 'Grant is unmarried'. But this seems wrong. Perhaps the first sentence "analytically" or "conceptually" implies the second sentence, but the implication doesn't seem *logical*. And it's natural to put this by saying that, whatever exactly logical implication amounts to, logical implications must at least hold by virtue of form.[6]

But what does that mean? Consider an implication that, one is inclined to say, *does* hold by virtue of form: the implication from 'Leisel is a swimmer and Leisel is famous' to 'Leisel is a swimmer'. This holds by virtue of form, one might think, because (i) it has the form "ϕ and ψ; so, ϕ"; and (ii) for *any* pair of sentences of this form, the first logically implies the second. But the defender of the modal conception of logical consequence could say the following:

> The inference from 'Grant is a bachelor' to 'Grant is unmarried' also holds in virtue of form. For: (i) it has the form "α is a bachelor; so, α is unmarried"; and (ii) for any pair of sentences of this form, the first sentence logically implies the second (since it's impossible for the first to be true while the second is false).

[4] Quine (1960); p. 103 in Quine (1966).

[5] Perhaps semantic/model-theoretic formalisms can be regarded as being inspired by the modal account.

[6] A hybrid of the modal and Quinean accounts of logical consequence respects this: ϕ is a logical consequence of $\psi_1, \psi_2 \dots$ iff it's impossible for $\psi_1', \psi_2' \dots$ to be true while ϕ' is false, for any ϕ' and $\psi_1', \psi_2' \dots$ that result from ϕ and $\psi_1, \psi_2 \dots$ by uniform substitution for nonlogical expressions.

What's wrong with saying this? We normally think of the "forms" of inferences as being things like "ϕ and ψ; so, ϕ", and *not* things like "α is a bachelor; so, α is unmarried", but why not?

When we assign a form to an inference, we focus on some phrases while ignoring others. The phrases we ignore disappear into the schematic letters (ϕ, ψ, and α in the previous paragraph); the phrases on which we focus remain ('and', 'bachelor', 'unmarried'). Now, logicians do not focus on just any old phrases. They focus on 'and', 'or', 'not', 'if...then', and so on, in propositional logic; on 'all' and 'some' in addition in predicate logic; and on a few others. But they do *not* focus on 'bachelor' and 'unmarried'. Call the words on which logicians focus—the words they leave intact when constructing forms, and the words for which they introduce special symbolic correlates, such as $\wedge$, $\vee$, and $\forall$—the *logical constants*. (These are what I was calling "logical expressions" in the previous section.)

We can speak of natural language logical constants ('and', 'or', 'all', 'some'...) as well as symbolic logical constants ($\wedge$, $\vee$, $\forall$, $\exists$...). The symbolic logical constants get special treatment in formal systems. For example, in proof systems for propositional logic there are special rules governing $\wedge$; and these rules differ from the rules governing $\vee$. This reflects the fact that $\wedge$ and $\vee$ have fixed interpretations in propositional logic. Unlike P, Q, and so on, which are not symbolic logical constants, and which do not fixedly represent any particular natural language sentences, $\wedge$ and $\vee$ fixedly represent 'and' and 'or'.

In terms of the notion of a logical constant, then, we can say why the inference from 'Grant is a bachelor' to 'Grant is unmarried' is not a logical one. When we say that logical implications hold by virtue of form, we mean that they hold by virtue of *logical* form; and the form "α is a bachelor; so, α is unmarried" is not a logical form. A logical form must consist exclusively of logical constants (plus punctuation and schematic variables); and the fact is that logicians do not treat 'bachelor' and 'unmarried' as logical constants.

But this just pushes the question back: why don't they? What's so special about 'and', 'or', 'all', and 'some'? Just as the meaning of 'and' guarantees that whenever 'Leisel is a swimmer and Leisel is famous' is true, 'Leisel is a swimmer' is true as well, so the meanings of 'bachelor' and 'unmarried' guarantee that whenever 'Grant is a bachelor' is true, 'Grant is unmarried' is true as well. Why not expand logic beyond propositional and predicate logic to include the logic of bachelorhood and unmarriage?

On the one hand there's no formal obstacle to doing just that. We could develop mathematical models of the inferential behavior of 'bachelor' and 'unmarried', by analogy to our models of the behavior of the usual logical constants. To our predicate logic containing the special symbols $\wedge$, $\vee$, $\forall$, $\exists$, and the rest, we could add the special predicates B (for 'bachelor') and U (for 'unmarried'). To our derivation systems, in addition to rules like $\wedge$-elimination (which lets us infer ϕ (and also ψ) from $\phi \wedge \psi$) we could add a rule that lets us infer Uα from Bα. But on the other hand, there are, intuitively, significant differences between the expressions usually regarded as logical constants and words like 'bachelor' and 'unmarried'. The question of what, exactly, these differences amount to is a philosophical question in its own right.[7]

1.7 Extensions, deviations, variations

"Standard logic" is what is usually studied in introductory logic courses. It includes propositional logic (logical constants: $\wedge, \vee, \sim, \rightarrow, \leftrightarrow$), and predicate logic (logical constants: $\forall, \exists$, variables). In this book we'll consider various modifications of standard logic. Following Gamut (1991*a*, pp. 156–158), it is helpful to distinguish three sorts: extensions, deviations, and variations.

In an *extension* we *add* to standard logic. We add new symbolic logical constants (for example, the $\square$ of modal logic), and new cases of logical consequence and logical truth that we can model using the new logical constants. We do this in order to represent more facets of the notion of logical consequence. We extend propositional logic, after all, to get predicate logic. Propositional logic is great as far as it goes, but it cannot represent the logical implication of 'someone is male' by 'Grant is male'. That is why we add quantifiers, variables, predicates, and so on to propositional logic (new symbols), and add means to deal with these new symbols in semantics and proof theory (new cases of logical consequence and logical truth we model), to obtain predicate logic.

As we saw in the previous section, logicians don't treat just any old words as logical constants. They never treat 'bachelor' as a logical constant, for example. But many logicians do allow some logical constants in addition to the familiar ones from propositional and predicate logic. Many consider modal logic, for example, in which one treats 'necessarily' as a logical constant (symbolized by the new symbol $\square$) to be part of logic.

In a *deviation* we retain the usual set of logical constants, but change what we say about them. We keep standard logic's symbols, but alter its proof theory and semantics, thereby offering a different model of logical consequence and logical truth.

Why do this? Perhaps because we think that standard logic is *wrong*. For example, the standard semantics for propositional logic counts the sentence $P \vee \sim P$ as a tautology. But some philosophers resist the idea that natural-language sentences like the following are logically true:

> Either Jones is bald or Jones is not bald

> Either there will be a sea battle tomorrow or there will not be a sea battle tomorrow

If these philosophers are right, then the standard notion of a tautology is an imperfect model of genuine logical truth, and we need a better model.

Variations also change standard logic, but here the changes are, roughly speaking, merely notational; they leave the content of standard logic unaltered. For example, in Polish notation, instead of writing $P \rightarrow (Q \wedge R)$, we write $\rightarrow P \wedge QR$; binary connectives go in front of the sentences they connect rather than between them.

---

[7] See MacFarlane (2005) for a survey of the issues here.

1.8 Set theory

I said earlier that modern logic uses "mathematical techniques" to study formal languages. The mathematical techniques in question are those of set theory. Only the most elementary set-theoretic concepts and assumptions will be needed, and you may already be familiar with them; but nevertheless, here is a brief overview.

Sets have *members*. Consider the set, A, of even integers between 2 and 6. 2 is a member of A, 4 is a member of A, 6 is a member of A; and nothing else is a member of A. We use the expression "$\in$" for membership; thus, we can say: $2 \in A$, $4 \in A$, and $6 \in A$. We often name a set by putting names of its members between braces: "$\{2, 4, 6\}$" is another name of A.

We can also speak of sets with infinitely many members. Consider $\mathbb{N}$, the set of natural numbers. Each natural number is a member of $\mathbb{N}$; thus, $0 \in \mathbb{N}, 1 \in \mathbb{N}$, and so on. We can informally name this set with the brace notation as well: "$\{0, 1, 2, 3, \dots\}$", so long as it is clear which continued series the ellipsis signifies.

The members of a set need not be mathematical entities; anything can be a member of a set.[8] Sets can contain people, or cities, or—to draw nearer to our intended purpose—sentences and other linguistic entities.

There is also the empty set, $\emptyset$. This is the one set with no members. That is, for each object u, u is not a member of $\emptyset$ (i.e.: for each u, $u \notin \emptyset$).

Though the notion of a set is an intuitive one, Russell's paradox (discovered by Bertrand Russell) shows that it must be employed with care. Russell asks us to consider the set, R, of all and only those sets that are not members of themselves. That is, R is the set of non-self-members. Russell then asks: is R a member of itself? There are two possibilities:

- $R \notin R$. Thus, R is a non-self-member. But R was said to contain *all* non-self-members, and so $R \in R$. *Contradiction.*

- $R \in R$. So R is *not* a non-self-member. But R was said to contain *only* non-self-members, and so $R \notin R$. *Contradiction.*

Each possibility leads to a contradiction. But there are no remaining possibilities—either R is a member of itself or it isn't! So it looks like the very idea of sets is paradoxical.

Since Russell's time, set theorists have developed theories of sets that avoid Russell's paradox (as well as other related paradoxes). They do this chiefly by imposing rigid restrictions on when sets exist. So far we have been blithely assuming that there exist various sets: the set $\mathbb{N}$, sets containing people, cities, and sentences, Russell's set R. That got us into trouble. So what we want is a theory of when sets exist that blocks the Russell paradox by saying that set R simply doesn't exist (for then Russell's argument falls apart), but which says that the sets we need to do mathematics and metalogic *do* exist. The details of set theory are beyond the scope of this book. Here, we will help ourselves to intuitively "safe" sets, sets that aren't anything like

---

[8]Well, some set theories bar certain "very large collections" from being members of sets. This issue won't be relevant here.

the Russell set. We'll leave the task of what "safe" amounts to, exactly, to the set theorists.

Various other useful set-theoretic notions can be defined in terms of the notion of membership. Set A is a *subset* of set B ("$A \subseteq B$") when every member of A is a member of B. The *intersection* of A and B ("$A \cap B$") is the set that contains all and only those things that are members of both A and B; the *union* of A and B ("$A \cup B$") is the set containing all and only those things that are members of either A or B (or both[9]).

Suppose we want to refer to the set of the so-and-sos—that is, the set containing all and only those objects, u, that satisfy the condition "so-and-so". We'll do this with the term "$\{u : u$ is a so-and-so$\}$". Thus, we could write: "$\mathbb{N} = \{u : u$ is a natural number$\}$". And we could restate the definitions of $\cap$ and $\cup$ from the previous paragraph as follows:

$$A \cap B = \{u : u \in A \text{ and } u \in B\}$$
$$A \cup B = \{u : u \in A \text{ or } u \in B\}$$

Sets have members, but they don't contain them in any particular order. For example, the set containing me and Barack Obama doesn't have a "first" member. "$\{$Ted, Obama$\}$" and "$\{$Obama, Ted$\}$" are two different names for the same set—the set containing just Obama and me. (This follows from the "criterion of identity" for sets: sets are identical if and only if they have exactly the same members.) But sometimes we need to talk about set-*like* things containing objects in a particular order. For this purpose we use *ordered sets*.[10] Two-membered ordered sets are called ordered pairs. To name the ordered pair of Obama and Ted, we use: "$\langle$Obama, Ted$\rangle$". Here, the order is significant: $\langle$Obama, Ted$\rangle$ and $\langle$Ted, Obama$\rangle$ are *not* the same ordered pair. The three-membered ordered set of u, v, and w (in that order) is written: $\langle u, v, w \rangle$; and similarly for ordered sets of any finite size. An n-membered ordered set is called an n-*tuple*. (For the sake of convenience, let's define the 1-tuple $\langle u \rangle$ to be just the object u itself.)

A further concept we'll need is that of a *relation*. A relation is just a feature of multiple objects taken together. The taller-than relation is one example: when one person is taller than another, that's a feature of those two objects taken together. Another example is the less-than relation for numbers. When one number is less than another, that's a feature of those two numbers taken together.

"Binary" relations apply to two objects at a time. The taller-than and less-than relations are binary relations, or "two-place" relations, as we might say. We can also speak of three-place relations, four-place relations, and so on. An example of a

---

[9]In this book I always use 'or' in its inclusive sense.

[10]There's a trick for defining ordered sets in terms of sets. First, define the ordered pair $\langle u, v \rangle$ as the set $\{\{u\}, \{u, v\}\}$. (We can recover the information that u is intended to be the *first* member because u "appears twice".) Then define the n-tuple $\langle u_1 \ldots u_n \rangle$ as the ordered pair $\langle u_1, \langle u_2 \ldots u_n \rangle \rangle$, for each $n \geq 3$. But henceforth I'll ignore this trick and just speak of ordered sets without worrying about how they're defined.

three-place relation would be the *betweenness* relation for numbers: the relation that holds among 2, 5, and 23 (in that order), for example.

We can use ordered sets to give an official definition of what a relation is.

DEFINITION OF RELATION: An n-place relation is a set of n-tuples.

So a binary (two-place) relation is a set of ordered pairs. For example, the taller-than relation may be taken to be the set of ordered pairs $\langle u, v \rangle$ such that u is a taller person than v. The *less-than* relation for positive integers is the set of ordered pairs $\langle m, n \rangle$ such that m is a positive integer less than n, another positive integer. That is, it is the following set:

$$\{\langle 1,2 \rangle, \langle 1,3 \rangle, \langle 1,4 \rangle \ldots \langle 2,3 \rangle, \langle 2,4 \rangle \ldots\}$$

When $\langle u, v \rangle$ is a member of relation R, we say, equivalently, that u and v "stand in" R, or R "holds between" u and v, or that u "bears" R to v. Most simply, we write "Ruv".[11]

Some more definitions:

DEFINITION OF DOMAIN, RANGE, OVER: Let R be any binary relation and A be any set.

- The domain of R ("dom(R)") is the set $\{u:$ for some $v, Ruv\}$
- The range of R ("ran(R)") is the set $\{u:$ for some $v, Rvu\}$
- R is over A iff dom(R) $\subseteq A$ and ran(R) $\subseteq A$

In other words, the domain of R is the set of all things that bear R to something; the range is the set of all things that something bears R to; and R is over A iff the members of the -tuples in R are all drawn from A.

Binary relations come in different kinds, depending on the patterns in which they hold:

DEFINITION OF KINDS OF BINARY RELATIONS: Let R be any binary relation over some set A.

- R is serial (in A) iff for every $u \in A$, there is some $v \in A$ such that Ruv
- R is reflexive (in A) iff for every $u \in A, Ruu$
- R is symmetric iff for every u, v, if Ruv then Rvu
- R is transitive iff for every u, v, w, if Ruv and Rvw then Ruw
- R is an equivalence relation (in A) iff R is symmetric, transitive, and reflexive (in A)
- R is total (in A) iff for every $u, v \in A, Ruv$

Notice that we relativize some of these relation types to a given set A. We do this in the case of reflexivity, for example, because the alternative would be to say that a relation is reflexive *simpliciter* if *everything* bears R to itself; but that would require the domain and range of any reflexive relation to be the set of absolutely all objects. It's better to introduce the notion of being reflexive relative to a set, which is applicable

---

[11]This notation is like that of predicate logic; but here I'm speaking the metalanguage, not displaying sentences of a formalized language.

to relations with smaller domains. (I will sometimes omit the qualifier 'in *A*' when it is clear which set that is.) Why don't symmetry and transitivity have to be relativized to a set? Because they only say what must happen *if R* holds among certain things. Symmetry, for example, says merely that *if R* holds between *u* and *v*, then it must also hold between *v* and *u*, and so we can say that a relation is symmetric absolutely, without implying that everything is in its domain.

We'll also need the concept of a *function*. A function "takes in" an object or objects (in a certain order), and "spits out" a further object. For example, the addition function takes in two numbers, and spits out their sum. As with sets, ordered sets, and relations, functions are not limited to mathematical entities: they can take in and spit out any objects whatsoever. We can speak of the *father-of* function, for example, which takes in a person, and spits out the father of that person. (The more common way of putting this is: the function "maps" the person to his or her father.) And later in this book we will be considering functions that take in and spit out linguistic entities.

Some functions must take in more than one object before they are ready to spit out something. For example, you need to give the addition function two numbers in order to get it to spit out something; for this reason it is called a *two-place* function. The father-of function, on the other hand, needs to be given only one object, so it is a one-place function. Let's simplify this by thinking of an *n*-place function as simply being a one-place function that takes in only *n*-tuples. Thus, if you give the addition function the ordered pair $\langle 2, 5 \rangle$, it spits out 7.

The objects that a function takes in are called its *arguments*, and the objects it spits out are called its *values*. If *u* is an argument of *f*, we write "$f(u)$" for the value of function *f* as applied to the argument *u*. $f(u)$ is the object that *f* spits out, if you feed it *u*. For example, where *f* is the father-of function, since Ron is my father we can write: $f(\text{Ted}) = \text{Ron}$. When *f* is an *n*-place function—i.e., its arguments are *n*-tuples—instead of writing $f(\langle u_1, \ldots, u_n \rangle)$ we write simply $f(u_1, \ldots, u_n)$. So where *a* is the addition function, we can write: $a(2, 3) = 5$. The *domain* of a function is the set of its arguments, and its *range* is the set of its values. If *u* is not in function *f*'s domain (i.e., *u* is not one of *f*'s arguments), then *f* is *undefined* for *u*. The father-of function, for example, is undefined for numbers (since numbers have no fathers). These concepts may be pictured for (a part of) the father-of function thus:

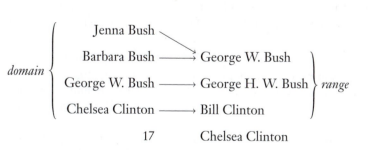

The number 17 and the state of Massachusetts are excluded from the domain because, being a number and a political entity, they don't have fathers. Chelsea Clinton and Cygnus X-1 are excluded from the range because, being a woman and a black hole, they aren't fathers of anyone. The number 17 and Massachusetts aren't in the range either; and Cygnus X-1 isn't in the domain. But Chelsea Clinton is in the domain, since she has a father.

It's part of the definition of a function that a function can never map an argument to two distinct values. That is, $f(u)$ cannot be equal both to v and also to v' when v and v' are two different objects. That is, a function always has a unique value, given any argument for which the function is defined. (So there is no such function as the *parent-of* function: people typically have more than one parent.) Functions *are* allowed to map two distinct arguments to the same value. (The father-of function is an example: two people can have the same father.) But if a given function happens never to do this, then it is called *one-to-one*. That is, a function f is one-to-one iff for any u and v in its domain, if $u \neq v$ then $f(u) \neq f(v)$. (The function of natural numbers f defined by the equation $f(n) = n + 1$ is an example.) This all may be pictured as follows:

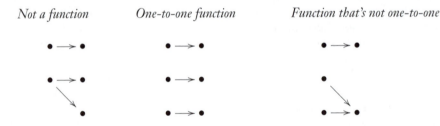

| *Not a function* | *One-to-one function* | *Function that's not one-to-one* |

As with the notion of a relation, we can use ordered sets to give official definitions of function and related notions:

DEFINITION OF FUNCTION-THEORETIC NOTIONS:

- A function is a set of ordered pairs, f, obeying the condition that if $\langle u, v \rangle$ and $\langle u, w \rangle$ are both members of f, then $v = w$
- When $\langle u, v \rangle \in f$, we say that u is an argument of f, v is a value of f, and that f maps u to v; and we write: "$f(u) = v$"
- The domain of a function is the set of its arguments; its range is the set of its values
- A function is n-place when every member of its domain is an n-tuple

Thus a function is just a certain kind of binary relation—one that never relates a single thing u to two distinct objects v and w. (Notice that the definition of "domain" and "range" for functions yields the same results as the definition given earlier for relations.)

The topic of infinity is perhaps set theory's most fascinating part. And one of the most fascinating things about infinity is the matter of sizes of infinity. Compare the set $\mathbb{N}$ of natural numbers and the set $\mathbb{E}$ of even natural numbers ($\{0, 2, 4, 6, \ldots\}$).

Which set is bigger—which has more members? You might think that $\mathbb{N}$ has got to be bigger, since it contains all the members of $\mathbb{E}$ and then the odd natural numbers in addition. But in fact these sets have the same size. For we can line up their members as follows:

$$\mathbb{N}: 0\ 1\ 2\ 3\ 4\ 5\ \ldots$$
$$\mathbb{E}: 0\ 2\ 4\ 6\ 8\ 10 \ldots$$

If two sets can be "lined up" in this way, then they have the same size. Indeed, this is how set theorists define 'same size'. Or rather, they give a precise definition of sameness of size (they call it "equinumerosity", or sameness of "cardinality") which captures this intuitive idea:

DEFINITION OF EQUINUMEROSITY: Sets A and B are equinumerous iff there exists some one-to-one function whose domain is A and whose range is B.

Intuitively: sets are equinumerous when each member of either set can be associated with a unique member of the other set. You can line up their members.

The picture in which the members of $\mathbb{N}$ and the members of $\mathbb{E}$ were lined up is actually a picture of a function: the function that maps each member of $\mathbb{N}$ to the member of $\mathbb{E}$ immediately below it in the picture. Mathematically, this function, f, may be defined thus:

$$f(n) = 2n \hspace{3cm} \text{(for any } n \in \mathbb{N})$$

This function is one-to-one (since if two natural numbers are distinct then doubling each results in two distinct numbers). So $\mathbb{N}$ and $\mathbb{E}$ are equinumerous. It's quite surprising that a set can be equinumerous with a mere subset of itself. But that's how it goes with infinity.

Even more surprising is the fact that the rational numbers are equinumerous with the natural numbers. A (nonnegative) rational number is a number that can be written as a fraction $\frac{n}{m}$ where n and m are natural numbers and $m \neq 0$. To show that $\mathbb{N}$ is equinumerous with the set $\mathbb{Q}$ of rational numbers, we must find a one-to-one function whose domain is $\mathbb{N}$ and whose range is $\mathbb{Q}$. At first this seems impossible, since the rationals are "dense" (between every two fractions there is another fraction) whereas the naturals are not. But we must simply be clever in our search for an appropriate one-to-one function.

Each rational number is represented in the following grid:

denominators

numerators		1	2	3	4	5	...
	0	$\frac{0}{1}$	$\frac{0}{2}$	$\frac{0}{3}$	$\frac{0}{4}$	$\frac{0}{5}$	...
	1	$\frac{1}{1}$	$\frac{1}{2}$	$\frac{1}{3}$	$\frac{1}{4}$	$\frac{1}{5}$	...
	2	$\frac{2}{1}$	$\frac{2}{2}$	$\boxed{\frac{2}{3}}$	$\frac{2}{4}$	$\frac{2}{5}$	...
	3	$\frac{3}{1}$	$\frac{3}{2}$	$\frac{3}{3}$	$\frac{3}{4}$	$\frac{3}{5}$	...
	4	$\frac{4}{1}$	$\frac{4}{2}$	$\frac{4}{3}$	$\frac{4}{4}$	$\frac{4}{5}$	...
	⋮	⋮	⋮	⋮	⋮	⋮	⋱

Any rational number $\frac{n}{m}$ can be found in the row for n and the column for m. For example, $\frac{2}{3}$ (circled in the grid) is in the row for 2 (the third row, since the first row is for 0) and the column for 3 (the third column). Every rational number appears multiple times in the grid (infinitely many times, in fact). For example, the rational number $\frac{1}{2}$, which occurs in the second row, second column, is the same as the rational number $\frac{2}{4}$, which occurs in the third row, fourth column. (It's also the same as $\frac{3}{6}, \frac{4}{8}, \frac{5}{10} \cdots$.)

Our goal is to find a way to line up the naturals with the rationals—to find a one-to-one function, f, with domain $\mathbb{N}$ and range $\mathbb{Q}$. Since each rational number appears in the grid, all we need to do is go through all of the (infinitely many!) points on the grid, one by one, and count off a corresponding natural number for each; we'll then let our function f map the natural numbers we count off to the rational numbers that appear at the corresponding points on the grid. Let's start at the top left of the grid, and count off the first natural number, 0. So we'll have f map 0 to the rational number at the top left of the grid, namely, $\frac{0}{1}$. That is, $f(0) = \frac{0}{1}$. We can depict this by labeling $\frac{0}{1}$ with the natural number we counted off, 0:

denominators

numerators		1	2	3	4	5	...
	0	$\frac{0}{1}(0)$	$\frac{0}{2}$	$\frac{0}{3}$	$\frac{0}{4}$	$\frac{0}{5}$	...
	1	$\frac{1}{1}$	$\frac{1}{2}$	$\frac{1}{3}$	$\frac{1}{4}$	$\frac{1}{5}$	...
	2	$\frac{2}{1}$	$\frac{2}{2}$	$\frac{2}{3}$	$\frac{2}{4}$	$\frac{2}{5}$	...
	3	$\frac{3}{1}$	$\frac{3}{2}$	$\frac{3}{3}$	$\frac{3}{4}$	$\frac{3}{5}$	...
	4	$\frac{4}{1}$	$\frac{4}{2}$	$\frac{4}{3}$	$\frac{4}{4}$	$\frac{4}{5}$	...
	⋮	⋮	⋮	⋮	⋮	⋮	⋱

Next, ignoring a certain wrinkle which I'll get to in a moment, let's count off natural numbers for the rationals in the uppermost "ring" around the top left of the grid, in counterclockwise order, beginning at the left:

denominators

		1	2	3	4	5	
	0	$\frac{0}{1}(0)$	$\frac{0}{2}(3)$	$\frac{0}{3}$	$\frac{0}{4}$	$\frac{0}{5}$	$\cdots$
	1	$\frac{1}{1}(1)$	$\frac{1}{2}(2)$	$\frac{1}{3}$	$\frac{1}{4}$	$\frac{1}{5}$	$\cdots$
numerators	2	$\frac{2}{1}$	$\frac{2}{2}$	$\frac{2}{3}$	$\frac{2}{4}$	$\frac{2}{5}$	$\cdots$
	3	$\frac{3}{1}$	$\frac{3}{2}$	$\frac{3}{3}$	$\frac{3}{4}$	$\frac{3}{5}$	$\cdots$
	4	$\frac{4}{1}$	$\frac{4}{2}$	$\frac{4}{3}$	$\frac{4}{4}$	$\frac{4}{5}$	$\cdots$
	$\vdots$	$\vdots$	$\vdots$	$\vdots$	$\vdots$	$\vdots$	$\ddots$

Then (continuing to ignore the wrinkle) let's count off the next ring of numbers, again in counterclockwise order beginning at the left:

denominators

		1	2	3	4	5	
	0	$\frac{0}{1}(0)$	$\frac{0}{2}(3)$	$\frac{0}{3}(8)$	$\frac{0}{4}$	$\frac{0}{5}$	$\cdots$
	1	$\frac{1}{1}(1)$	$\frac{1}{2}(2)$	$\frac{1}{3}(7)$	$\frac{1}{4}$	$\frac{1}{5}$	$\cdots$
numerators	2	$\frac{2}{1}(4)$	$\frac{2}{2}(5)$	$\frac{2}{3}(6)$	$\frac{2}{4}$	$\frac{2}{5}$	$\cdots$
	3	$\frac{3}{1}$	$\frac{3}{2}$	$\frac{3}{3}$	$\frac{3}{4}$	$\frac{3}{5}$	$\cdots$
	4	$\frac{4}{1}$	$\frac{4}{2}$	$\frac{4}{3}$	$\frac{4}{4}$	$\frac{4}{5}$	$\cdots$
	$\vdots$	$\vdots$	$\vdots$	$\vdots$	$\vdots$	$\vdots$	$\ddots$

And so on infinitely. For each new ring, we begin at the left, and move through the ring counterclockwise, continuing to count off natural numbers.

Every point on the grid will eventually be reached by one of these increasingly large (but always finite) rings. Since every rational number appears on the grid, every rational number eventually gets labeled with a natural number. So the range of our function f is the entirety of $\mathbb{Q}$! There are two tricks that make this work. First, even though the rational numbers are dense, they can be laid out in a discrete grid. Second, even though the grid is two-dimensional and the natural numbers are only one-dimensional, there is a way to cover the whole grid with naturals since there is a one-dimensional path that covers the entire grid: the path along the expanding rings.

The wrinkle is that this procedure, as we've laid it out so far, doesn't deliver a one-to-one function, because rational numbers appear multiple times in the grid. For example, given our definition, f maps 0 to $\frac{0}{1}$ and 3 to $\frac{0}{2}$. But $\frac{0}{2}$ is the same rational number as $\frac{0}{1}$—namely, 0—so f isn't one-to-one. (f also maps 8 to 0; and it maps both 1 and 5 to 1, etc.) But it's easy to modify the procedure to fix this problem. In our trek through the rings, whenever we hit a rational number that we've already encountered, let's now simply skip it, and go on to the next rational number on the trek. Thus, the new diagram looks as follows (the skipped rational numbers are struck out):

denominators

		1	2	3	4	5	
	0	$\frac{0}{1}$(0)	$\frac{\not0}{\not2}$	$\frac{\not0}{\not3}$	$\frac{\not0}{\not4}$	$\frac{\not0}{\not5}$	...
	1	$\frac{1}{1}$(1)	$\frac{1}{2}$(2)	$\frac{1}{3}$(5)	$\frac{1}{4}$(9)	$\frac{1}{5}$(15)	...
numerators	2	$\frac{2}{1}$(3)	$\frac{\not2}{\not2}$	$\frac{2}{3}$(4)	$\frac{\not2}{\not4}$	$\frac{2}{5}$(14)	...
	3	$\frac{3}{1}$(6)	$\frac{3}{2}$(7)	$\frac{\not3}{\not3}$	$\frac{3}{4}$(8)	$\frac{3}{5}$(13)	...
	4	$\frac{4}{1}$(10)	$\frac{\not4}{\not2}$	$\frac{4}{3}$(11)	$\frac{\not4}{\not4}$	$\frac{4}{5}$(12)	...
	$\vdots$	$\vdots$	$\vdots$	$\vdots$	$\vdots$	$\vdots$	$\ddots$

We've now got our desired function f: it is the function that maps each natural number to the rational number in the grid labeled by that natural number. (Notice, incidentally, that f could be displayed in this way instead:

$$n: \quad 0\ 1\ 2\ 3\ 4\ 5\ 6\ 7\ 8\ 9\ 10\ 11\ 12\ 13\ 14\ 15 \ldots$$
$$f(n): 0\ 1\ \tfrac{1}{2}\ 2\ \tfrac{2}{3}\ \tfrac{1}{3}\ 3\ \tfrac{3}{2}\ \tfrac{3}{4}\ \tfrac{1}{4}\ 4\ \tfrac{4}{3}\ \tfrac{4}{5}\ \tfrac{3}{5}\ \tfrac{2}{5}\ \tfrac{1}{5} \ldots$$

This is just a different picture of the same function.) Since each rational number is labeled by some natural number, f's range is $\mathbb{Q}$. f's domain is clearly $\mathbb{N}$. And f is clearly one-to-one (since our procedure skips previously encountered rational numbers). So f is our desired function; $\mathbb{N}$ and $\mathbb{Q}$ are the same size.

If even a dense set like $\mathbb{Q}$ is no bigger than $\mathbb{N}$, are *all* infinite sets the same size? The answer is in fact no. Some infinite sets are bigger than $\mathbb{N}$; there are different sizes of infinity.

One such set is the set of real numbers. Real numbers are numbers that can be represented by decimals. All rational numbers are real numbers; and their decimal representations either terminate or eventually repeat in some infinitely recurring pattern. (For example, $\frac{1}{3}$ has the repeating decimal representation $0.3333\ldots$; $\frac{7}{4}$ has the terminating decimal representation 1.75.) But some real numbers are not rational numbers. These are the real numbers with decimal representations that never repeat. One example is the real number π, whose decimal representation begins: 3.14159....

We'll prove that there are more real than natural numbers by proving that there are more real numbers between 0 and 1 than there are natural numbers. Let R be the set of real numbers in this interval. Now, consider the function f which maps each natural number n to $\frac{1}{n+2}$. This is a one-to-one function whose domain is $\mathbb{N}$ and whose range is $\{\frac{1}{2}, \frac{1}{3}, \frac{1}{4}, \dots\}$. But this latter set is a subset of R. So R is *at least* as big as $\mathbb{N}$. So all we need to do is show that R is not the same size as $\mathbb{N}$. And we can do this by showing that the assumption that $\mathbb{N}$ and R *are* the same size would lead to a contradiction.

So, suppose that $\mathbb{N}$ and R are equinumerous. Given the definition of equinumerosity, there must exist some one-to-one function, f, whose domain is $\mathbb{N}$ and whose range is R. We can represent f on a grid as follows:

$$f(0) = 0 \, . \, a_{0,0} \, a_{0,1} \, a_{0,2} \dots$$
$$f(1) = 0 \, . \, a_{1,0} \, a_{1,1} \, a_{1,2} \dots$$
$$f(2) = 0 \, . \, a_{2,0} \, a_{2,1} \, a_{2,2} \dots$$
$$\vdots \quad \vdots \quad \vdots \quad \vdots \quad \vdots \quad \ddots$$

The grid represents the real numbers in the range of f by their decimal representations.[12] The as are the digits in these decimal representations. For any natural number i, $f(i)$ is represented as the decimal $0.a_{i,0}a_{i,1}a_{i,2}\dots$. Thus $a_{i,j}$ is the $(j+1)^{\text{st}}$ digit in the decimal representation of $f(i)$. Consider $f(2)$, for example. If $f(2)$ happens to be the real number $0.2562894\dots$, then $a_{2,0} = 2$, $a_{2,1} = 5$, $a_{2,2} = 6$, $a_{2,3} = 2$, and so on.

The right-hand part of the grid (everything except the column beginning with "$f(0) =$") is a list of real numbers. The first real number on this list is $0.a_{0,0}a_{1,1}a_{0,2}\dots$, the second is $0.a_{1,0}a_{1,1}a_{1,2}\dots$, the third is $0.a_{2,0}a_{2,1}a_{2,2}\dots$, and so on. The real numbers in this list, in fact, comprise the range of f. But we have supposed, remember, that the range of f is the entirety of R. Thus we have an important consequence of our supposition: this list is a *complete* list of R. That is, every member of R occurs somewhere on the list, as the decimal $0.a_{i,0}a_{i,1}a_{i,2}\dots$, for some natural number i.

But we can show that this *can't* be a complete list of R, by showing that there is at least one real number between 0 and 1 that does not appear on the list. We're going to do this in a crafty way: we'll look at the grid above, and construct our real number as a function of the grid in such a way that it's guaranteed not to be anywhere on the list.

I'll call the real number I'm after "d"; to specify d, I'm going to specify its decimal representation $0.d_0d_1d_2\dots$. Here is my definition of the jth digit in this decimal representation:

---

[12] If a decimal representation terminates, we can think of it as nevertheless being infinite: there are infinitely many zeros after the termination point.

$$d_j = \begin{cases} 6 & \text{if } a_{j,j} = 5 \\ 5 & \text{otherwise} \end{cases}$$

The "$a_{j,j}$"s refer to the grid depicting f above; thus, what real number d we have defined depends on the nature of the grid, and thus on the nature of the function f.

To get a handle on what's going on here, think about it geometrically. Consider the digits on the following *diagonal line* in the grid:

$$f(0) = 0 . \boxed{a_{0,0}} \quad a_{0,1} \quad a_{0,2} \quad \cdots$$
$$f(1) = 0 . \quad a_{1,0} \quad \boxed{a_{1,1}} \quad a_{1,2} \quad \cdots$$
$$f(2) = 0 . \quad a_{2,0} \quad a_{2,1} \quad \boxed{a_{2,2}} \quad \cdots$$
$$\vdots \quad \vdots \quad \vdots \quad \vdots \quad \vdots \quad \ddots$$

To these diagonal digits, there corresponds a real number: $0.a_{0,0}a_{1,1}a_{2,2}\ldots$. Call this real number a. What we did to arrive at our number d (so called because we are giving a "diagonal argument") was to begin with a's decimal representation and change each of its digits. We changed each of its digits to 5, except when the digit was already 5, in which case we changed it to 6.

We now approach the punchline. d's definition insures that it cannot be anywhere on the list. Let $f(i)$ be *any* member of the list. We can prove that d and $f(i)$ are not the same number. If they were, then their decimal representations $0.d_0d_1d_2\ldots$ and $0.a_{i,0}a_{i,1}a_{i,2}\ldots$ would also be the same. So each digit d_j in d's decimal representation would equal its corresponding digit $a_{i,j}$ in $f(i)$'s decimal representation. But this can't be. There is one place in particular where the digits must differ: the ith place. d_i is defined to be 6 if $a_{i,i}$ is 5, and defined to be 5 if $a_{i,i}$ is not 5. Thus d_i is not the same digit as $a_{i,i}$. So d's decimal representation differs in at least one place from $f(i)$'s decimal representation; so d is different from $f(i)$. But $f(i)$ was an arbitrarily chosen member of the list. Thus we have our conclusion: d isn't anywhere on the list. But d is a real number between 0 and 1. So if our initial assumption that the range of f were all of R were correct, d would have to be on the list. So that initial assumption was false, and we've completed our argument: it's impossible for there to be a one-to-one function whose domain is $\mathbb{N}$ and whose range is all of R. Even though $\mathbb{N}$ and R are both infinite sets, R is a bigger infinite set.

To grasp the argument's final phase, think again in geometric terms. If d were on the list, its decimal representation would intersect the diagonal. Suppose, for instance, that d were $f(3)$:

$$f(0) = 0 . \boxed{a_{0,0}} \quad a_{0,1} \quad a_{0,2} \quad a_{0,3} \quad a_{0,4} \quad \cdots$$
$$f(1) = 0 . \quad a_{1,0} \quad \boxed{a_{1,1}} \quad a_{1,2} \quad a_{1,3} \quad a_{1,4} \quad \cdots$$
$$f(2) = 0 . \quad a_{2,0} \quad a_{2,1} \quad \boxed{a_{2,2}} \quad a_{2,3} \quad a_{2,4} \quad \cdots$$
$$d = f(3) = 0 . \boxed{a_{3,0}} \quad \boxed{a_{3,1}} \quad \boxed{a_{3,2}} \quad \boxed{a_{3,3}} \quad \boxed{a_{3,4}} \quad \cdots$$
$$f(4) = 0 . \quad a_{4,0} \quad a_{4,1} \quad a_{4,2} \quad a_{4,3} \quad \boxed{a_{4,4}} \quad \cdots$$

Then, given d's definition, its decimal representation would be guaranteed to differ from the diagonal series in its fourth digit, the point of intersection.

It's natural to voice the following misgiving about the argument: "if d was left off the list, then why can't you just add it in? You could add it in at the beginning, bumping all the remaining members of the list down one slot to make room for it":

initial list	make room for d	new list
$f(0)$		d
	$\downarrow$	
$f(1)$	$f(0)$	$f(0)$
	$\downarrow$	
$f(2)$	$f(1)$	$f(1)$
	$\downarrow$	
$\vdots$	$f(2)$	$f(2)$
	$\downarrow$	
$\vdots$	$\vdots$	$\vdots$

Natural as it is, the misgiving is misguided. It's true that, given any list, one could add d to that list using the method described. But this fact is irrelevant to the argument. The argument wasn't that there is some *unlistable real number*, d—some real number d that is somehow prevented from occurring in the range of any one-to-one function whose domain is $\mathbb{N}$. That would be absurd. The argument was rather that no single list can be complete: any list (i.e., any one-to-one function whose domain is $\mathbb{N}$) will leave out some real numbers. The left-out real numbers can appear on *other* lists, but that's beside the point. Compare: if a thousand people show up to eat at a small restaurant, many people will be left out. That's not to say that any individual person is incapable of entering; it's just to say that not everyone can enter at once. No matter who enters, others will be left out in the cold.

Exercise 1.4* For any set, A, the powerset of A is defined as the set of all A's subsets. Write out the definition of the powerset of A in the "$\{u : \ldots\}$" notation. Write out the powerset of $\{2, 4, 6\}$ in the braces notation (the one where you list each member of the set).

Exercise 1.5* Is $\mathbb{N}$ equinumerous with the set $\mathbb{Z}$ of all integers, negative, positive, and zero: $\{\cdots - 3, -2, -1, 0, 1, 2, 3, \ldots\}$?

2

PROPOSITIONAL LOGIC

WE BEGIN with the simplest logic commonly studied: propositional logic (PL). Despite its simplicity, it has great power and beauty.

2.1 Grammar of PL

We're going to approach propositional logic by studying a formal language. And the first step in the study of a formal language is always to rigorously define the language's grammar.

If all you want to do is to use and understand the language of logic, you needn't be so careful about grammar. For even without a precisely formulated grammar, you can intuitively recognize that things like this make sense:

$$P \rightarrow Q$$
$$R \wedge (\sim S \leftrightarrow P)$$

whereas things like this do not:

$$\rightarrow PQR\sim$$
$$(P\sim Q\sim (\vee$$
$$P \oplus Q$$

But to make any headway in metalogic, we will need more than an intuitive understanding of what makes sense and what does not. We will need a precise definition that has the consequence that only the strings of symbols in the first group "make sense".

Grammatical strings of symbols (i.e., ones that "make sense") are called *well-formed formulas*, or "formulas" or "wffs" for short. We define these by first carefully defining exactly which symbols are allowed to occur in wffs (the "primitive vocabulary"), and second, carefully defining exactly which strings of these symbols count as wffs. Here is the official definition; I'll explain what it means in a moment:

PRIMITIVE VOCABULARY:

- Connectives:[13] $\rightarrow$, $\sim$
- Sentence letters: $P, Q, R \ldots$, with or without numerical subscripts
- Parentheses: (,)

---

[13] Some books use $\supset$ instead of $\rightarrow$, or $\neg$ instead of $\sim$. Other common symbols include & or · for conjunction, | for disjunction, and $\equiv$ for the biconditional.

Definition of wff:

   (i) Every sentence letter is a PL-wff

  (ii) If ϕ and ψ are PL-wffs, then $(\phi\rightarrow\psi)$ and $\sim\!\phi$ are also PL-wffs

 (iii) Only strings that can be shown to be PL-wffs using (i) and (ii) are PL-wffs

(We allow numerical subscripts on sentence letters so that we don't run out when constructing increasingly complex formulas. Since $P_1, P_2, P_3 \ldots$ are all sentence letters, we have infinitely many to choose from.)

    We will be discussing a number of different logical systems throughout this book, with differing grammars. What we have defined here is the notion of a wff for one particular language, the language of PL. So strictly, we should speak of *PL-wffs*, as the official definition does. But usually I'll just say "wff" if there is no danger of ambiguity.

    Here is how the definition works. Its core is clauses (i) and (ii) (they're sometimes called the formation rules). Clause (i) says that if you write down a sentence letter on its own, that counts as a wff. So, for example, the sentence letter P, all by itself, is a wff. (So is Q, so is P_{147}, and so on. Sentence letters are often called "atomic" wffs, because they're not made up of smaller wffs.) Next, clause (ii) tells us how to build complex wffs from smaller wffs. It tells us that we can do this in two ways. First, it says that if we already have a wff, then we can put a $\sim$ in front of it to get another wff. (The resulting wff is often called a "negation".) For example, since P is a wff (we just used clause (i) to establish this), then $\sim\!P$ is also a wff. Second, clause (ii) says that if we already have two wffs, then we can put an $\rightarrow$ between them, enclose the whole thing in parentheses, and we get another wff. (The resulting wff is often called a "conditional", whose "antecedent" is the wff before the $\rightarrow$ and whose "consequent" is the wff after the $\rightarrow$.) For example, since we know that Q is a wff (clause (i)), and that $\sim\!P$ is a wff (we just showed this a moment ago), we know that $(Q\rightarrow\sim\!P)$ is also a wff. This process can continue. For example, we could put an $\rightarrow$ between the wff we just constructed and R (which we know to be a wff from clause (i)) to construct another wff: $((Q\rightarrow\sim\!P)\rightarrow R)$. By iterating this procedure, we can demonstrate the wff-hood of arbitrarily complex strings.

    Why the Greek letters in clause (ii)? Well, it wouldn't be right to phrase it, for example, in the following way: "if P and Q are wffs, then $\sim\!P$ and $(P\rightarrow Q)$ are also wffs". That would be too narrow, for it would apply only in the case of the sentence letters P and Q. It wouldn't apply to any other sentence letters (it wouldn't tell us that $\sim\!R$ is a wff, for example), nor would it allow us to construct negations and conditionals from complex wffs (it wouldn't tell us that $(P\rightarrow\sim\!Q)$ is a wff). We want to say that for *any* wff (not just P), if you put a $\sim$ in front of it you get another wff; and for *any* two wffs (not just P and Q), if you put an $\rightarrow$ between them (and enclose the result in parentheses) you get another wff. That's why we use the *metalinguistic variables* "ϕ" and "ψ".[14] The practice of using variables to express generality is familiar; we can say, for example, "for any integer n, if n is even, then $n+2$ is even as well". Just as "n" here is a variable for numbers, metalinguistic variables are variables

---

[14]Strictly speaking clause (ii) ought to be phrased using corner quotes; see exercise 1.2b.

for linguistic items. (We call them *meta*linguistic because they are variables we use in our metalanguage, in order to talk generally about the object language, which is in this case the formal language of propositional logic.)

What's the point of clause (iii)? Clauses (i) and (ii) provide only sufficient conditions for being a wff, and therefore do not on their own exclude nonsense combinations of primitive vocabulary like $P{\sim}Q{\sim}R$, or even strings like $P \oplus Q$ that include disallowed symbols. Clause (iii) rules these strings out, since there is no way to build up either of these strings from clauses (i) and (ii), in the way that we built up the wff $({\sim}P{\rightarrow}(P{\rightarrow}Q))$.

Notice an interesting feature of this definition: the very expression we are trying to define, 'wff', appears on the right-hand side of clause (ii) of the definition. In a sense, we are using the expression 'wff' in its own definition. But this "circularity" is benign, because the definition is *recursive*. A recursive (or "inductive") definition of a concept F contains a circular-seeming clause, often called the "inductive" clause, which specifies that *if* such-and-such objects are F, then so-and-so objects are also F. But a recursive definition also contains a "base clause", which specifies noncircularly that certain objects are F. Even though the inductive clause rests the status of certain objects as being Fs on whether certain other objects are Fs (whose status as Fs might in turn depend on the status of still other objects…), this eventually traces back to the base clause, which secures F-hood all on its own. Thus, recursive definitions are anchored by their base clauses; that's what distinguishes them from viciously circular definitions. In the definition of wffs, clause (i) is the base, and clause (ii) is the inductive clause. The wff-hood of the string of symbols $((P{\rightarrow}Q){\rightarrow}{\sim}R)$, for example, rests on the wff-hood of $(P{\rightarrow}Q)$ and of ${\sim}R$ by clause (ii); and the wff-hood of these, in turn, rests on the wff-hood of P, Q, and R, again by clause (ii). But the wff-hood of P, Q, and R doesn't rest on the wff-hood of anything else; clause (i) specifies directly that all sentence letters are wffs.

It's common to have symbols representing "and", "or", and "if and only if", for example: $\wedge$, $\vee$, and $\leftrightarrow$. But the only connectives in our primitive vocabulary are $\rightarrow$ and $\sim$; expressions like $P{\wedge}Q$, $P{\vee}Q$, and $P{\leftrightarrow}Q$ therefore do not officially count as wffs. However, we can still use $\wedge$, $\vee$, and $\leftrightarrow$ unofficially, since we can define those connectives in terms of $\sim$ and $\rightarrow$:

DEFINITIONS OF $\wedge$, $\vee$, AND $\leftrightarrow$:

- "$\phi{\wedge}\psi$" is short for "$\sim(\phi{\rightarrow}{\sim}\psi)$"
- "$\phi{\vee}\psi$" is short for "$\sim\phi{\rightarrow}\psi$"
- "$\phi{\leftrightarrow}\psi$" is short for "$(\phi{\rightarrow}\psi){\wedge}(\psi{\rightarrow}\phi)$" (which is in turn short for "$\sim((\phi{\rightarrow}\psi) \rightarrow \sim(\psi{\rightarrow}\phi))$")

So, whenever we subsequently write down an expression that includes one of the defined connectives, we can regard it as being short for an expression that includes only the official connectives, $\sim$ and $\rightarrow$. (Why did we choose these particular definitions? We'll show below that they generate the usual truth conditions for $\wedge$, $\vee$, and $\leftrightarrow$.)

Our choice to begin with $\rightarrow$ and $\sim$ as our official connectives was somewhat arbitrary. We could have started with $\sim$ and $\wedge$, and defined the others as follows:

- "$\phi \lor \psi$" is short for "$\sim(\sim\phi \land \sim\psi)$"
- "$\phi \rightarrow \psi$" is short for "$\sim(\phi \land \sim\psi)$"
- "$\phi \leftrightarrow \psi$" is short for "$(\phi \rightarrow \psi) \land (\psi \rightarrow \phi)$"

And other alternate choices are possible. (Why did we choose only a small number of primitive connectives, rather than including all of the usual connectives? Because, as we will see, it makes metalogic easier.)

The definition of wff requires conditionals to have outer parentheses. $P \rightarrow Q$, for example, is officially not a wff; one must write $(P \rightarrow Q)$. But informally, I'll often omit those outer parentheses. And I'll sometimes write square brackets instead of the official round ones (for example, "$[(P \rightarrow Q) \rightarrow R] \rightarrow P$") to improve readability.

2.2 The semantic approach to logic

In the next section I will introduce a "semantics" for propositional logic, and formal representations of logical truth and logical consequence of the semantic (model-theoretic) variety (recall section 1.5).

On the semantic conception, logical consequence amounts to: "truth-preservation in virtue of the meanings of the logical constants". This isn't perfectly clear, but it does lead to a clearer thought. Suppose we keep the meanings of an argument's logical constants fixed, but vary *everything else*. If the argument remains truth-preserving no matter how we vary everything else, then it would seem to preserve truth "in virtue of" the meanings of its logical constants. But what is to be included in "everything else"?

Here is an attractive picture of truth and meaning. The truth of a sentence is determined by two factors, *meaning* and *the world*. A sentence's meaning determines the conditions under which it is true—the ways the world would have to be in order for that sentence to be true. If the world *is* one of the ways picked out by the sentence's truth conditions, then the sentence is true; otherwise, not. Furthermore, a sentence's meaning is typically determined by the meanings of its parts—both its logical constants and its nonlogical expressions. So three elements determine whether a sentence is true: the world, the meanings of its nonlogical expressions, and the meanings of its logical constants.[15]

Now we can say what "everything else" means. Since we're holding constant the third element (the meanings of logical constants), varying everything else means varying the first two elements. The clearer thought about logical consequence, then, is that if an argument remains truth-preserving no matter how we vary (i) the world, and (ii) the meanings of nonlogical expressions, then its premises logically imply its conclusion.

To turn this clearer, but still not perfectly clear, thought into a formal approach, we need to do two things. First, we need mathematical representations—I'll call them *configurations*—of variations of types (i) and (ii). A configuration is a mathematical representation, both of the world and of the meanings of nonlogical expressions. Second, we need to define the conditions under which a sentence of the formal

---

[15] And also a fourth element: its syntax. We hold this constant as well.

language in question is *true in* one of these configurations. When we've done both things, we'll have a semantics for our formal language.

One thing such a semantics is good for is giving a formalization, of the semantic variety, of the notions of logical consequence and logical truth. This formalization represents one formula as being a logical consequence of others iff it is true in any configuration in which the latter formulas are true, and represents a formula as being a logical truth iff it is true in all configurations.

But a semantics for a formal language is good for something else as well. Defining configurations, and truth-in-a-configuration, can shed light on meaning in natural and other interpreted languages. Philosophers disagree over how to understand the notion of meaning in general. But meaning surely has *something* to do with truth conditions, as in the attractive picture above. If so, a formal semantics can shed light on meaning, if the ways in which configurations render formal sentences true and false are parallel to the ways in which the real world plus the meanings of words render corresponding interpreted sentences true and false. Expressions in formal languages are typically intended to represent bits of interpreted languages. The PL logical constant $\sim$, for example, represents the English logical constant 'not'; the sentence letters represent English declarative sentences, and so on. Part of specifying a configuration will be specifying what the nonlogical expressions mean in that configuration. And the definition of truth-in-a-configuration will be constructed so that the contributions of the symbolic logical constants to truth conditions will mirror the contributions to truth conditions of the logical constants that they represent.

2.3 Semantics of PL

Our semantics for PL is really just a more rigorous version of the method of truth tables from introductory logic books. What a truth table does is depict how the truth value of a given formula is determined by the truth values of its sentence letters, for *each* possible combination of truth values for its sentence letters. To do this nonpictorially, we need to define a notion corresponding to "a possible combination of truth values for sentence letters":

DEFINITION OF INTERPRETATION: A PL-interpretation is a function $\mathscr{I}$, that assigns to each sentence letter either 1 or 0.

The numbers 1 and 0 are our truth values. (Sometimes the letters 'T' and 'F' are used instead.) So an interpretation assigns truth values to sentence letters. Instead of saying "let P be false, and Q be true", we can say: let $\mathscr{I}$ be an interpretation such that $\mathscr{I}(P) = 0$ and $\mathscr{I}(Q) = 1$. (As with the notion of a wff, we will have different definitions of interpretations for different logical systems, so strictly we must speak of *PL-interpretations*. But usually it will be fine to speak simply of interpretations when it's clear which system is at issue.)

An interpretation assigns a truth value to each of the infinitely many sentence letters. To picture one such interpretation we could begin as follows:

$$\mathscr{I}(P)=1$$
$$\mathscr{I}(Q)=1$$
$$\mathscr{I}(R)=0$$
$$\mathscr{I}(P_1)=0$$
$$\mathscr{I}(P_2)=1$$

but since there are infinitely many sentence letters, the picture could not be completed. And this is just one interpretation among infinitely many; any other combination of assigned 1s and 0s to the infinitely many sentence letters counts as a new interpretation.

Once we settle what truth values a given interpretation assigns to the sentence letters, the truth values of complex sentences containing those sentence letters are thereby fixed. The usual, informal, method for saying exactly how those truth values are fixed is by giving truth tables for each connective. The standard truth tables for the $\rightarrow$ and $\sim$ are the following:[16]

What we will do, instead, is write out a formal definition of a function—the *valuation* function—that assigns truth values to complex sentences as a function of the truth values of their sentence letters—i.e., as a function of a given intepretation $\mathscr{I}$. But the idea is the same as for the truth tables: truth tables are really just pictures of the definition of a valuation function.

DEFINITION OF VALUATION: For any PL-interpretation, $\mathscr{I}$, the PL-valuation for $\mathscr{I}$, $V_{\mathscr{g}}$, is defined as the function that assigns to each wff either 1 or 0, and which is such that, for any sentence letter α and any wffs ϕ and ψ:

$$V_{\mathscr{g}}(\alpha)=\mathscr{I}(\alpha)$$
$$V_{\mathscr{g}}(\phi\rightarrow\psi)=1 \text{ iff either } V_{\mathscr{g}}(\phi)=0 \text{ or } V_{\mathscr{g}}(\psi)=1$$
$$V_{\mathscr{g}}(\sim\phi)=1 \text{ iff } V_{\mathscr{g}}(\phi)=0$$

Intuitively: we begin by choosing an interpretation function, which fixes the truth values for sentence letters. Then the valuation function assigns corresponding truth values to complex sentences depending on what connectives they're built up from: a negation is true iff the negated formula is false, and a conditional is true when its antecedent is false or its consequent is true.

---

[16]The $\rightarrow$ table, for example, shows what truth value $\phi\rightarrow\psi$ takes on depending on the truth values of its parts. Rows correspond to truth values for ϕ, columns to truth values for ψ. Thus, to ascertain the truth value of $\phi\rightarrow\psi$ when ϕ is 1 and ψ is 0, we look in the 1 row and the 0 column. The value listed there is 0—the conditional is false in this case. The $\sim$ table has only one "input-column" and one "result-column" because $\sim$ is a one-place connective.

We have here another recursive definition: the valuation function's values for complex formulas are determined by its values for smaller formulas; and this procedure bottoms out in the values for sentence letters, which are determined directly by the interpretation function $\mathscr{I}$.

Notice how the definition of the valuation function contains the English logical connectives 'either...or', and 'iff'. I used these English connectives rather than the logical connectives $\lor$ and $\leftrightarrow$, because at that point I was *not* writing down wffs of the language of study (in this case, the language of PL). I was rather using sentences of English—our metalanguage, the informal language we're using to discuss the formal language of PL—to construct my definition of the valuation function. My definition needed to employ the logical notions of disjunction and biconditionalization, the English words for which are 'either...or' and 'iff'.

One might again worry that something circular is going on. We defined the symbols for disjunction and biconditionalization, $\lor$ and $\leftrightarrow$, in terms of $\sim$ and $\rightarrow$ in section 2.1, and now we've defined the valuation function in terms of disjunction and biconditionalization. So haven't we given a circular definition of disjunction and biconditionalization? No. When we define the valuation function, we're not trying to *define* logical concepts such as negation, conjunction, disjunction, conditionalization, biconditionalization, and so on, at all. Reductive definition of these very basic concepts is probably impossible (though one can define some of them in terms of the others). What we are doing is starting with the assumption that we *already* understand the logical concepts, and then using those concepts to provide a semantics for a formal language. This can be put in terms of object language and metalanguage: we use metalanguage connectives, such as 'iff' and 'or', which we simply take ourselves to understand, to provide a semantics for the object-language connectives $\sim$ and $\rightarrow$.

An elementary fact will be important in what follows: for every wff ϕ and every PL-interpretation $\mathscr{I}$, $V_{\mathscr{I}}(\phi)$ is either 0 or 1, but not both.[17] Equivalently: a formula has one of the truth values iff it lacks the other. That this is a fact is built into the definition of the valuation function for PL. First of all, $V_{\mathscr{I}}$ is defined as a *function*, and so it can't assign *both* the number 0 and the number 1 to a wff. And second, $V_{\mathscr{I}}$ is defined as a function that *assigns either 1 or 0 to each wff* (thus, in the case of the second and third clauses, if a complex wff fails the condition for getting assigned 1, it automatically gets assigned 0).

Back to the definition of the valuation function. The definition applies only to official wffs, which can contain only the primitive connectives $\rightarrow$ and $\sim$. But sentences containing $\land$, $\lor$, and $\leftrightarrow$ are abbreviations for official wffs, and are therefore indirectly governed by the definition. In fact, given the abbreviations defined in section 2.1, we can show that the definition assigns the intuitively correct truth values to sentences containing $\land$, $\lor$, and $\leftrightarrow$. In particular, we can show that for any PL-interpretation $\mathscr{I}$, and any wffs ψ and χ,

---

[17] This fact won't hold for all the valuation functions we'll consider in this book; in Chapter 3 we will consider "trivalent" semantic systems in which some formulas are assigned neither 1 nor 0.

$$V_\mathscr{I}(\psi \wedge \chi) = 1 \text{ iff } V_\mathscr{I}(\psi) = 1 \text{ and } V_\mathscr{I}(\chi) = 1$$
$$V_\mathscr{I}(\psi \vee \chi) = 1 \text{ iff either } V_\mathscr{I}(\psi) = 1 \text{ or } V_\mathscr{I}(\chi) = 1$$
$$V_\mathscr{I}(\psi \leftrightarrow \chi) = 1 \text{ iff } V_\mathscr{I}(\psi) = V_\mathscr{I}(\chi)$$

I'll show that the first statement is true here; the others are exercises for the reader. I'll write out this proof in excessive detail, to make it clear exactly how the reasoning works.

Example 2.1: Proof that $\wedge$ gets the right truth condition. We are to show that for any wffs ψ and χ, and any PL-interpretation $\mathscr{I}$, $V_\mathscr{I}(\psi \wedge \chi) = 1$ iff $V_\mathscr{I}(\psi) = 1$ and $V_\mathscr{I}(\chi) = 1$. So, let ψ and χ be any wffs, and let $\mathscr{I}$ be any PL-interpretation; we must show that: $V_\mathscr{I}(\psi \wedge \chi) = 1$ iff $V_\mathscr{I}(\psi) = 1$ and $V_\mathscr{I}(\chi) = 1$. The expression $\psi \wedge \chi$ is an abbreviation for the expression $\sim(\psi \rightarrow \sim\chi)$. So what we must show is this: $V_\mathscr{I}(\sim(\psi \rightarrow \sim\chi)) = 1$ iff $V_\mathscr{I}(\psi) = 1$ and $V_\mathscr{I}(\chi) = 1$.

Now, in order to show that a statement A holds iff a statement B holds, we must first show that if A holds, then B holds; then we must show that if B holds, then A holds. So, first we must establish that if $V_\mathscr{I}(\sim(\psi \rightarrow \sim\chi)) = 1$, then $V_\mathscr{I}(\psi) = 1$ and $V_\mathscr{I}(\chi) = 1$. So, we begin by *assuming* that $V_\mathscr{I}(\sim(\psi \rightarrow \sim\chi)) = 1$, and we then attempt to show that $V_\mathscr{I}(\psi) = 1$ and $V_\mathscr{I}(\chi) = 1$. Well, since $V_\mathscr{I}(\sim(\psi \rightarrow \sim\chi)) = 1$, by definition of the valuation function, clause for $\sim$, we know that $V_\mathscr{I}(\psi \rightarrow \sim\chi) = 0$. Now, we earlier noted the principle that a wff has one of the two truth values iff it lacks the other; thus $V_\mathscr{I}(\psi \rightarrow \sim\chi)$ is *not* 1. (Henceforth I won't mention it when I make use of this principle.) But then, by the clause in the definition of $V_\mathscr{I}$ for the $\rightarrow$, we know that it's not the case that: either $V_\mathscr{I}(\psi) = 0$ or $V_\mathscr{I}(\sim\chi) = 1$. So, $V_\mathscr{I}(\psi) = 1$ and $V_\mathscr{I}(\sim\chi) = 0$. From the latter, by the clause for $\sim$, we know that $V_\mathscr{I}(\chi) = 1$. So now we have what we wanted: $V_\mathscr{I}(\psi) = 1$ and $V_\mathscr{I}(\chi) = 1$.

Next we must show that if $V_\mathscr{I}(\psi) = 1$ and $V_\mathscr{I}(\chi) = 1$, then $V_\mathscr{I}(\sim(\psi \rightarrow \sim\chi)) = 1$. This is sort of like undoing the previous half. Suppose that $V_\mathscr{I}(\psi) = 1$ and $V_\mathscr{I}(\chi) = 1$. Since $V_\mathscr{I}(\chi) = 1$, by the clause for $\sim$, $V_\mathscr{I}(\sim\chi) = 0$; but now since $V_\mathscr{I}(\psi) = 1$ and $V_\mathscr{I}(\sim\chi) = 0$, by the clause for $\rightarrow$ we know that $V_\mathscr{I}(\psi \rightarrow \sim\chi) = 0$; then by the clause for $\sim$, we know that $V_\mathscr{I}(\sim(\psi \rightarrow \sim\chi)) = 1$, which is what we were trying to show.   □

Example 2.1 is the first of many *metalogic proofs* we will be constructing in this book. (The symbol □ marks the end of such a proof.) It is an informal argument, phrased in the metalanguage, which establishes a fact about a formal language. As noted in section 1.3, metalogic proofs must be distinguished from proofs in formal systems—from the derivations and truth trees of introductory logic, and from the axiomatic and sequent proofs we will introduce below. Although there are no explicit guidelines for how to present metalogic proofs, they are generally given in a style that is common within mathematics. Constructing such proofs can at first be difficult. I offer the following pointers. First, keep in mind exactly what you are trying to prove. (In your first few proofs, it might be a good idea to begin by writing down: "what I am trying to prove is…".) Second, keep in mind the definitions of all the relevant technical terms (the definition of $\psi \wedge \chi$, for instance.) Third, keep in mind exactly what you are *given*. (In the preceding, for example, the important bit of information you are given is the definition of the valuation function; that definition tells you the conditions under which valuation functions assign 1s and 0s to negations and conditionals.) Fourth, keep in mind the canonical methods for establishing claims of various forms. (For example, if you want to show that a certain claim holds for *every* two wffs, begin with "let ψ and χ be any wffs"; show that the claim holds for ψ and χ; and conclude that the claim holds for all pairs of wffs. If you want to establish something of the form "if A, then B", begin by saying "suppose A", go on to reason your way to "B", and conclude: "and so, if A, then B". Often it can be helpful to reason by *reductio ad absurdum*: assume the opposite of the assertion you are trying to prove, reason your way to a contradiction, and conclude that the assertion is true since its opposite leads to contradiction.) Fifth: practice, practice, practice. As we progress, I'll gradually speed up the presentation of such proofs, omitting more and more details when they seem obvious. You should feel free to do the same; but it may be best to begin by constructing proofs very deliberately, so that later on you know exactly what details you are omitting.

Let's reflect on what we've done so far. We have defined the notion of a PL-interpretation, which assigns 1s and 0s to sentence letters of the formal language of PL. And we have also defined, for any PL-interpretation, a corresponding PL-valuation function, which extends the interpretation's assignment of 1s and 0s to complex wffs of PL. Note that we have been informally speaking of these assignments as assignments of *truth values*. That's because the assignment of 1s and 0s to complex wffs mirrors the way complex natural-language sentences get their truth values, as a function of the truth values of their parts. For example, the $\sim$ of PL is supposed to represent the English phrase 'it is not the case that'. Accordingly, just as an English sentence "It is not the case that ϕ" is true iff ϕ is false, one of our valuation functions assigns 1 to $\sim\phi$ iff it assigns 0 to ϕ. But strictly, it's probably best not to think of wffs of our formal language as genuinely having truth values. They don't genuinely have meanings after all. Our assignments of 1 and 0 *represent* the having of truth values.

A semantics for a formal language, recall, defines two things: configurations and truth-in-a-configuration. In the PL-semantics we have laid out, the configurations are the interpretation functions. A configuration is supposed to represent a way for the world to be, plus the meanings of nonlogical expressions. The only nonlogical expressions in PL are the sentence letters; and, for the purposes of PL anyway, their meanings can be represented simply as truth values. And once we've specified a truth value for each sentence letter, we've already represented the world as much as we can in PL. Thus PL-interpretations are appropriate configurations. As for truth-in-a-configuration, this is accomplished by the valuation functions. For any PL-interpretation, its corresponding valuation function specifies, for each complex wff, what truth value that wff has in that interpretation. Thus, for each wff (ϕ) and each configuration ($\mathscr{I}$), we have specified the truth value of that wff in that configuration ($V_{\mathscr{I}}(\phi)$).

Onward. We are now in a position to define the semantic versions of the notions of logical truth and logical consequence for propositional logic. The semantic notion of a logical truth is that of a *valid formula*:

DEFINITION OF VALIDITY: A wff ϕ is PL-valid iff for every PL-interpretation, $\mathscr{I}$, $V_{\mathscr{I}}(\phi) = 1$.

We write "$\vDash_{PL} \phi$" for "ϕ is PL-valid". (When it's obvious which system we're talking about, we'll omit the subscript on $\vDash$.) The valid formulas of PL are also called *tautologies*.

As for logical consequence, the semantic version of this notion is that of a single formula's being a *semantic consequence* of a set of formulas:

DEFINITION OF SEMANTIC CONSEQUENCE: A wff ϕ is a PL-semantic consequence of a set of wffs Γ iff for every PL-interpretation, $\mathscr{I}$, if $V_{\mathscr{I}}(\gamma) = 1$ for each γ such that $\gamma \in \Gamma$, then $V_{\mathscr{I}}(\phi) = 1$.

That is, ϕ is a PL-semantic-consequence of Γ iff ϕ is true whenever each member of Γ is true. We write "$\Gamma \vDash_{PL} \phi$" for "ϕ is a PL-semantic-consequence of Γ". (As usual we'll often omit the "PL" subscript; and further, let's improve readability by writing "$\phi_1, \ldots, \phi_n \vDash \psi$" instead of "$\{\phi_1, \ldots, \phi_n\} \vDash \psi$". That is, let's drop the set braces when it's convenient to do so.)

A related concept is that of *semantic equivalence*. Formulas ϕ and ψ are said to be (PL-) semantically equivalent iff each (PL-) semantically implies the other. For example, $\phi \rightarrow \psi$ and $\sim\psi \rightarrow \sim\phi$ are semantically equivalent. Notice that we could just as well have worded the definition thus: semantically equivalent formulas are those that have exactly the same truth value in every interpretation. Thus there is a sense in which semantically equivalent formulas "say the same thing": they have the same truth-conditional content.

Just as it's probably best not to think of sentences of our formal language as genuinely having truth values, it's probably best not to think of them as genuinely being logically true or genuinely standing in the relation of logical consequence. The notions we have just defined, of PL-validity and PL-semantic-consequence, are just formal representations of logical truth and logical consequence (semantically conceived). Indeed, the definitions we have given are best thought of as representing, rather than really being, a semantics. Further, when we get to formal provability, the definitions we will give are probably best thought of as representing facts about provability, rather than themselves defining a kind of provability. But forgive me if I sometimes speak loosely as if formal sentences really do have these features, rather than just representing them.

By the way, we can now appreciate why it was important to set up our grammar so carefully. The valuation function assigns truth values to complex formulas based on their form. One clause in its definition kicks in for atomic wffs, another clause kicks in for wffs of the form $\sim\phi$, and a third kicks in for wffs of the form $\phi \rightarrow \psi$. This works only if each wff has exactly one of these three forms; only a precise definition of wff guarantees this.

Exercise 2.1 Given the definitions of the defined symbols ∨ and ↔, show that for any PL-interpretation, $\mathscr{I}$, and any wffs ψ and χ,

$$V_{\mathscr{I}}(\psi \vee \chi) = 1 \text{ iff either } V_{\mathscr{I}}(\psi) = 1 \text{ or } V_{\mathscr{I}}(\chi) = 1$$
$$V_{\mathscr{I}}(\psi \leftrightarrow \chi) = 1 \text{ iff } V_{\mathscr{I}}(\psi) = V_{\mathscr{I}}(\chi)$$

2.4 Establishing validity and invalidity in PL

Now that we have set up a semantics, we can establish semantic facts about particular wffs. For example:

Example 2.2: Proof that $\vDash_{PL} (P \rightarrow Q) \rightarrow (\sim Q \rightarrow \sim P)$. To show a wff to be PL-valid, we must show that it is true in every PL-interpretation. So, let $\mathscr{I}$ be any PL-interpretation, and suppose for reductio that $V_{\mathscr{I}}((P \rightarrow Q) \rightarrow (\sim Q \rightarrow \sim P)) = 0$. This assumption leads to a contradiction, as the following argument shows:

(i) $V_{\mathscr{I}}((P \rightarrow Q) \rightarrow (\sim Q \rightarrow \sim P)) = 0$ (reductio assumption).
(ii) So, by the definition of a valuation function, clause for the $\rightarrow$, $V_{\mathscr{I}}(P \rightarrow Q) = 1$ and...
(iii) ...$V_{\mathscr{I}}(\sim Q \rightarrow \sim P) = 0$.
(iv) Given (iii), again by the clause for the $\rightarrow$, $V_{\mathscr{I}}(\sim Q) = 1$ and ...
(v) ...$V_{\mathscr{I}}(\sim P) = 0$.
(vi) Given (iv), by the clause for the $\sim$, $V_{\mathscr{I}}(Q) = 0$.
(vii) Similarly, (v) tells us that $V_{\mathscr{I}}(P) = 1$.
(viii) From (vii) and (vi), by the clause for the $\rightarrow$ we know that $V_{\mathscr{I}}(P \rightarrow Q) = 0$, which contradicts line (ii).

Here again we have given a metalogic proof: an informal mathematical argument establishing a fact about one of our formal languages. (The conclusion of the argument was not sufficiently impressive to merit the □ flourish.) There is nothing special about the form that this argument took. One could just as well have established the fact that $\vDash_{PL} (P \rightarrow Q) \rightarrow (\sim Q \rightarrow \sim P)$ by constructing a truth table, as one does in introductory textbooks, for such a construction is in effect a pictorial metalogic proof that a certain formula is PL-valid.

Arguments establishing facts of semantic consequence are parallel (in this example we will proceed more briskly):

Example 2.3: Proof that $P \rightarrow (Q \rightarrow R) \vDash Q \rightarrow (P \rightarrow R)$. We must show that in any PL-interpretation in which $P \rightarrow (Q \rightarrow R)$ is true, $Q \rightarrow (P \rightarrow R)$ is true as well. Let $\mathscr{I}$ be any PL-interpretation; we then reason as follows:

(i) Suppose for reductio that $V_{\mathscr{I}}(P \rightarrow (Q \rightarrow R)) = 1$ but...
(ii) ...$V_{\mathscr{I}}(Q \rightarrow (P \rightarrow R)) = 0$. (From now on we'll omit the subscripted $\mathscr{I}$.)
(iii) Line (ii) tells us that $V(Q) = 1$ and $V(P \rightarrow R) = 0$, and hence that $V(R) = 0$. So $V(Q \rightarrow R) = 0$.

(iv) Since $V(P \to R) = 0$ (line (iii)), $V(P) = 1$. So then, by (iii), $V(P \to (Q \to R)) = 0$. This contradicts (i).

One can also establish facts of invalidity and failures of semantic consequence:

Example 2.4: Proof that $\nvDash ((P \land R) \to Q) \to (R \to Q)$. To be valid is to be true in all interpretations; so to be *invalid* (i.e., not valid) is to be false in at least one interpretation. So all we must do is find one interpretation in which this wff is false. Let $\mathscr{I}$ be an interpretation such that $\mathscr{I}(R) = 1$ and $\mathscr{I}(P) = \mathscr{I}(Q) = 0$. Then $V_{\mathscr{I}}(P \land R) = 0$ (example 2.1), so $V_{\mathscr{I}}((P \land R) \to Q) = 1$. But since $V_{\mathscr{I}}(R) = 1$ and $V_{\mathscr{I}}(Q) = 0$, $V_{\mathscr{I}}(R \to Q) = 0$. So $V_{\mathscr{I}}((P \land R) \to Q) \to (R \to Q)) = 0$.

Example 2.5: Proof that $P \to R \nvDash (P \lor Q) \to R$. Consider a PL-interpretation in which P and R are false, and in which Q is true. $P \to R$ is then true (since its antecedent is false), but $P \lor Q$ is true (since Q is true—see exercise 2.1) while R is false, so $(P \lor Q) \to R$ is false.

I'll end this section by noting a certain fact about validity in PL: it is mechanically "decidable". That is, a computer program could be written that is capable of telling, for any given formula, whether or not that formula is PL-valid. The program would simply construct a complete truth table for the formula in question. A rigorous proof of this fact would take us too far afield (we would need, for example, to give a rigorous definition of what counts as a computer program), but the point is intuitively clear.

Exercise 2.2 Establish each of the following facts:

(a) $\vDash [P \land (Q \lor R)] \to [(P \land Q) \lor (P \land R)]$

(b) $(P \leftrightarrow Q) \lor (R \leftrightarrow S) \nvDash P \lor R$

(c) $\sim(P \land Q)$ and $\sim P \lor \sim Q$ are semantically equivalent.

2.4.1 *Schemas, validity, and invalidity*

Example 2.2 showed that a particular wff is valid: $(P \to Q) \to (\sim Q \to \sim P)$. But the argument for this depended only on the fact that the wff had the form $(\phi \to \psi) \to (\sim \psi \to \sim \phi)$. We could argue for a more general conclusion, namely that *any* wff of that form is valid, simply by replacing each "P" in the argument with "ϕ", and each "Q" with "ψ". This general conclusion is more useful than a conclusion concerning just one particular wff. Similarly, instead of showing particular wffs to semantically imply one another (as in example 2.3), we can show types of wffs to semantically imply one another (we can show, for example, that $\phi \to (\psi \to \chi) \vDash \psi \to (\phi \to \chi)$, for any wffs ϕ, ψ, and χ). And instead of showing particular wffs to be semantically equivalent, we can show types of wffs to be semantically equivalent.

It's tempting to think of general proofs of this sort as establishing facts about *schemas*—strings like "$(\phi \to \psi) \to (\sim \psi \to \sim \phi)$". For example, once the proof of example 2.2 has been appropriately generalized, it's tempting to think of it as showing that the schema $(\phi \to \psi) \to (\sim \psi \to \sim \phi)$ is valid. But strictly speaking such talk is incorrect since the notion of validity does not apply to schemas. Validity is defined in terms of truth in interpretations, and truth in interpretations is defined only for wffs. And schemas are not wffs, since schemas contain metalinguistic variables like ϕ, ψ, and χ, which are not part of the primitive vocabulary of the language of PL. Rather, schemas are "blueprints", which become wffs when we substitute particular wffs in for the metalinguistic variables.

Now, a schema can have a property that's closely related to validity. The schema $(\phi{\to}\psi){\to}(\sim\psi{\to}\sim\phi)$ has the following feature: all of its *instances* (that is, all formulas resulting from replacing ϕ and ψ with wffs) are valid. So one can informally speak of schemas as being valid when they have this closely related property. But we must take great care when speaking of the *in*validity of schemas. One might think to say that the schema $\phi{\to}\psi$ is invalid. But what would that mean? If it means that every instance of the schema is invalid, then the statement would be wrong. The wffs $P{\to}P$ and $P{\to}(Q{\to}Q)$, for example, are instances of $\phi{\to}\psi$, but each is valid. What's true about the schema $\phi{\to}\psi$ is that *some* of its instances are invalid (for example $P{\to}Q$).

So when dealing with schemas, it will often be of interest to ascertain whether each instance of the schema is valid; it will rarely (if ever) be of interest to ascertain whether each instance of the schema is invalid.

2.5 Sequent proofs in PL

The definitions of section 2.3 were inspired by the semantic conception of logical truth and logical consequence. An alternate conception is proof-theoretic. On this conception, the logical consequences of a set are those statements that can be proved if one takes the members of the set as premises; and a logical truth is a sentence that can be proved without using any premises at all. A proof procedure is a method of reasoning one's way, step by step, according to mechanical rules, from some premises to a conclusion. The formal systems inspired by this conception introduce mathematical models of proof procedures, which apply to sentences of formal languages.

There are different methods for defining what a proof procedure is. One is the method of *natural deduction*. This method is popular in introductory logic textbooks, since it allows reasoning with assumptions. For example, in order to prove a conditional, one assumes its antecedent for the sake of conditional proof, and goes on to establish its consequent on that basis. Natural-deduction proofs often look like this:

1.	$P{\to}(Q{\to}R)$	
2.	$P{\wedge}Q$	
3.	P	2, $\wedge$E
4.	Q	2, $\wedge$E
5.	$Q{\to}R$	1, 3, $\to$E
6.	R	4, 5, $\to$E
7.	$(P{\wedge}Q){\to}R$	2–6, $\to$I

or like this:

1. $P \rightarrow (Q \rightarrow R)$ Pr.
2. ~~show~~ $(P \wedge Q) \rightarrow R$ CD

3. | $P \wedge Q$ As.
4. | ~~show~~ R DD

5. | | P 3, $\wedge$E
6. | | Q 3, $\wedge$E
7. | | $Q \rightarrow R$ 1, 5, $\rightarrow$E
8. | | R 6, 7 $\rightarrow$E

The system we will examine in this section is a bit different. Our "sequent proofs" will look different from natural-deduction proofs:

1. $P \rightarrow (Q \rightarrow R) \Rightarrow P \rightarrow (Q \rightarrow R)$ RA
2. $P \wedge Q \Rightarrow P \wedge Q$ RA
3. $P \wedge Q \Rightarrow P$ 2, $\wedge$E
4. $P \wedge Q \Rightarrow Q$ 2, $\wedge$E
5. $P \rightarrow (Q \rightarrow R), P \wedge Q \Rightarrow Q \rightarrow R$ 1, 3, $\rightarrow$E
6. $P \rightarrow (Q \rightarrow R), P \wedge Q \Rightarrow R$ 4, 5, $\rightarrow$E
7. $P \rightarrow (Q \rightarrow R) \Rightarrow (P \wedge Q) \rightarrow R$ 6, $\rightarrow$I

Nevertheless, the underlying idea is quite similar. As we will see, sequent proofs also let us reason with assumptions.

2.5.1 Sequents

How does everyday reasoning work? Most simply, we reason in a step-by-step fashion from premises to a conclusion, each step being sanctioned by a *rule of inference*. For example, suppose that you begin with the premise $P \wedge (P \rightarrow Q)$. You already know this premise to be true, or you are supposing it to be true for the sake of argument. You can then reason your way to the conclusion that Q is also true, as follows:

1. $P \wedge (P \rightarrow Q)$ premise
2. P from line 1
3. $P \rightarrow Q$ from line 1
4. Q from lines 2 and 3

In this kind of proof, each step is a tiny, indisputably correct, logical inference. Consider the moves from 1 to 2 and from 1 to 3, for example. These are indisputably correct because a conjunctive statement clearly logically implies each of its conjuncts. Likewise for the move from 2 and 3 to 4: it is clear that a conditional statement together with its antecedent imply its consequent. Proof systems consist in part of simple *rules of inference*, which allow one to infer further formulas from formulas already contained in the proof. One example of a rule of inference (the one used to derive lines 2 and 3 in the above example) might be stated thus: "from a conjunctive statement one may infer either of the conjuncts".

In addition to rules of inference, ordinary reasoning employs a further technique: the use of *assumptions*. In order to establish a conditional claim "if *A*, then *B*", one would ordinarily (i) *assume A*, (ii) reason one's way to *B*, and then (iii) on that basis conclude that the conditional claim "if *A*, then *B*" is true. Once the assumption of *A* is shown to lead to *B*, the conditional claim "if *A*, then *B*" may be concluded. Another example: to establish a claim of the form "not-*A*", one would ordinarily (i) assume *A*, (ii) reason one's way to a contradiction, and (iii) on that basis conclude that "not-*A*" is true. Once the assumption of *A* is shown to lead to a contradiction, "not-*A*" may be concluded. The first sort of reasoning is called conditional proof, the second, reductio ad absurdum.

When you reason with assumptions, you write down sentences that you don't know to be true. Suppose you write down the sentence 'Jones is a bachelor' as an assumption for a conditional proof, with the goal of using it to prove the statement 'Jones is male' and thus to conclude that the conditional 'if Jones is a bachelor, then Jones is male' is true. In this context, you do not know 'Jones is a bachelor' to be true. You're merely assuming it for the sake of establishing the conditional. Outside of this conditional proof, the assumption need not hold. Once you've established the conditional, you stop assuming that Jones is a bachelor. To model this sort of reasoning formally, we need a way to keep track of how the conclusions we establish depend on the assumptions we have made. Natural-deduction systems in introductory textbooks tend to do this geometrically (by placement on the page), with special markers (e.g., 'show'), and by drawing lines or boxes around parts of the proof once the assumptions that led to those parts are no longer operative. We will do it differently: we will keep track of the dependence of conclusions on assumptions by writing down explicitly, for each conclusion, which assumptions it depends on. We will do this using what are known as *sequents*.[18]

A sequent looks like this:

$$\Gamma \Rightarrow \phi$$

Γ is a set of formulas; these formulas are called the *premises* of the sequent. ϕ is a single formula, called the *conclusion* of the sequent. "$\Rightarrow$" is a sign that goes between the sequent's premises and its conclusion, to indicate that the whole thing is a sequent. Think intuitively of a sequent as meaning that its conclusion is a logical consequence of its premises.[19]

---

[18]The method of sequents (as well as the method of natural deduction) was invented by Gerhard Gentzen (1935).

[19]For reasons I won't go into, multiple formulas are sometimes allowed on the right-hand side of a sequent. Also, the premises of a sequent are usually taken to be an ordered sequence (or some other ordered structure) of wffs rather than a set of wffs. This is to allow for nonstandard logics in which order

In the proof system that I am about to introduce, one constructs proofs out of sequents, rather than out of wffs. The lines of a sequent proof are sequents; the conclusion of a sequent proof is a sequent; and the rules of inference in sequent proofs let us infer new sequents from earlier sequents in a proof. Reasoning with sequents might initially seem weird. For example, one normally infers formulas from formulas; what does it *mean* to infer sequents from sequents? Well, think of it this way. Call a *natural-language sequent* one in which ϕ and the members of Γ are natural-language sentences; and call a natural-language sequent *logically correct* iff ϕ is a (genuine) logical consequence of the members of Γ. Natural-language sequent proofs can then be thought of as attempts to show that natural-language sequents are logically correct, and thus as attempts to establish that some sentences are logical consequences of others. On this conception, a good natural-language sequent rule ought to *preserve logical correctness*. That is, if the rule lets us infer a new sequent from some old sequents, then if the old sequents are logically correct, so must be the new sequent. Natural-language sequent proofs, thus understood, let us establish new cases of logical consequence on the basis of old cases of logical consequence—we reason about logical consequence. The symbolic sequent proof system we are about to define can be thought of as modeling this sort of reasoning.

We have seen how to think of reasoning with sequents as reasoning about logical consequence. But notice that this is, in effect, reasoning with assumptions. For whenever one makes some assumptions Γ, and on that basis establishes ϕ, ϕ will be a logical consequence of Γ if the reasoning is any good. Assumptions that lead to a conclusion are just statements that logically imply that conclusion. So, one can think of reasoning to ϕ on the basis of assumptions Γ as a sequent proof of the sequent $\Gamma \Rightarrow \phi$.

2.5.2 Rules

The first step in developing our system is to write down sequent rules. A sequent rule is a permission to move *from* certain sequents *to* another sequent. Our first rule will be "$\wedge$ introduction", or "$\wedge$I" for short:[20]

$$\frac{\Gamma \Rightarrow \phi \quad \Delta \Rightarrow \psi}{\Gamma, \Delta \Rightarrow \phi \wedge \psi} \ \wedge\text{I}$$

Above the line go the "from-sequents"; below the line goes the "to-sequent". (The comma between Γ and Δ in the to-sequent simply means that the premises of this sequent are all the members of Γ plus all the members of Δ. Strictly speaking we should write this in set-theoretic notation: $\Gamma \cup \Delta \Rightarrow \phi \wedge \psi$.) Thus $\wedge$I permits us to move from the sequents $\Gamma \Rightarrow \phi$ and $\Delta \Rightarrow \psi$ to the sequent $\Gamma, \Delta \Rightarrow \phi \wedge \psi$. We say that

---

and repetition of premises can affect the correctness of arguments. To recover logics in which order and repetition do *not* matter, one must then introduce "structural" rules of inference, for example a rule allowing one to infer $\phi, \psi \Rightarrow \chi$ from $\psi, \phi \Rightarrow \chi$ and a rule allowing one to infer $\phi, \phi \Rightarrow \psi$ from $\phi \Rightarrow \psi$. In the sequent systems we'll be discussing, order and repetition of premises don't matter, and so I'll just treat premises as sets. See Restall (2000) for more on sequent proof systems and structural rules.

[20]We have rules for $\wedge$ and $\vee$, even though they're not grammatically primitive connectives.

the to-sequent ($\Gamma, \Delta \Rightarrow \phi \wedge \psi$ in this case) *follows from* the from-sequents (in this case $\Gamma \Rightarrow \phi$ and $\Delta \Rightarrow \psi$) *via* the rule (in this case, $\wedge$I.)

Remember that our sequent rules are supposed to represent natural-language sequent rules that preserve logical correctness. So intuitively, our rules ought to have the following feature: if all of the from-sequents are (represent) logically correct sequents, then the to-sequent is guaranteed to be (represent) a logically correct sequent. Intuitively, $\wedge$I has this feature. For if some assumptions Γ logically imply ϕ, and some assumptions Δ logically imply ψ, then (since $\phi \wedge \psi$ intuitively follows from ϕ and ψ taken together) the conclusion $\phi \wedge \psi$ should indeed logically follow from all the assumptions together, the ones in Γ and the ones in Δ.

Our next sequent rule is $\wedge$E:

$$\frac{\Gamma \Rightarrow \phi \wedge \psi}{\Gamma \Rightarrow \phi} \quad \frac{\Gamma \Rightarrow \phi \wedge \psi}{\Gamma \Rightarrow \psi} \quad \wedge\text{E}$$

This has two forms. The first lets one move from the sequent $\Gamma \Rightarrow \phi \wedge \psi$ to the sequent $\Gamma \Rightarrow \phi$; the second lets one move from $\Gamma \Rightarrow \phi \wedge \psi$ to $\Gamma \Rightarrow \psi$. Again, each appears to preserve logical correctness. If the members of Γ imply the conjunction $\phi \wedge \psi$, then (since $\phi \wedge \psi$ intuitively implies both ϕ and ψ individually) it must be that the members of Γ imply ϕ, and they must also imply ψ.

The rule $\wedge$I is known as an *introduction rule* for $\wedge$, since it allows us to move *to* a sequent of the form $\Gamma \Rightarrow \phi \wedge \psi$. Likewise, the rule $\wedge$E is known as an *elimination rule* for $\wedge$, since it allows us to move *from* a sequent of that form. In fact our sequent system contains introduction and elimination rules for the other connectives as well: $\sim$, $\vee$, and $\rightarrow$ (let's forget the $\leftrightarrow$ here). We'll present those rules in turn.

First $\vee$I and $\vee$E:

$$\frac{\Gamma \Rightarrow \phi}{\Gamma \Rightarrow \phi \vee \psi} \quad \frac{\Gamma \Rightarrow \phi}{\Gamma \Rightarrow \psi \vee \phi} \quad \vee\text{I} \qquad \frac{\Gamma \Rightarrow \phi \vee \psi \quad \Delta_1, \phi \Rightarrow \chi \quad \Delta_2, \psi \Rightarrow \chi}{\Gamma, \Delta_1, \Delta_2 \Rightarrow \chi} \quad \vee\text{E}$$

$\vee$E embodies reasoning by separation of cases. Here, intuitively, is why it is a good sequent rule. Suppose we know that the three from-sequents of $\vee$E are logically correct. We can then give an intuitive argument that the to-sequent $\Gamma, \Delta_1, \Delta_2 \Rightarrow \chi$ is also logically correct; that is, that χ is a logical consequence of the formulas in Γ, Δ_1, and Δ_2. Suppose the formulas in Γ, Δ_1, and Δ_2 are all true. The first from-sequent tells us that the disjunction $\phi \vee \psi$ is true. So either ϕ or ψ is true. Now, if ϕ is true then the second from-sequent tells us that χ is true. And if ψ is true then the third from-sequent tells us that χ is again true. Either way, we learn that χ is true (there's the separation of cases reasoning).

Next, we have double negation:

$$\frac{\Gamma \Rightarrow \phi}{\Gamma \Rightarrow \sim\sim\phi} \quad \frac{\Gamma \Rightarrow \sim\sim\phi}{\Gamma \Rightarrow \phi} \quad \text{DN}$$

In connection with negation, we also have the rule of reductio ad absurdum:

$$\frac{\Gamma, \phi \Rightarrow \psi \wedge \sim\psi}{\Gamma \Rightarrow \sim\phi} \quad \text{RAA}$$

That is, if ϕ (along with perhaps some other assumptions, Γ) leads to a contradiction, we can conclude that $\sim\phi$ is true (given the assumptions in Γ). RAA and DN together are our introduction and elimination rules for $\sim$.

And finally we have $\rightarrow$I and $\rightarrow$E:

$$\frac{\Gamma, \phi \Rightarrow \psi}{\Gamma \Rightarrow \phi \rightarrow \psi} \quad \rightarrow\text{I} \qquad \frac{\Gamma \Rightarrow \phi \rightarrow \psi \quad \Delta \Rightarrow \phi}{\Gamma, \Delta \Rightarrow \psi} \quad \rightarrow\text{E}$$

$\rightarrow$E is perfectly straightforward; it's just the familiar rule of modus ponens. $\rightarrow$I is the principle of conditional proof. Suppose you can get to ψ on the assumption that ϕ (plus perhaps some other assumptions Γ). Then, you should be able to conclude that the conditional $\phi \rightarrow \psi$ is true (assuming the formulas in Γ). Put another way: if you want to establish the conditional $\phi \rightarrow \psi$, all you need to do is *assume* that ϕ is true, and reason your way to ψ.

We add, finally, one more sequent rule, the *rule of assumptions*:

$$\frac{}{\phi \Rightarrow \phi} \quad \text{RA}$$

This is the one sequent rule that requires no from-sequents (there are no sequents above the line). The rule permits us to move from no sequents at all to a sequent of the form $\phi \Rightarrow \phi$. (Strictly, this sequent should be written "$\{\phi\} \Rightarrow \phi$".) Intuitively, any such sequent is logically correct since any statement logically implies itself.

2.5.3 Sequent proofs

We have assembled all the sequent rules. Now we'll see how to construct sequent proofs with them.

DEFINITION OF SEQUENT PROOF: A sequent proof is a series of sequents, each of which is either of the form $\phi \Rightarrow \phi$, or follows from earlier sequents in the series by some sequent rule.

So, for example, the following is a sequent proof:

1. $P \wedge Q \Rightarrow P \wedge Q$ RA
2. $P \wedge Q \Rightarrow P$ 1, $\wedge$E
3. $P \wedge Q \Rightarrow Q$ 1, $\wedge$E
4. $P \wedge Q \Rightarrow Q \wedge P$ 2, 3, $\wedge$I

Though the definition of a sequent proof doesn't strictly require it, we write a line number to the left of each sequent in the series, and to the right of each line we write the sequent rule that justifies it, together with the line or lines (if any) that contained the "from" sequents required by the sequent rule in question. (The rule of assumptions requires no "from" sequents, recall.)

To reiterate a distinction I've been making, it's important to distinguish sequent proofs from metalogic proofs. Sequent proofs (and also the axiomatic proofs we will introduce in section 2.6) are proofs in formal systems. They consist of wffs in a formal language (plus the sequent sign, $\Rightarrow$), and are structured according to a carefully formulated definition (the definition of a sequent proof). Moreover, only the system's official rules of inference may be used. Metalogic proofs are very different. Recall the argument I gave in section 2.3 that any PL-valuation assigns 1 to $\phi \wedge \psi$ iff it assigns 1 to ϕ and 1 to ψ. The sentences in the argument were sentences of English, and the argument used informal reasoning. ("Informal" means merely that the reasoning doesn't follow a formally stipulated set of rules; it doesn't imply lack of rigor. The argument conforms to the standards of good argumentation that generally prevail in mathematics.)

Next we introduce the notion of a "provable sequent": ·

DEFINITION OF PROVABLE SEQUENT: A provable sequent is a sequent that is the last line of some sequent proof.

So, for example, the sequent proof given above establishes that $P \wedge Q \Rightarrow Q \wedge P$ is a provable sequent. We call a sequent proof whose last line is $\Gamma \Rightarrow \phi$ a sequent proof *of* $\Gamma \Rightarrow \phi$.

Note that it would be equivalent to define a provable sequent as any line in any sequent proof, because at any point in a sequent proof one may simply stop adding lines; the proof up until that point counts as a legal sequent proof.

The definitions we have given in this section give us a formal model (of the proof-theoretic variety) of the core logical notions, as applied to PL. The formal model of ϕ being a logical consequence of the formulas in set Γ is: the sequent $\Gamma \Rightarrow \phi$ is a provable sequent. The formal model of ϕ being a logical truth is: the sequent $\varnothing \Rightarrow \phi$ is a provable sequent ($\varnothing$ is the empty set).

2.5.4 *Example sequent proofs*

Let's explore how to construct sequent proofs. (You may find this initially awkward, but a little experimentation will show that the techniques familiar from proof systems in introductory textbooks will work here.)

Example 2.6: Let's return to the sequent proof of $P \wedge Q \Rightarrow Q \wedge P$:

1. $P \wedge Q \Rightarrow P \wedge Q$ RA
2. $P \wedge Q \Rightarrow P$ 1, $\wedge$E
3. $P \wedge Q \Rightarrow Q$ 1, $\wedge$E
4. $P \wedge Q \Rightarrow Q \wedge P$ 2, 3, $\wedge$I

Notice the strategy. We're trying to prove the sequent $P \wedge Q \Rightarrow Q \wedge P$. The premise of this sequent is $P \wedge Q$, so our first step is to use the rule of assumptions to introduce this wff into our proof (line 1). We now have a sequent with a conjunction as its conclusion, but its conjuncts are in the wrong order (we want $Q \wedge P$, not $P \wedge Q$). So first we take the conjuncts apart using $\wedge$E (lines 2 and 3), and then we put them back together in the other order (line 4).

Example 2.7: Next an example to illustrate conditional proof. Let's construct a sequent proof of $P{\rightarrow}Q, Q{\rightarrow}R \Rightarrow P{\rightarrow}R$:

1. $P{\rightarrow}Q \Rightarrow P{\rightarrow}Q$ RA
2. $Q{\rightarrow}R \Rightarrow Q{\rightarrow}R$ RA
3. $P \Rightarrow P$ RA   (for conditional proof)
4. $P{\rightarrow}Q, P \Rightarrow Q$ 1, 3, $\rightarrow$E
5. $P{\rightarrow}Q, Q{\rightarrow}R, P \Rightarrow R$ 2, 4, $\rightarrow$E
6. $P{\rightarrow}Q, Q{\rightarrow}R \Rightarrow P{\rightarrow}R$ 5, $\rightarrow$I

Here we are trying to establish a sequent whose premises are $P{\rightarrow}Q$ and $Q{\rightarrow}R$, so we start by using RA to get these two wffs into the proof. Then, since the conclusion of the sequent we're after is a conditional ($P{\rightarrow}R$), we use RA to introduce its antecedent (P), and our goal then is to get a sequent whose conclusion is the conditional's consequent (R). (To prove a conditional you assume the antecedent and then try to establish the consequent.) When we achieve this goal in line 5, we've shown that R follows from various assumptions, including P. The rule $\rightarrow$I (in essence, the principle of conditional proof) then lets us conclude that the conditional $P{\rightarrow}R$ follows from those other assumptions alone, without the help of P.

Notice how dependencies sometimes get added and sometimes get subtracted when we use sequent rules. The sequent on line 5 has P among its premises, but when we use $\rightarrow$I to move to line 6, P is no longer present as a premise. Whereas the conclusion of line 5 (R) depends on P, the conclusion of line 6 ($P{\rightarrow}R$) does not. A dependency is subtracted. (In compensation, the conclusion weakens, from R to $P{\rightarrow}R$.) But the move from 1 and 3 to 4 adds dependencies: the conclusion of line 4 depends on the premises from lines 1 and 3 taken together. (The rule $\rightarrow$E requires this.)

Example 2.8: Next a "DeMorgan" sequent, $\sim(P{\vee}Q) \Rightarrow \sim P{\wedge}\sim Q$:

1. $\sim(P{\vee}Q) \Rightarrow \sim(P{\vee}Q)$ RA
2. $P \Rightarrow P$ RA   (for reductio)
3. $P \Rightarrow P{\vee}Q$ 2, VI
4. $\sim(P{\vee}Q), P \Rightarrow (P{\vee}Q){\wedge}\sim(P{\vee}Q)$ 1, 3, $\wedge$I
5. $\sim(P{\vee}Q) \Rightarrow \sim P$ 4, RAA
6. $Q \Rightarrow Q$ RA   (for reductio)
7. $Q \Rightarrow P{\vee}Q$ 6, VI
8. $\sim(P{\vee}Q), Q \Rightarrow (P{\vee}Q){\wedge}\sim(P{\vee}Q)$ 1, 7, $\wedge$I
9. $\sim(P{\vee}Q) \Rightarrow \sim Q$ 8, RAA
10. $\sim(P{\vee}Q) \Rightarrow \sim P{\wedge}\sim Q$ 5, 9, $\wedge$I

Notice the two main strategies here. First, in order to establish a conjunction (such as $\sim P{\wedge}\sim Q$), you independently establish the conjuncts and then put them together using $\wedge$I. Second, in order to establish a negation (such as $\sim P$), you use reductio ad absurdum.

Example 2.9: Next let's establish $\varnothing \Rightarrow P{\vee}{\sim}P$:

1. ${\sim}(P{\vee}{\sim}P) \Rightarrow {\sim}(P{\vee}{\sim}P)$ RA   (for reductio)
2. $P \Rightarrow P$ RA   (for reductio)
3. $P \Rightarrow P{\vee}{\sim}P$ 2, VI
4. ${\sim}(P{\vee}{\sim}P), P \Rightarrow (P{\vee}{\sim}P) \wedge {\sim}(P{\vee}{\sim}P)$ 1, 3, ∧I
5. ${\sim}(P{\vee}{\sim}P) \Rightarrow {\sim}P$ 4, RAA
6. ${\sim}(P{\vee}{\sim}P) \Rightarrow P{\vee}{\sim}P$ 5, VI
7. ${\sim}(P{\vee}{\sim}P) \Rightarrow (P{\vee}{\sim}P) \wedge {\sim}(P{\vee}{\sim}P)$ 1, 6, ∧I
8. $\varnothing \Rightarrow {\sim}{\sim}(P{\vee}{\sim}P)$ 7, RAA
9. $\varnothing \Rightarrow P{\vee}{\sim}P$ 8, DN

Here my overall goal was to assume ${\sim}(P{\vee}{\sim}P)$ and then derive a contradiction. And my route to the contradiction was to first establish ${\sim}P$ (by a reductio argument, in lines 2–5), and then to get my contradiction from that.

Example 2.10: Finally, let's establish a sequent corresponding to a way that ∨E is sometimes formulated: $P{\vee}Q, {\sim}P \Rightarrow Q$:

1. $P{\vee}Q \Rightarrow P{\vee}Q$ RA
2. ${\sim}P \Rightarrow {\sim}P$ RA
3. $Q \Rightarrow Q$ RA   (for use with ∨E)
4. $P \Rightarrow P$ RA   (for use with ∨E)
5. ${\sim}Q \Rightarrow {\sim}Q$ RA   (for reductio)
6. ${\sim}P, P \Rightarrow P \wedge {\sim}P$ 2, 4, ∧I
7. ${\sim}P, P, {\sim}Q \Rightarrow (P \wedge {\sim}P) \wedge Q$ 5, 6, ∧I
8. ${\sim}P, P, {\sim}Q \Rightarrow P \wedge {\sim}P$ 7, ∧E
9. ${\sim}P, P \Rightarrow {\sim}{\sim}Q$ 8, RAA
10. ${\sim}P, P \Rightarrow Q$ 9, DN
11. $P{\vee}Q, {\sim}P \Rightarrow Q$ 1, 3, 10, ∨E

The basic idea of this proof was to use ∨E on line 1 to get Q. That called, in turn, for showing that each disjunct of $P{\vee}Q$ leads to Q. Showing that Q leads to Q is easy; that was line 3. Showing that P leads to Q took lines 4–10; line 10 states the result of that reasoning, namely that Q follows from P (given also the other premise of the whole argument, ${\sim}P$). I began at line 4 by assuming P. Then my strategy was to establish Q by reductio, so I assumed ${\sim}Q$ in line 5, and then got a contradiction in line 6. But there was a minor hitch. I wanted next to use RAA to conclude ${\sim}{\sim}Q$. But look carefully at how RAA is formulated. It says that if we have $\Gamma, \phi \Rightarrow \psi \wedge {\sim}\psi$, we can conclude $\Gamma \Rightarrow {\sim}\phi$. So to use RAA to infer $\Gamma \Rightarrow {\sim}\phi$, Γ *together with* ϕ must imply a contradiction. So in the present case, in order to finish the reductio argument and conclude ${\sim}{\sim}Q$, the contradiction $P \wedge {\sim}P$ needed to depend on the reductio assumption ∼Q. But on line 6, the contradiction depended only on ∼P and P. To get around this, I used a little trick in lines 7 and 8. I used ∧I to pop ∼Q onto the end of the contradiction (thus adding a dependency on ∼Q), and then I used ∧E to pop it off (retaining the dependency). One can always use this trick to add a dependency—to add any desired wff to the premises of a sequent.[21] (If the wff you want to add isn't in the proof already, just use RA to get it in there.)

Exercise 2.3 Prove the following sequents:

(a) $P{\rightarrow}(Q{\rightarrow}R) \Rightarrow (Q{\wedge}{\sim}R){\rightarrow}{\sim}P$

(b) $P, Q, R \Rightarrow P$

(c) $P{\rightarrow}Q, R{\rightarrow}Q \Rightarrow (P{\vee}R){\rightarrow}Q$

2.6 Axiomatic proofs in PL

In this section we consider a different approach to proof theory, the axiomatic approach. An axiomatic (or "Hilbert-style") proof consists of step-by-step reasoning governed by rules of inference, just like a sequent proof. But axiomatic systems do not allow reasoning with assumptions, and therefore do not allow conditional proof or reductio ad absurdum. Moreover, they have very few rules of inference. (They have axioms instead—see below.) These differences make axiomatic proofs much harder to construct, but there is a compensatory advantage in metalogic: in many cases it is easier to prove things *about* axiomatic systems.

Let's first think about axiomatic systems informally. An axiomatic proof will be defined as a series of formulas (not sequents—we no longer need them since we're not reasoning with assumptions anymore), the last of which is the conclusion of the proof. Each line in the proof must be justified in one of two ways: it may be inferred by a rule of inference from earlier lines in the proof (rules of inference now relate formulas, not sequents), or it may be an *axiom*. An axiom is a certain kind of formula, a formula that one is allowed to enter into a proof without any further justification. Axioms are the "starting points" of proofs, the foundation on which proofs rest. Since axioms are to play this role, the axioms in a *good* axiomatic system ought to represent indisputable logical truths. (For example, "$P{\rightarrow}P$" would be a good axiom, since sentences like "if it is raining then it is raining" and "if snow is white then snow is white" are obviously logical truths. But we won't choose this particular axiom; we'll choose other axioms from which it may be proved.) Similarly, a rule of inference in a good axiomatic system ought to represent an argument form in which the premises clearly logically imply the conclusion.

Actually we'll employ a slightly more general notion of a proof: a proof *from* a given set of wffs Γ. A proof from Γ will be allowed to contain members of Γ, in

---

[21] Adding arbitrary dependencies is not allowed in *relevance logic*, where a sequent is provable only when all of its premises are, intuitively, relevant to its conclusion. Relevance logicians modify various rules of standard logic, including the rule of ∧E.

addition to axioms and wffs that follow from earlier lines by a rule. Think of the members of Γ as premises, which in the context of a proof from Γ are temporarily treated as axioms, in that they are allowed to be entered into the proof without any justification. (Premises are a *bit* like the assumptions in sequent proofs, but they're not the same: a proof of ϕ from set of premises Γ cannot contain any further assumptions beyond those in Γ. You can't just assume a formula for the sake of conditional proof or reductio—there simply is no conditional proof or proof by reductio in an axiomatic system.) The intuitive point of a proof from Γ is to demonstrate its conclusion *on the assumption that the members of Γ are true*, in contrast to a proof simpliciter (i.e. a proof in the sense of the previous paragraph), whose point is to demonstrate its conclusion unconditionally. (Note that we can regard a proof simpliciter as a proof *from* the empty set ∅.)

Formally, to apply the axiomatic method, we must choose (i) a set of rules, and (ii) a set of axioms. In choosing a set of axioms, we simply choose any set of wffs, although as we saw, in a good axiomatic system the axioms should represent logical truths. A rule is simply a permission to infer one sort of sentence from other sentences. For example, the rule *modus ponens* can be stated thus: "*From $\phi \rightarrow \psi$ and ϕ you may infer ψ*", and pictured as follows:

$$\frac{\phi \rightarrow \psi \quad \phi}{\psi} \quad \text{MP}$$

(There typically are very few rules, often just modus ponens. Modus ponens corresponds to the sequent rule →E.) Given any chosen axioms and rules, we can define the following concepts:

DEFINITION OF AXIOMATIC PROOF FROM A SET: Where Γ is a set of wffs and ϕ is a wff, an axiomatic proof from Γ is a finite sequence of wffs whose last line is ϕ, in which each line either (i) is an axiom, (ii) is a member of Γ, or (iii) follows from earlier wffs in the sequence via a rule.

DEFINITION OF AXIOMATIC PROOF: An axiomatic proof of ϕ is an axiomatic proof of ϕ *from* ∅ (i.e., a finite sequence of wffs whose last line is ϕ, in which each line either (i) is an axiom, or (ii) follows from earlier wffs in the sequence via a rule).

It is common to write "Γ ⊢ ϕ" to mean that ϕ is provable from Γ, i.e., that there exists some axiomatic proof of ϕ from Γ. We also write "⊢ ϕ" to mean that ∅ ⊢ ϕ, i.e. that ϕ is provable, i.e., that there exists some axiomatic proof of ϕ from no premises at all. (Formulas provable from no premises at all are often called theorems.) This notation can be used for any axiomatic system, i.e. any choice of axioms and rules. The symbol ⊢ may be subscripted with the name of the system in question. Thus, for our axiom system for PL below, we may write: ⊢$_{PL}$. (We'll omit this subscript when it's clear which axiomatic system is being discussed.)

Here is an axiomatic system for PL:

AXIOMATIC SYSTEM FOR PL:

- *Rule*: MP
- *Axioms*: The result of substituting wffs for ϕ, ψ, and χ in any of the following schemas is an axiom:

$$\phi \rightarrow (\psi \rightarrow \phi) \tag{PL1}$$

$$(\phi \rightarrow (\psi \rightarrow \chi)) \rightarrow ((\phi \rightarrow \psi) \rightarrow (\phi \rightarrow \chi)) \tag{PL2}$$

$$(\sim\psi \rightarrow \sim\phi) \rightarrow ((\sim\psi \rightarrow \phi) \rightarrow \psi) \tag{PL3}$$

Thus a PL-theorem is any formula that is the last of a sequence of formulas, each of which is either a PL1-, PL2-, or PL3-axiom, or follows from earlier formulas in the sequence by MP. And a formula is PL-provable *from* some set Γ if it is the last of a sequence of formulas, each of which is either a member of Γ, a PL1-, PL2-, or PL3-axiom, or follows from earlier formulas in the sequence by MP.

The axiom "schemas" PL1–PL3 are not themselves axioms. They are, rather, "recipes" for constructing axioms. Take PL1, for example:

$$\phi \rightarrow (\psi \rightarrow \phi)$$

This string of symbols isn't itself an axiom because it isn't a wff; it isn't a wff because it contains Greek letters, which aren't allowed in wffs (since they're not on the list of PL primitive vocabulary). ϕ and ψ are variables of our metalanguage; you only get an axiom when you replace these variables with wffs. $P \rightarrow (Q \rightarrow P)$, for example, is an axiom (well, officially it requires outer parentheses). It results from PL1 by replacing ϕ with P and ψ with Q. (Note: since you can put in any wff for these variables, and there are infinitely many wffs, there are infinitely many axioms.)

A few points of clarification about how to construct axioms from schemas. First point: you can stick in the same wff for two different Greek letters. Thus you can let both ϕ and ψ in PL1 be P, and construct the axiom $P \rightarrow (P \rightarrow P)$. (But of course, you don't *have* to stick in the same thing for ϕ as for ψ.) Second point: you can stick in complex formulas for the Greek letters. Thus $(P \rightarrow Q) \rightarrow (\sim(R \rightarrow S) \rightarrow (P \rightarrow Q))$ is an axiom (I put in $P \rightarrow Q$ for ϕ and $\sim(R \rightarrow S)$ for ψ in PL1). Third point: within a single axiom, you can't substitute different wffs for a single Greek letter. For example, $P \rightarrow (Q \rightarrow R)$ is *not* an axiom; you can't let the first ϕ in PL1 be P and the second ϕ be R. Final point: even though you can't substitute different wffs for a single Greek letter *within* a single axiom, you *can* let a Greek letter become one wff when making *one* axiom, and let it become a different wff when making *another* axiom; and you can use each of these axioms within a single axiomatic proof. For example, each of the following is an instance of PL1; you could use both within a single axiomatic proof:

$$P \rightarrow (Q \rightarrow P)$$

$$\sim P \rightarrow ((Q \rightarrow R) \rightarrow \sim P)$$

In the first case, I made ϕ be P and ψ be Q; in the second case I made ϕ be $\sim P$ and ψ be $Q \rightarrow R$. This is fine because I kept ϕ and ψ constant *within* each axiom. (The type of symbol replacement described in this paragraph is sometimes called uniform substitution.)

Thus we have developed another formalism that is inspired by the proof-theoretic conception of the core logical notions. The PL-theorems represent the logical truths, and PL-provability represents logical consequence.

Axiomatic proofs are much harder to construct than sequent proofs. Some are easy, of course. Here is a proof of $(P{\to}Q){\to}(P{\to}P)$:

1. $P{\to}(Q{\to}P)$ PL1
2. $(P{\to}(Q{\to}P)){\to}((P{\to}Q){\to}(P{\to}P))$ PL2
3. $(P{\to}Q){\to}(P{\to}P)$ 1, 2, MP

The existence of this proof shows that $(P{\to}Q){\to}(P{\to}P)$ is a theorem. (The line numbering and explanations of how the lines were obtained aren't required, but they make the proofs easier to read.)

Building on the previous proof, we can construct a proof of $P{\to}P$ *from* $\{P{\to}Q\}$. (In a proof *from* a set, when we write down a member of the set we'll annotate it "premise".)

1. $P{\to}(Q{\to}P)$ PL1
2. $(P{\to}(Q{\to}P)){\to}((P{\to}Q){\to}(P{\to}P))$ PL2
3. $(P{\to}Q){\to}(P{\to}P)$ 1, 2, MP
4. $P{\to}Q$ premise
5. $P{\to}P$ 3, 4, MP

Thus we have shown that $\{P{\to}Q\} \vdash P{\to}P$. (Let's continue with our practice of dropping the set-braces in such statements. In this streamlined notation, what we just showed is: $P{\to}Q \vdash P{\to}P$.)

The next example is a little harder: $(R{\to}P){\to}(R{\to}(Q{\to}P))$

1. $[R{\to}(P{\to}(Q{\to}P))]{\to}[(R{\to}P){\to}(R{\to}(Q{\to}P))]$ PL2
2. $P{\to}(Q{\to}P)$ PL1
3. $[P{\to}(Q{\to}P)]{\to}[R{\to}(P{\to}(Q{\to}P))]$ PL1
4. $R{\to}(P{\to}(Q{\to}P))$ 2, 3, MP
5. $(R{\to}P){\to}(R{\to}(Q{\to}P))$ 1, 4, MP

Here's how I approached this problem. The formula I was trying to prove, namely $(R{\to}P){\to}(R{\to}(Q{\to}P))$, is a conditional whose antecedent and consequent both begin: $(R{\to}$. That looks like the consequent of PL2. So I wrote out an instance of PL2 whose consequent was the formula I was trying to prove; that gave me line 1 of the proof. Then I tried to figure out a way to get the antecedent of line 1; namely, $R{\to}(P{\to}(Q{\to}P))$. And that turned out to be pretty easy. The consequent of this formula, $P{\to}(Q{\to}P)$, is an axiom (line 2 of the proof). And if you can get a formula ϕ, then you choose anything you like—say, R,—and then get $R{\to}\phi$, by using PL1 and modus ponens; that's what I did in lines 3 and 4.

As you can see, the proofs are getting harder. And they get harder still. Fortunately, we will be able to develop some machinery to make them easier; but that will need to wait for a couple of sections.

> **Exercise 2.4** Establish each of the following facts. For these problems, do not use the "toolkit" assembled below; construct the axiomatic proofs "from scratch". However, you may use a fact you prove in an earlier problem in later problems.
>
> (a) $\vdash P {\to} P$
>
> (b) $\vdash ({\sim}P {\to} P) {\to} P$
>
> (c) ${\sim}{\sim}P \vdash P$

2.7 Soundness of PL and proof by induction

Note: the next three sections are more difficult than the preceding sections. You might at first skip them; but if you decide to work through the more difficult sections on metalogic later in the book (for example sections 6.5 and 6.6, or the bits dealing with proof by induction), you should first return here.

In this chapter we have taken both a proof-theoretic and a semantic approach to propositional logic. In each case, we introduced formal notions of logical truth and logical consequence. For the semantic approach, these notions involved truth in PL-interpretations. For the proof-theoretic approach, we considered two formal definitions, one involving sequent proofs, the other involving axiomatic proofs.

An embarrassment of riches! We have multiple formal accounts of our logical notions. But in fact, it can be shown that *all three of our definitions yield exactly the same results*. Here I'll prove this just for the notion of a *theorem* (last line of an axiomatic proof) and the notion of a *valid* formula (true in all PL-interpretations). I'll do this by proving the following two statements:

Soundness of PL: Every PL-theorem is PL-valid.

Completeness of PL: Every PL-valid wff is a PL-theorem.

Soundness is pretty easy to prove; we'll do that in a moment. Completeness is harder; we'll prove that in section 2.9. Soundness and completeness together tell us that PL-validity and PL-theoremhood exactly coincide.

But first a short detour: we need to introduce a method of proof that is ubiquitous throughout metalogic (as well as mathematics generally): the method of induction. The basic idea, in its simplest form, is this. Suppose we have infinitely many objects lined up like this:

$$\bullet \quad \bullet \quad \bullet \quad \bullet \quad \cdots$$

And suppose we want to show that each of these objects has a certain property. How to do it?

The method of induction directs us to proceed in two steps. First, show that the *first* object has the property:

$$\odot \quad \bullet \quad \bullet \quad \bullet \quad \cdots$$

This is called the "base case" of the inductive proof. Next, show that whenever any of the objects in the line has the property, the next object in the line must have the property as well. This is called the "inductive step" of the proof. The method of induction then says: if you've established those two things, you can go ahead and conclude that *all* the objects in the line have the property. Why is this conclusion justified? Well, since the first object has the property, the second object must have the property as well, given the inductive step:

But then another application of the inductive step tells us that the third object has the property as well:

And so on; all objects in the line have the property:

That is how induction works when applied to objects lined up in the manner depicted: there is a first object in line; after each object there is exactly one further object; and each object appears some finite number of jumps after the first object. Induction can also be applied to objects structured in different ways. Consider, for example, the following infinite grid of objects:

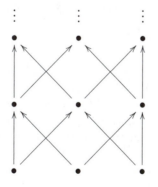

At the bottom of this grid there are three dots. Every pair of these three dots combines to produce one new dot. (For example, the leftmost dot on the second from the bottom level is produced by the leftmost two dots on the bottom level.) The resulting three dots (formed from the three pairs drawn from the three dots on the bottom level) form the second level of the grid. These three dots on the second level produce the third level in the same way, and so on. Suppose, now, that one could prove that the bottom three dots have some property:

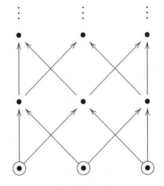

(This is the "base case".) And suppose further that one could prove that whenever two dots with the property combine, the resulting dot also has the property ("inductive step"). Then, just as in the previous example, induction allows us to conclude that all the dots in the grid have the property. Given the base case and the inductive step, we know that the dots on the second level of the grid have the property:

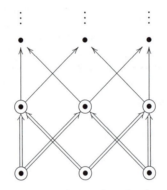

But then, given the inductive step, we know that the dots on the third level have the property. And so on, for all the other levels.

In general, induction is a method for proving that each member of a certain collection of objects has a property. It works when (but only when) each object in the collection results from some "starting objects" by a finite number of iterations of some "operations". In the base case one proves that the starting objects have the property; in the inductive step one proves that the operations *preserve* the property, in the sense that whenever one of the operations is applied to some objects with the property, the resulting new object has the property as well; and finally one concludes that all objects have the property.

This idea manifests itself in logic in a few ways. One is in a style of proof sometimes called "induction on formula construction" (or: induction "on the number of connectives" of the formula). Suppose we want to establish that absolutely every PL-wff has a certain property, p. The method of proof by induction on formula construction tells us to first establish the following two claims:

(B) Every atomic wff (i.e. every sentence letter) has property p

(I) For any wffs ϕ and ψ, *if* both ϕ and ψ have property p, *then* the wffs $\sim\phi$ and $\phi\rightarrow\psi$ also have property p

Once these are established, proof by induction allows us to conclude that every wff has property p. Why is this conclusion justified? Recall the definition of a wff from section 2.1: each wff is built up from atomic wffs by repeated application of clause (ii): "if ϕ and ψ are wffs then $\sim\phi$ and $\phi\rightarrow\psi$ are also wffs". So each wff is the culmination of a finite process that starts with atomic wffs and continues by building conditionals and negations from wffs formed in previous steps of the process. But claim (B) (the base case) shows that the *starting points* of this process all have property p. And claim (I) (the inductive step) shows that the subsequent steps in this process *preserve* property p: if the formulas one has built up so far have property p, then the next formula in the process (built up of previous formulas using either $\rightarrow$ or $\sim$) is guaranteed to also have p. So all wffs have property p. In terms of the general idea of inductive proof, the atomic wffs are our "starting objects" (like the bottom three dots in the grid), and the rules of grammar for $\sim$ and $\rightarrow$ which generate complex wffs from simpler wffs are the "operations".

Here is a simple example of proof by induction on formula construction:

Proof that every wff contains a finite number of different sentence letters. We are trying to prove a statement of the form: every wff has property p. The property p in this case is *having a finite number of different sentence letters*. Our proof has two steps:

Base case: here we must show that each atomic wff—i.e., each sentence letter—has p. This is obvious, since each sentence letter contains just one sentence letter: itself.

Inductive step: here we must show that *if* wffs ϕ and ψ have property p, then so do $\sim\phi$ and $\phi\rightarrow\psi$. So we begin by *assuming*:

> formulas ϕ and ψ each have finitely many different sentence letters   (ih)

This assumption is often called the "inductive hypothesis". We must then show that both $\sim\phi$ and $\phi\rightarrow\psi$ have finitely many different sentence letters. This, too, is easy. $\sim\phi$ has as many different sentence letters as does ϕ; (ih) tells us that ϕ has finitely many; $\sim\phi$ therefore has finitely many as well. As for $\phi\rightarrow\psi$, it has, at most, $n+m$ sentence letters, where n and m are the number of different sentence letters in ϕ and ψ, respectively; (ih) tells us that n and m are finite, and so $n+m$ is finite as well.

We've shown that every atomic formula has the property *having a finite number of different sentence letters*; and we've shown that the property is inherited by complex formulas built according to the formation rules. But every wff is either atomic, or built from atomics by a finite series of applications of the formation rules. Therefore, by induction, every wff has the property.   □

The following proof of soundness requires a different form of inductive proof:

Proof of soundness for PL. Unlike the previous proof, what we are trying to prove here does not have the form "Every wff has property p". Instead, it has the form "Every *theorem* has property *p*". We can still use induction, but it will have to be induction of a type other than induction on formula construction. Consider: a theorem is any line of a proof. And every line of every proof is the culmination of a finite series of wffs in which each wff is either an axiom, or follows from earlier lines by MP. So the conditions are right for an inductive proof. The "starting points" are the axioms; and the "operation" is the inference of a new line from earlier lines using MP. If we can show that the starting points (axioms) have the property of validity, and that the operation (MP) preserves the property of validity, then we can conclude that every wff in every proof—i.e., every theorem—has the property of validity. This sort of inductive proof is called induction "on the proof of a formula" (or induction "on the length of the formula's proof").

Base case: here we need to show that every PL-axiom is valid. This is tedious but straightforward. Take PL1, for example. Suppose for reductio that some instance of PL1 is invalid, i.e., for some PL-interpretation $\mathscr{I}$, $V_\mathscr{I}(\phi\rightarrow(\psi\rightarrow\phi)) = 0$. Thus $V_\mathscr{I}(\phi) = 1$ and $V_\mathscr{I}(\psi\rightarrow\phi) = 0$. Given the latter, $V_\mathscr{I}(\phi) = 0$; contradiction. One can similarly show that all instances of PL2 and PL3 are also valid (exercise 2.5).

Inductive step: here we begin by *assuming* that every line in a proof up to a certain point is valid (the "inductive hypothesis"); we then show that if one adds another line that follows from earlier lines by the rule modus ponens, that line must be valid too. That is, we're trying to show that "modus ponens preserves validity". So, assume the inductive hypothesis: that all the earlier lines in the proof are valid. And now, consider the result of applying modus ponens. That means that the new line we've added to the proof is some formula ψ, which we've inferred from two earlier lines that have the forms $\phi\rightarrow\psi$ and ϕ. We must show that ψ is a valid formula, i.e., is true in every interpretation. So let $\mathscr{I}$ be any interpretation. By the inductive hypothesis, all earlier lines in the proof are valid, and hence both $\phi\rightarrow\psi$ and ϕ are valid. Thus $V_\mathscr{I}(\phi) = 1$ and $V_\mathscr{I}(\phi\rightarrow\psi) = 1$. But if $V_\mathscr{I}(\phi) = 1$, then $V_\mathscr{I}(\psi)$ can't be 0, for if it were, then $V_\mathscr{I}(\phi\rightarrow\psi)$ would be 0, and it isn't. Thus $V_\mathscr{I}(\psi) = 1$.

(If our system had included rules other than modus ponens, we would have needed to show that they too preserve validity. The paucity of rules in axiomatic systems makes the construction of proofs within those systems a real pain in the neck, but now we see how it makes metalogical life easier.)

We've shown that the axioms are valid, and that modus ponens preserves validity. All theorems are generated from the axioms via modus ponens in a finite series of steps. So, by induction, every theorem is valid.   □

Soundness gives us a way to establish *unprovability*. Soundness says "if $\vdash \phi$ then $\vDash \phi$", or equivalently: "if $\nvDash \phi$ then $\nvdash \phi$". So, to show that a wff isn't a theorem, it suffices to show that it isn't valid. Consider, for example, $(P\rightarrow Q)\rightarrow(Q\rightarrow P)$. This wff is false in a PL-interpretation in which P is 0 and Q is 1. So it's not valid. But then soundness tells us that it isn't a theorem either. In general: given soundness, in order to show that a wff isn't a theorem, all you need to do is find an interpretation in which it isn't true.

Before we leave this section, let me reiterate the distinction between the two types of induction most commonly used in metalogic. Induction on the proof of a formula (the type of induction used to establish soundness) is used when one is establishing a fact of the form: *every **theorem** has a certain property p*. Here the base case consists of showing that the axioms (PL1–PL3 in the case of PL) have the property p, and the inductive step consists of showing that the rules of inference preserve p—in the case of PL, that *if ϕ and $\phi{\rightarrow}\psi$ both have property p, then so does ψ*. (Induction on proofs can also be used to show that all wffs *provable from* a given set Γ have a given property; in that case the base case would also need to include a demonstration that all members of Γ have the property.) Induction on formula construction (the type of induction used to show that all formulas have finitely many sentence letters), on the other hand, is used when one is trying to establish a fact of the form: *every **formula** has a certain property p*. Here the base case consists of showing that all atomic wffs—sentence letters, in the case of PL—have property p; and the inductive step consists of showing that the rules of formation preserve p—in the case of PL, that *if ϕ and ψ both have property p, then both $(\phi{\rightarrow}\psi)$ and $\sim\phi$ also will have property p*.

If you're ever proving something by induction, it's important to identify what sort of inductive proof you're constructing. What are the entities you're dealing with? What is the property p? What are the starting points, and what are the operations generating new entities from the starting points? If you're trying to construct an inductive proof and get stuck, you should return to these questions and make sure you're clear about their answers.

Exercise 2.5 Finish the soundness proof by showing that all instances of axiom schemas PL2 and PL3 are valid.

Exercise 2.6 Consider a (strange) axiomatic system whose axiom schemas are "$\phi{\rightarrow}\phi$" and "$(\phi{\rightarrow}\psi){\rightarrow}(\psi{\rightarrow}\phi)$" rather than PL1–PL3 (MP is still the sole rule of inference). Show that (a) every theorem of this system has an even number of "$\sim$"s; and (b) soundness is false for this system—i.e., some theorems are not PL-valid.

Exercise 2.7 Show by induction that the truth value of a wff depends only on the truth values of its sentence letters. That is, show that for any wff ϕ and any PL-interpretations $\mathscr{I}$ and $\mathscr{I}'$, if $\mathscr{I}(\alpha) = \mathscr{I}'(\alpha)$ for each sentence letter α in ϕ, then $V_{\mathscr{I}}(\phi) = V_{\mathscr{I}'}(\phi)$.

Exercise 2.8** Show that if wff ϕ has no repetitions of sentence letters (i.e., each sentence letter occurs at most once in ϕ) then $\nvDash \phi$.

Exercise 2.9 Prove "strong soundness": for any set of formulas, Γ, and any formula ϕ, if $\Gamma \vdash \phi$ then $\Gamma \vDash \phi$ (i.e., if ϕ is provable from Γ then ϕ is a semantic consequence of Γ).

Exercise 2.10** Prove the soundness of the sequent calculus. That is, show that if $\Gamma \Rightarrow \phi$ is a provable sequent, then $\Gamma \vDash \phi$. (No need to go through each and every detail of the proof once it becomes repetitive.)

2.8 PL-proofs and the deduction theorem

Before attempting to prove completeness we need to get better at establishing theoremhood. And the way to do that is to assemble a "toolkit": a collection of techniques for doing bits of proofs, techniques that are applicable in a wide range of situations. These techniques will save time and make proofs easier to construct.

To assemble the toolkit, we'll need to change our focus from constructing proofs to constructing *proof schemas*. Recall the proof of the formula $(R{\to}P){\to}(R{\to}(Q{\to}P))$ from section 2.6:

1. $[R{\to}(P{\to}(Q{\to}P))]{\to}[(R{\to}P){\to}(R{\to}(Q{\to}P))]$ PL2
2. $P{\to}(Q{\to}P)$ PL1
3. $[P{\to}(Q{\to}P)]{\to}[R{\to}(P{\to}(Q{\to}P))]$ PL1
4. $R{\to}(P{\to}(Q{\to}P))$ 2, 3, MP
5. $(R{\to}P){\to}(R{\to}(Q{\to}P))$ 1, 4, MP

Consider the result of replacing the sentence letters P, Q, and R in this proof with metalinguistic variables ϕ, ψ, and χ:

1. $[\chi{\to}(\phi{\to}(\psi{\to}\phi))]{\to}[(\chi{\to}\phi){\to}(\chi{\to}(\psi{\to}\phi))]$ PL2
2. $\phi{\to}(\psi{\to}\phi)$ PL1
3. $[\phi{\to}(\psi{\to}\phi)]{\to}[\chi{\to}(\phi{\to}(\psi{\to}\phi))]$ PL1
4. $\chi{\to}(\phi{\to}(\psi{\to}\phi))$ 2, 3, MP
5. $(\chi{\to}\phi){\to}(\chi{\to}(\psi{\to}\phi))$ 1, 4, MP

Given our official definition, this does *not* count as a proof: proofs must be made up of wffs, and the symbols ϕ, ψ, and χ can't occur in wffs. But it becomes a proof if we substitute in wffs for ϕ, ψ, and χ. (As with the construction of axioms, the substitution must be "uniform". Uniform throughout the proof, in fact: each Greek letter must be changed to the same wff throughout the proof.) So let's call it a proof schema—a proof schema *of* the wff-schema $(\chi{\to}\phi){\to}(\chi{\to}(\psi{\to}\phi))$ (call this latter schema "weakening the consequent"). The existence of this proof schema shows that each instance of weakening the consequent is a theorem.

A proof schema is more useful than a proof because it shows that *any* instance of a certain schema can be proved. Suppose you're laboring away on a proof, and you find that you need $(P{\to}{\sim}P){\to}[P{\to}((R{\to}R){\to}{\sim}P)]$ to complete the proof. This wff is an instance of weakening the consequent. So you know that you can construct a five-line proof of it anytime you like, by beginning with the proof schema of weakening the consequent, and substituting P for χ, ${\sim}P$ for ϕ, and $R{\to}R$ for ψ. Instead of actually inserting those five lines into your proof, why not instead just write down the line:

   i. $(P{\to}{\sim}P){\to}[P{\to}((R{\to}R){\to}{\sim}P)]$ weakening the consequent

? You know that you could always replace this line, if you wanted to, with the five-line proof.

Citing previously proved theorem schemas saves time and writing. Let's introduce another time-saving practice: that of doing two or more steps at once. We'll allow ourselves to do this, and annotate in some perspicuous way, when it's reasonably obvious what the skipped steps are. For example, let's rewrite the proof of the weakening-the-consequent schema thus:

1. $\phi \rightarrow (\psi \rightarrow \phi)$ PL1
2. $\chi \rightarrow (\phi \rightarrow (\psi \rightarrow \phi))$ PL1, 1, MP
3. $(\chi \rightarrow \phi) \rightarrow (\chi \rightarrow (\psi \rightarrow \phi))$ PL2, 2, MP

So the first tools in our toolkit are the weakening-the-consequent schema and doing multiple steps at once. Once the kit is full, we'll try to reduce a given problem to a few chunks, each of which can be accomplished by citing a tool from the kit.

Notice that as soon as we start using the toolkit, the proofs we construct cease to be official proofs—not every line will be either an axiom or premise or follow from earlier lines by MP. They will instead be informal proofs, or proof sketches. A proof sketch is in essence a metalogic argument for the conclusion that *there exists* some proof or other of the desired type. It is a blueprint that an ambitious reader could always use to construct an official proof, by filling in the details.

We're now ready to make a more significant addition to our toolkit. Suppose we already have $\phi \rightarrow \psi$ and $\phi \rightarrow (\psi \rightarrow \chi)$. The following technique then shows us how to move to $\phi \rightarrow \chi$. Let's call it the "MP technique", since it lets us do modus ponens "within the consequent of the conditional $\phi \rightarrow$":

1. $\phi \rightarrow \psi$
2. $\phi \rightarrow (\psi \rightarrow \chi)$
3. $(\phi \rightarrow (\psi \rightarrow \chi)) \rightarrow ((\phi \rightarrow \psi) \rightarrow (\phi \rightarrow \chi))$ PL2
4. $(\phi \rightarrow \psi) \rightarrow (\phi \rightarrow \chi)$ 2, 3, MP
5. $\phi \rightarrow \chi$ 1, 4, MP

In effect we have given a metalogic proof of the following fact: "for any wffs ϕ, ψ, and χ: $\phi \rightarrow \psi, \phi \rightarrow (\psi \rightarrow \chi) \vdash \phi \rightarrow \chi$".

Let's add a "meta-tool" to the kit:

Cut: If $\Gamma_1 \vdash \delta_1, \ldots, \Gamma_n \vdash \delta_n$, and $\Sigma, \delta_1 \ldots \delta_n \vdash \phi$, then $\Gamma_1 \ldots, \Gamma_n, \Sigma \vdash \phi$

Think of Cut as saying that one can "cut out the middleman". Suppose $\Gamma_1 \ldots \Gamma_n$ lead to some intermediate conclusions, $\delta_1 \ldots \delta_n$ (the middleman). And suppose one can go from those intermediate conclusions to some ultimate conclusion ϕ (perhaps with the help of some auxiliary premises Σ). Then, Cut says, you can go directly from $\Gamma_1 \ldots \Gamma_n$ to the ultimate conclusion ϕ (with the help of Σ if needed). I call this a meta-tool because it facilitates use of other tools in the kit. For example, suppose you know that $\Gamma_1 \vdash P \rightarrow Q$ and $\Gamma_2 \vdash P \rightarrow (Q \rightarrow R)$. We know from the MP technique that $P \rightarrow Q, P \rightarrow (Q \rightarrow R) \vdash P \rightarrow R$. Cut then tells us that $\Gamma_1, \Gamma_2 \vdash P \rightarrow R$ (δ_1 is $P \rightarrow Q$, δ_2 is $P \rightarrow (Q \rightarrow R)$; Σ is null in this case).

Proof of Cut. We are given that there exists a proof A_i of δ_i from Γ_i, for $i = 1 \ldots n$, and that there exists a proof B of ϕ from $\Sigma, \delta_1 \ldots \delta_n$. Let C be the result of concatenating all these proofs, in that order. That is, C begins with a first phase, consisting of the formulas of proof A_1, followed by the formulas of proof A_2, and so on, finishing with the formulas of proof A_n. Then, in the second phase, C concludes with the formulas of proof B. The last formula of C is the last formula of B, namely, ϕ. So all we need to show is that C counts as a proof from $\Gamma_1 \ldots, \Gamma_n, \Sigma$—that is, that each line of C is either an axiom, a member of Γ_1, or of $\Gamma_2, \ldots$, or of Γ_n, or of Σ, or follows from earlier lines in C by MP. For short, we must show that each line of C is "legit". Clearly, each line j of the first phase of C is legit: j is from one of the A_i segments; A_i is a proof from Γ_i; so the formula on line j is either an axiom, a member of Γ_i, or follows from earlier lines in that A_i segment by MP. Consider, finally, the second phase of C, namely, the B portion. Since B is a proof from $\Sigma, \delta_1 \ldots \delta_n$, the formula on any line j here is either (i) an axiom, (ii) a member of Σ, (iii) one of the δ_is, or (iv) follows from earlier lines of the B portion by MP. Line j is clearly legit in cases (i), (ii), and (iv). In case (iii), the formula on line j is some δ_i. But δ_i also occurred in the first phase of C, as the last line, k, of the A_i portion. So δ_i is either an axiom, or a member of Γ_i, or follows from earlier lines in the A_i portion—which are before k—by MP. In either of the first two cases, line j is legit; and it's also legit in the last case because lines before k in C are also lines before j. □

We're now ready for the most important addition to our toolkit: the deduction theorem. As you have been learning (perhaps to your dismay), constructing axiomatic proofs is much harder than constructing sequent proofs. It's hard to prove things when you're not allowed to reason with assumptions! Nevertheless, one can prove a metalogical theorem *about* our axiomatic system that is closely related to one method of reasoning with assumptions, namely conditional proof:

Deduction theorem for PL: If $\Gamma, \phi \vdash_{PL} \psi$, then $\Gamma \vdash_{PL} \phi \rightarrow \psi$

That is: whenever there exists a proof from Γ and $\{\phi\}$ to ψ, then there *also* exists a proof of $\phi \rightarrow \psi$ from Γ alone.

Suppose we want to prove $\phi \rightarrow \psi$. Our axiomatic system does not allow us to assume ϕ in a conditional proof of $\phi \rightarrow \psi$. But once we've proved the deduction theorem, we'll be able to do the next best thing. Suppose we succeed in constructing a proof of ψ *from* $\{\phi\}$. That is, we write down a proof in which each line is either (i) a member of $\{\phi\}$ (that is, ϕ itself), or (ii) an axiom, or (iii) follows from earlier lines in the proof by modus ponens. The deduction theorem then lets us conclude that *some proof of* $\phi \rightarrow \psi$ *exists*. We won't have constructed such a proof ourselves; we only constructed the proof from ϕ to ψ. Nevertheless the deduction theorem assures us that it exists. More generally, whenever we can construct a proof of ψ from ϕ plus some other premises (the formulas in some set Γ), then the deduction theorem assures us that some proof of $\phi \rightarrow \psi$ from those other premises also exists.

Proof of deduction theorem. Suppose $\Gamma \cup \{\phi\} \vdash \psi$. Thus there exists some proof, A, from $\Gamma \cup \{\phi\}$ to ψ. Each line α_i of A is either a member of $\Gamma \cup \{\phi\}$, an axiom, or follows from earlier lines in the proof by MP; the last line of A is ψ. Our strategy will be to establish that:

$$\text{for each } \alpha_i \text{ in proof } A, \Gamma \vdash \phi \rightarrow \alpha_i \qquad (*)$$

We already know that each line of proof A is provable from $\Gamma \cup \phi$; what (*) says is that if you stick "$\phi \rightarrow$" in front of any of those lines, the result is provable from Γ all by itself. Once we succeed in establishing (*), we will have proved the deduction theorem. For since the last line of proof A is ψ, (*) tells us that $\phi \rightarrow \psi$ is provable from Γ.

(*) says that each line of proof A has a certain property, namely, the property of: *being provable from Γ when prefixed with "$\phi \rightarrow$"*. Just as in the proof of soundness, this calls for the method of proof by induction, and in particular, induction on ϕ's proof. Here goes.

Base case: we must show that all the "starting points"—axioms and premises—of A have the property. So first, suppose that line α_i in A is an axiom. We must show that α_i has the property—that is, show that $\Gamma \vdash \phi \rightarrow \alpha_i$. Well, consider this:

1. α_i axiom
2. $\phi \rightarrow \alpha_i$ PL1, 1, MP

This is a proof (sketch) of $\phi \rightarrow \alpha_i$ from Γ. It's true that we didn't actually use any members of Γ in the proof, but that's OK. If you look back at the definition of a proof from a set, you'll see that this counts officially as a proof from Γ.

Next suppose that line α_i is a premise—that is, a member of $\Gamma \cup \{\phi\}$. This subdivides into two subcases. The first is where α_i is ϕ itself. Here, $\phi \rightarrow \alpha_i$ is $\phi \rightarrow \phi$, which can be proved from no premises at all using the method of exercise 2.4a; so $\Gamma \vdash \phi \rightarrow \phi$. The second subcase is where $\alpha_i \in \Gamma$. But here we can prove $\phi \rightarrow \alpha_i$ from Γ as follows:

1. α_i premise
2. $\phi \rightarrow \alpha_i$ PL1, 1, MP

Inductive step: here we simply *assume* that all earlier lines of the proof have the property we're interested in (this assumption is the inductive hypothesis; the property, recall, is: *being provable from Γ when prefixed with "$\phi \rightarrow$"*) and we show that the result of applying MP to any of those earlier lines has the property as well. So suppose that α_i follows from earlier lines in the proof by MP. That means that the earlier lines have to have the forms $\chi \rightarrow \alpha_i$ and χ. Furthermore, the inductive hypothesis tells us that the result of prefixing either of these earlier lines with "$\phi \rightarrow$" is provable from Γ. Thus $\Gamma \vdash \phi \rightarrow (\chi \rightarrow \alpha_i)$ and $\Gamma \vdash \phi \rightarrow \chi$. But then, given the MP technique and Cut, $\Gamma \vdash \phi \rightarrow \alpha_i$.

So by induction, (*) is established; and we're done. $\square$

Once we've got the deduction theorem for PL in our toolkit, we can really get going. For we can now, in effect, use conditional proof. As an illustration, I'll show how to use the deduction theorem to establish that $\phi \rightarrow \psi, \psi \rightarrow \chi \vdash \phi \rightarrow \chi$. That is: conditionals are transitive (a useful addition to the toolkit). Consider the following proof schema:

1. $\phi\to\psi$ premise
2. $\psi\to\chi$ premise
3. ϕ premise
4. ψ 1, 3, MP
5. χ 2, 4, MP

This is a proof of χ *from* the set $\{\phi\to\psi,\psi\to\chi,\phi\}$. Thus, $\phi\to\psi,\psi\to\chi,\phi\vdash\chi$. The deduction theorem then tells us that $\phi\to\psi,\psi\to\chi\vdash\phi\to\chi$. That's all it takes!—much easier than constructing from scratch a proof of $\phi\to\chi$ from $\phi\to\psi$ and $\psi\to\chi$.

Let's call this last addition to the toolkit, the fact that $\phi\to\psi,\psi\to\chi\vdash\phi\to\chi$, "transitivity". The transitivity schema tells us that certain wffs are provable from certain other wffs. It does not tell us that certain wffs are theorems. That is, it's not a theorem schema. However, there is a theorem schema corresponding to transitivity: $(\phi\to\psi)\to[(\psi\to\chi)\to(\phi\to\chi)]$. The theoremhood of this schema follows immediately from the transitivity schema via two applications of the deduction theorem. In general, if the toolkit includes a provability-from schema $\phi_1\ldots\phi_n\vdash\psi$ rather than the corresponding theorem schema $\vdash\phi_1\to(\phi_2\to\ldots(\phi_n\to\psi))$, one can always infer the existence of the latter, if one wants it, by using the deduction theorem repeatedly.

Example 2.11: More additions to the toolkit:

$\sim\psi\to\sim\phi\vdash\phi\to\psi$ ("contraposition 1"):

The following proof shows that $\sim\psi\to\sim\phi,\phi\vdash\psi$:

1. $\sim\psi\to\sim\phi$ premise
2. ϕ premise
3. $\sim\psi\to\phi$ PL1, 2, MP
4. ψ PL3, 1, MP, 3, MP

The desired result then follows by the deduction theorem.

$\phi\to\psi\vdash\sim\psi\to\sim\phi$ ("contraposition 2"):

1. $\phi\to\psi$ premise
2. $\psi\to\sim\sim\psi$ exercise 2.11d
3. $\sim\sim\phi\to\phi$ exercise 2.11c
4. $\sim\sim\phi\to\sim\sim\psi$ 3, 1, 2, transitivity
5. $\sim\psi\to\sim\phi$ 3, contraposition 1

$\phi,\sim\phi\vdash\psi$ ("ex falso quodlibet"):

1. ϕ premise
2. $\sim\phi$ premise
3. $\sim\psi\rightarrow\phi$ PL1, 1, MP
4. $\sim\psi\rightarrow\sim\phi$ PL1, 2, MP
5. ψ PL3, 4, MP, 3, MP

$\sim(\phi\rightarrow\psi)\vdash\phi$ and $\sim(\phi\rightarrow\psi)\vdash\sim\psi$ ("negated conditional"):

To demonstrate the first: by two applications of the deduction theorem to ex falso quodlibet, we know that $\vdash\sim\phi\rightarrow(\phi\rightarrow\psi)$. So, begin a proof with a proof of this wff, and then continue as follows:

1. $\sim\phi\rightarrow(\phi\rightarrow\psi)$
2. $\sim(\phi\rightarrow\psi)\rightarrow\sim\sim\phi$ 1, contraposition 2
3. $\sim(\phi\rightarrow\psi)$ premise
4. $\sim\sim\phi$ 2, 3, MP
5. ϕ 4, exercise 2.4c

As for the second:

1. $\psi\rightarrow(\phi\rightarrow\psi)$ PL1
2. $\sim(\phi\rightarrow\psi)\rightarrow\sim\psi$ 1, contraposition 2
3. $\sim(\phi\rightarrow\psi)$ premise
4. ψ 2, 3, MP

$\phi\rightarrow\psi,\sim\phi\rightarrow\psi\vdash\psi$ ("excluded-middle MP")

1. $\phi\rightarrow\psi$ premise
2. $\sim\phi\rightarrow\psi$ premise
3. $\sim\psi\rightarrow\sim\phi$ 1, contraposition 2
4. $\sim\psi\rightarrow\sim\sim\phi$ 2, contraposition 2
5. $\sim\psi\rightarrow\phi$ 4, exercise 2.11c, transitivity
6. ψ PL3, 3, MP, 5, MP

Exercise 2.11 Establish each of the following. You may use the toolkit, including the deduction theorem.

    (a) $\vdash \phi \to [(\phi \to \psi) \to \psi]$

    (b) $\vdash [\phi \to (\psi \to \chi)] \to [\psi \to (\phi \to \chi)]$ ("permutation")

    (c) $\vdash {\sim}{\sim}\phi \to \phi$ ("double-negation elimination")

    (d) $\vdash \phi \to {\sim}{\sim}\phi$ ("double-negation introduction")

Exercise 2.12 (Long.) Establish the axiomatic correctness of the rules of inference from our sequent system. For example, in the case of $\wedge$E, show that $\phi, \psi \vdash \phi \wedge \psi$—i.e., give an axiomatic proof of ${\sim}(\phi \to {\sim}\psi)$ from $\{\phi, \psi\}$. You may use the toolkit.

2.9 Completeness of PL

We're finally ready for the completeness proof. We will give what is known as a "Henkin proof", after Leon Henkin, who used similar methods to demonstrate completeness for predicate logic. Most of the proof will consist of assembling various pieces—various definitions and facts. The point of these pieces will become apparent at the end, when we put them all together.

2.9.1 Maximal consistent sets of wffs

Let "$\perp$" abbreviate "${\sim}(P \to P)$". (The idea of $\perp$ is that it stands for a generic contradiction. The choice of ${\sim}(P \to P)$ was arbitrary; all that matters is that $\perp$ is the negation of a theorem.) Here are the central definitions we'll need:

DEFINITION OF CONSISTENCY AND MAXIMALITY:

- A set of wffs, Γ, is inconsistent iff $\Gamma \vdash \perp$. Γ is consistent iff it is not inconsistent.
- A set of wffs, Γ, is maximal iff for every wff ϕ, either ϕ or ${\sim}\phi$ (or perhaps both) is a member of Γ.

Intuitively: a maximal set is so large that it contains each formula or its negation; and a consistent set is one from which you can't prove a contradiction. Note the following lemmas:

Lemma 2.1 For any set of wffs Γ and wff ϕ, if ϕ is provable from Γ, then ϕ is provable from some finite subset of Γ. That is, if $\Gamma \vdash \phi$, then $\gamma_1 \ldots \gamma_n \vdash \phi$ for some $\gamma_1 \ldots \gamma_n \in \Gamma$ (or else $\vdash \phi$).

Proof. If $\Gamma \vdash \phi$, then there is some proof, A, of ϕ from Γ. Like every proof, A is a finite series of wffs. Thus only finitely many of Γ's members can have occurred as lines in A. Let $\gamma_1 \ldots \gamma_n$ be those members of Γ. (If no member of Γ occurs in A, then A proves ϕ from no premises at all, in which case $\vdash \phi$.) In addition to counting as a proof of ϕ from Γ, proof A is also a proof of ϕ from $\{\gamma_1 \ldots \gamma_n\}$. Thus $\gamma_1 \ldots \gamma_n \vdash \phi$. $\square$

Lemma 2.2 For any set of wffs Γ, if $\Gamma \vdash \phi$ and $\Gamma \vdash {\sim}\phi$ for some ϕ then Γ is inconsistent.

Proof. Follows immediately from ex falso quodlibet (example 2.11) and Cut.　□

Note that the first lemma tells us that a set is inconsistent iff some finite subset of that set is inconsistent.

2.9.2 *Maximal consistent extensions*

Suppose we begin with a consistent set Δ that isn't maximal—for at least one wff ϕ, Δ contains neither ϕ nor $\sim\phi$. Is there some way of adding wffs to Δ to make it maximal, without destroying its consistency? That is, is Δ guaranteed to have some maximal consistent "extension"? The following theorem tells us that the answer is *yes*:

Theorem 2.3 If Δ is a consistent set of wffs, then there exists some maximal consistent set of wffs, Γ, such that $\Delta \subseteq \Gamma$.

Proof of theorem 2.3. In outline, we're going to build up Γ as follows. We're going to start by dumping the wffs that are in Δ into Γ. Then we will go through all the PL-wffs—*all* of them, not just those in Δ—one at a time. For each one, we're going to dump either it or its negation into Γ, depending on which choice would be consistent. After we're done, our set Γ will obviously be maximal; it will obviously contain Δ as a subset; and, we'll show, it will also be consistent.

So, let $\phi_1, \phi_2,\dots$ be a list—an infinite list, of course—of all the wffs.[22] To construct Γ, our strategy is to start with Δ, and then go through this list one by one, at each point adding either ϕ_i or $\sim\phi_i$. Here's how we do this more carefully. We first define an infinite sequence of sets, $\Gamma_0, \Gamma_1,\dots$:

---

[22]We need to be sure that there is some way of arranging all the wffs into such a list. Here is one method. First, begin with a list of the primitive expressions of the language. In the case of PL this can be done as follows:

$$(\;) \; \sim \; \rightarrow \; P_1 \; P_2 \; \dots$$
$$1 \; 2 \; 3 \; 4 \; \; 5 \; \; 6 \; \dots$$

(For simplicity, get rid of all the sentence letters except for $P_1, P_2,\dots$.) Since we'll need to refer to what *position* an expression has in this list, the positions of the expressions are listed underneath those expressions. (E.g., the position of the $\rightarrow$ is 4.) Now, where ϕ is any wff, call the *rating* of ϕ the sum of the positions of the occurrences of its primitive expressions. (The rating for the wff $(P_1 \rightarrow P_1)$, for example, is $1+5+4+5+2 = 17$.) We can now construct the listing of all the wffs of PL by an infinite series of stages: stage 1, stage 2, etc. In stage n, we append to our growing list all the wffs of rating n, *in alphabetical order*. The notion of alphabetical order here is the usual one, given the ordering of the primitive expressions laid out above. (E.g., just as 'and' comes before 'dna' in alphabetical order, since 'a' precedes 'd' in the usual ordering of the English alphabet, $(P_1 \rightarrow P_2)$ comes before $(P_2 \rightarrow P_1)$ in alphabetical order since P_1 comes before P_2 in the ordering of the alphabet of PL. Note that each of these wffs is inserted into the list in stage 18, since each has rating 18.) In stages 1–4 no wffs are added at all, since every wff must have at least one sentence letter and P_1 is the sentence letter with the smallest position. In stage 5 there is one wff: P_1. Thus the first member of our list of wffs is P_1. In stage 6 there is one wff: P_2, so P_2 is the second member of the list. In every subsequent stage there are only finitely many wffs; so each stage adds finitely many wffs to the list; each wff gets added at some stage; so each wff eventually gets added to this list after some finite amount of time.

$$\Gamma_0 = \Delta$$

$$\Gamma_{n+1} = \begin{cases} \Gamma_n \cup \{\phi_{n+1}\} & \text{if } \Gamma_n \cup \{\phi_{n+1}\} \text{ is consistent} \\ \Gamma_n \cup \{\sim\phi_{n+1}\} & \text{if } \Gamma_n \cup \{\phi_{n+1}\} \text{ is not consistent} \end{cases}$$

This definition is recursive, notice. We begin with a noncircular definition of the first member of the sequence of sets, Γ_0, and after that, we define each subsequent member Γ_{n+1} in terms of the previous member Γ_n: we add ϕ_{n+1} to Γ_n if the result of doing so would be consistent; otherwise we add $\sim\phi_{n+1}$.

Next let's prove that each member in this sequence—that is, each Γ_i—is a consistent set. We do this inductively, by first showing that Γ_0 is consistent, and then showing that if Γ_n is consistent, then so will be Γ_{n+1}. This is a different sort of inductive proof from what we've seen so far, neither an induction on formula construction nor on formula proof. Nevertheless we have the required structure for proof by induction: each of the objects of interest (the Γ_is) is generated from a starting point (Γ_0) by a finite series of operations (the operation taking us from Γ_n to Γ_{n+1}).

Base case: Γ_0 is obviously consistent, since Δ was stipulated to be consistent.

Inductive step: we suppose that Γ_n is consistent (inductive hypothesis), and then show that Γ_{n+1} is consistent. Look at the definition of Γ_{n+1}. What Γ_{n+1} gets defined as depends on whether $\Gamma_n \cup \{\phi_{n+1}\}$ is consistent. If $\Gamma_n \cup \{\phi_{n+1}\}$ *is* consistent, then Γ_{n+1} gets defined as that very set $\Gamma_n \cup \{\phi_{n+1}\}$. So of course Γ_{n+1} is consistent in that case.

The remaining possibility is that $\Gamma_n \cup \{\phi_{n+1}\}$ is *in*consistent. In that case, Γ_{n+1} gets defined as $\Gamma_n \cup \{\sim\phi_{n+1}\}$. So we must show that in this case, $\Gamma_n \cup \{\sim\phi_{n+1}\}$ is consistent. Suppose for reductio that it isn't. Then $\perp$ is provable from $\Gamma_n \cup \{\sim\phi_{n+1}\}$, and so, given lemma 2.1, is provable from some finite subset of this set; and the finite subset must contain $\sim\phi_{n+1}$ since Γ_n was consistent. Letting $\psi_1 \ldots \psi_m$ be the remaining members of the finite subset, we have, then: $\psi_1 \ldots \psi_m, \sim\phi_{n+1} \vdash \perp$, from which we get $\psi_1 \ldots \psi_m \vdash \sim\phi_{n+1} \rightarrow \perp$ by the deduction theorem. Since $\Gamma_n \cup \{\phi_{n+1}\}$ is inconsistent, similar reasoning tells us that $\chi_1 \ldots \chi_p \vdash \phi_{n+1} \rightarrow \perp$, for some $\chi_1 \ldots \chi_p \in \Gamma_n$. It then follows by "excluded-middle MP" (example 2.11) and Cut that $\psi_1 \ldots \psi_m, \chi_1 \ldots \chi_p \vdash \perp$. Since $\psi_1 \ldots \psi_m, \chi_1 \ldots \chi_p$ are all members of Γ_n, this contradicts the fact that Γ_n is consistent.

We have shown that all the sets in our sequence Γ_i are consistent. Let us now define Γ to be the *union* of all the sets in the infinite sequence—i.e., $\{\phi : \phi \in \Gamma_i \text{ for some } i\}$. We must now show that Γ is the set we're after: that (i) $\Delta \subseteq \Gamma$, (ii) Γ is maximal, and (iii) Γ is consistent.

Any member of Δ is a member of Γ_0 (since Γ_0 was defined as Δ), hence is a member of one of the Γ_is, and hence is a member of Γ. So $\Delta \subseteq \Gamma$.

Any wff is in the list of all the wffs somewhere—i.e., it is ϕ_i for some i. But by definition of Γ_i, either ϕ_i or $\sim\phi_i$ is a member of Γ_i; and so one of these is a member of Γ. Γ is therefore maximal.

Suppose for reductio that Γ is inconsistent. Given lemma 2.1, there are $\psi_1 \ldots \psi_m \in$

Γ such that $\psi_1 \ldots \psi_m \vdash \perp$. By definition of Γ, each $\psi_i \in \Gamma_{j_i}$, for some j_i. Let k be the largest of $j_1 \ldots j_m$. Given the way the $\Gamma_0, \Gamma_1, \ldots$ series is constructed, each set in the series is a subset of all subsequent ones. Thus each of $\psi_1 \ldots \psi_m$ is a member of Γ_k, and thus Γ_k is inconsistent. But we showed that each member of the series $\Gamma_0, \Gamma_1, \ldots$ is consistent. $\qquad\square$

2.9.3 Features of maximal consistent sets

Next we'll establish two facts about maximal consistent sets that we'll need for the completeness proof:

Lemma 2.4 Where Γ is any maximal consistent set of wffs:

    2.4a for any wff ϕ, exactly one of ϕ, $\sim\phi$ is a member of Γ

    2.4b $\phi \rightarrow \psi \in \Gamma$ iff either $\phi \notin \Gamma$ or $\psi \in \Gamma$

Proof of lemma 2.4a. Since Γ is maximal it must contain at least one of ϕ or $\sim\phi$. But it cannot contain both; otherwise each would be provable from Γ, whence by lemma 2.2, Γ would be inconsistent. $\qquad\square$

Proof of lemma 2.4b. Suppose first that $\phi \rightarrow \psi$ is in Γ, and suppose for reductio that ϕ is in Γ but ψ is not. Then we can prove ψ from Γ (begin with ϕ and $\phi \rightarrow \psi$ as premises, and then use MP). But since $\psi \notin \Gamma$ and Γ is maximal, $\sim\psi$ is in Γ, and hence is provable from Γ. Given lemma 2.2, this contradicts Γ's consistency.

    Suppose for the other direction that either $\phi \notin \Gamma$ or $\psi \in \Gamma$, and suppose for reductio that $\phi \rightarrow \psi \notin \Gamma$. Since Γ is maximal, $\sim(\phi \rightarrow \psi) \in \Gamma$. Then $\Gamma \vdash \sim(\phi \rightarrow \psi)$, and so by "negated conditional" (example 2.11) and Cut, $\Gamma \vdash \phi$ and $\Gamma \vdash \sim\psi$. Now, if $\phi \notin \Gamma$ then $\sim\phi \in \Gamma$ and so $\Gamma \vdash \sim\phi$; and if on the other hand $\psi \in \Gamma$, then $\Gamma \vdash \psi$. Each possibility contradicts Γ's consistency, given lemma 2.2. $\qquad\square$

2.9.4 The proof

Now it's time to put together all the pieces that we've assembled.

Proof of PL-completeness. Completeness says: if $\vDash \phi$, then $\vdash \phi$. We'll prove this by proving the equivalent statement: if $\nvdash \phi$, then $\nvDash \phi$. So, suppose that $\nvdash \phi$. We must construct some PL-interpretation in which ϕ isn't true.

    Since $\nvdash \phi$, $\{\sim\phi\}$ must be consistent. For suppose otherwise. Then $\sim\phi \vdash \perp$; so $\vdash \sim\phi \rightarrow \perp$ by the deduction theorem. That is, given the definition of $\perp$: $\vdash \sim\phi \rightarrow \sim(P \rightarrow P)$. Then by contraposition 1 (example 2.11), $\vdash (P \rightarrow P) \rightarrow \phi$. But $\vdash P \rightarrow P$ (exercise 2.4a), and so $\vdash \phi$; contradiction.

    Since $\{\sim\phi\}$ is consistent, theorem 2.3 tells us that it is a subset of some maximal consistent set of wffs Γ. Next, let's use Γ to construct a somewhat odd PL-interpretation. This PL-interpretation decides whether a sentence letter is true or false by looking to see whether that sentence letter *is a member of* Γ. What we will do next is show that *all* formulas, not just sentence letters, are true in this odd interpretation iff they are members of Γ.

So, let $\mathscr{I}$ be the PL-interpretation in which for any sentence letter α, $\mathscr{I}(\alpha) = 1$ iff $\alpha \in \Gamma$. We must show that:

$$\text{for every wff } \phi, \; V_{\mathscr{I}}(\phi) = 1 \text{ iff } \phi \in \Gamma \tag{*}$$

We do this by induction on formula construction. The base case, that the assertion holds for sentence letters, follows immediately from the definition of $\mathscr{I}$. Next we make the inductive hypothesis (ih): that wffs ϕ and ψ are true in $\mathscr{I}$ iff they are members of Γ, and we show that the same is true of $\sim\phi$ and $\phi{\rightarrow}\psi$.

First, $\sim\phi$: we must show that $V_{\mathscr{I}}(\sim\phi) = 1$ iff $\sim\phi \in \Gamma$:[23]

$$
\begin{array}{llr}
V_{\mathscr{I}}(\sim\phi) = 1 & \text{iff } V_{\mathscr{I}}(\phi) = 0 & (\text{truth cond. for } \sim) \\
& \text{iff } \phi \notin \Gamma & (\text{ih}) \\
& \text{iff } \sim\phi \in \Gamma & (\text{lemma 2.4a})
\end{array}
$$

Next, $\rightarrow$: we must show that $V_{\mathscr{I}}(\phi{\rightarrow}\psi) = 1$ iff $\phi{\rightarrow}\psi \in \Gamma$:

$$
\begin{array}{llr}
V_{\mathscr{I}}(\phi{\rightarrow}\psi) = 1 & \text{iff either } V_{\mathscr{I}}(\phi) = 0 \text{ or } V_{\mathscr{I}}(\psi) = 1 & (\text{truth cond. for } \rightarrow) \\
& \text{iff either } \phi \notin \Gamma \text{ or } \psi \in \Gamma & (\text{ih}) \\
& \text{iff } \phi{\rightarrow}\psi \in \Gamma & (\text{lemma 2.4b})
\end{array}
$$

The inductive proof of (*) is complete. But now, since $\{\sim\phi\} \subseteq \Gamma$, $\sim\phi \in \Gamma$, and so by lemma 2.4a, $\phi \notin \Gamma$. Thus, by (*), ϕ is not true in $\mathscr{I}$. So we have succeeded in constructing an interpretation in which ϕ isn't true. □

---

[23] Here we continue to use the fact that a formula has one truth value iff it lacks the other.

3

BEYOND STANDARD PROPOSITIONAL LOGIC

A s PROMISED, we will study more than the standard logical systems familiar from introductory textbooks. In this chapter we'll examine some variations and deviations from standard propositional logic. (In later chapters we will discuss several extensions of standard propositional logic.)

In this chapter, let's treat all connectives as primitive unless otherwise specified. (So, for example, our recursive definition of a wff now has a clause saying that if ϕ and ψ are wffs, then so are $(\phi \wedge \psi)$, $(\phi \vee \psi)$, and $(\phi \leftrightarrow \psi)$, and our official definition of a PL-valuation now contains the semantic clauses for the $\wedge$, $\vee$, and $\leftrightarrow$ that were derived in Chapter 2.) The main reason for doing this is that in some nonstandard logics, the definitions of the defined connectives given in section 2.1 are inappropriate.

3.1 Alternate connectives

3.1.1 Symbolizing truth functions in PL

Standard propositional logic is in a sense "expressively complete". To get at this idea, let's introduce the idea of a *truth function*. A truth function is a function that maps truth values (i.e., 0s and 1s) to truth values. For example:

$$f(1) = 0$$
$$f(0) = 1$$

f is a one-place function because it takes only one truth value as input. We have an English name for this truth function: 'negation'; and we have a symbol for it: $\sim$. Consider next the two-place conjunction truth function:

$$g(1,1) = 1$$
$$g(1,0) = 0$$
$$g(0,1) = 0$$
$$g(0,0) = 0$$

We have a symbol for this truth function as well: $\wedge$.

The language of PL we have been using doesn't have a symbol for every truth function. It has no symbol for the "not-both" truth function, for example:[24]

---

[24]Though we'll consider below the addition of a symbol, |, for this truth function.

$$h(1,1) = 0$$
$$h(1,0) = 1$$
$$h(0,1) = 1$$
$$h(0,0) = 1$$

But in a sense that I'll introduce in a moment, we can "symbolize" this truth function using a complex sentence: $\sim(P{\wedge}Q)$. In fact, we can symbolize (in this sense) *any* truth function (of any finite number of places) using just $\wedge, \vee$, and $\sim$.

Proof that every truth function can be symbolized using just $\wedge$, $\vee$, and $\sim$. We need to define what it means to say that a wff "symbolizes" a truth function. The rough idea is that the wff has the right truth table. Here's a precise definition:

DEFINITION OF SYMBOLIZING: Wff ϕ symbolizes n-place truth function f iff ϕ contains the sentence letters $P_1 \ldots P_n$ and no others, and for any PL-interpretation $\mathscr{I}$, $V_{\mathscr{I}}(\phi) = f(\mathscr{I}(P_1) \ldots \mathscr{I}(P_n))$.

The sentence letters $P_1 \ldots P_n$ represent the n inputs to the truth function f. (The choice of these letters (and this order) is arbitrary; but given the choice, $\sim(P{\wedge}Q)$ doesn't officially symbolize not-both; we must instead use $\sim(P_1{\wedge}P_2)$.)

Now let's prove that for every truth function, there exists some wff containing no connectives other than $\wedge$, $\vee$, and $\sim$ that symbolizes the truth function. I'll do this informally. Let's begin with an example. Suppose we want to symbolize the following three-place truth function:

$$i(1,1,1) = 0$$
$$i(1,1,0) = 1$$
$$i(1,0,1) = 0$$
$$i(1,0,0) = 1$$
$$i(0,1,1) = 0$$
$$i(0,1,0) = 0$$
$$i(0,0,1) = 1$$
$$i(0,0,0) = 0$$

We must construct a sentence whose truth value is the same as the output of function i, whenever the sentence letters P_1, P_2, and P_3 are given i's inputs. Now, if we ignore everything but the numbers in the above picture of function i, we can think of it as a kind of truth table for the sentence we're after. The first column of numbers represents the truth values of P_1, the second column, the truth values of P_2, and the third column, the truth values of P_3; and the far right column represents the truth values that the desired formula should have. Each row represents a possible combination of truth values for these sentence letters. Thus the second row ("$i(1,1,0) = 1$") is the combination where P_1 is 1, P_2 is 1, and P_3 is 0; the fact that the fourth column in this row is 1 indicates that the desired formula should be true here.

Since function i returns the value 1 in just three cases (rows two, four, and seven), the sentence we're after should be true in exactly those three cases. Now, we can construct a sentence that is true in the case of row two (i.e. when P_1, P_2, and P_3 are 1, 1, and 0, respectively) and false otherwise: $P_1 {\wedge} P_2 {\wedge}{\sim}P_3$. And we can do the same for rows four and seven: $P_1 {\wedge}{\sim}P_2 {\wedge}{\sim}P_3$ and ${\sim}P_1 {\wedge}{\sim}P_2 {\wedge}P_3$. But then we can simply disjoin these three sentences to get the sentence we want:

$$(P_1 {\wedge} P_2 {\wedge}{\sim}P_3) \vee (P_1 {\wedge}{\sim}P_2 {\wedge}{\sim}P_3) \vee ({\sim}P_1 {\wedge}{\sim}P_2 {\wedge}P_3)$$

(Strictly speaking the three-way conjunctions, and the three-way disjunction, need parentheses. But it doesn't matter where they're added since conjunction and disjunction are associative. That is, $\phi {\wedge}(\psi {\wedge}\chi)$ and $(\phi {\wedge}\psi){\wedge}\chi$ are semantically equivalent, as are $\phi \vee (\psi \vee \chi)$ and $(\phi \vee \psi)\vee\chi$.)

This strategy is in fact purely general. Any n-place truth function, f, can be represented by a chart like the one above. Each row in the chart consists of a certain combination of n truth values, followed by the truth value returned by f for those n inputs. For each such row, construct a conjunction whose i^{th} conjunct is P_i if the ith truth value in the row is 1, and ${\sim}P_i$ if the ith truth value in the row is 0. Notice that the conjunction just constructed is true if and only if its sentence letters have the truth values corresponding to the row in question. The desired formula is then simply the disjunction of all and only the conjunctions for rows where the function f returns the value 1.[25] Since the conjunction for a given row is true iff its sentence letters have the truth values corresponding to that row, the resulting disjunction is true iff its sentence letters have truth values corresponding to one of the rows where f returns the value true, which is what we want. □

Say that a set of connectives is *adequate* iff all truth functions can be symbolized using sentences containing no connectives not in that set. What we just showed was that the set $\{{\wedge}, \vee, {\sim}\}$ is adequate. We can now use this fact to prove that other sets of connectives are adequate. Take $\{{\wedge}, {\sim}\}$, for example. Where f is any truth function, we must find some wff χ that symbolizes f whose only connectives are ${\wedge}$ and ${\sim}$. Since $\{{\wedge}, \vee, {\sim}\}$ is adequate, some sentence χ' containing only ${\wedge}$, $\vee$, and ${\sim}$ symbolizes f. But it's easy to see that any wff of the form $\phi \vee \psi$ is (PL-) semantically equivalent to ${\sim}({\sim}\phi {\wedge}{\sim}\psi)$; so we can obtain our desired χ by replacing all wffs in χ' of the form $\phi \vee \psi$ with ${\sim}({\sim}\phi {\wedge}{\sim}\psi)$.[26]

Similar arguments can be made to show that other connective sets are adequate as well. For example, the ${\wedge}$ can be eliminated in favor of the $\rightarrow$ and the ${\sim}$ (since $\phi {\wedge}\psi$ is semantically equivalent to ${\sim}(\phi \rightarrow {\sim}\psi)$); therefore, since $\{{\wedge}, {\sim}\}$ is adequate, $\{\rightarrow, {\sim}\}$ is also adequate.

---

[25] Special case: if there are no such rows—i.e., if the function returns 0 for all inputs—then let the formula simply be any always-false formula containing $P_1 \ldots P_n$, for example $P_1 {\wedge}{\sim}P_1 {\wedge}P_2 {\wedge}P_3 {\wedge}\cdots {\wedge}P_n$.

[26] Here I'm using the obvious fact that semantically equivalent wffs represent the same truth functions, and also the slightly less obvious but still obvious fact that substituting semantically equivalent wffs inside a wff α results in a wff that is semantically equivalent to α.

3.1.2 Sheffer stroke

All of the adequate connective sets we've seen so far contain more than one connective. But consider next a new connective, called the "Sheffer stroke": |. $\phi|\psi$ means that *not both* ϕ and ψ are true; thus its truth table is:

$$
\begin{array}{c|cc}
| & 1 & 0 \\
\hline
1 & 0 & 1 \\
0 & 1 & 1
\end{array}
$$

In fact, | is an adequate connective all on its own; one can symbolize all the truth functions using just |! (One other binary connective is adequate all on its own; see exercise 3.2.)

Proof that {|} is an adequate connective set. $\psi|\psi$ is semantically equivalent to $\sim\psi$. Furthermore, $\psi\rightarrow\chi$ is semantically equivalent to $\sim(\psi\wedge\sim\chi)$, and thus to $\psi|\sim\chi$, and thus to $\psi|(\chi|\chi)$. So: take any truth function, f. We showed earlier that $\{\sim,\rightarrow\}$ is adequate; so some sentence ϕ containing just $\rightarrow$ and $\sim$ symbolizes f. Replace each occurrence of $\psi\rightarrow\chi$ in ϕ with $\psi|(\chi|\chi)$, and each occurrence of $\sim\psi$ with $\psi|\psi$; the resulting wff contains only | and symbolizes f. □

3.1.3 Inadequate connective sets

Can we show that certain sets of connectives are *not* adequate?

We can quickly answer *yes*, for a trivial reason. The set $\{\sim\}$ isn't adequate, for the simple reason that, since $\sim$ is a one-place connective, no sentence with more than one sentence letter can be built using just $\sim$. So there's no hope of symbolizing n-place truth functions, for $n > 1$, using just the $\sim$.

More interestingly, we can show that there are inadequate connective sets containing two-place connectives. One example is $\{\wedge,\rightarrow\}$.

Proof that $\{\wedge,\rightarrow\}$ is not an adequate set of connectives. Suppose for reductio that the set *is* adequate. Then there exists some wff, ϕ, containing just the sentence letter P_1 and no connectives other than $\wedge$ and $\rightarrow$ that symbolizes the negation truth function. But there can be no such wff ϕ. For ϕ would have to be false whenever P_1 is true, whereas we can prove the following by induction:

> Each wff ϕ whose only sentence letter is P_1, and which contains no connectives other than $\wedge$ and $\rightarrow$, is true in any PL-interpretation in which P_1 is true.

Base case: if ϕ has no connectives, then ϕ is just the sentence letter P_1 itself, in which case it's clearly true in any PL-interpretation in which P_1 is true. Next we assume the inductive hypothesis, that wffs ϕ and ψ are true in any PL-interpretation in which P_1 is true; we must now show that $\phi\wedge\psi$ and $\phi\rightarrow\psi$ are true in any such PL-interpretation. But this follows immediately from the truth tables for $\wedge$ and $\rightarrow$. □

Exercise 3.1 For each of the following two truth functions, (i) find a sentence with just $\sim$, $\wedge$, $\vee$, $\leftrightarrow$, or $\rightarrow$ that symbolizes it; and (ii) find a sentence containing just the Sheffer stroke that symbolizes it. You may save time by making abbreviations and saying things like "make such-and-such substitutions throughout".

$$f(1,1) = 1 \qquad\qquad g(1,1,0) = 0$$
$$f(1,0) = 0 \qquad\qquad g(0,0,1) = 0$$
$$f(0,1) = 0 \qquad\qquad g(x,y,z) = 1 \text{ otherwise}$$
$$f(0,0) = 1$$

Exercise 3.2 Show that all truth functions can be symbolized using just $\downarrow$ (nor). $\phi \downarrow \psi$ is 1 when both ϕ and ψ are 0, and 0 otherwise.

Exercise 3.3 Can all the truth functions be symbolized using just the following connective? (Give a proof to justify your answer.)

%	1	0
1	0	1
0	1	0

3.2 Polish notation

Reformulating standard logic using the Sheffer stroke is a mere variation (section 1.7) of standard logic, since in a sense it's a mere notational change. Another variation is Polish notation. In Polish notation, the connectives all go *before* the sentences they connect. Instead of writing $P \wedge Q$, we write $\wedge PQ$. Instead of writing $P \vee Q$ we write $\vee PQ$. Formally, we redefine the wffs as follows:

DEFINITION OF WFFS FOR POLISH NOTATION:

- sentence letters are wffs
- if ϕ and ψ are wffs, then so are: $\sim\phi$, $\wedge\phi\psi$, $\vee\phi\psi$, $\rightarrow\phi\psi$, and $\leftrightarrow\phi\psi$

What's the point? This notation eliminates the need for parentheses. With the usual notation, in which we put the connectives between the sentences they connect, we need parentheses to distinguish, e.g.:

$$(P \wedge Q) \rightarrow R$$
$$P \wedge (Q \rightarrow R)$$

But with Polish notation, these are distinguished without parentheses:

$$\rightarrow \wedge PQR$$
$$\wedge P \rightarrow QR$$

Exercise 3.4 Translate each of the following into Polish notation:

(a) $P\leftrightarrow\sim P$

(b) $(P\rightarrow(Q\rightarrow(R\rightarrow\sim\sim(S\vee T))))$

(c) $[(P\wedge\sim Q)\vee(\sim P\wedge Q)]\leftrightarrow\sim[(P\vee\sim Q)\wedge(\sim P\vee Q)]$

3.3 Nonclassical propositional logics

In the rest of this chapter we will examine certain deviations from standard propositional logic. These are often called "nonclassical" logics, "classical" logic being the standard type of propositional and predicate logic studied in introductory courses and presented here in Chapters 2 and 4.[27] These nonclassical logics use the standard *language* of logic, but they offer different semantics and/or proof theories.

There are many reasons to get interested in nonclassical logic, but one exciting one is the belief that classical logic is *wrong*—that it provides an inadequate model of (genuine) logical truth and logical consequence. For example, every wff of the form $\phi\vee\sim\phi$ is PL-valid and a PL-theorem. But mathematical intuitionists (section 3.5) claim that for certain mathematical statements ϕ, the sentence "either ϕ or it is not the case that ϕ" is not even one we are entitled to assert, let alone a logical truth. As elsewhere in this book, our primary concern is to understand how formalisms work, rather than to evaluate philosophical claims about genuine logical truth and logical consequence. However, to explain why nonclassical formalisms have been developed, and to give them some context, in each case we'll dip briefly into the relevant philosophical issues.

In principle, a critic of classical logic could claim either that classical logic recognizes too many logical consequences (or logical truths), or that it recognizes too few. But in practice, the latter is rare. In nearly every case, the nonclassicalist's concern is to scale back classical logic's set of logical truths or logical consequences. Intuitionists and many other nonclassical logicians want to remove $\phi\vee\sim\phi$, the so-called law of the excluded middle, from the set of logical truths; paraconsistent logicians (section 3.4.4) want to remove ex falso quodlibet (ϕ; $\sim\phi$; therefore, ψ) from the set of logical implications; and so on.

Like classical logic, one can approach a given nonclassical logic in various ways. One can take a proof-theoretic approach (using axioms, sequents, or some other proof system). Or one can take a semantic approach. I'll take different approaches to different logics, depending on which approach seems most natural.

Nonclassical logic can seem dizzying. It challenges assumptions that we normally regard as utterly unproblematic, assumptions we normally make without even noticing, assumptions that form the very bedrock of rational thought. Can these assumptions sensibly be questioned? Some nonclassical logicians even say that there

---

[27] Extensions to standard propositional logic, such as modal logic, are also sometimes called nonclassical; but by 'nonclassical' I'll have in mind just deviations.

are true contradictions! (See section 3.4.4.) If even the law of noncontradiction is up for grabs, one might worry: how is argumentation possible at all?

My own view is that even the most radical challenges to classical logic can coherently be entertained, and need not amount to intellectual suicide. But if you're more philosophically conservative, fear not: from a *formal* point of view there's nothing at all dizzying about nonclassical logic. In the previous chapter we gave various mathematical definitions: of the notion of a PL-interpretation, the notion of a sequent proof, and so on. Formally speaking, nonclassical logics result simply from giving different definitions. As we'll see, these different definitions are easy to give and to understand. Furthermore, when I give the definitions and reason about them, I will myself be assuming "classical logic in the metalanguage". For example, even when we discuss the formalism accepted by the defenders of true contradictions, I won't myself accept any true contradictions. I will reason normally in the course of developing a formal system that represents abnormal patterns of inference, much as a sane psychologist might develop a model of insanity. Thus, even if there's something philosophically perplexing about the claims about (genuine) logical consequence made by nonclassical logicians, there's nothing mathematically perplexing about the formal systems that represent those claims.

3.4 Three-valued logic

For our first foray into nonclassical logic, we will take a semantic approach. Various logicians have considered adding a third truth value to the usual two. In addition to truth (1) and falsity (0), they add a third truth value, #. The third truth value is (in most cases anyway) supposed to represent sentences that are neither true nor false, but rather have some other status. This other status could be taken in various ways, depending on the intended application, for example: "meaningless", "undefined", or "indeterminate".

Classical logic is "bivalent": there are exactly two truth values, and each formula is assigned exactly one of them in any interpretation. So, admitting a third truth value is one way to deny bivalence. There are others. One could admit four, five, or even infinitely many truth values. Or one could stick with two truth values but allow formulas to have both truth values, or to lack both. (Some would argue that there's no real difference between allowing formulas to lack both of two truth values, and admitting a third truth value thought of as meaning "neither true nor false".) Here we will only discuss *trivalent* systems—systems in which each formula has exactly one of three truth values.

Why introduce a third truth value? Various philosophical reasons have been given. One concerns vagueness. Donald Trump is rich. Pete the peasant is not. Somewhere in the middle there are people who are hard to classify. Perhaps middling Mary, who has $50,000, is an example. Is she rich? We're reluctant to say either that she is rich, or that she is not rich. 'Rich' is vague, and Mary is on the borderline, in a grey area. (If you think $50,000 clearly makes you rich, choose a somewhat smaller amount for the example; if you think it clearly doesn't, choose a larger amount.) So there's pressure to say that the statement "Mary is rich" can be neither true nor false.

Others say we need a third truth value for statements about the future. If it is in some sense "not yet determined" whether there will be a sea battle tomorrow, then, it has been argued, the sentence:

There will be a sea battle tomorrow

is neither true nor false. In general, this viewpoint says, statements about the future are neither true nor false if there is nothing about the present that determines their truth value one way or the other.[28]

Yet another alleged counterinstance to bivalence involves *failed presupposition*. Consider this sentence:

Ted stopped beating his dog

In fact, I've never beaten a dog. I've never beaten anything. I don't even have a dog. So is it true that I stopped beating my dog? Obviously not. But on the other hand, is this statement false? Certainly no one would want to assert its negation: "Ted has not stopped beating his dog". "Ted stopped beating his dog" *presupposes* that I was beating a dog in the past; since this presupposition is false, the sentence does not rise to the level of truth or falsity.

For a final challenge to bivalence, consider the sentence:

Sherlock Holmes has a mole on his left leg

'Sherlock Holmes' doesn't refer to a real entity. Further, Sir Arthur Conan Doyle does not specify in his Sherlock Holmes stories whether Holmes has such a mole. For either of these reasons, one might argue, the displayed sentence is neither true nor false.

It's an open question whether any of these arguments against bivalence is any good. Moreover, powerful arguments can be given *against* the idea that some sentences are neither true nor false. First, it is natural to identify the falsity of a sentence with the truth of its negation. So, if we say that 'Mary is rich' is neither true nor false, i.e., not true and not false, we must also say that:

'Mary is rich' is not true, and 'not: Mary is rich' is not true

Second, the notion of truth is often thought to be "transparent", in that for any (meaningful) sentence ϕ, the sentences ϕ and " 'ϕ' is true" are interchangeable, even when (nonquotationally) embedded inside other expressions. If truth is transparent then " 'ϕ' is not true"—i.e., "not: ϕ is true"—implies "not-ϕ". Thus the previously displayed sentence commits us to saying:

not: Mary is rich, and not: not: Mary is rich

Saying that 'Mary is rich' is neither true nor false has apparently committed us to a contradiction!

---

[28] There is an alternate view that upholds the "open future" without denying bivalence. According to this view, both 'There will be a sea battle tomorrow' and 'There will fail to be a sea battle tomorrow' are *false*; "It will be the case tomorrow that not-ϕ" and "Not: it will be the case tomorrow that ϕ" are not equivalent. See Prior (1957, chapter X).

So there is controversy about whether some sentences are neither true nor false. But rather than spending more time on such philosophical questions, let's now concentrate on a certain sort of formalism that is intended to represent the failure of bivalence. The idea is simple: give three-valued truth tables for the connectives of propositional logic. The classical truth tables give you the truth values of complex formulas based on whether their constituent sentences are true or false (1 or 0), whereas the new truth tables will take into account new cases: cases where sentences are #.

3.4.1 *Łukasiewicz's system*

Here is one set of three-valued truth tables, due to Jan Łukasiewicz (who also invented the Polish notation of section 3.2):

$\sim$		$\wedge$	1	0	#		$\vee$	1	0	#		$\rightarrow$	1	0	#
1	0	1	1	0	#		1	1	1	1		1	1	0	#
0	1	0	0	0	0		0	1	0	#		0	1	1	1
#	#	#	#	0	#		#	1	#	#		#	1	#	1

(In our discussion of three-valued logic, let $\phi \leftrightarrow \psi$ abbreviate $(\phi \rightarrow \psi) \wedge (\psi \rightarrow \phi)$.) Using these truth tables, one can calculate truth values of wholes based on truth values of parts.

Example 3.1: Where P is 1, Q is 0, and R is #, calculate the truth value of $(P \vee Q) \rightarrow \sim(R \rightarrow Q)$. First, what is $R \rightarrow Q$? The truth table for $\rightarrow$ tells us that #$\rightarrow$0 is #. So, since the negation of a # is #, $\sim(R \rightarrow Q)$ is # as well. Next, $P \vee Q$: that's 1$\vee$0—i.e., 1. Finally, the whole thing: 1$\rightarrow$#, i.e., #.

We can formalize this a bit more by defining new interpretation and valuation functions:

DEFINITION OF TRIVALENT INTERPRETATION: A trivalent interpretation is a function that assigns to each sentence letter exactly one of the values: 1, 0, #.

DEFINITION OF VALUATION: For any trivalent interpretation, $\mathscr{I}$, the Łukasiewicz-valuation for $\mathscr{I}$, $ŁV_{\mathscr{I}}$, is defined as the function that assigns to each wff one of 1, 0, or #, and which is such that, for any wffs ϕ and ψ,

$$ŁV_{\mathscr{I}}(\phi) = \mathscr{I}(\phi) \text{ if } \phi \text{ is a sentence letter}$$

$$ŁV_{\mathscr{I}}(\phi \wedge \psi) = \begin{cases} 1 & \text{if } ŁV_{\mathscr{I}}(\phi) = 1 \text{ and } ŁV_{\mathscr{I}}(\psi) = 1 \\ 0 & \text{if } ŁV_{\mathscr{I}}(\phi) = 0 \text{ or } ŁV_{\mathscr{I}}(\psi) = 0 \\ \# & \text{otherwise} \end{cases}$$

$$ŁV_{\mathscr{I}}(\phi \vee \psi) = \begin{cases} 1 & \text{if } ŁV_{\mathscr{I}}(\phi) = 1 \text{ or } ŁV_{\mathscr{I}}(\psi) = 1 \\ 0 & \text{if } ŁV_{\mathscr{I}}(\phi) = 0 \text{ and } ŁV_{\mathscr{I}}(\psi) = 0 \\ \# & \text{otherwise} \end{cases}$$

$$ \text{ŁV}_{\mathscr{g}}(\phi \rightarrow \psi) = \begin{cases} 1 & \text{if ŁV}_{\mathscr{g}}(\phi) = 0, \text{ or ŁV}_{\mathscr{g}}(\psi) = 1, \text{ or ŁV}_{\mathscr{g}}(\phi) = \text{ŁV}_{\mathscr{g}}(\psi) = \# \\ 0 & \text{ŁV}_{\mathscr{g}}(\phi) = 1 \text{ and ŁV}_{\mathscr{g}}(\psi) = 0 \\ \# & \text{otherwise} \end{cases} $$

$$ \text{ŁV}_{\mathscr{g}}(\sim\phi) = \begin{cases} 1 & \text{if ŁV}_{\mathscr{g}}(\phi) = 0 \\ 0 & \text{if ŁV}_{\mathscr{g}}(\phi) = 1 \\ \# & \text{otherwise} \end{cases} $$

Let's define validity and semantic consequence for Łukasiewicz's system much like we did for standard PL:

DEFINITIONS OF VALIDITY AND SEMANTIC CONSEQUENCE:

- ϕ is Łukasiewicz-valid ("$\vDash_{\text{Ł}} \phi$") iff $\text{ŁV}_{\mathscr{g}}(\phi) = 1$ for every trivalent interpretation $\mathscr{g}$
- ϕ is a Łukasiewicz-semantic-consequence of Γ ("$\Gamma \vDash_{\text{Ł}} \phi$") iff for every trivalent interpretation, $\mathscr{g}$, if $\text{ŁV}_{\mathscr{g}}(\gamma) = 1$ for each $\gamma \in \Gamma$, then $\text{ŁV}_{\mathscr{g}}(\phi) = 1$

Example 3.2: Is $P \vee \sim P$ Łukasiewicz-valid? Answer: no, it isn't. Suppose P is #. Then $\sim P$ is #; but then the whole thing is # (since #∨# is #).

Example 3.3: Is $P \rightarrow P$ Łukasiewicz-valid? Answer: yes. P could be 1, 0, or #. From the truth table for $\rightarrow$, we see that $P \rightarrow P$ is 1 in all three cases.

Notice that even if a formula can never be false, it doesn't follow that the formula is valid—perhaps the formula is sometimes #. "Valid" (on the definition just given) means *always true*; it does *not* mean *never false*. (Similarly, the notion of semantic consequence that we defined is that of truth-preservation, *not* nonfalsity-preservation.)

One *could* define validity differently, as meaning never-false. (And one could define semantic consequence as nonfalsity-preservation.) Such definitions would generate a very different system; they would generate a very different range of valid formulas and semantic consequences. This illustrates an important fact. Once one chooses to introduce extra truth values (and extra truth tables based on them), one then faces a second choice: how should validity and semantic consequence be understood? New theories of the nature of validity and semantic consequence do not result solely from the first choice, only from a combination of the two choices.

There is a helpful terminology for talking about the second of these choices. Consider any semantics that employs some set $\mathscr{V}$ of truth values. (In standard logic $\mathscr{V} = \{1, 0\}$; in our trivalent systems $\mathscr{V} = \{1, 0, \#\}$.) We can select some subset of $\mathscr{V}$ and call the members of that subset the *designated* truth values. Once the designated values have been selected, we can then say: a valid formula is one that has a designated truth value in every interpretation; and Γ semantically implies ϕ iff ϕ has a designated truth value in every interpretation in which each $\gamma \in \Gamma$ has a designated truth value. Our definition of Łukasiewicz-validity (as meaning always-true) takes 1 to be the sole designated value; defining "valid" to mean never-false would amount to taking both 1 and # as designated.

Now is perhaps as good a time as any to make a general point about semantic definitions of logical truth and logical consequence. In this section we used a three-valued semantics to define a certain property of wffs (Łukasiewicz-validity) and a certain relation between sets of wffs and wffs (Łukasiewicz-semantic-consequence). It would be possible to sharply distinguish the semantic means from the resulting end. Imagine a philosopher who says the following:

> The three-valued Łukasiewicz-semantics does not represent the real semantics of natural language, since no (meaningful) natural language sentences are neither true nor false. (I accept the argument at the end of section 3.4: the claim that a sentence is neither true nor false would lead to a contradiction.) Nevertheless, I do think that Łukasiewicz-validity and Łukasiewicz-semantic-consequence do a pretty good job of modeling genuine logical truth and logical consequence. If you ignore the internal workings of the definitions, and focus just on their outputs—that is, if you focus just on which wffs count as Łukasiewicz-valid and which sets of wffs Łukasiewicz-semantically-imply which other wffs—you get the right results. For example, $P{\rightarrow}P$ is Łukasiewicz-valid whereas $P{\vee}{\sim}P$ is not; and sure enough, on my view, "if there will be a sea battle tomorrow then there will be a sea battle tomorrow" is a logical truth whereas "either there will be a sea battle tomorrow or there won't" is not.

There may be philosophical tensions within such a position, but it is, at least on its face, a position someone might take. The moral is that the properties and relations we define using a formal semantics have a "life of their own" beyond the semantics.

Exercise 3.5 We noted that it seems in-principle possible for a formula to be "never-false", given the Łukasiewicz tables, without being "always-true". Give an example of such a formula.

Exercise 3.6 Show that no wff ϕ whose sentence letters are just P and Q and which has no connectives other than $\wedge$, $\vee$, and $\sim$ has the same Łukasiewicz truth table as $P{\rightarrow}Q$—i.e., that for no such ϕ is $ŁV_{\mathscr{I}}(\phi) = ŁV_{\mathscr{I}}(P{\rightarrow}Q)$ for each trivalent interpretation $\mathscr{I}$.

3.4.2 Kleene's tables

Łukasiewicz's tables are not the only three-valued truth tables one can give. Stephen C. Kleene gave three-valued tables that are just like Łukasiewicz's except for the following different table for the $\rightarrow$:[29]

---

[29] These are sometimes called Kleene's "strong tables". Kleene also gave another set of tables known as his "weak" tables, which assign # whenever any constituent formula is # (and are classically otherwise). Perhaps # in the weak tables can be thought of as representing "nonsense": any nonsense in a part of a sentence is infectious, making the entire sentence nonsense.

→	1	0	#
1	1	0	#
0	1	1	1
#	1	#	#

As in the previous section, we could write out a corresponding definition of a Kleene valuation function $KV_{\mathscr{I}}$, relative to a trivalent assignment $\mathscr{I}$. But let's not bother. To define Kleene-validity and Kleene-semantic-consequence ("$\vDash_K$"), we continue to take 1 as the sole designated value; thus we have: $\vDash_K \phi$ iff $KV_{\mathscr{I}}(\phi) = 1$ for all trivalent interpretations $\mathscr{I}$; and $\Gamma \vDash_K \phi$ iff $KV_{\mathscr{I}}(\phi) = 1$ for each trivalent interpretation $\mathscr{I}$ in which $KV_{\mathscr{I}}(\gamma) = 1$ for all $\gamma \in \Gamma$.

Here is the intuitive idea behind the Kleene tables. Let's call the truth values 0 and 1 the "classical" truth values. If the immediate parts of a complex formula have only classical truth values, then the truth value of the whole formula is just the classical truth value determined by the classical truth values of those parts. But if some of those parts are #, then we must consider the result of turning each # into one of the classical truth values. If the entire formula would sometimes be 1 and sometimes be 0 after doing this, then the entire formula is #. But if the entire formula always takes the same truth value, X, no matter which classical truth value any #s are turned into, then the entire formula gets this truth value X. Intuitively: if there is "enough information" in the classical truth values of a formula's immediate parts to settle on one particular classical truth value, then that truth value is the formula's truth value.

Take Kleene's truth table for $\phi \rightarrow \psi$, for example. When ϕ is 0 and ψ is #, the table says that $\phi \rightarrow \psi$ is 1—because the false antecedent is classically sufficient to make $\phi \rightarrow \psi$ true, no matter what classical truth value we convert ψ's # to. On the other hand, when ϕ is 1 and ψ is #, then $\phi \rightarrow \psi$ is #—because which classical truth value we substitute in for ψ's # affects the truth value of $\phi \rightarrow \psi$. If the # becomes a 0, then $\phi \rightarrow \psi$ is 0; but if the # becomes a 1 then $\phi \rightarrow \psi$ is 1.

Let me mention two important differences between the Łukasiewicz and Kleene systems. First, unlike Łukasiewicz's system, Kleene's system makes the formula $P \rightarrow P$ invalid. (This might be regarded as an advantage for Łukasiewicz.) The reason is that in Kleene's system, $\# \rightarrow \#$ is #; thus, $P \rightarrow P$ isn't true in all valuations (it is # in the valuation where P is #). In fact, it's easy to show that there are *no* valid formulas in Kleene's system (exercise 3.7). Nevertheless, there are cases of semantic consequence. For example, $P \land Q \vDash_K P$, since the only way for $P \land Q$ to be 1 is for both P and Q to be 1.

Second, in Kleene's system, $\rightarrow$ is interdefinable with the $\sim$ and $\lor$, in that $\phi \rightarrow \psi$ has exactly the same truth table as $\sim \phi \lor \psi$. (Look at the truth tables to verify that this is true.) That's not true in Łukasiewicz's system (exercise 3.6).

Exercise 3.7* Show that there are no Kleene-valid wffs.

Exercise 3.8** Say that one trivalent interpretation $\mathscr{J}$ *refines* another, $\mathscr{I}$, iff for any sentence letter α, if $\mathscr{I}(\alpha) = 1$ then $\mathscr{J}(\alpha) = 1$, and if $\mathscr{I}(\alpha) = 0$ then $\mathscr{J}(\alpha) = 0$. That is, $\mathscr{J}$ preserves all of $\mathscr{I}$'s classical values (though it may assign some additional classical values, in cases where $\mathscr{I}$ assigns #). Show that refining a trivalent interpretation preserves classical values for all wffs, given the Kleene tables. That is, if $\mathscr{J}$ refines $\mathscr{I}$ then for every wff, ϕ, if $KV_{\mathscr{I}}(\phi) = 1$ then $KV_{\mathscr{J}}(\phi) = 1$, and if $KV_{\mathscr{I}}(\phi) = 0$ then $KV_{\mathscr{J}}(\phi) = 0$.

Exercise 3.9 Show that the claim in exercise 3.8 does not hold if you valuate using Łukasiewicz's tables rather than Kleene's.

3.4.3 *Determinacy*

As we saw at the beginning of section 3.4, one potential application of three-valued logic is to vagueness. Here we think of 1 as representing *determinate*, or nonvague, truth ("Donald Trump is rich"), 0 as representing determinate falsehood ("Pete the peasant is rich"), and # as representing *indeterminacy* ("Middling Mary is rich").[30]

1, 0, and # are values that are possessed by sentences (relative to three-valued interpretations). To attribute one of these values to a sentence is thus to say something about that sentence. So these values represent statements about determinacy that we make in the metalanguage, by quoting sentences and attributing determinacy-statuses to them:

> 'Donald Trump is rich' is determinately true
> 'Pete the peasant is rich' is determinately false
> 'Middling Mary is rich' is indeterminate

But we can speak of determinacy directly, in the object language, without quoting sentences, by using the adverb 'definitely':

> Donald Trump is definitely rich
> Pete the peasant is definitely not rich
> Middling Mary is indefinitely rich (neither definitely rich nor definitely not)

How might we represent this use of 'definitely' within logic?

We could add a new symbol to the language of propositional logic. The usual choice is a one-place sentence operator, $\triangle$. We read "$\triangle\phi$" as meaning "definitely, ϕ" (or: "determinately, ϕ").[31] (Being a one-place sentence operator, $\triangle$ has the same grammar as $\sim$: it's governed in the definition of a wff by the clause that if ϕ is a wff

---

[30]Indeterminacy can be viewed as being more general than vagueness, encompassing other phenomena (e.g., indeterminacy of the future); and the operator $\triangle$ can be construed in a correspondingly general way.

[31]Some distinguish "definiteness" from "determinacy". I'll be ignoring this and other subtleties.

Logic for Philosophy

then so is $\triangle\phi$. A corresponding operator for indefiniteness could be defined in terms of $\triangle$: "$\nabla\phi$" is short for "$\sim\triangle\phi \wedge \sim\triangle\sim\phi$".)

The next question is how to treat $\triangle$ semantically. It's easy to see how to extend the systems of Łukasiewicz and Kleene to cover $\triangle$; we simply adopt the following new truth table:

$$
\begin{array}{c|c}
\triangle & \\
\hline
1 & 1 \\
0 & 0 \\
\# & 0 \\
\end{array}
$$

Thus $\triangle\phi$ is 1 whenever ϕ is 1, and is 0 otherwise. (And $\nabla\phi$ is 1 when ϕ is #; 0 otherwise.)

This approach to the semantics of $\triangle$ has an apparently serious shortcoming: $\triangle\phi$ can never have the value #. This is a shortcoming because some statements about definiteness seem themselves to be indeterminate. Donald Trump is definitely rich; but if in a fit of philanthropy he started giving money away, one dollar at a time, eventually it would become unclear whether he was still definitely rich. Letting R symbolize "Philanthropic Trump is rich", it's natural to think that $\triangle R$ should here be #.

"Higher-order vagueness" is vagueness about vagueness. The shortcoming of our three-valued approach to $\triangle$ is in essence that it doesn't allow for higher-order vagueness. This deficiency comes out in other ways as well. For example, it's natural to describe philanthropic Trump as being an indefinite case of definite richness—he's neither definitely definitely rich nor definitely not definitely rich. But $\sim\triangle\triangle R \wedge \sim\triangle\sim\triangle R$ (i.e., $\nabla\triangle R$) comes out 0 no matter what value R has, given the above truth table for $\triangle$. Our semantics does a bad job with $\triangle$s embedded within $\triangle$s. Furthermore, $\triangle R \vee \sim\triangle R$ comes out 1 no matter what value R has, whereas, one might think, 'Philanthropic Trump is either definitely rich or not definitely rich' is neither true nor false.

The root of these problems is that the approach to vagueness that we have taken in the last three sections lets us represent only three states for a given sentence letter: determinate truth (1), determinate falsity (0), and indeterminacy (#); this leaves out states distinctive of higher-order vagueness such as determinate determinate falsity, indeterminate determinate falsity, and so on. More sophisticated approaches to vagueness and the logic of $\triangle$ than those we will consider in this book do a better job of allowing for higher-order vagueness.[32]

3.4.4 *Priest's logic of paradox*

Suppose we keep Kleene's tables, but take both # and 1 to be designated truth values. Thus we call a wff valid iff it is either 1 or # in every trivalent interpretation; and we say that a set of wffs Γ semantically implies wff ϕ iff ϕ is either 1 or # in every

---

[32] See for example Fine (1975); Williamson (1999*b*).

trivalent interpretation in which each member of Γ is either 1 or #. The resulting logic is Graham Priest's (1979) "logic of paradox" (LP). The official definitions:

DEFINITIONS OF VALIDITY AND SEMANTIC CONSEQUENCE:

- ϕ is LP-valid ("$\vDash_{LP} \phi$") iff $KV_{\mathscr{I}}(\phi) \neq 0$ for each trivalent interpretation $\mathscr{I}$
- ϕ is an LP-semantic-consequence of Γ ("Γ $\vDash_{LP} \phi$") iff for every trivalent interpretation, $\mathscr{I}$, if $KV_{\mathscr{I}}(\gamma) \neq 0$ for each $\gamma \in \Gamma$, then $KV_{\mathscr{I}}(\phi) \neq 0$

Priest calls this the "logic of paradox" because of the philosophical interpretation he gives to #. For Priest, # represents the state of being *both true and false* (a truth-value "glut"), rather than the state of being *neither true nor false* (a truth-value "gap"). Correspondingly, he takes 1 to represent *true and only true*, and 0 to represent *false and only false*.

For Priest, LP is not an idle formal game, since, according to him, some natural language sentences really are both true and false. (This position is known as dialetheism.) Consider, for example, the liar sentence "this sentence is false". The liar sentence presents a challenging paradox to everyone. Is it true? Well, if so, then since what it says is that it is false, it must be false as well. Is it false? Well, if so, then since what it says is that it is false, it must then be true as well. We've shown that in each alternative—the alternative that the liar sentence is true and the alternative that the liar sentence is false—the liar sentence comes out both true and false. These are the only alternatives; hence the formula is both true and false. That's the liar paradox. Most people conclude that something has gone wrong along the way, whereas Priest embraces the paradoxical conclusion.

It's natural for a dialetheist like Priest to embrace a logic like LP. For it's natural to think of logical consequence as truth-preservation; LP represents logical consequence as the preservation of *either 1 or #*; and in LP, a formula is thought of as being true iff it is either 1 or # (in the latter case the formula is false as well). Further, a look at the Kleene tables shows that their assignments to # seem, intuitively, to mesh with Priest's "both true and false" interpretation.

Further, Priest embraces some contradictions. That is, for some sentences ϕ, he accepts both ϕ and also "not-ϕ".[33] But in standard propositional logic, everything follows from a contradiction, via the principle of ex falso quodlibet: $\phi, \sim\phi \vDash_{PL} \psi$. Priest does not of course want to have to accept every sentence ψ, and so he needs a logic that does not let you infer any old sentence from a contradiction. That is, he needs a *paraconsistent* logic. But LP is a paraconsistent logic (there are others). For it's easy to check that $P, \sim P \nvDash_{LP} Q$. In a trivalent interpretation in which P is # and Q is 0, both P and $\sim P$ are #, but Q is 0. So in this trivalent interpretation, the premises (P and $\sim P$) have designated values whereas the conclusion (Q) does not.

Ex falso quodlibet is not the only classical inference that fails in LP. Modus ponens is another (exercise 3.10d). So LP's relation of logical consequence differs

---

[33] Accepting "Sentence 'ϕ' is both true and false" is not exactly the same as accepting both ϕ and "not-ϕ"; but the former leads to the latter given the principles about truth and falsity described at the end of section 3.4.

drastically from that of classical logic. However, LP generates precisely the same results as classical propositional logic when it comes to the validity of individual formulas (exercise 3.11).

Exercise 3.10 Demonstrate each of the following:

(a) $P \wedge Q \vDash_{LP} Q \wedge P$

(b) $P \rightarrow (Q \rightarrow R) \vDash_{LP} Q \rightarrow (P \rightarrow R)$

(c) $\sim(P \wedge Q) \vDash_{LP} \sim P \vee \sim Q$

(d) $P, P \rightarrow Q \nvDash_{LP} Q$

(e) $\sim P, P \vee Q \nvDash_{LP} Q$

Exercise 3.11** Show that a formula is PL-valid iff it is LP-valid.

3.4.5 Supervaluationism

Recall the guiding thought behind the Kleene tables: if a formula's classical truth values fix a particular truth value, then that is the value that the formula takes on. There is a way to take this idea a step further, which results in a new and interesting way of thinking about three-valued logic.

According to the Kleene tables, we get a classical truth value for $\phi C \psi$, where C is any connective, only when we have "enough classical information" in the truth values of ϕ and ψ to fix a classical truth value for $\phi C \psi$. Consider $\phi \wedge \psi$ for example: if either ϕ or ψ is false, then since the falsehood of a conjunct is classically sufficient for the falsehood of the whole conjunction, the entire formula is false. But if, on the other hand, both ϕ and ψ are #, then neither ϕ nor ψ has a classical truth value, we do *not* have enough classical information to settle on a classical truth value for $\phi \wedge \psi$, and so the whole formula is #.

But now consider a special case of the situation in the previous paragraph: let ϕ be P, ψ be $\sim P$, and consider a trivalent interpretation $\mathscr{I}$ in which P is #. According to the Kleene tables, the conjunction $P \wedge \sim P$ is #, since it is the conjunction of two formulas that are #. But there is a way of thinking about truth values of complex sentences according to which the truth value ought to be 0, not #. Consider changing the truth value that $\mathscr{I}$ assigns to P from # to a classical truth value. No matter which classical value we choose, the whole sentence $P \wedge \sim P$ would then become 0. If we changed $\mathscr{I}$ to make P 0, then $P \wedge \sim P$ would be $0 \wedge \sim 0$—that is 0; and if we made P 1, then $P \wedge \sim P$ would be $1 \wedge \sim 1$—0 again. $P \wedge \sim P$ becomes false no matter what classical truth value we give to its sentence letter P—isn't that a reason to think that, contrary to what Kleene says, $P \wedge \sim P$ is false?

The general thought here is this: suppose a sentence ϕ contains some sentence letters $P_1 \ldots P_n$ that are #. If ϕ would be false no matter how we assigned classical truth values to $P_1 \ldots P_n$—that is, no matter how we *precisified* ϕ—then ϕ is in fact false. Further, if ϕ would be true no matter how we precisified it, then ϕ is in fact true. But if precisifying ϕ would sometimes make it true and sometimes make it false, then ϕ is #.

The idea here can be thought of as an extension of the idea behind the Kleene tables. Consider a formula $\phi C \psi$, where C is any connective. If there is enough classical information in the *truth values* of ϕ and ψ to fix on a particular classical truth value, then the Kleene tables assign $\phi C \psi$ that truth value. Our new idea goes further, and says: if there is enough classical information *within* ϕ and ψ to fix a particular classical truth value, then $\phi C \psi$ gets that truth value. Information "within" ϕ and ψ includes, not only the truth values of ϕ and ψ, but also a certain sort of information about sentence letters that occur in both ϕ and ψ. For example, in $P \wedge \sim P$, when P is #, there is insufficient classical information in the truth values of P and of $\sim P$ to settle on a truth value for the whole formula $P \wedge \sim P$ (since each is #). But when we look *inside* P and $\sim P$, we get more classical information: we can use the fact that P occurs in each to reason as we did above: whenever we turn P to 0, we turn $\sim P$ to 1, and so $P \wedge \sim P$ becomes 0; and whenever we turn P to 1, we turn $\sim P$ to 0, and so again, $P \wedge \sim P$ becomes 0.

This new idea—that a formula has a classical truth value iff every way of precisifying it results in that truth value—is known as *supervaluationism*. Let us lay out this idea formally. We begin with the notion of a *precisification*:

DEFINITION OF PRECISIFICATION: Where $\mathscr{I}$ is a trivalent interpretation, $\mathscr{C}$ is a precisification of $\mathscr{I}$ iff $\mathscr{C}$ is a PL-interpretation (as defined in section 2.3) such that for any sentence letter α, if $\mathscr{I}(\alpha) = 1$ then $\mathscr{C}(\alpha) = 1$, and if $\mathscr{I}(\alpha) = 0$ then $\mathscr{C}(\alpha) = 0$.

Here's the idea. Begin with a trivalent interpretation, $\mathscr{I}$—an assignment of 1s, 0s, and #s to sentence letters. Now construct a *bivalent* interpretation by (i) leaving all 1s and 0s assigned by $\mathscr{I}$ (if there are any) alone, and changing any #s assigned by $\mathscr{I}$ to 1s or 0s in any way you like. The result is a precisification of $\mathscr{I}$. Thus precisifications of $\mathscr{I}$ agree with $\mathscr{I}$ whenever $\mathscr{I}$ assigns classical values; but if $\mathscr{I}$ assigns any #s to any sentence letters then its precisifications will disagree with it on those sentence letters (since precisifications are bivalent and therefore may assign only 1s and 0s). Note, finally, that different precisifications of $\mathscr{I}$ will change $\mathscr{I}$'s #s to classical values in different ways.

We can now say how the supervaluationist assigns truth values to complex formulas relative to a given trivalent interpretation.

DEFINITION OF SUPERVALUATION: When ϕ is any wff and $\mathscr{I}$ is a trivalent interpretation, the supervaluation of ϕ relative to $\mathscr{I}$ is the function $SV_{\mathscr{I}}(\phi)$ that assigns 0, 1, or # to each wff as follows:

$$SV_{\mathscr{I}}(\phi) = \begin{cases} 1 & \text{if } V_{\mathscr{C}}(\phi) = 1 \text{ for every precisification, } \mathscr{C}, \text{ of } \mathscr{I} \\ 0 & \text{if } V_{\mathscr{C}}(\phi) = 0 \text{ for every precisification, } \mathscr{C}, \text{ of } \mathscr{I} \\ \# & \text{otherwise} \end{cases}$$

Here $V_{\mathscr{C}}$ is the valuation for PL-interpretation $\mathscr{C}$, as defined in section 2.3.

When $SV_{\mathscr{I}}(\phi) = 1$, we say that ϕ is *supertrue* in $\mathscr{I}$; when $SV_{\mathscr{I}}(\phi) = 0$, we say that ϕ is *superfalse* in $\mathscr{I}$. Supervaluational notions of validity and semantic consequence may be defined thus:

DEFINITIONS OF VALIDITY AND SEMANTIC CONSEQUENCE:

- ϕ is supervaluationally valid ("$\vDash_S \phi$") iff ϕ is supertrue in every trivalent interpretation
- ϕ is a supervaluational semantic consequence of Γ ("$\Gamma \vDash_S \phi$") iff ϕ is supertrue in each trivalent interpretation in which every member of Γ is supertrue

Example 3.4: Let $\mathscr{I}$ be a trivalent interpretation where $\mathscr{I}(P) = \mathscr{I}(Q) = \#$. What is $SV_{\mathscr{I}}(P \wedge Q)$? Answer: $\#$. Let $\mathscr{C}$ be a precisification of $\mathscr{I}$ that assigns 1 whenever $\mathscr{I}$ assigns $\#$; let $\mathscr{C}'$ be a precisification of $\mathscr{I}$ that assigns 0 whenever $\mathscr{I}$ assigns $\#$. Since $\mathscr{C}(P) = \mathscr{C}(Q) = 1$, $V_{\mathscr{C}}(P \wedge Q) = 1$. Since $\mathscr{C}'(P) = \mathscr{C}'(Q) = 0$, $V_{\mathscr{C}'}(P \wedge Q) = 0$. So $P \wedge Q$ is 1 on some precisifications of $\mathscr{I}$ and 0 on others.

Example 3.5: Where $\mathscr{I}$ is the trivalent interpretation considered in example 3.4, what is $SV_{\mathscr{I}}(P \wedge {\sim}P)$? Answer: 0. (A different result, notice, from that delivered by the Kleene and Łukasiewicz tables.) For any precisification of $\mathscr{I}$ is a PL-interpretation, and $P \wedge {\sim}P$ is 0 in each PL-interpretation. So $P \wedge {\sim}P$ is superfalse in $\mathscr{I}$.

Supervaluation is a formalism, a way of assigning 1s, 0s, and #s to wffs of the language of PL relative to trivalent interpretations. While this formalism can be applied in many ways—not all of them involving vagueness—the following philosophical idea is often associated with it. For any vague, interpreted language, we can consider various *sharpenings*: ways of making its vague terms precise without disturbing their determinate semantic features. For example, to sharpen the vague term 'rich', we go through everyone who is on the borderline of being rich and arbitrarily classify each one either as being rich or as not being rich; but we must continue to classify all the definitely rich people as being rich and all the definitely not rich people as being not rich. Some sentences come out true on some sharpenings and false on others. For example, since middling Mary is a borderline case of being rich, we are free to sharpen 'rich' so that 'Mary is rich' comes out true, and we are free to sharpen 'rich' so that 'Mary is rich' comes out false. But since Donald Trump is definitely rich, we are not free to sharpen 'rich' so that 'Trump is rich' comes out false; 'Trump is rich' is true on all sharpenings. Also, the disjunction 'Mary is either rich or not rich' comes out true on all sharpenings, even though Mary is on the borderline, since each sharpening will count one or the other of its disjuncts, and hence the whole disjunction, as being true. And still other sentences come out false on all sharpenings, for instance 'Pete the peasant is rich' and 'Mary is both rich and not rich'. The philosophical idea is this: truth *is* truth-on-all-sharpenings, and falsity *is* falsity-on-all-sharpenings. 'Trump is rich' is true because it is true on all sharpenings; 'Pete is rich' is false because it is false on all sharpenings; 'Mary is rich' is neither true nor false because it is neither true on all sharpenings nor false on all sharpenings. And supervaluationism is a good formal model of this philosophical idea. Precisifications are good formal models of sharpenings; supertruth relative to trivalent interpretations is a good formal model of truth-on-all-sharpenings, and hence of truth itself; so supervaluational validity and semantic consequence are good formal models of (genuine) logical truth and logical consequence.[34]

Let's close by noticing two important facts about supervaluationism. The first is that the supervaluation functions SV are not in general *truth-functional*. To say that a valuation function is truth-functional is to say that the value it assigns to any complex wff is a function of the values it assigns to that wff's immediate constituents. Now, the valuation functions associated with the Łukasiewicz and Kleene tables *are* truth-functional. (What a truth table *is*, is a specification of how the values of a type of complex wff depend on the values of its parts.) But not so for supervaluations. Examples 3.4 and 3.5 show that if trivalent interpretation $\mathscr{I}$ assigns # to both P and Q, then $SV_{\mathscr{I}}(P{\wedge}Q) = \#$ whereas $SV_{\mathscr{I}}(P{\wedge}{\sim}P) = 0$. But $SV_{\mathscr{I}}({\sim}P)$ is obviously # (the precisifications of $\mathscr{I}$ considered in example 3.4 show this). So $P{\wedge}Q$ and $P{\wedge}{\sim}P$ are both conjunctions, each of whose conjuncts is # in $SV_{\mathscr{I}}$, and yet they are assigned different values by $SV_{\mathscr{I}}$. So $SV_{\mathscr{I}}$ isn't truth-functional: the values it assigns to conjunctions aren't a function of the values it assigns to their conjuncts. (Similar arguments can be made for other connectives as well; see for example exercise 3.12.)

The second important fact is this: supervaluational logic is in a sense classical, even though supervaluations are three-valued. For example, every tautology (PL-valid formula) turns out to be supervaluationally valid. (Precisifications are PL-interpretations; tautologies are defined as wffs that are true in each PL-interpretation; so every tautology is true in every precisification of every three-valued interpretation; so every tautology is supertrue in every three-valued interpretation.) Similarly, any PL-consequence of a set is also a supervaluational consequence of that set (exercise 3.13).

So, in a sense, supervaluationism preserves classical logic. However, when we add the operator $\triangle$ for determinacy, and extend the supervaluational semantics in a natural way to handle $\triangle$, there's a sense in which classical logic is violated. The details of this semantics and argument can be found in Williamson (1994, section 5.3); here I will argue informally. Specifically, I'll argue for two claims with respect to English, assuming that truth is truth-on-all-sharpenings, and then I'll draw a conclusion about supervaluationism.

Assume that truth is truth-on-all-sharpenings. Claim 1: any English sentence ϕ logically implies "definitely, ϕ". Argument: assume ϕ is true. Then ϕ is true on all sharpenings. But then, surely, "definitely, ϕ" is true. Claim 2: the sentence 'If middling Mary is rich, then middling Mary is definitely rich' is not true, and so is not a logical truth. Argument: on some sharpenings, the antecedent of this conditional is true while its consequent is false (assume Mary is a definite case of indefinite richness; so the consequent is false on all sharpenings).

Given claims 1 and 2, if a supervaluational semantics for $\triangle$ is to model English, it must have these two features: $P \vDash \triangle P$ and $\nvDash P{\rightarrow}\triangle P$. But it is a law of classical logic

[34]See Fine (1975) for a fuller presentation and Williamson (1994, chapter 5) for a critique. Some supervaluationists do not identify truth with truth-on-all-sharpenings; see McGee and McLaughlin (1995).

that whenever $\phi \vDash_{PL} \psi$, it's also true that $\vDash_{PL} \phi \rightarrow \psi$. So this classical law—the law of "conditional proof" (compare the deduction theorem)—fails supervaluationally. Analogous arguments can be made for other classical laws. For example, the following forms of contraposition and reductio hold for classical logic:

- If $\phi \vDash_{PL} \psi$, then $\sim\psi \vDash_{PL} \sim\phi$
- If $\phi \vDash_{PL} \psi \wedge \sim\psi$, then $\vDash_{PL} \sim\phi$

But they too can be argued to fail, given a supervaluational semantics for $\triangle$ (exercise 3.16). These discrepancies with classical logic involve, in effect, laws about sequent validity—reasoning with assumptions. When it comes to reasoning with assumptions, then, a supervaluational logic for $\triangle$ will be nonclassical, if it is inspired by the identification of truth with truth-on-all-sharpenings.

> **Exercise 3.12** Show that supervaluations aren't truth-functional with respect to conditionals. That is, find a trivalent interpretation, $\mathscr{I}$, and wffs ϕ_1, ϕ_2, ψ_1, and ψ_2, such that $SV_{\mathscr{I}}(\phi_1) = SV_{\mathscr{I}}(\phi_2)$ and $SV_{\mathscr{I}}(\psi_1) = SV_{\mathscr{I}}(\psi_2)$, but $SV_{\mathscr{I}}(\phi_1 \rightarrow \psi_1) \neq SV_{\mathscr{I}}(\phi_2 \rightarrow \psi_2)$.
>
> **Exercise 3.13** Show that if $\Gamma \vDash_{PL} \phi$, then $\Gamma \vDash_S \phi$.
>
> **Exercise 3.14** Show that any wff that is true in a trivalent interpretation given the Kleene truth tables is supertrue in that interpretation.
>
> **Exercise 3.15**** Our definition of supervaluational semantic consequence is sometimes called the "global" definition. The "local" definition says rather that ϕ is a supervaluational semantic consequence of Γ iff for every trivalent interpretation, $\mathscr{I}$, and every precisification, $\mathscr{C}$, of $\mathscr{I}$, if $V_{\mathscr{C}}(\gamma) = 1$ for each $\gamma \in \Gamma$, then $V_{\mathscr{C}}(\phi) = 1$. Show that the global and local definitions are equivalent. (Equivalent, that is, before $\triangle$ is introduced. Under some supervaluational semantics for $\triangle$, the global and local definitions are not equivalent.)
>
> **Exercise 3.16*** Argue on intuitive grounds that a supervaluational semantics for $\triangle$ should violate the forms of contraposition and reductio just mentioned.

3.5 Intuitionistic propositional logic: proof theory

Intuitionism is a philosophy of mathematics according to which there are no mind-independent mathematical facts. Rather, mathematical facts and entities are mental constructs that owe their existence to the activities of mathematicians constructing proofs.

In addition to espousing this constructivist philosophy of mathematics, intuitionists also reject classical logic in favor of a nonclassical logic known as "intuitionistic logic". This logic rejects various classical laws, most notoriously the law of the excluded middle, which says that each statement of the form "ϕ or not-ϕ" is a logical truth, and double-negation elimination, which says that a statement of the form "not-not-ϕ" logically implies the statement ϕ. Intuitionistic logic has been highly influential within philosophy in a way that transcends its connection with constructivist mathematics, in large part because it is often regarded as a logic appropriate to "anti-realism".

While intuitionistic logic itself will be our main focus, let me first say a bit about why mathematical intuitionists are drawn to it. Consider the decimal expansion of π: 3.14159... Little is known about the patterns occurring in it. We do not know, for example, whether the sequence 0123456789 eventually appears. This sequence has not been observed in the trillion or so digits to which π has so far been expanded; but no one has proved that it cannot appear. Now, from a mathematical realist (platonist) point of view, we should say nevertheless that: either this sequence eventually appears or it does not. That is, where P is the statement "The sequence 0123456789 occurs somewhere in the decimal expansion of π", we should accept this instance of the law of the excluded middle: "P or not-P". Mathematical reality includes a certain infinite object, the decimal expansion of π, which either contains or fails to contain the sequence 0123456789. But facts about infinite totalities of this sort are precisely what intuitionists reject. According to intuitionists, there are no "completed infinities". In the case of π, we have the potential to construct longer and longer initial segments of its decimal expansion, but we should not think of the entire infinite expansion as "already existing". As a result, according to intuitionists, until we either observe the sequence 0123456789 (thus proving P) or show that it cannot appear (thus proving $\sim P$), we cannot assume that "P or not-P" is true. To assume this would be to assume that facts about π's decimal expansion are "already out there", independently of our constructing proofs.

But these vague thoughts are not an argument. And turning them into an argument is not straightforward. For example, we cannot formulate the intuitionist's challenge to "P or not-P" as follows: "Since mathematical truth is constituted by proof, and we have no proof of either disjunct, neither disjunct is true, and so the disjunction is not true." This challenge leads to a three-valued approach to propositional logic (if neither P nor "not-P" is true, then P is neither true nor false) whereas intuitionistic logic is not a three-valued approach. It is not based on constructing truth tables of any sort, and it embraces a different set of logical truths and logical consequences from all the three-valued approaches we have considered so far (see exercises 3.17 and 7.10).

What then is the intuitionist's complaint about "P or not-P", if not that its disjuncts are untrue? Here is one thought.[35] Intuitionist philosophy of mathematics requires acceptance of the following two conditionals:

If P, then it is provable that P

If not-P, then it is provable that not-P

---

[35] Here I follow Wright (1992, pp. 37–44). For some other thoughts on this matter, see the works by Brouwer, Heyting, and Dummett in Benacerraf and Putnam (1983).

So if we were entitled to assume "*P* or not-*P*", we could infer that: "it is provable that *P* or it is provable that not-*P*". But we're not entitled to this conclusion. We don't have any guarantee that our methods of proof are powerful enough to settle the question of whether *P* is true.[36] Conclusion: we are not entitled to assume "*P* or not-*P*", so it's not a logical truth.

So: intuitionists are unwilling to accept "*P* or not-*P*". Interestingly, they do not accept its denial "not: *P* or not-*P*", since they accept the denial of this denial: "not-not: *P* or not-*P*". Why? Consider the following argument.[37]

> Assume for reductio: "not: *P* or not-*P*". Now, if *P* were true, then we would have "*P* or not-*P*", contradicting the assumption. So "not-*P*" must be true. But from "not-*P*" it follows that "*P* or not-*P*"—contradiction. So, "not-not: *P* or not-*P*".

The reasoning in this argument is hard to resist (in essence it uses only reductio ad absurdum and disjunction-introduction) and is accepted by intuitionists. So even intuitionists have reason to accept that "not-not: *P* or not-*P*" is a logical truth. Since intuitionists reject double-negation elimination, this is consistent with their refusal to accept "*P* or not-*P*".[38]

In the classical semantics for propositional logic, $\phi \vee \sim\phi$ is of course assigned the truth value 1 no matter what truth value ϕ is assigned, and ϕ is assigned 1 whenever $\sim\sim\phi$ is. But this does not faze the intuitionist, since classical semantics is by her lights based on a mistaken picture: the picture of mathematical statements being statements about independently existing mathematical reality (such as the infinite decimal expansion of π), and thus as being appropriately represented as having truth values (either 1 or 0) depending on the nature of this reality.

So much for philosophical justification; now on to the logic itself. I'm going to approach this proof-theoretically, with sequents. (A semantics will have to wait until section 7.4.) Two simple modifications to the sequent-proof system of section 2.5 generate a proof system for intuitionistic propositional logic. First, we need to split up the double-negation rule, DN, into two halves, double-negation introduction and double-negation elimination:

$$\frac{\Gamma \vdash \sim\sim\phi}{\Gamma \vdash \phi} \quad \text{DNE} \qquad \frac{\Gamma \vdash \phi}{\Gamma \vdash \sim\sim\phi} \quad \text{DNI}$$

---

[36] Beware: the intuitionist will *not* say "it is not provable that *P* nor is it provable that not-*P*"—that would lead, via the two conditionals, to a contradiction: "not-*P* and not-not-*P*".

[37] Compare the first 8 lines of example 2.9.

[38] To get more of a feel for the intuitionist's rejection of double-negation elimination, suppose we could show that the assumption of "not-*P*"—that 0123456789 never occurs—leads to a contradiction. This would establish "not-not-*P*", but it would not establish *P*. To establish *P*, we would need to construct enough of π's decimal expansion to observe 0123456789. (Relatedly, intuitionistic predicate logic (which we won't consider further in this book) rejects the inference from "not everything is *F*" to "something is not-*F*". To prove the former one must merely show that "everything is *F*" leads to contradiction; to prove the latter one must prove an instance—some particular sentence of the form "*a* is not-*F*".)

In the classical system of section 2.5 we were allowed to use both DNE and DNI; but in the intuitionistic system, only DNI is allowed. Second, to make up for the dropped rule DNE, our intuitionist system adds the rule "ex falso":

$$\frac{\Gamma \vdash \phi \wedge \sim\phi}{\Gamma \vdash \psi} \quad \text{EF}$$

In the move from our old classical sequent system to the new intuitionistic system, the only rule we have *added* is EF. And any use of EF can be replicated in the old system: simply use RAA and then DNE. That means that every sequent proof in the new system can be replicated in the old system; every intuitionistically provable sequent is also classically provable.

Notice how dropping DNE blocks proofs of various classical theorems the intuitionist wants to avoid. The proof of $\varnothing \vdash P \vee \sim P$ (example 2.9), for instance, used DNE. Of course, for all we've said so far, there might be some other way to prove this sequent that doesn't use DNE. Only when we have a semantics for intuitionistic logic, and a soundness proof relative to that semantics, can we show that this sequent is not intuitionistically provable (section 7.4).

It is interesting to note that even though intuitionists reject the inference from $\sim\sim P$ to P, they *accept* the inference from $\sim\sim\sim P$ to $\sim P$, since its proof requires only the half of DN that they accept, namely DNI:

1. $\sim\sim\sim P \Rightarrow \sim\sim\sim P$ RA
2. $P \Rightarrow P$ RA   (for reductio)
3. $P \Rightarrow \sim\sim P$ 2, DNI
4. $\sim\sim\sim P, P \Rightarrow \sim\sim P \wedge \sim\sim\sim P$ 1, 3, $\wedge$I
5. $\sim\sim\sim P \Rightarrow \sim P$ 4, RAA

Note that you can't use this sort of proof to establish $\sim\sim P \vdash P$. Given the way RAA is stated, its application always results in a formula beginning with $\sim$.

> **Exercise 3.17*** Show that our intuitionistic proof system generates a different logic from the three-valued systems of Łukasiewicz, Kleene, and Priest. For each of those three-valued systems S_3, find an intuitionistically provable sequent $\Gamma \Rightarrow \phi$ such that $\Gamma \nvDash_{S_3} \phi$ (if your chosen Γ is the empty set this means showing that $\nvDash_{S_3} \phi$).

4

PREDICATE LOGIC

L ET'S NOW TURN from propositional logic to predicate logic, the logic of "all" and "some". As with propositional logic, our plan is to formalize. We'll first do grammar, then semantics, then proof theory. We've already called our system of propositional logic "PL", so we'll use "PC" here, for "the predicate calculus", as our formal system for predicate logic is sometimes called.

4.1 Grammar of PC

As before, we start by specifying the primitive vocabulary—the symbols that may be used in (well-formed) formulas of PC. Then we define the formulas as strings of primitive vocabulary that have the right form.

PRIMITIVE VOCABULARY:

- Connectives: $\rightarrow$, $\sim$, $\forall$
- variables $x, y \ldots$, with or without numerical subscripts
- for each $n > 0$, n-place predicates $F, G \ldots$, with or without numerical subscripts
- individual constants (names) $a, b \ldots$, with or without numerical subscripts
- parentheses

No symbol of one type is a symbol of any other type. Let's call any variable or constant a *term*.

Note how we allow numerical subscripts on predicates, variables, and names, just as we did with sentence letters in propositional logic. We do this so that we'll never run out of vocabulary when constructing increasingly complex sentences, such as $\forall x \forall y \forall z \forall x_{259} \forall y_{47} (Rxyzx_{259} \rightarrow \sim R_3 x y_{47})$.

DEFINITION OF WFF:

(i) If Π is an n-place predicate and $\alpha_1 \ldots \alpha_n$ are terms, then $\Pi \alpha_1 \ldots \alpha_n$ is a PC-wff
(ii) If ϕ and ψ are PC-wffs, and α is a variable, then $\sim\phi, (\phi \rightarrow \psi)$, and $\forall \alpha \phi$ are PC-wffs
(iii) Only strings that can be shown to be PC-wffs using (i) and (ii) are PC-wffs

We'll call wffs generated by clause (i) "atomic" formulas.

$\forall$ is called the "universal quantifier". Read $\forall x \ldots$ as saying "everything x is such that …". So "$\forall x Fx$" is read as "everything is F", "$\sim\forall x(Fx \rightarrow Gx)$" as "not all Fs are Gs", and so on.

Notice that in addition to familiar-looking wffs such as Fa and $\forall x \sim \forall y Rxy$, our definition also counts the following as wffs:

$$Fx$$
$$\forall x Rxy$$

What is distinctive about such wffs is that they contain variables that don't "belong" to any quantifier in the formula. In the first formula, for example, the variable x doesn't belong to any quantifier; and in the second formula, whereas the second x belongs to the quantifier $\forall x$, the variable y doesn't belong to any quantifier. Variables that don't belong to quantifiers are called *free*; variables that do belong to quantifiers are called *bound*.

More carefully: we must speak of variables as being free or bound *in given formulas* (since x is free in Fx but bound in $\forall x Fx$). Still more carefully, we must speak of individual *occurrences* of variables being free or bound (in formulas). For example, in the formula $Fx \rightarrow \forall x Fx$, the first occurrence of x is free (in the whole formula) whereas the third is bound. (We also count the second occurrence of x, within the quantifier $\forall x$ itself, as being bound.) Even more carefully: we may define the notions as follows.

DEFINITION OF FREE AND BOUND VARIABLES: An occurrence of variable α in wff ϕ is bound in ϕ iff that occurrence is within an occurrence of some wff of the form $\forall \alpha \psi$ within ϕ. Otherwise the occurrence is free in ϕ.

When a formula has no free occurrences of variables, we'll say that it is a closed formula, or sentence; otherwise it is an open formula.

Our concern is normally with closed formulas, since it is those formulas that represent quantificational statements of everyday language. Open formulas, by contrast, are "semantically incomplete". Nevertheless, they are useful for certain purposes, especially in proof theory (section 4.4).

We have the same defined connectives: $\land, \lor, \leftrightarrow$. We also add the following definition of the existential quantifier:

DEFINITION OF $\exists$: "$\exists \alpha \phi$" is short for "$\sim \forall \alpha \sim \phi$" (where α is a variable and ϕ is a wff).

This is an intuitively correct definition, given that $\exists$ is supposed to represent "some": there are some pigs if and only if not everything is a non-pig.

4.2 Semantics of PC

Recall from section 2.2 the semantic approach to logic, in which we (i) define configurations, which are mathematical representations of ways for the world to be, and of the meanings of nonlogical expressions; and (ii) define the notion of truth for formulas in these configurations. We thereby shed light on meaning, and we are thereby able to define formal analogs of the notions of logical truth and logical consequence.

In propositional logic, the configurations were assignments of truth values to atomic wffs. This strategy breaks down in predicate logic, for various reasons. First, atomic wffs now include formulas with free variables, and we shouldn't assign truth values to such wffs. A variable like x doesn't stand for any fixed thing; variables are rather used to express generality when combined with quantifiers, as in sentences like

$\forall x F x$ and $\forall x(Fx{\rightarrow}Gx)$. But when a variable is *not* combined with a quantifier, as in wffs like Fx and Rxy, the result is, intuitively, semantically incomplete, and incapable of truth or falsity. Second, configurations generally assign meanings to the smallest meaningful bits of language, so as to enable the calculation of truth values of complex sentences. In propositional logic, sentence letters were the smallest meaningful bits of language, and so it was appropriate for the configurations there to assign semantic values to them (and truth values are appropriate semantic values for sentence letters). But here in predicate logic, the smallest meaningful bits of language are the names and predicates, for example a, b, F, and R, so the configurations here ought to assign semantic values to names and predicates, so as to enable the calculation of truth values of complex sentences like Fa, Rab, and $\forall x F x$. But truth values are not appropriate semantic values for names and predicates.

As a first step towards solving these problems, let's begin by adopting a new conception of a configuration, that of a *model*:

DEFINITION OF MODEL: A PC-model is an ordered pair $\langle \mathcal{D}, \mathcal{I} \rangle$ such that:

- $\mathcal{D}$ is a non-empty set ("the domain")
- $\mathcal{I}$ is a function ("the interpretation function") obeying the following constraints:
  - if α is a constant, then $\mathcal{I}(\alpha) \in \mathcal{D}$
  - if Π is an n-place predicate, then $\mathcal{I}(\Pi)$ is an n-place relation over $\mathcal{D}$

(Recall the notion of a relation from section 1.8.)

A configuration is supposed to represent a way for the world to be, as well as meanings for nonlogical expressions. The part of a model that represents a way for the world to be is its domain, $\mathcal{D}$, which contains, intuitively, the individuals that exist in the configuration.[39] The part of a model that represents the meanings of nonlogical expressions is its interpretation function, $\mathcal{I}$, which tells us what names and predicates mean in the configuration. $\mathcal{I}$ assigns to each name a member of the domain—its referent. For example, if the domain is the set of persons, then $\mathcal{I}$ might assign me to the name 'a'. An n-place predicate gets assigned an n-place relation over $\mathcal{D}$—that is, a set of n-tuples drawn from $\mathcal{D}$. This set is called the *extension* of the predicate in the model. Think of the extension of a predicate as the set of -tuples to which the predicate applies. One-place predicates get assigned sets of 1-tuples of $\mathcal{D}$—that is, sets of members of $\mathcal{D}$. If the extension of 'F' is the set of males, then 'F' might be thought of as symbolizing "is male". Two-place predicates get assigned binary relations over the domain. If a two-place predicate 'R' is assigned the set of ordered pairs of persons $\langle u, v \rangle$ such that u is taller than v, we might think of 'R' as symbolizing "is taller than". Similarly, three-place predicates get assigned sets of ordered triples, and so on.

---

[39]There's more to the world than which objects exist; there are also the features those objects have. Predicate logic models blur their representation of this second aspect of the world with their representation of the meanings of predicates (much as PL-interpretations blur their representation of the world with their representation of the meanings of sentence letters).

Relative to any PC-model $\langle \mathcal{D}, \mathcal{I} \rangle$, we want to define what it is for wffs to be true in that model. It's easy to see how this should go for certain wffs. Take, for example, an atomic wff without free variables such as Fa. $\mathcal{I}$ assigns a member of the domain to a—call that member u. $\mathcal{I}$ also assigns a subset of the domain to F—let's call that subset S. The sentence Fa should be true iff $u \in S$—that is, iff the referent of a is a member of the extension of F. That is, Fa should be true iff $\mathcal{I}(a) \in \mathcal{I}(F)$. Similarly, Rab should be true iff $\langle \mathcal{I}(a), \mathcal{I}(b) \rangle \in \mathcal{I}(R)$. And as before, we can give recursive clauses for the truth values of negations and conditionals. $\phi \rightarrow \psi$, for example, will be true iff either ϕ is false or ψ is true. But we encounter a problem when we try to specify the truth value of $\forall x Fx$. It should, intuitively, be true if and only if 'Fx' is true, no matter what we put in place of 'x'. But what does "no matter what we put in place of 'x'" mean? Does it mean "no matter what *name* (constant) we put in place of 'x'"? No, because we don't want to assume that we've got a name for everything in the domain (Fx might be true for all the objects we have names for, but false for one of the nameless things). Does it mean, "no matter what *object from the domain* we put in place of 'x'"? No; objects from the domain needn't be part of our primitive vocabulary, so the result of literally replacing 'x' in 'Fx' with an object from the domain won't in general be a wff.

The way forward here is due to Alfred Tarski. First step: we let the variables temporarily refer to certain things in the domain. Second step: we show how to compute the truth value of a formula like Fx, relative to a temporary referent of the variable x. Third step: we say that $\forall x Fx$ is true iff for all objects u in the domain $\mathcal{D}$, Fx is true when x temporarily refers to u.

We implement this idea of temporary reference with the idea of a "variable assignment" (Tarski did it a bit differently):

DEFINITION OF VARIABLE ASSIGNMENT: g is a variable assignment for model $\langle \mathcal{D}, \mathcal{I} \rangle$ iff g is a function that assigns to each variable some object in $\mathcal{D}$.

When $g(x) = u$, think of u as the object to which the variable x temporarily refers. Notice that a variable assignment assigns a value to each of the infinitely many variables that are allowed to occur in PC-wffs. We define variable assignments in this way because we need to be ready to evaluate any formula for a truth value, no matter what variables it contains. When we evaluate the formula $Fxy \rightarrow Gzx_1 y_{47} x_{191}$, for example, we'll need temporary referents for all its variables: $x, y, z, x_1, y_{47}, x_{191}$. Other formulas contain other variables. So we take the safe course and assign temporary referents to all variables.

We need a further bit of notation. Let u be some object in $\mathcal{D}$, let g be some variable assignment, and let α be a variable. We then define "g_u^α" to be the variable assignment that is just like g, except that it assigns u to α. (If g already assigns u to α, then g_u^α will be the same function as g.) Note the following important fact about variable assignments: g_u^α, when applied to α, must give the value u. (Work through the definitions to see that this is so.) That is:

$$g_u^\alpha(\alpha) = u$$

One more bit of apparatus:

DEFINITION OF DENOTATION: Let $\mathcal{M}\,(=\langle\mathcal{D},\mathcal{I}\rangle)$ be a model, g be a variable assignment, and α be a term. $[\alpha]_{\mathcal{M},g}$, i.e., the denotation of α (relative to $\mathcal{M}$ and g), is defined thus:

$$[\alpha]_{\mathcal{M},g} = \begin{cases} \mathcal{I}(\alpha) & \text{if } \alpha \text{ is a constant} \\ g(\alpha) & \text{if } \alpha \text{ is a variable} \end{cases}$$

The subscripts $\mathcal{M}$ and g on $[\alpha]$ indicate that denotations are assigned relative to a model ($\mathcal{M}$), and relative to a variable assignment (g).

Now we are ready to define truth in a model. That is, we're ready to define the valuation function for a given model, $\mathcal{M}$. The valuation function will assign truth values to formulas *relative to variable assignments*. This relativization is crucial to Tarski's strategy. The second step of that strategy, recall, was to show how to compute truth values of formulas relative to choices of temporary referents for their variables—i.e., relative to variable assignments.

DEFINITION OF VALUATION: The PC-valuation function, $V_{\mathcal{M},g}$, for PC-model $\mathcal{M}\,(=\langle\mathcal{D},\mathcal{I}\rangle)$ and variable assignment g, is defined as the function that assigns to each wff either 0 or 1 subject to the following constraints:

(i) For any n-place predicate Π and any terms $\alpha_1\ldots\alpha_n$, $V_{\mathcal{M},g}(\Pi\alpha_1\ldots\alpha_n)=1$ iff $\langle[\alpha_1]_{\mathcal{M},g}\ldots[\alpha_n]_{\mathcal{M},g}\rangle\in\mathcal{I}(\Pi)$

(ii) For any wffs ϕ, ψ, and any variable α:

$$V_{\mathcal{M},g}(\sim\phi)=1 \text{ iff } V_{\mathcal{M},g}(\phi)=0$$
$$V_{\mathcal{M},g}(\phi\rightarrow\psi)=1 \text{ iff either } V_{\mathcal{M},g}(\phi)=0 \text{ or } V_{\mathcal{M},g}(\psi)=1$$
$$V_{\mathcal{M},g}(\forall\alpha\phi)=1 \text{ iff for every } u\in\mathcal{D}, V_{\mathcal{M},g_u^\alpha}(\phi)=1$$

The valuation functions of propositional logic defined a kind of relativized truth: truth relative to a PL-interpretation. Predicate logic valuation functions are relativized to variable assignments as well as to interpretations (which are now models), and so define a doubly relativized kind of truth; think of $V_{\mathcal{M},g}(\phi)=1$ as meaning that ϕ is true in $\mathcal{M}$ *relative to* g. But we'd also like a singly relativized notion of truth that is relativized only to models, not valuation functions. (We want this because we want to define, e.g., a valid formula as one that is true in all models.) How are we to define such a notion? Consider an example. What must be true in order for the formula $\forall xFx$ to be true in some model $\mathcal{M}\,(=\langle\mathcal{D},\mathcal{I}\rangle)$, relative to some variable assignment g? Working through our various definitions:

$$V_{\mathcal{M},g}(\forall xFx)=1 \text{ iff for every } u\in\mathcal{D}, V_{\mathcal{M},g_u^x}(Fx)=1 \qquad \text{(truth condition for } \forall)$$
$$\text{iff for every } u\in\mathcal{D}, [x]_{g_u^x}\in\mathcal{I}(F) \qquad \text{(t.c. for atomics)}$$
$$\text{iff for every } u\in\mathcal{D}, g_u^x(x)\in\mathcal{I}(F) \qquad \text{(def. of denotation)}$$
$$\text{iff for every } u\in\mathcal{D}, u\in\mathcal{I}(F) \qquad \text{(def. of } g_u^x)$$

Notice how, by the end, the function g with which we began has dropped out. The values that g assigns, as a result, do not affect whether $\forall x F x$ is true relative to g in this model. In fact, this happens for every formula that, like $\forall x F x$, lacks free variables: whether the formula is true in a model relative to variable assignment g does not depend at all on g (exercise 4.1). So we might as well define the singly relativized notion of truth thus:

DEFINITION OF TRUTH IN A MODEL: ϕ is *true in* PC-model $\mathcal{M}$ iff $V_{\mathcal{M},g}(\phi) = 1$, for each variable assignment g for $\mathcal{M}$.

(So as far as closed formulas are concerned, we would have gotten the same result if we had required truth relative to *some* variable assignment.)

What about formulas with free variables, such as Fx? These aren't generally the formulas we're interested in; but nevertheless, what does our definition of singly relativized truth say about them? It's fairly easy to see that these formulas turn out true in a model iff they are true for all values of their variables in that model's domain. Thus a formula with free variables is true in a model iff its "universal closure", the result of prefixing the formula with universal quantifiers for each of its free variables, is true in that model. For example, Fx is true in a model iff $\forall x F x$ is true in that model.

Next, we can give definitions of validity and consequence:

DEFINITION OF VALIDITY: ϕ is PC-valid ("$\vDash_{PC} \phi$") iff ϕ is true in all PC-models.

DEFINITION OF SEMANTIC CONSEQUENCE: ϕ is a PC-semantic-consequence of set of wffs Γ ("$\Gamma \vDash_{PC} \phi$") iff for every PC-model $\mathcal{M}$ and every variable assignment g for $\mathcal{M}$, if $V_{\mathcal{M},g}(\gamma) = 1$ for each $\gamma \in \Gamma$, then $V_{\mathcal{M},g}(\phi) = 1$.

Note: exercise 4.1 tells us that if a closed formula is true in a model relative to one variable assignment, then it's true relative to every variable assignment. Thus, when ϕ and the members of Γ are all closed formulas, an equivalent definition of semantic consequence would be this: *if every member of Γ is true in $\mathcal{M}$, then so is ϕ*.

Since PC-valuation functions treat the propositional connectives $\rightarrow$ and $\sim$ in the same way as PL-valuations do, they also treat the defined connectives $\wedge$, $\vee$, and $\leftrightarrow$ in the same way:

$$V_{\mathcal{M},g}(\phi \wedge \psi) = 1 \text{ iff } V_{\mathcal{M},g}(\phi) = 1 \text{ and } V_{\mathcal{M},g}(\psi) = 1$$
$$V_{\mathcal{M},g}(\phi \vee \psi) = 1 \text{ iff } V_{\mathcal{M},g}(\phi) = 1 \text{ or } V_{\mathcal{M},g}(\psi) = 1$$
$$V_{\mathcal{M},g}(\phi \leftrightarrow \psi) = 1 \text{ iff } V_{\mathcal{M},g}(\phi) = V_{\mathcal{M},g}(\psi)$$

Moreover, we can also prove that $\exists$ gets the correct truth condition:

Example 4.1: Let's show that

$$V_{\mathcal{M},g}(\exists \alpha \phi) = 1 \text{ iff there is some } u \in \mathcal{D} \text{ such that } V_{\mathcal{M},g_u^\alpha}(\phi) = 1$$

The definition of $\exists \alpha \phi$ is: $\sim\forall\alpha\sim\phi$. So, we must show that for any model, $\mathcal{M}$ ($= \langle \mathcal{D}, \mathcal{I} \rangle$), and any variable assignment g for $\mathcal{M}$, $V_{\mathcal{M},g}(\sim\forall\alpha\sim\phi) = 1$ iff there is some

$u \in \mathscr{D}$ such that $V_{\mathscr{M},g_u^a}(\phi) = 1$. (I'll sometimes stop writing the subscript $\mathscr{M}$ in order to reduce clutter. It should be obvious from the context what the relevant model is.) Here's the argument:

$$V_g(\sim\forall a\sim\phi) = 1 \text{ iff } V_g(\forall a\sim\phi) = 0 \qquad \text{(t.c. for } \sim)$$
$$\text{iff for some } u \in \mathscr{D},\, V_{g_u^a}(\sim\phi) = 0 \qquad \text{(t.c. for } \forall)$$
$$\text{iff for some } u \in \mathscr{D},\, V_{g_u^a}(\phi) = 1 \qquad \text{(t.c. for } \sim)$$

> **Exercise 4.1**** Show that if ϕ has no free variables, then for any model $\mathscr{M}$ and variable assignments g and h for $\mathscr{M}$, $V_{\mathscr{M},g}(\phi) = V_{\mathscr{M},h}(\phi)$

4.3 Establishing validity and invalidity in PC

Given our definitions, we can establish that particular formulas are valid.

Example 4.2: Show that $\forall x Fx \rightarrow Fa$ is valid. That is, show that this formula is true relative to any model and any variable assignment for that model:

(i) Suppose otherwise; then $V_{\mathscr{M},g}(\forall xFx \rightarrow Fa) = 0$, for some model $\mathscr{M} = \langle \mathscr{D}, \mathscr{I} \rangle$ and variable assignment g for $\mathscr{M}$. So (dropping the $\mathscr{M}$ subscript henceforth) $V_g(\forall xFx) = 1$ and $V_g(Fa) = 0$.

(ii) Given the latter, $[a]_g \notin \mathscr{I}(F)$. But $[a]_g = \mathscr{I}(a)$; so $\mathscr{I}(a) \notin \mathscr{I}(F)$.

(iii) Given the former, for any $u \in \mathscr{D}$, $V_{g_u^x}(Fx) = 1$. But $\mathscr{I}(a) \in \mathscr{D}$, so $V_{g_{\mathscr{I}(a)}^x}(Fx) = 1$. So, by the truth condition for atomics, $[x]_{g_{\mathscr{I}(a)}^x} \in \mathscr{I}(F)$. But $[x]_{g_{\mathscr{I}(a)}^x} = g_{\mathscr{I}(a)}^x(x) = \mathscr{I}(a)$. Thus, $\mathscr{I}(a) \in \mathscr{I}(F)$, contradicting (ii).

The claim in step (iii) that $\mathscr{I}(a) \in \mathscr{D}$ comes from the definition of an interpretation function: the interpretation of a name is always a member of the domain. Notice that "$\mathscr{I}(a)$" is a term of our metalanguage; that's why, when I learned that "for any $u \in \mathscr{D}$..." in step (ii), I could set u equal to $\mathscr{I}(a)$.

Example 4.3: Show that $\models \forall x \forall y Rxy \rightarrow \forall x Rxx$ (moving more quickly now):

(i) Suppose for reductio that $V_g(\forall x \forall y Rxy \rightarrow \forall x Rxx) = 0$ (for some assignment g in some model). Then $V_g(\forall x \forall y Rxy) = 1$ and ...

(ii) ...$V_g(\forall x Rxx) = 0$. So for some $v \in \mathscr{D}$, $V_{g_v^x}(Rxx) = 0$. Call one such v "u". So we have: $V_{g_u^x}(Rxx) = 0$.

(iii) Given (ii), $\langle [x]_{g_u^x}, [x]_{g_u^x} \rangle \notin \mathscr{I}(R)$. $[x]_{g_u^x}$ is $g_u^x(x)$, i.e., u. So $\langle u, u \rangle \notin \mathscr{I}(R)$.

(iv) Given (i), for every member of $\mathscr{D}$, and so for u in particular, $V_{g_u^x}(\forall y Rxy) = 1$. So for every member of $\mathscr{D}$, and so for u in particular, $V_{g_{uu}^{xy}}(Rxy) = 1$. So $\langle [x]_{g_{uu}^{xy}}, [y]_{g_{uu}^{xy}} \rangle \in \mathscr{I}(R)$. But $[x]_{g_{uu}^{xy}}$ and $[y]_{g_{uu}^{xy}}$ are each just u. Hence $\langle u, u \rangle \in \mathscr{I}(R)$, contradicting (iii).

Line (ii) of example 4.3 illustrates an elementary inferential practice that is ubiquitous in mathematical reasoning. Suppose you learn that there exists some object of a certain type, T. Immediately afterwards you should give one of these objects of type T a name. Say: "call one such object 'u'". Then continue your proof, using the name u.[40]

Once this practice becomes familiar, I'll streamline proofs by no longer explicitly saying "call one such object u". Instead, after writing down an initial line of the form "there exists some u of type T", I'll subsequently use 'u' as a name of one such object. But strictly one ought always to say "call one of the objects of type T 'u'", to mark this change in how 'u' is being used, since in the initial line 'u' is not a name, but is rather a bound metalanguage variable (bound to the metalanguage quantifier 'there is some'). (A common mistake to avoid: using an expression like 'u' initially as a metalanguage variable, but then drifting into using it as if it's a name, where it isn't clear which object it names.)

This practice needs to be employed with care. Suppose you introduce 'u' as a name for some object of type T, and suppose that later in the same proof, you learn that there exists an object of a certain other type T'. You *cannot* then introduce the same name 'u' for some object of type T'—what if nothing is both of type T and of type T'? You must instead give the new object a new name: 'v', say.

The practice of introducing a name for an object of a certain type is for use with existentially quantified statements of the metalanguage—statements of the form "there exists *some* object of such and such type". It's not for use with universally quantified statements; if you learn that *every* object is of a certain type, it's usually not a good idea to say: "call one such object 'u'". Instead, wait. Wait until some particular object or objects of interest have emerged in the proof—until, for example, you've learned some existentially quantified statements, and have introduced corresponding names. Only then should you use the universally quantified statement—you can now apply it to the objects of interest. For example, if you introduced a name 'u', you could use a universally quantified statement 'everything is of type T' to infer that u is of type T. (Compare line (iv) in example 4.3.) In general: deal with existentially quantified metalanguage statements first, and universally quantified metalanguage statements later. (Note that statements of the form $V_g(\forall\alpha\phi) = 1$ and $V_g(\exists\alpha\phi) = 0$ imply universally quantified metalanguage statements, whereas statements of the form $V_g(\exists\alpha\phi) = 1$ and $V_g(\forall\alpha\phi) = 0$ imply existentially quantified metalanguage statements. So deal with the latter first.)

We've seen how to establish that particular formulas are valid. How do we show that a formula is *invalid*? All we must do is exhibit a single model in which the formula is false. (A valid formula must be true in *all* models; therefore, it only takes one model in which a formula is false to make that formula invalid.)

---

[40]You haven't really attached the name 'u' to any particular one of the objects of type T. But this doesn't matter, so long as you only use the name u to derive conclusions that could be derived for any object of type T. The practice I'm describing is often called the rule of "existential elimination" in introductory logic texts.

Example 4.4: Show that the formula $(\exists x Fx \wedge \exists x Gx) \rightarrow \exists x(Fx \wedge Gx)$ isn't valid. We need to find a model in which this formula is false. My model will contain letters in its domain:

$$\mathcal{D} = \{u, v\}$$
$$\mathcal{I}(F) = \{u\}$$
$$\mathcal{I}(G) = \{v\}$$

It is intuitively clear that the formula is false in this model. In this model, something is F (namely, u), and something is G (namely, v), but nothing in the model's domain is both F and G.

Example 4.5: Show that $\forall x \exists y Rxy \nvDash \exists y \forall x Rxy$. We must show that the first formula does not semantically imply the second. So we must come up with a model and variable assignment in which the first formula is true and the second is false. (Since these formulas are closed, as noted above it won't matter which variable assignment we choose; so all we need is a model in which the premise is true and the conclusion is false.) It helps to think about natural language sentences that these formulas might represent. If R symbolizes "respects", then the first formula says that "everyone respects someone or other", and the second says that "there is someone whom everyone respects". Clearly, the first can be true while the second is false: suppose that each person respects a different person, so that no one person is respected by everyone. A simple case of this occurs when there are just two people, each of whom respects the other, but neither of whom respects him/herself:

Here is a model based on this idea:

$$\mathcal{D} = \{u, v\}$$
$$\mathcal{I}(R) = \{\langle u, v\rangle, \langle v, u\rangle\}$$

Exercise 4.2 Show that:

(a) $\vDash \forall x(Fx \rightarrow (Fx \vee Gx))$

(b) $\vDash \forall x(Fx \wedge Gx) \rightarrow (\forall x Fx \wedge \forall x Gx)$

(c) $\forall x(Fx \rightarrow Gx), \forall x(Gx \rightarrow Hx) \vDash \forall x(Fx \rightarrow Hx)$

(d) $\vDash \exists x \forall y Rxy \rightarrow \forall y \exists x Rxy$

Exercise 4.3 Show that:

(a) $\nvDash \forall x(Fx \rightarrow Gx) \rightarrow \forall x(Gx \rightarrow Fx)$

(b) $\nvDash \forall x(Fx \vee {\sim}Gx) \rightarrow (\forall x Fx \vee {\sim}\exists x Gx)$

(c) $Rab \nvDash \exists x Rxx$

(d)** $Fx \nvDash \forall x Fx$

(e) $\forall x \forall y \forall z[(Rxy \wedge Ryz) \rightarrow Rxz], \forall x \exists y Rxy \nvDash \exists x Rxx$

4.4 Axiomatic proofs in PC

Let's turn now to proof theory for predicate logic. One can construct natural deduction, sequent, or axiomatic systems of proof for predicate logic, just as with propositional logic. (And there are other approaches as well.) Although axiomatic proofs are less intuitive than the others, we'll take the axiomatic approach since this will be convenient for use with modal logic later on.

We'll continue to use section 2.6's definitions of the key concepts of the axiomatic approach: a proof from a set of wffs Γ is defined as a sequence of wffs, each of which is either a member of Γ, an axiom, or follows from earlier lines in the proof by a rule; ϕ is provable from Γ iff ϕ is the last line of a proof from Γ; ϕ is a theorem iff ϕ is provable from the empty set—i.e. provable using only the axioms and rules. Once we have given appropriate axioms and rules for predicate logic, we will have defined provability in predicate logic ($\vdash_{PC} \phi$ and $\Gamma \vdash_{PC} \phi$).

Our axioms and rules for predicate logic will include our axioms and rules for propositional logic, plus additional ones dealing with quantifiers:[41]

AXIOMATIC SYSTEM FOR PC:

- *Rules*: MP plus *universal generalization* (UG):

$$\frac{\phi}{\forall \alpha \phi}$$

- *Axioms*: all instances (with PC-wffs) of PL1–PL3, plus:

$$\forall \alpha \phi \rightarrow \phi(\beta / \alpha) \tag{PC1}$$
$$\forall \alpha(\phi \rightarrow \psi) \rightarrow (\phi \rightarrow \forall \alpha \psi) \tag{PC2}$$

where:

- ϕ, ψ, and χ are any PC-wffs, α is any variable, and β is any term
- $\phi(\beta / \alpha)$ results from ϕ by "correct substitution" of β for α (see below)
- in PC2, no occurrences of variable α may be free in ϕ

Let's examine the new predicate logic axioms and rule. The rule UG is based on the idea that proving an arbitrary instance of a universal generalization suffices to prove that universal generalization. To prove that every F is an F, for example, one picks an "arbitrary" object, x, proves that $Fx \rightarrow Fx$, and then concludes by UG that $\forall x(Fx \rightarrow Fx)$. (See also example 4.6.)

Axiomatic proof systems tend to handle inferences using free variables a bit unsteadily. (It's easier with natural deduction and sequent systems to smooth out the wrinkles.) For example, our system allows the following proof of $\forall x Fx$ *from* Fx:

1. Fx premise
2. $\forall x Fx$ 1, UG

---

[41] See Mendelson (1987, pp. 55–56).

Hence $Fx \vdash \forall x Fx$. This is an undesirable result. Since $\nvdash Fx \rightarrow \forall x Fx$ (I won't prove this here, but it's true), and since $Fx \nvDash \forall x Fx$ (exercise 4.3d), it follows that unless they are restricted in certain ways, the deduction theorem (section 2.9) and a generalized version of soundness ("$\Gamma \vDash \phi$ whenever $\Gamma \vdash \phi$"—compare exercise 2.9) both fail for our axiomatic system. (The needed restrictions are of a sort familiar from introductory logic books, which require variables used in connection with UG to be "new" to proofs.) Let's not worry about this glitch; our interest will be solely in *theoremhood*, and in inferences $\Gamma \vdash \phi$ where ϕ and all the members of Γ are closed wffs; and UG doesn't lead to undesirable results in those cases.[42]

PC1 embodies the familiar principle of substitution (often called "universal instantiation"). It yields axioms like $\forall x Fx \rightarrow Fa$ (and $\forall x Fx \rightarrow Fb$, $\forall x Fx \rightarrow Fx$, etc.). To construct an instance of PC1, you: (i) begin with $\forall \alpha \phi$, (ii) strip off the quantifier $\forall \alpha$ to get ϕ, (iii) choose a term (variable or constant) β, called the "instantial term", (iv) change the αs in ϕ to βs to arrive at $\phi(\beta/\alpha)$, and then (v) write down the conditional $\forall \alpha \phi \rightarrow \phi(\beta/\alpha)$. But steps (iii) and (iv) need to be restricted. First, only the αs that are free in ϕ are to be changed in step (iv). For example, if ϕ is $Fx \rightarrow \forall x Rxx$ and the instantial term is a, you change only the first x to a. (Thus the resulting axiom is $\forall x(Fx \rightarrow \forall x Rxx) \rightarrow (Fa \rightarrow \forall x Rxx)$. It's *not* $\forall x(Fx \rightarrow \forall x Rxx) \rightarrow (Fa \rightarrow \forall a Raa)$— that's not even a wff.) Second, *all* free occurrences of α in ϕ must be changed to the instantial term. ($\forall x Rxx \rightarrow Rxa$ is not an instance of PC1.) Third, if the instantial term is a variable, none of the occurrences of that variable that would result from the substitution can be bound in the axiom. For example, $\forall x \exists y Rxy \rightarrow \exists y Ryy$ isn't an instance of PC1 (even after $\exists$ is replaced with its definition). You can't choose y as the instantial term here, since the occurrence of y that would result from the substitution in the consequent (the underlined one: $\forall x \exists y Rxy \rightarrow \exists y R\underline{y}y$) is bound in the would-be axiom, not free. (This wff *shouldn't* count as an axiom: it would symbolize, for example, the sentence "If everyone respects someone (or other), then someone respects him- or herself", which isn't a logical truth.) "Correct substitutions" are those that meet these three restrictions.

The importance of PC2 will be illustrated in the examples below.

As we saw in section 2.6, constructing axiomatic proofs in propositional logic can be tedious. We paid our dues in that section, so now let's give ourselves a break. Suppose, for example, that we want to get the formula $(\forall x Fx \rightarrow \forall x Gx) \rightarrow (\forall x Fx \rightarrow \forall x Fx)$ into one of our PC-proofs. Recall from section 2.6 that we were able to construct an axiomatic proof in *propositional* logic of $(P \rightarrow Q) \rightarrow (P \rightarrow P)$. But if we take that proof and change each P to $\forall x Fx$ and each Q to $\forall x Gx$, the result is a legal PC-proof of $(\forall x Fx \rightarrow \forall x Gx) \rightarrow (\forall x Fx \rightarrow \forall x Fx)$, since our PC axiomatic system includes the axiom schemas and rules of PL. Instead of actually inserting this proof of $(\forall x Fx \rightarrow \forall x Gx) \rightarrow (\forall x Fx \rightarrow \forall x Fx)$ into our PC-proof, let's allow ourselves to write merely:

    i. $(\forall x Fx \rightarrow \forall x Gx) \rightarrow (\forall x Fx \rightarrow \forall x Fx)$ PL

---

[42]A similar issue will be raised by modal logic's rule of necessitation.

In essence, writing "PL" means: "I could prove this line using just PL1–PL3 and MP if I wanted to."

Since our focus in this section is on predicate rather than propositional logic, let's be quite liberal about when this time-saving expedient may be used: let's allow it for any formula that is a "PC-tautology". By this I mean the following. Suppose that ψ is a tautology—i.e., a valid wff of PL. And suppose that there is some way of uniformly substituting PC-wffs for ψ's sentence letters to obtain a PC-wff ϕ. In such a case, we'll say that ϕ is a PC-tautology. For example, in the previous paragraph, $(\forall x Fx \rightarrow \forall x Gx) \rightarrow (\forall x Fx \rightarrow \forall x Fx)$ is a PC-tautology, resulting from the tautology $(P \rightarrow Q) \rightarrow (P \rightarrow P)$. (I call ϕ a *PC*-tautology rather than a tautology full stop because tautologies have to be PL-wffs, whereas ϕ is a PC-wff.) Breezily writing "PL" beside any such ϕ is justified because (i) our axiom system for PL is complete (section 2.9), so ψ has a PL-proof, and (ii) that proof can be converted into a PC-proof of ϕ as in the previous paragraph.

Furthermore, suppose in some PC-proof we have some formulas $\phi_1 \ldots \phi_n$ on separate lines. And suppose that formula ψ is a "PC-tautological-consequence" of formulas $\phi_1 \ldots \phi_n$, in the sense that the formula

$$(\phi_1 \rightarrow (\phi_2 \rightarrow \ldots (\phi_n \rightarrow \psi)))$$

is a PC-tautology. Then, let's allow ourselves to enter ψ into our proof, annotating "PL" and referencing the lines on which $\phi_1 \ldots \phi_n$ occurred. This too is a harmless shortcut, for since $(\phi_1 \rightarrow (\phi_2 \rightarrow \ldots (\phi_n \rightarrow \psi)))$ is a PC-tautology, we know that a proof of it exists, which we could insert and then use modus ponens n times from the lines containing $\phi_1 \ldots \phi_n$ to obtain ψ by more legitimate means.

When annotating "PL", how do we figure out whether something is a tautology? Any way we like: with truth tables, natural-deduction derivations, memory—whatever. For future reference, table 4.1 lists some helpful tautologies. Henceforth, when I annotate a line "PL" I will sometimes refer parenthetically to one or more of the tautologies in this table, to clarify how I obtained the line. (The line won't always come exactly or solely from the cited tautology; my goal here is to make proofs easier to understand, not to introduce a rigorous convention.) Also, notice this fact about PL: if $\phi \leftrightarrow \psi$ is a tautology, then the result of substituting ϕ for ψ in any tautology is itself a tautology.[43] This fact makes table 4.1 all the more useful. For example, since $(P \rightarrow Q) \leftrightarrow (\sim Q \rightarrow \sim P)$ is a tautology (contraposition), we can substitute $\sim Q \rightarrow \sim P$ for $P \rightarrow Q$ in the tautology $((P \rightarrow R) \wedge (R \rightarrow Q)) \rightarrow (P \rightarrow Q)$ (syllogism) to conclude that the following is also a tautology: $((P \rightarrow R) \wedge (R \rightarrow Q)) \rightarrow (\sim Q \rightarrow \sim P)$.

And while we're on the topic of shortcuts, let's also continue in the practice of doing two or more steps at once, as in section 2.8. (As noted in that section, whenever we use any of these shortcuts, we are constructing proof sketches rather than official proofs.)

Example 4.6: As our first example, let's show that $\forall x Fx, \forall x (Fx \rightarrow Gx) \vdash_{PC} \forall x Gx$:

---

[43] See note 26.

TABLE 4.1. Some tautologies

$$\phi \leftrightarrow \sim\sim\phi \qquad \text{(double negation)}$$
$$(\phi \rightarrow \psi) \leftrightarrow (\sim\psi \rightarrow \sim\phi) \qquad \text{(contraposition)}$$
$$((\phi \rightarrow \psi) \wedge (\psi \rightarrow \chi)) \rightarrow (\phi \rightarrow \chi) \qquad \text{(syllogism)}$$
$$(\phi \rightarrow (\psi \rightarrow \chi)) \leftrightarrow ((\phi \wedge \psi) \rightarrow \chi) \qquad \text{(import/export)}$$
$$(\phi \rightarrow (\psi \rightarrow \chi)) \leftrightarrow (\psi \rightarrow (\phi \rightarrow \chi)) \qquad \text{(permutation)}$$
$$((\phi \rightarrow \psi) \wedge (\phi \rightarrow \chi)) \leftrightarrow (\phi \rightarrow (\psi \wedge \chi)) \qquad \text{(composition)}$$
$$((\phi \rightarrow \chi) \wedge (\psi \rightarrow \chi)) \leftrightarrow ((\phi \vee \psi) \rightarrow \chi) \qquad \text{(dilemma)}$$
$$((\phi \rightarrow \psi) \wedge (\psi \rightarrow \phi)) \leftrightarrow (\phi \leftrightarrow \psi) \qquad \text{(biconditional)}$$
$$(\sim\phi \rightarrow \psi) \leftrightarrow (\phi \vee \psi) \qquad \text{(disjunction)}$$
$$(\phi \rightarrow \sim\psi) \leftrightarrow \sim(\phi \wedge \psi) \qquad \text{(negated conjunction)}$$

1. $\forall x F x$ premise
2. $\forall x(Fx \rightarrow Gx)$ premise
3. $\forall x Fx \rightarrow Fx$ PC1
4. Fx 1, 3 MP
5. $Fx \rightarrow Gx$ PC1, 2, MP
6. Gx 4, 5 MP
7. $\forall x Gx$ 6, UG

This proof illustrates the main method for proving universally quantified formulas: to prove $\forall x \phi$, first prove ϕ; and then use UG. Here we wanted to prove $\forall x Gx$, so we first proved Gx (line 6) and then used UG. To do this, notice, we must include formulas with free variables in our proofs. We must use free variables as instantial terms when using PC1 (lines 3 and 5), we must apply propositional logic's axiom schemas and rules to formulas with free variables (lines 4–6), and we must apply UG to such formulas (line 7). This may seem odd. What does a formula with a free variable *mean*? Well, intuitively, think of a free variable as denoting some particular but unspecified object. Thus, think of line 3, $\forall x Fx \rightarrow Fx$ (in which the final occurrence of x is free), as saying "if everything is F, then *this particular object* is F". And think of the whole proof as follows. Since we want to prove $\forall x Gx$, we choose an arbitrary object, x, and try to show that x is G. Once we do so (line 6), we can conclude that everything is G because x was arbitrarily chosen.[44]

---

[44]If any of the premises contained free occurrences of x, then x wouldn't really have been "arbitrarily chosen". Such cases are precisely the ones where UG gets restricted in introductory books; but as I said, I'm not worrying here about this glitch.

Example 4.7: Let's show that $\vdash_{PC} \forall x \forall y Rxy \rightarrow \forall y \forall x Rxy$ (this will illustrate the need for PC2):

1. $\forall x \forall y Rxy \rightarrow \forall y Rxy$ PC1
2. $\forall y Rxy \rightarrow Rxy$ PC1
3. $\forall x \forall y Rxy \rightarrow Rxy$ 1, 2, PL (syllogism)
4. $\forall x(\forall x \forall y Rxy \rightarrow Rxy)$ 3, UG
5. $\forall x \forall y Rxy \rightarrow \forall x Rxy$ 4, PC2, MP
6. $\forall x \forall y Rxy \rightarrow \forall y \forall x Rxy$ 5, UG, PC2, MP

Example 4.8: A theorem schema that will be useful is the following:

$$\vdash_{PC} \forall \alpha (\phi \rightarrow \psi) \rightarrow (\forall \alpha \phi \rightarrow \forall \alpha \psi) \qquad \text{(distribution)}$$

Any instance of distribution can be established as follows:

1. $\forall \alpha (\phi \rightarrow \psi) \rightarrow (\phi \rightarrow \psi)$ PC1
2. $\forall \alpha \phi \rightarrow \phi$ PC1
3. $\forall \alpha (\phi \rightarrow \psi) \rightarrow (\forall \alpha \phi \rightarrow \psi)$ 1, 2 PL (see below)
4. $\forall \alpha (\forall \alpha (\phi \rightarrow \psi) \rightarrow (\forall \alpha \phi \rightarrow \psi))$ 3, UG
5. $\forall \alpha (\phi \rightarrow \psi) \rightarrow \forall \alpha (\forall \alpha \phi \rightarrow \psi))$ PC2, 4, MP
6. $\forall \alpha (\forall \alpha \phi \rightarrow \psi) \rightarrow (\forall \alpha \phi \rightarrow \forall \alpha \psi)$ PC2
7. $\forall \alpha (\phi \rightarrow \psi) \rightarrow (\forall \alpha \phi \rightarrow \forall \alpha \psi)$ 5, 6, PL (syllogism)

(Line 3 is via the tautology $(P \rightarrow (Q \rightarrow R)) \rightarrow ((S \rightarrow Q) \rightarrow (P \rightarrow (S \rightarrow R)))$.) Note that steps 1 and 2 are legal instances of PC1, regardless of what ϕ and ψ look like. In step 2, for example, we strip off the $\forall \alpha$ from $\forall \alpha \phi$, and leave ϕ alone. If you go back and look at the two restrictions on PC, you will see that since no occurrences of α within ϕ are changed, those two restrictions are satisfied. And notice further why the uses of PC2 are correct. Line 6, for example, is a legal instance of PC2 because the variable α is not free in $\forall \alpha \phi$—any free occurrences of α in ϕ get bound to the quantifier $\forall \alpha$.

Example 4.9: One thing distribution is good for is proving wffs of the form $\forall x \phi \rightarrow \forall x \psi$ where $\phi \rightarrow \psi$ is provable. For example:

1. $(Fx \wedge Gx) \rightarrow Fx$ PL
2. $\forall x((Fx \wedge Gx) \rightarrow Fx)$ 1, UG
3. $\forall x(Fx \wedge Gx) \rightarrow \forall x Fx$ distribution, 2, MP

Example 4.10: Show that $\exists x \forall y Rxy \vdash_{PC} \forall y \exists x Rxy$. Given the definition of $\exists$, this means showing that $\sim \forall x \sim \forall y Rxy \vdash_{PC} \forall y \sim \forall x \sim Rxy$:

1. $\sim\forall x\sim\forall y Rxy$ premise
2. $\forall y Rxy \rightarrow Rxy$ PC1
3. $\sim Rxy \rightarrow \sim\forall y Rxy$ 2, PL (contraposition)
4. $\forall x(\sim Rxy \rightarrow \sim\forall y Rxy)$ 3, UG
5. $\forall x\sim Rxy \rightarrow \forall x\sim\forall y Rxy$ distribution, 4, MP
6. $\sim\forall x\sim Rxy$ 1, 5 PL (contraposition)
7. $\forall y\sim\forall x\sim Rxy$ 6, UG

My approach to this problem was to work my way backwards. (This approach is often helpful.) I set myself an initial goal, and then thought about how to reach that goal. Whatever I would need to reach that initial goal became my new goal. Then I thought about how to reach this new goal. I continued in this way until I got a goal I knew how to reach. In this case, this thought process went as follows:

- goal 1: get $\forall y\sim\forall x\sim Rxy$ (since this is the conclusion of the argument)
- goal 2: get $\sim\forall x\sim Rxy$ (since then I can get goal 1 by UG)
- goal 3: get $\forall x\sim Rxy \rightarrow \forall x\sim\forall y Rxy$ (since then I can get goal 2 from the argument's premise and PL)
- goal 4: get $\sim Rxy \rightarrow \sim\forall y Rxy$ (since then I can get goal 3 by UG and distribution)

Once I had written down goal 4, I had something I knew how to achieve, so then I started work on the actual proof. I then worked backwards toward the ultimate goal: goal 1. Notice in particular goal 3. Something like this strategy is often needed in connection with negation. I figured that at some point I would need to use the argument's premise, which was a negation. And a natural way to use a negation, $\sim\phi$, is to attempt to prove some conditional $\psi\rightarrow\phi$, and then conclude $\sim\psi$ by modus tollens. This is what happened in goal 3.

> **Exercise 4.4** Construct axiomatic proofs to establish each of the following facts. You may use the various shortcuts introduced in this chapter; and you may use the principle of distribution.
>
> (a) $\forall x(Fx\rightarrow Gx), \forall x(Gx\rightarrow Hx) \vdash_{PC} \forall x(Fx\rightarrow Hx)$
> (b) $\vdash_{PC} Fa\rightarrow\exists x Fx$
> (c) $\vdash_{PC} \forall x Rax\rightarrow\forall x\exists y Ryx$
> (d) $\exists x Rax, \forall y(Ray\rightarrow\forall z Rzy) \vdash_{PC} \exists x\forall z Rzx$

4.5 Metalogic of PC

We have given a semantics and a proof theory for predicate logic. Mathematical logicians have proved fascinating metalogical results about this semantics and proof theory. Although the *raison d'être* of this book is to not focus on these matters in detail, the results are important to appreciate. I'll state—informally and without proof—and comment on some of the most significant results.[45] Needless to say, our discussion will only scratch the surface.

Soundness and Completeness. When ϕ and Γ contain only closed wffs, then it can be shown that $\Gamma \vdash_{PC} \phi$ iff $\Gamma \vDash_{PC} \phi$.[46] That is, provability and semantic consequence coincide. Thus one can establish facts of the form $\Gamma \nvdash \phi$ by exhibiting a model in which all members of Γ are true and ϕ is false, and then citing soundness; and one can establish facts of the form $\Gamma \vdash \phi$ while avoiding the agonies of axiomatic proofs by reasoning directly about models to conclusions about semantic consequence, and then citing completeness.

Compactness. Say that a set of sentences is *satisfiable* iff there is some model in which each of its members is true. It can be shown that if each finite subset of a set Γ of sentences is satisfiable, then Γ itself must be satisfiable. This result, known as compactness, is intuitively surprising because it holds even in the case where Γ contains infinitely many sentences. One might have thought that there could be some contradiction latent within some infinite set Γ, preventing it from being satisfiable, but which only emerges when you consider all of its infinitely many members together—a contradiction that does not emerge, that is, if you consider only finite subsets of Γ. Compactness says that this can never happen.

Compactness is a sign of a kind of expressive weakness in PC. The weakness pertains to infinity: intuitively speaking, you can't say anything in PC whose logical significance would emerge only in connection with infinitely many other sentences. For example, after we add the identity sign to PC in section 5.1, we will show how to symbolize the sentences "there are at least two Fs", "there are at least three Fs", and so on. Call these symbolizations $F^2, F^3, \ldots$. These "symbolize" the various numeric claims in the sense that F^n is true in a model iff the extension of F in that model has at least n members. Given compactness, there is no way to symbolize, in this same sense of 'symbolize', "there are finitely many Fs". For if there existed a sentence, ϕ, that is true in a given model iff the extension of F in that model is finite, then the following infinite set would violate compactness: $\{\phi, F^2, F^3 \ldots\}$ (exercise 4.5).

Undecidability says roughly that there is no mechanical procedure for deciding whether a given sentence of PC is valid. Intuitively, this means that there is no way to write a computer program that will tell you whether an arbitrary sentence is valid or invalid, in the sense that:

(i) you feed the program sentences; it can give answers of the form "valid" or "invalid"

(ii) it never answers incorrectly. That is, if it says "valid", then the sentence is indeed valid; if it says "invalid", then the sentence is indeed invalid

(iii) if you feed it a valid sentence it eventually answers "valid"

(iv) if you feed it an invalid sentence it eventually answers "invalid"

---

[45] See, for example, Boolos *et al.* (2007) or Mendelson (1987) for the details.

[46] Other axiomatic systems for predicate logic can be given that are sound and complete even for inferences involving free variables.

The intuitive idea of a "mechanical procedure" needs to be precisely defined, of course. But, it turns out, all reasonable ways of defining it are equivalent. (One common definition is that of a "Turing Machine".) So the upshot is: on any reasonable construal of "mechanical procedure", there's no mechanical procedure for figuring out whether an arbitrary sentence is PC-valid. (Given soundness and completeness, it follows that there's no mechanical procedure to figure out whether an arbitrary sentence is a PC-theorem.) There *are*, it turns out, mechanical "positive" tests for validity, in the sense of computer programs satisfying (i)–(iii). A program of this sort would be guaranteed to correctly classify any valid formula as such. But if you fed it an invalid formula, it might just go on churning away forever, never delivering an answer.

Gödel's incompleteness theorem. One can write down axioms from which one can prove all and only the *valid sentences of PC*. (That is what the soundness and completeness theorems say.) This axiomatic approach has been attempted in other areas as well. Euclid, for example, attempted to write down axioms for plane geometry. The intent was that one could prove all and only the *truths of plane geometry* using his axioms. What Kurt Gödel showed is that this axiomatic approach will not work for the *truths of arithmetic*. Arithmetic is the theory of multiplication and addition over natural numbers. One can represent statements of arithmetic using the language of predicate logic.[47] Can we write down axioms for arithmetic? That is, are there axioms from which one can prove all and only the truths of arithmetic? In a trivial sense there are: we could just say "let each truth of arithmetic be an axiom". But such an "axiomatic system" would be useless: there would be no way of telling what counts as an axiom! Gödel's (first) incompleteness theorem tells us that there is no set S of axioms such that (i) there is a mechanical procedure for telling what is a member of S, and (ii) one can prove all and only the truths of arithmetic from S. (It can also be shown that there exists no mechanical procedure for figuring out whether an arbitrary sentence of arithmetic is true.)

> **Exercise 4.5*** Show that the set $\{\phi, F^2, F^3 \ldots\}$ mentioned above would violate compactness.

---

[47]Including identity—see section 5.1.

5

BEYOND STANDARD PREDICATE LOGIC

S TANDARD PREDICATE LOGIC is powerful. It captures a wide variety of logical truths and inferences. Still, it isn't perfect. In this chapter we consider some of its limitations, and discuss extensions that make up for the deficits.[48]

5.1 Identity

How might we symbolize "Only Ted is happy" using PC? "Ht" gets half of it right—we've said that Ted is happy—but we've left out the "only" part. We can't say $Ht \land \sim\exists x Hx$, because that's a logical falsehood: if the first part, "Ted is happy", is true, then the second part, "it's not the case that someone is happy", can't be right, since Ted is a someone, and we just said that he's happy. What we want to add to Ht is that it's not the case that someone *else* is happy. But how to say "someone *else*"?

"Someone else" means: someone *not identical to*. So we need a predicate for identity. Now, we could simply choose some two-place predicate to symbolize "is identical to"—I, say. Then we could symbolize "Only Ted is happy" as meaning $Ht \land \sim\exists x(Hx \land \sim Ixt)$. But treating "is identical to" as just another predicate sells it short. For surely it's a *logical* truth that everything is self-identical, whereas the sentence $\forall x I x x$ is not PC-valid.

In order to recognize distinctive logical truths and logical consequences issuing from the meaning of "is identical to", we must treat that predicate as a logical constant (recall section 1.6); and we must symbolize it in our formal system with a symbolic logical constant. Grammatically this new symbol will be a predicate; but to set it apart from other predicates we'll use a distinctive symbol, "$=$", and we'll write it between its two arguments rather than before them: we'll write $\alpha=\beta$ rather than $=\alpha\beta$. We can now symbolize "Only Ted is happy" thus: $Ht \land \sim\exists x(Hx \land \sim x=t)$.

5.1.1 Grammar for the identity sign

We first need to expand the grammar of PC to allow for the new symbol $=$. Two changes are needed. First, we need to add $=$ to the primitive vocabulary. Then we need to add the following clause to the definition of a well-formed formula:

- If α and β are terms, then $\alpha=\beta$ is a wff

We are now using the symbol '$=$' as the object-language symbol for identity. But we've also been using '$=$' as the metalanguage symbol for identity, for instance when we write things like "$\mathscr{I}(P) = 1$". This shouldn't generally cause confusion, but if

---

[48]Actually "standard" predicate logic is often taken to already include the identity sign, and sometimes function symbols as well.

there's a danger of misunderstanding, I'll clarify by writing things like: "$\mathscr{I}(P) =$ (i.e., is the same object as) 1", to make clear that it's the metalanguage's identity predicate I'm using.

5.1.2 Semantics for the identity sign

This is easy. We keep the notion of a PC-model from the last chapter, and simply add a clause to the definition of a valuation function telling it what truth values to give to sentences containing the $=$ sign. Here is the clause:

$$V_{\mathscr{M},g}(\alpha = \beta) = 1 \text{ iff: } [\alpha]_{\mathscr{M},g} = \text{ (i.e., is the same object as) } [\beta]_{\mathscr{M},g}$$

That is, the wff $\alpha = \beta$ is true iff the terms α and β refer to the same object.

Example 5.1: Show that the formula $\forall x \exists y\, x = y$ is valid. Let g be any variable assignment for any model, and suppose for reductio that $V_g(\forall x \exists y\, x = y) = 0$. Given the clause for $\forall$, we know that for some object in the domain, call it "u", $V_{g_u^x}(\exists y\, x = y) = 0$. Given the clause for $\exists$, for every member of the domain, and so for u in particular, $V_{g_{uu}^{xy}}(x = y) = 0$. So, given the clause for "$=$", $[x]_{g_{uu}^{xy}}$ is not the same object as $[y]_{g_{uu}^{xy}}$. But $[x]_{g_{uu}^{xy}}$ and $[y]_{g_{uu}^{xy}}$ *are* the same object. $[x]_{g_{uu}^{xy}}$ is $g_{uu}^{xy}(x)$, i.e., u; and $[y]_{g_{uu}^{xy}}$ is $g_{uu}^{xy}(y)$, i.e., u.

5.1.3 Symbolizations with the identity sign

In this section, we'll have a quick look at the kinds of sentences we can symbolize using '$=$'.

Most obviously, there are sentences that explicitly concern identity, such as "Mark Twain is identical to Samuel Clemens":

$$t = c$$

and "Every man fails to be identical to George Sand":

$$\forall x(Mx \rightarrow {\sim}x = s)$$

(It will be convenient to abbreviate ${\sim}\alpha = \beta$ as $\alpha \neq \beta$. Thus the second symbolization can be rewritten as: $\forall x(Mx \rightarrow x \neq s)$.) But many other sentences involve the concept of identity in subtler ways.

For example, there are sentences involving 'only', as the example "Only Ted is happy" illustrated. Next, consider "Every lawyer hates every other lawyer". The 'other' signifies nonidentity; we have, therefore:

$$\forall x(Lx \rightarrow \forall y[(Ly \wedge x \neq y) \rightarrow Hxy])$$

Another interesting class of sentences concerns number. We cannot symbolize "There are at least two dinosaurs" as: "$\exists x \exists y(Dx \wedge Dy)$", since this would be true even if there were only one dinosaur: x and y could be the same dinosaur. The identity sign to the rescue:

$$\exists x \exists y (Dx \land Dy \land x \neq y)$$

This says that there are two *different* objects, x and y, each of which is a dinosaur. To say "There are at least three dinosaurs" we say:

$$\exists x \exists y \exists z (Dx \land Dy \land Dz \land x \neq y \land x \neq z \land y \neq z)$$

Indeed, for any n, one can construct a sentence F^n that symbolizes "there are at least n Fs":

$$F^n: \quad \exists x_1 \dots \exists x_n (Fx_1 \land \cdots \land Fx_n \land \delta)$$

where δ is the conjunction of all sentences "$x_i \neq x_j$" where i and j are integers between 1 and n (inclusive) and $i < j$. (The sentence δ says in effect that no two of the variables $x_1 \dots x_n$ stand for the same object.)

Since we can construct each F^n, we can symbolize other sentences involving number as well. To say that there are *at most* n Fs, we write: $\sim F^{n+1}$. To say that there are between n and m Fs (where $m > n$), we write: $F^n \land \sim F^{m+1}$. To say that there are *exactly* n Fs, we write: $F^n \land \sim F^{n+1}$.

These methods for constructing sentences involving number will always *work*; but one can often construct shorter numerical symbolizations by other methods. For example, to say "there are exactly two dinosaurs", instead of saying "there are at least two dinosaurs, and it's not the case that there are at least three dinosaurs", we could say instead:

$$\exists x \exists y (Dx \land Dy \land x \neq y \land \forall z [Dz \rightarrow (z = x \lor z = y)])$$

Exercise 5.1 Demonstrate each of the following:

(a) $Fab \vDash \forall x (x = a \rightarrow Fxb)$

(b) $\exists x \exists y \exists z (Fx \land Fy \land Fz \land x \neq y \land x \neq z \land y \neq z)$, $\forall x (Fx \rightarrow (Gx \lor Hx)) \nvDash \exists x \exists y \exists z (Gx \land Gy \land Gz \land x \neq y \land x \neq z \land y \neq z)$

Exercise 5.2 Symbolize each of the following, using predicate logic with identity.

(a) Everyone who loves someone else loves everyone

(b) The only truly great player who plays in the NBA is Allen Iverson

(c) If a person shares a solitary confinement cell with a guard, then they are the only people in the cell

(d) There are at least five dinosaurs (What is the shortest symbolization you can find?)

5.2 Function symbols

A singular term, such as 'Ted', 'New York City', 'George W. Bush's father', or 'the sum of 1 and 2', is a term that purports to refer to a single entity. Notice that some of these have semantically significant internal structure. 'George W. Bush's father', for example, means what it does because of the meaning of 'George W. Bush' and the meaning of 'father' (and the meaning of the possessive construction). But PC's only singular terms are its names and variables, which do *not* have semantically significant parts and are therefore inadequate representations of semantically complex English singular terms.

Suppose, for example, that we give the following symbolizations:

"3 is the sum of 1 and 2": $a = b$

"George W. Bush's father was a politician": Pc

By symbolizing 'the sum of 1 and 2' as simply 'b', the first symbolization ignores the fact that '1', '2', and 'sum' are semantically significant constituents of 'the sum of 1 and 2'; and by symbolizing "George W. Bush's father" as 'c', we ignore the semantically significant constituents 'George W. Bush' and 'father'. These constituents are responsible for the sentence's logical relations, for example the fact that "George W. Bush's father was a politician" logically implies "Someone's father was a politician". This ought to be reflected in the symbolizations: the first sentence's symbolization ought to semantically imply the second sentence's symbolization.

One way of doing this is via an extension of PC: we add *function symbols* to its primitive vocabulary. Think of "George W. Bush's father" as the result of plugging "George W. Bush" into the blank in "__'s father". "__'s father" is an English function symbol. Function symbols are like predicates in some ways. The predicate "__ is happy" has a blank in it, in which you can put a name. "__'s father" is similar in that you can put a name into its blank. But there is a difference: when you put a name into the blank of "__ is happy", you get a complete sentence, such as "Ted is happy", whereas when you put a name into the blank of "__'s father", you get a noun phrase, such as "George W. Bush's father".

Corresponding to English function symbols, we'll add symbolic function symbols to the language of predicate logic. We'll symbolize "__'s father" as $f(\_\_)$. We can put names or variables into the blank here. Thus we will symbolize "George W. Bush's father" as "$f(a)$", where "a" symbolizes "George W. Bush".

This story needs to be revised in two ways. First, what goes into the blank doesn't have to be a name or variable; it could be something that itself contains a function symbol. For example, in English one can say: "George W. Bush's father's father". We'd symbolize this as: $f(f(a))$. Second, just as we have multi-place predicates, we have multi-place function symbols. "The sum of 1 and 2" contains the function symbol "the sum of __ and __". When you fill in the blanks with the names "1" and "2", you get the noun phrase "the sum of 1 and 2". So, we symbolize this using the two-place function symbol, "s(__,__). If we let "a" symbolize "1" and "b" symbolize "2", then "the sum of 1 and 2" becomes: $s(a, b)$.

The result of plugging names into function symbols in English is a noun phrase.

Noun phrases combine with predicates to form complete sentences. Function symbols in logic work analogously. Once you combine a function symbol with a name, you can take the whole thing, apply a predicate to it, and get a complete sentence. Thus the sentence "George W. Bush's father was a politician" becomes:

$$Pf(a)$$

And "3 is the sum of 1 and 2" becomes:

$$c = s(a, b)$$

(here "c" symbolizes "3"). We can put variables into the blanks of function symbols, too. Thus we can symbolize "Someone's father was a politician" as

$$\exists x P f(x)$$

Example 5.2: Symbolize the following sentences using PC with identity and function symbols:

Everyone loves his or her father
$\forall x L x f(x)$

No one's father is also his or her mother
$\sim \exists x f(x){=}m(x)$

No one is his or her own father
$\sim \exists x \, x{=}f(x)$

A person's maternal grandfather hates that person's paternal grandmother
$\forall x \, H f(m(x)) \, m(f(x))$

Every even number is the sum of two prime numbers
$\forall x (Ex \rightarrow \exists y \exists z (Py \land Pz \land x{=}s(y, z)))$

Exercise 5.3 Symbolize each of the following, using PC with identity and function symbols.

(a) The product of an even number and an odd number is an even number.

(b) If the father of a person is friends with each of his (the father's) co-workers, then that person's mother has at least two sisters.

5.2.1 Grammar for function symbols

We need to update our grammar to allow for function symbols. First, we need to add function symbols to our primitive vocabulary:

- For each $n > 0$, n-place function symbols $f, g, \ldots$, with or without numerical subscripts

The definition of a wff, actually, stays the same. But our definition of a term needs to get a little more complicated. Before, terms were just names or variables. But now, terms can have arbitrarily complex form. For example, each of the following is a term: $f(a), f(f(a)), f(f(f(a))) \ldots$. To account for this we need a recursive definition:[49]

DEFINITION OF TERMS:

- Names and variables are terms
- If f is an n-place function symbol and $\alpha_1 \ldots \alpha_n$ are terms, then $f(\alpha_1 \ldots \alpha_n)$ is a term
- Only strings that can be shown to be terms by the preceding clauses are terms

5.2.2 Semantics for function symbols

We now need to update our definition of a PC-model by saying what the interpretation of a function symbol is. That's easy: the interpretation of an n-place function symbol ought to be an n-place function defined on the model's domain—i.e., a rule that maps any n members of the model's domain to another member of the model's domain. For example, in a model in which the domain is a set of people and the one-place function symbol $f(\_)$ is to represent "$\_$'s father", the interpretation of f will be the function that assigns to any member of the domain that object's father. So we must add to our definition of a model the following clause (call the new models "PC+FS-models", for "predicate calculus plus function symbols"):

- If f is an n-place function symbol, then $\mathscr{I}(f)$ is an n-place (total) function over $\mathscr{D}$.

Calling the function a "total" function "over $\mathscr{D}$" means that the function must have a well-defined output (which is a member of $\mathscr{D}$) whenever it is given as inputs any n members of $\mathscr{D}$. So if, for example, $\mathscr{D}$ contains both numbers and people, $\mathscr{I}(f)$ could not be the father-of function, since that function is undefined for numbers.

The definition of the valuation function stays the same; all we need to do is update the definition of denotation to accommodate our new complex terms:

DEFINITION OF DENOTATION: For any model $\mathscr{M}(= \langle \mathscr{D}, \mathscr{I} \rangle)$, variable assignment g for $\mathscr{M}$, and term α, $[\alpha]_{\mathscr{M},g}$ is defined as follows:

$$[\alpha]_{\mathscr{M},g} = \begin{cases} \mathscr{I}(\alpha) & \text{if } \alpha \text{ is a constant} \\ g(\alpha) & \text{if } \alpha \text{ is a variable} \\ \mathscr{I}(f)([\alpha_1]_{\mathscr{M},g} \ldots [\alpha_n]_{\mathscr{M},g}) & \text{if } \alpha \text{ is a complex term } f(\alpha_1 \ldots \alpha_n) \end{cases}$$

Note the recursive nature of this definition: the denotation of a complex term is defined in terms of the denotations of its smaller parts. Let's think carefully about

---

[49]Complex terms formed from function symbols with more than one place do not, officially, contain commas. But to improve readability I will write, for example, $f(x,y)$ instead of $f(xy)$.

what the final clause says. It says that, in order to calculate the denotation of the complex term $f(\alpha_1 \ldots \alpha_n)$ (relative to assignment g), we must first figure out what $\mathscr{I}(f)$ is—that is, what the interpretation function $\mathscr{I}$ assigns to the function symbol f. This object, the new definition of a model tells us, is an n-place function on the domain. We then take this function, $\mathscr{I}(f)$, and apply it to n arguments: namely, the denotations (relative to g) of the terms $\alpha_1 \ldots \alpha_n$. The result is our desired denotation of $f(\alpha_1 \ldots \alpha_n)$.

It may help to think about a simple case. Suppose that f is a one-place function symbol; suppose our domain consists of the set of natural numbers; suppose that the name a denotes the number 3 in this model (i.e., $\mathscr{I}(a) = 3$), and suppose that f denotes the successor function (i.e., $\mathscr{I}(f)$ is the function, *successor*, that assigns to any natural number n the number $n + 1$). In that case, the definition tells us that:

$$[f(a)]_g = \mathscr{I}(f)([a]_g)$$
$$= \mathscr{I}(f)(\mathscr{I}(a))$$
$$= successor(3)$$
$$= 4$$

Example 5.3: Here's a sample metalanguage argument that makes use of the new definitions. As mentioned earlier, 'George W. Bush's father was a politician' logically implies 'Someone's father was a politician'. Let's show that these sentences' symbolizations stand in the relation of semantic implication. That is, let's show that $Pf(c) \models \exists x Pf(x)$.

(i) Suppose for reductio that for some model and some variable assignment g, we have $V_g(Pf(c)) = 1$, but...

(ii) ...$V_g(\exists x Pf(x)) = 0$

(iii) By line (i), $V_g(Pf(c)) = 1$, and so $[f(c)]_g \in \mathscr{I}(P)$. $[f(c)]_g$ is just $\mathscr{I}(f)([c]_g)$, and $[c]_g$ is just $\mathscr{I}(c)$. So $\mathscr{I}(f)(\mathscr{I}(c)) \in \mathscr{I}(P)$.

(iv) By (ii), for every member of $\mathscr{D}$, and so for $\mathscr{I}(c)$ in particular, $V_{g^x_{\mathscr{I}(c)}}(Pf(x)) = 0$. So $[f(x)]_{g^x_{\mathscr{I}(c)}} \notin \mathscr{I}(P)$. But $[f(x)]_{g^x_{\mathscr{I}(c)}} = \mathscr{I}(f)([x]_{g^x_{\mathscr{I}(c)}})$, and $[x]_{g^x_{\mathscr{I}(c)}} = g^x_{\mathscr{I}(c)}(x) = \mathscr{I}(c)$. So $\mathscr{I}(f)(\mathscr{I}(c)) \notin \mathscr{I}(P)$, which contradicts line (iii).

Exercise 5.4 Demonstrate each of the following:

(a) $\models \forall x Fx \rightarrow Ff(a)$

(b) $\{\forall x f(x) \neq x\} \not\models \exists x \exists y (f(x) = y \wedge f(y) = x)$

5.3 Definite descriptions

Our logic has gotten more powerful with the addition of function symbols, but it still isn't perfect. Function symbols let us "break up" certain complex singular terms, such as "Bush's father". But there are others we still can't break up. Consider "the black cat". Even with function symbols, we can do no better than symbolizing it with a simple name, such as "a". But this symbolization ignores the fact that "the black cat" contains "black" and "cat" as semantically significant constituents. It therefore fails to capture this term's logical behavior. For example, 'The black cat is happy' logically implies 'Some cat is happy'. But the simple-minded symbolization of the first sentence, Ha, obviously does not semantically imply $\exists x(Cx \wedge Hx)$.

One response is to introduce another extension of predicate logic. We introduce a new symbol, ι, to stand for "the". The grammatical function of "the" in English is to turn predicates into noun phrases. "Black cat" is a predicate of English; "the black cat" is a noun phrase that refers to the thing that satisfies the predicate "black cat". Similarly, in logic, given a predicate F, we'll let $\iota x Fx$ be a term that means: the thing that is F.

We'll want to let ιx attach to complex wffs, not just simple predicates. To symbolize "the black cat"—i.e., the thing that is both black and a cat—we want to write: $\iota x(Bx \wedge Cx)$. In fact, we'll let ιx attach to wffs with arbitrary complexity. To symbolize "the fireman who saved someone", we'll write: $\iota x(Fx \wedge \exists y Sxy)$.

5.3.1 Grammar for ι

To the primitive vocabulary of the previous section, we add one further expression: ι. And we revise our definition of terms and wffs, as follows:

DEFINITION OF TERMS AND WFFS:

  (i) Names and variables are terms
 (ii) If ϕ is a wff and α is a variable, then $\iota \alpha \phi$ is a term
(iii) If f is an n-place function symbol, and $\alpha_1 \ldots \alpha_n$ are terms, then $f(\alpha_1 \ldots \alpha_n)$ is a term
 (iv) If Π is an n-place predicate and $\alpha_1 \ldots \alpha_n$ are terms, then $\Pi \alpha_1 \ldots \alpha_n$ is a wff
  (v) If α and β are terms, then $\alpha = \beta$ is a wff
 (vi) If ϕ and ψ are wffs and α is a variable, then $\sim\phi$, $(\phi \rightarrow \psi)$, and $\forall \alpha \phi$ are wffs
(vii) Only strings that can be shown to be terms or wffs using (i)–(vi) are terms or wffs

Notice how we needed to combine the recursive definitions of term and wff into a single recursive definition of wffs and terms together. The reason is that we need the notion of a wff to define what counts as a term containing the ι operator (clause (ii); but we need the notion of a term to define what counts as a wff (clause (iv)). The way we accomplish this is not circular. The reason it isn't is that we can always decide, using these rules, whether a given string counts as a wff or term by looking at whether *smaller* strings count as wffs or terms. And the smallest strings are said to be wffs or terms in non-circular ways.

5.3.2 Semantics for ι

We need to update the definition of denotation so that $\iota x \phi$ will denote the one and only thing in the domain that is ϕ. But there's a snag. What if there is no such thing as "the one and only thing in the domain that is ϕ"? Suppose that 'K' symbolizes "king of" and 'a' symbolizes "USA". Then what should '$\iota x K x a$' denote? It is trying to denote the king of the USA, but there is no such thing. Further, what if more than one thing satisfies the predicate? What should 'the daughter of George W. Bush' denote, given that Bush has more than one daughter? In short, what do we say about "empty descriptions"?

One approach is to say that every atomic sentence with an empty description is false.[50] To implement this thought, we keep the definition of a PC+FS-model from before, but rework the definition of truth in a model as follows:

DEFINITION OF DENOTATION AND VALUATION: The denotation and valuation functions, $[\,]_{\mathcal{M},g}$ and $V_{\mathcal{M},g}$, for PC+FS-model $\mathcal{M}$ $(=\langle \mathcal{D},\mathcal{I}\rangle)$ and variable assignment g, are defined as the functions that satisfy the following constraints:

(i) $V_{\mathcal{M},g}$ assigns to each wff either 0 or 1
(ii) For any term α,

$$[\alpha]_{\mathcal{M},g} = \begin{cases} \mathcal{I}(\alpha) & \text{if } \alpha \text{ is a constant} \\[4pt] g(\alpha) & \text{if } \alpha \text{ is a variable} \\[4pt] \mathcal{I}(f)([\alpha_1]_{\mathcal{M},g}\cdots[\alpha_n]_{\mathcal{M},g}) & \begin{array}{l}\text{if } \alpha \text{ has the form } f(\alpha_1\ldots\alpha_n) \\ \text{and } [\alpha_1]_{\mathcal{M},g}\cdots[\alpha_n]_{\mathcal{M},g} \\ \text{are all defined}\end{array} \\[4pt] \text{undefined} & \begin{array}{l}\text{if } \alpha \text{ has the form } f(\alpha_1\ldots\alpha_n) \\ \text{and not all of } [\alpha_1]_{\mathcal{M},g}\cdots \\ [\alpha_n]_{\mathcal{M},g} \text{ are defined}\end{array} \\[4pt] \text{the } u \in \mathcal{D} \text{ such that } V_{\mathcal{M},g_u^\beta}(\phi)=1 & \begin{array}{l}\text{if } \alpha \text{ has the form } \iota\beta\phi \text{ and} \\ \text{there is a unique such } u\end{array} \\[4pt] \text{undefined} & \begin{array}{l}\text{if } \alpha \text{ has the form } \iota\beta\phi \text{ and} \\ \text{there is no such } u\end{array} \end{cases}$$

(iii) for any n-place predicate Π and any terms $\alpha_1\ldots\alpha_n$, $V_{\mathcal{M},g}(\Pi\alpha_1\ldots\alpha_n)=1$ iff $[\alpha_1]_{\mathcal{M},g}\cdots[\alpha_n]_{\mathcal{M},g}$ are all defined and $\langle [\alpha_1]_{\mathcal{M},g}\cdots[\alpha_n]_{\mathcal{M},g}\rangle \in \mathcal{I}(\Pi)$
(iv) $V_{\mathcal{M},g}(\alpha=\beta)=1$ iff: $[\alpha]_{\mathcal{M},g}$ and $[\beta]_{\mathcal{M},g}$ are each defined and are the same object
(v) for any wffs ϕ, ψ, and any variable α:

$$V_{\mathcal{M},g}(\sim\phi)=1 \text{ iff } V_{\mathcal{M},g}(\phi)=0$$
$$V_{\mathcal{M},g}(\phi\rightarrow\psi)=1 \text{ iff either } V_{\mathcal{M},g}(\phi)=0 \text{ or } V_{\mathcal{M},g}(\psi)=1$$
$$V_{\mathcal{M},g}(\forall\alpha\phi)=1 \text{ iff for every } u \in \mathcal{D}, V_{\mathcal{M},g_u^\alpha}(\phi)=1$$

---

[50] An alternate approach would treat atomic sentences with empty descriptions as being neither true nor false—i.e., #. We would then need to update the other semantic clauses to allow for #s, perhaps using one of the three-valued approaches from Chapter 3.

As with the grammar, we need to mix together the definition of denotation and the definition of the valuation function. The reason is that we need to define the denotations of definite descriptions using the valuation function (in clause (ii)), but we need to define the valuation function using the concept of denotation (in clauses (iii) and (iv)). As before, this is not circular.

Notice that the denotation of a term can now be "undefined". This means simply that there is no such thing as the denotation of such a term (put another way: such a term is not in the domain of the denotation function). The initial source of this status is the sixth case of clause (ii)—empty definite descriptions. But then the undefined status is inherited by complex terms formed from such terms using function symbols, via the fourth case of clause (ii). And then, finally, clauses (iii) and (iv) insure that atomic and identity sentences containing such terms all turn out false.

Note a consequence of this last feature of the semantics. There are now two ways for an atomic sentence to be false (similar remarks apply to identity sentences). There is the old way: the -tuple of the denotations of the terms can fail to be in the predicate's extension. But now there is a new way: one of the terms might have an undefined denotation. So you have to be careful when constructing validity proofs. Suppose, for example, that you learn that $V_g(F\alpha) = 0$ for some term α. You can't immediately conclude that $[\alpha]_g \notin \mathscr{I}(F)$, since $[\alpha]_g$ might not even be defined. To conclude that $[\alpha]_g \notin \mathscr{I}(F)$, you must first show that $[\alpha]_g$ is defined.

Example 5.4: Show that $\vDash G\iota x Fx \rightarrow \exists x(Fx \wedge Gx)$:

(i) Suppose for reductio that in some model, and some assignment g in that model, $V_g(G\iota x Fx \rightarrow \exists x(Fx \wedge Gx)) = 0$. So, $V_g(G\iota x Fx) = 1$ and ...

(ii) ...$V_g(\exists x(Fx \wedge Gx)) = 0$.

(iii) By (i), via the clause for atomics in the definition of truth in a model, $[\iota x Fx]_g$ is both defined and a member of $\mathscr{I}(G)$.

(iv) Since $[\iota x Fx]_g$ is defined, the definition of denotation for ι terms tells us that $[\iota x Fx]_g$ is the unique $u \in \mathscr{D}$ such that $V_{g_u^x}(Fx) = 1$. Call this object (i.e., $[\iota x Fx]_g$) henceforth: "u".

(v) Given (ii), for every member of $\mathscr{D}$, and so for u in particular, $V_{g_u^x}(Fx \wedge Gx) = 0$. So either $V_{g_u^x}(Fx) = 0$ or $V_{g_u^x}(Gx) = 0$. Since $V_{g_u^x}(Fx) = 1$ (line (iv)), $V_{g_u^x}(Gx) = 0$.

(vi) Since $V_{g_u^x}(Gx) = 0$, given the definition of truth for atomics, either $[x]_{g_u^x}$ is undefined or else it is defined and is not a member of $\mathscr{I}(G)$. But it *is* defined: the definition of denotation (second case) defines it as $g_u^x(u)$—i.e., u. So $u \notin \mathscr{I}(G)$, contradicting (iii).

Exercise 5.5 Establish the following:

(a)** $\models \forall x L x \iota y F x y \rightarrow \forall x \exists y L x y$

(b) $F \iota x \forall y L x y \models \forall x \forall y ((\forall z L x z \wedge \forall z L y z) \rightarrow x = y)$

(c) $\not\models G \iota x F x \rightarrow F \iota x G x$

Exercise 5.6* Show that the denotation of any term is either undefined or a member of $\mathscr{D}$.

5.3.3 Elimination of function symbols and descriptions

In a sense, we don't really need function symbols or the ι. Let's return to the English singular term 'the black cat'. The ι lets us symbolize this singular term in a way that takes into account its semantic structure (namely: $\iota x (B x \wedge C x)$). But even without the ι, there is a way to symbolize *whole sentences containing 'the black cat'*, using just standard predicate plus identity. We could, for example, symbolize "The black cat is happy" as:

$$\exists x [(B x \wedge C x) \wedge \forall y [(B y \wedge C y) \rightarrow x = y] \wedge H x]$$

That is, "there is something such that: (i) it is a black cat, (ii) any black cat is it (i.e., it is the only black cat), and (iii) it is happy".

This method for symbolizing sentences containing 'the' is called "Russell's theory of descriptions", in honor of its inventor Bertrand Russell (1905). The general idea is to symbolize: "the ϕ is ψ" as $\exists x [\phi(x) \wedge \forall y (\phi(y) \rightarrow x = y) \wedge \psi(x)]$. This method can be iterated so as to apply to sentences with two or more definite descriptions, such as "The 8-foot-tall man drove the 20-foot-long limousine", which becomes, letting 'E' stand for 'is 8 feet tall' and 'T' stand for 'is 20 feet long':

$$\exists x [E x \wedge M x \wedge \forall z ([E z \wedge M z] \rightarrow x = z) \wedge$$
$$\exists y [T y \wedge L y \wedge \forall z ([T z \wedge L z] \rightarrow y = z) \wedge D x y]]$$

An interesting question arises with negations of sentences involving definite descriptions, when we use Russell's method. Consider "The president is not bald". Does this mean "The president is such that he's non-bald", which is symbolized as follows:

$$\exists x [P x \wedge \forall y (P y \rightarrow x = y) \wedge \sim B x]$$

? Or does it mean "It is not the case that the President is bald", which is symbolized thus:

$$\sim \exists x [P x \wedge \forall y (P y \rightarrow x = y) \wedge B x]$$

? According to Russell, the original sentence is simply ambiguous. Symbolizing it the first way is called giving the description "wide scope" (relative to the $\sim$), since the $\sim$

is in the scope of the ∃. (That is, the ~ is "inside" the ∃; i.e., the formula has the form ∃xφ, and the ~ is part of the φ.) Symbolizing it in the second way is called giving the description "narrow scope" (relative to the ~), because the ∃ is in the scope of the ~ (the formula has the form ~ψ, and the ∃ is part of the ψ). These two symbolizations differ in meaning. The first says that there really is a unique president, and adds that he is not bald. So the first implies that there's a unique president. The second merely denies that there is a unique president who is bald. That doesn't imply that there's a unique president. It would be true if there's a unique president who is not bald, but it would also be true in two other cases: the case in which there are no presidents at all, and the case in which there is more than one president.

A similar issue arises with the sentence "The round square does not exist". We might think to symbolize it:

$$\exists x [Rx \wedge Sx \wedge \forall y([Ry \wedge Sy] \rightarrow x=y) \wedge \sim Ex]$$

letting "E" stand for "exists". In other words, we might give the description wide scope. But this symbolization says something very odd: that *there is* a certain round square that doesn't exist. This corresponds to reading the sentence as saying "The thing that is a round square is such that it does not exist". But that isn't the most natural way to read the sentence. The sentence would usually be interpreted to mean: "It is not true that the round square exists", —that is, as the negation of "the round square exists":

$$\sim \exists x [Rx \wedge Sx \wedge \forall y([Ry \wedge Sy] \rightarrow x=y) \wedge Ex]$$

with the ~ out in front. Here we've given the description narrow scope.

If we are willing to use Russell's method for translating definite descriptions, we can drop ι from our language. We would, in effect, not be treating "the F" as a syntactic unit. We would instead be symbolizing sentences that contain "the F" with wffs that contain no corresponding term. "The black cat is happy" gets symbolized as $\exists x [(Bx \wedge Cx) \wedge \forall y[(By \wedge Cy) \rightarrow x=y] \wedge Hx]$ See?—no term corresponds to "the black cat". The only terms in the symbolization are variables.

In fact, once we use Russell's method, we can get rid of function symbols too. Earlier we treated "father" as a function symbol, symbolized it with "f", and symbolized the sentence "George W. Bush's father was a politician" as $Pf(b)$. But instead, we could treat 'father of' as a two-place *predicate*, F, and regard the whole sentence as meaning: "The father of George W. Bush was a politician." Given the ι, this could be symbolized as:

$$P\iota x Fxb$$

But given Russell's method, we can symbolize the whole thing without using either function symbols or the ι:

$$\exists x (Fxb \wedge \forall y(Fyb \rightarrow x=y) \wedge Px)$$

We can get rid of all function symbols this way, if we want. Here's the method:

- Take any *n*-place function symbol f
- Introduce a corresponding $n+1$-place predicate R
- In any sentence containing the term "$f(\alpha_1 \ldots \alpha_n)$", replace each occurrence of this term with "the x such that $R(x, \alpha_1 \ldots \alpha_n)$"
- Finally, symbolize the resulting sentence using Russell's theory of descriptions

For example, let's go back to: "Every even number is the sum of two prime numbers." Our earlier symbolization, $\forall x(Ex \rightarrow \exists y \exists z(Py \wedge Pz \wedge x=s(y,z)))$, was obtained by thinking of the sentence as meaning "For every even number, x there are two prime numbers y and z such that x is identical to *the sum of y and z*", and then symbolizing the italicized definite description using a function symbol. Now, we instead symbolize the definite description using Russell's method. In place of the two-place function symbol s, let's introduce a three-place predicate letter S, where $Sxyz$ means "x is *a* sum of y and z". We then use Russell's method to symbolize the whole sentence thus:

$$\forall x(Ex \rightarrow \exists y \exists z[Py \wedge Pz \wedge \exists w(Swyz \wedge \forall w_1(Sw_1yz \rightarrow w=w_1) \wedge x=w)])$$

The end of the formula (beginning with $\exists w$) is the Russellian symbolization of "x is identical to the sum of y and z": "there exists some w such that w is a sum of y and z, and w is the only sum of y and z, and $w = x$".

> **Exercise 5.7** Symbolize each of the following, using predicate logic with identity, function symbols, and the ι operator. (Do *not* eliminate descriptions using Russell's method.)
>
> (a) If a person commits a crime, then the judge that sentences him/her wears a wig.
>
> (b) The tallest spy is a spy. (Use a two-place predicate to symbolize "is taller than".)
>
> **Exercise 5.8** For the sentence "The 10-feet-tall man is not happy", first symbolize with the ι operator. Then symbolize *two* readings using Russell's method. Explain the intuitive difference between those two readings. Which gives truth conditions like the ι symbolization?

5.4 Further quantifiers

The quantifiers of PC, $\forall$ and $\exists$, are so-called because they concern *quantity*. The natural-language phrases they represent, 'some' and 'all', are also called quantifiers. But there are other natural-language phrases with a similar grammar that also concern quantity. These, too, are called quantifiers. What is more, some of them cannot be represented using $\forall$ and $\exists$. For instance, it can be shown that there is no way to symbolize the following sentences using just $\forall$ and $\exists$:

> Most things are massive
> Most men are brutes
> There are infinitely many numbers
> Some critics admire only one another

In this section we introduce this broader conception of what a quantifier is, and new symbolic quantifiers with which we can symbolize these sentences.

5.4.1 Generalized monadic quantifiers

We will generalize the standard quantifiers $\exists$ and $\forall$ in two ways. To approach the first, let's introduce the following bit of terminology. For any PC-model, $\mathcal{M}$ (= $\langle \mathcal{D}, \mathcal{I} \rangle$), and wff, ϕ, let's introduce the name "$\phi^{\mathcal{M},g,\alpha}$" for (roughly speaking) the set of members of $\mathcal{M}$'s domain of which ϕ is true:

DEFINITION: $\phi^{\mathcal{M},g,\alpha} = \{u : u \in \mathcal{D} \text{ and } V_{\mathcal{M},g_u^\alpha}(\phi) = 1\}$.

Thus, if we begin with any variable assignment g, then $\phi^{\mathcal{M},g,\alpha}$ is the set of things u in $\mathcal{D}$ such that ϕ is true, relative to variable assignment g_u^α. Now, recall the truth conditions in a PC-model, $\mathcal{M}$, with domain $\mathcal{D}$, for $\forall$ and $\exists$:

$$V_{\mathcal{M},g}(\forall\alpha\phi) = 1 \text{ iff for every } u \in \mathcal{D}, V_{\mathcal{M},g_u^\alpha}(\phi) = 1$$
$$V_{\mathcal{M},g}(\exists\alpha\phi) = 1 \text{ iff for some } u \in \mathcal{D}, V_{\mathcal{M},g_u^\alpha}(\phi) = 1$$

Given our new terminology, we can write equivalent truth conditions as follows:

$$V_{\mathcal{M},g}(\forall\alpha\phi) = 1 \text{ iff } \phi^{\mathcal{M},g,\alpha} = \mathcal{D}$$
$$V_{\mathcal{M},g}(\exists\alpha\phi) = 1 \text{ iff } \phi^{\mathcal{M},g,\alpha} \neq \varnothing$$

Thus, the truth conditions for the familiar quantifiers $\forall$ and $\exists$ can be rewritten as conditions on $\phi^{\mathcal{M},g,\alpha}$. But then, why not introduce new symbols of the same grammatical type as the familiar quantifiers, but whose truth conditions lay down different conditions on $\phi^{\mathcal{M},g,\alpha}$? These would be new kinds of quantifiers. For instance, for any integer n, we could introduce a quantifier $\exists_n$ such that $\exists_n\phi$ means: "there are at least n ϕs". The definitions of a wff, and of truth in a model, would be updated with the following clauses:

- If α is a variable and ϕ is a wff, then $\exists_n\alpha\phi$ is a wff
- $V_{\mathcal{M},g}(\exists_n\alpha\phi) = 1 \text{ iff } |\phi^{\mathcal{M},g,\alpha}| \geq n$

For any set, A, the expression $|A|$ stands for the "cardinality" of set A—i.e., the number of members of A. Thus the expression $|\phi^{\mathcal{M},g,\alpha}|$ stands for the cardinality of the set $\phi^{\mathcal{M},g,\alpha}$, and so the truth condition says that $\exists_n\alpha\phi$ is true iff $\phi^{\mathcal{M},g,\alpha}$ has at least n members.

Now, the introduction of the symbols $\exists_n$ does not increase the expressive power of PC, for as we saw in section 5.1.3, we can symbolize "there are at least n Fs" using just PC (plus "="). The new notation is merely a space-saver. But other such additions are not mere space-savers. For example, by analogy with the symbols $\exists_n$, we can introduce a symbol $\exists_\infty$, meaning "there are infinitely many":

- If α is a variable and ϕ is a wff, then "$\exists_\infty \alpha \, \phi$" is a wff
- $V_{\mathcal{M},g}(\exists_\infty \alpha \, \phi) = 1$ iff $|\phi^{\mathcal{M},g,\alpha}|$ is infinite

As it turns out, the addition of $\exists_\infty$ genuinely enhances PC: no sentence of standard PC has the same truth condition as does $\exists_\infty x F x$.[51] One can then use this new generalized quantifier to symbolize new English sentences. For example, "The number of fish that have escaped some predator is infinite" could be symbolized thus: $\exists_\infty x(Fx \wedge \exists y(Py \wedge Exy))$. And "for every number, there are infinitely many greater numbers" could be symbolized thus: $\forall x(Nx \rightarrow \exists_\infty y(Ny \wedge Gyx))$.

Another generalized quantifier that is not symbolizable using standard PC is most:

- If α is a variable and ϕ is a wff, then "most $\alpha \, \phi$" is a wff
- $V_{\mathcal{M},g}(\text{most } \alpha \, \phi) = 1$ iff $|\phi^{\mathcal{M},g,\alpha}| > |\mathcal{D} - \phi^{\mathcal{M},g,\alpha}|$

The minus sign in the second clause is the symbol for set-theoretic difference: $A - B$ is the set of things that are in A but not in B. Thus the definition says that most $\alpha \, \phi$ is true iff more things in the domain $\mathcal{D}$ are ϕ than are not ϕ.

One could add all sorts of additional "quantifiers" Q in this way. Each would be, grammatically, just like $\forall$ and $\exists$, in that each would combine with a variable, α, and then attach to a sentence ϕ, to form a new sentence $Q\alpha\phi$. Each of these new quantifiers, Q, would be associated with a relation between sets, R_Q, such that $Q\alpha\phi$ would be true in a PC-model, $\mathcal{M}$, with domain $\mathcal{D}$, relative to variable assignment g, iff $\phi^{\mathcal{M},g,\alpha}$ bears R_Q to $\mathcal{D}$.

If such an added symbol Q is to count as a quantifier in any intuitive sense, then the relation R_Q can't be just any relation between sets. It should be a relation concerning the relative "quantities" of its relata. It shouldn't, for instance, "concern particular objects" in the way that the following symbol, $\exists_{\text{Ted-loved}}$, concerns particular objects:

$$V_{\mathcal{M},g}(\exists_{\text{Ted-loved}} \alpha \phi) = 1 \text{ iff } \phi^{\mathcal{M},g,\alpha} \cap \{u : u \in \mathcal{D} \text{ and Ted loves } u\} \neq \varnothing$$

So we should require the following of R_Q: if a subset X of some set D bears R_Q to D, and f is a one-to-one function with domain D and range D', then $f[X]$ must bear R_Q to D'. ($f[X]$ is the image of X under function f—i.e., $\{u : u \in D' \text{ and } u = f(v), \text{ for some } v \in D\}$. It is the subset of D' onto which f "projects" X.)

Exercise 5.9 Let the quantifier $\exists_{\text{prime}}$ mean "there is a prime number of". Using the notation of generalized quantifiers, write out the semantics of this quantifier.

---

[51] I won't prove this; but see the discussion of compactness in section 4.5.

5.4.2 *Generalized binary quantifiers*

We have seen how the standard quantifiers $\forall$ and $\exists$ can be generalized in one way: syntactically similar symbols may be introduced and associated with different semantic conditions of quantity. Our second way of generalizing the standard quantifiers is to allow two-place, or *binary*, quantifiers.

$\forall$ and $\exists$ are *monadic* in that $\forall\alpha$ and $\exists\alpha$ attach to a single open sentence ϕ. Compare the natural-language monadic quantifiers 'everything' and 'something':

> Everything is material
> Something is spiritual

Here, the predicates (verb phrases) 'is material' and 'is spiritual' correspond to the open sentences of logic; it is to these that 'everything' and 'something' attach. But in fact, monadic quantifiers in natural language are atypical. 'Every' and 'some' typically occur as follows:

> Every student is happy
> Some fish are tasty

The quantifiers 'every' and 'some' attach to *two* predicates. In the first sentence, 'every' attaches to '[is a] student' and 'is happy'; in the second, 'some' attaches to '[is a] fish' and '[is] tasty'. In these sentences, we may think of 'every' and 'some' as binary quantifiers. (Indeed, one might think of 'everything' and 'something' as the result of applying the binary quantifiers 'every' and 'some' to the predicate 'is a thing'.) A logical notation with a parallel structure can be introduced, in which $\forall$ and $\exists$ attach to *two* open sentences. In this notation we symbolize "every ϕ is a ψ" as $(\forall\alpha{:}\phi)\psi$, and "some ϕ is a ψ" as $(\exists\alpha{:}\phi)\psi$. The grammar and semantic clauses for these binary quantifiers are as follows:

- If ϕ and ψ are wffs and α is a variable, then $(\forall\alpha{:}\phi)\psi$ and $(\exists\alpha{:}\phi)\psi$ are wffs
- $V_{\mathcal{M},g}((\forall\alpha{:}\phi)\psi) = 1$ iff $\phi^{\mathcal{M},g,\alpha} \subseteq \psi^{\mathcal{M},g,\alpha}$
- $V_{\mathcal{M},g}((\exists\alpha{:}\phi)\psi) = 1$ iff $\phi^{\mathcal{M},g,\alpha} \cap \psi^{\mathcal{M},g,\alpha} \neq \varnothing$

A further important binary quantifier is the:

- If ϕ and ψ are wffs and α is a variable, then $(\text{the}\,\alpha{:}\phi)\psi$ is a wff
- $V_{\mathcal{M},g}((\text{the}\,\alpha{:}\phi)\psi) = 1$ iff $|\phi^{\mathcal{M},g,\alpha}| = 1$ and $\phi^{\mathcal{M},g,\alpha} \subseteq \psi^{\mathcal{M},g,\alpha}$

That is, $(\text{the}\,\alpha{:}\phi)\psi$ is true iff (i) there is exactly one ϕ, and (ii) every ϕ is a ψ. This truth condition, notice, is exactly the truth condition for Russell's symbolization of "the ϕ is a ψ"; hence the name the.

As with the monadic quantifiers $\exists_n$, the introduction of the binary existential and universal quantifiers, and of the, does not increase our expressive power, for the same effect can be achieved with $\forall$ and $\exists$ (and $=$). $(\forall\alpha{:}\phi)\psi$, $(\exists\alpha{:}\phi)\psi$, and $(\text{the}\,\alpha{:}\phi)\psi$ become, respectively:

$$\forall\alpha(\phi{\rightarrow}\psi)$$
$$\exists\alpha(\phi{\wedge}\psi)$$
$$\exists\alpha(\phi \wedge \forall\beta(\phi(\beta/\alpha){\rightarrow}\alpha{=}\beta) \wedge \psi)$$

But, as with the monadic quantifiers $\exists_\infty$ and **most**, there are binary quantifiers that genuinely increase expressive power. For example, most occurrences of 'most' in English are binary, as in:

Most fish swim

To symbolize such sentences, we can introduce a binary quantifier **most²**. We read the sentence $(\mathbf{most}^2\alpha{:}\phi)\psi$ as "most ϕs are ψs". The semantic clause for **most²** is:

$$V_{\mathcal{M},g}((\mathbf{most}^2\alpha{:}\phi)\psi) = 1 \text{ iff } |\phi^{\mathcal{M},g,\alpha} \cap \psi^{\mathcal{M},g,\alpha}| > |\phi^{\mathcal{M},g,\alpha} - \psi^{\mathcal{M},g,\alpha}|$$

The binary **most²** increases our expressive power, even relative to the monadic **most**: not every sentence expressible with the former is equivalent to a sentence expressible with the latter.[52] One can then use this binary quantifier to symbolize more complex sentences. For example, "Most people who love someone are loved by someone" could be symbolized as: $(\mathbf{most}^2 x : \exists y Lxy)\exists y Lyx$.

> **Exercise 5.10** Symbolize the following sentence:
>
> > The number of people multiplied by the number of cats that bite at least one dog is 198.
>
> You may invent any generalized quantifiers you need, provided you write out their semantics.

5.4.3 Second-order logic

We'll now briefly look at second-order predicate logic, a powerful extension to standard predicate logic in which we add *predicate variables*. Predicate variables differ from the familiar variables $x, y, \dots$ (which are called "individual variables") in syntactic and semantic ways.

Syntactically: individual variables are *terms*. That is, they behave grammatically like names: to produce a wff you must combine them with a predicate, not just other terms. Predicate variables, on the other hand, behave grammatically like predicates, resulting in well-formed formulas like the following:

$$\exists X Xa$$
$$\forall X \exists y Xy$$

Like predicates, predicate variables can be one-place, two-place, three-place, etc. Thus, to our primitive vocabulary we must add, for each n, n-place predicate variables $X, Y, \dots$; and we must add the following clause to the definition of a wff:

- If π is an n-place predicate variable and $\alpha_1 \dots \alpha_n$ are terms, then $\pi\alpha_1 \dots \alpha_n$ is a wff

[52]See Westerståhl (1989) for this and related results cited in this chapter.

Semantically: individual variables are assigned members of the domain by variable assignments. But in second-order logic, a variable assignment must in addition assign to each n-place predicate an n-place relation over the domain. (This is what one would expect: the semantic value of an n-place predicate is an n-place relation, and variable assignments assign temporary semantic values.) Then the following clauses to the definition of truth in a PC-model must be added:

- If π is an n-place predicate variable and $\alpha_1 \ldots \alpha_n$ are terms, then $V_{\mathcal{M},g}(\pi\alpha_1\ldots\alpha_n)=1$ iff $\langle [\alpha_1]_{\mathcal{M},g} \ldots [\alpha_n]_{\mathcal{M},g} \rangle \in g(\pi)$
- If π is a predicate variable and ϕ is a wff, then $V_{\mathcal{M},g}(\forall\pi\phi)=1$ iff for every set U of n-tuples from $\mathcal{D}$, $V_{\mathcal{M},g_U^\pi}(\phi)=1$

(where g_U^π is the variable assignment just like g except in assigning U to π). Notice that, as with the generalized monadic quantifiers, no alteration to the definition of a PC-model is needed. All we need to do is change grammar and the definition of the valuation function.

Since standard predicate logic contains only individual variables, it is often called "first-order logic" to distinguish it from second-order logic. (Logics with generalized quantifiers like **most** also contain only individual variables, but 'first-order logic' usually only refers to PC, perhaps with identity and function symbols.)

The metalogical properties of second-order logic are dramatically different from those metalogical properties of PC that we briefly mentioned in section 4.5. For instance, second-order logic is "incomplete" in the sense that there are no axioms from which one can prove all and only the second-order valid sentences. (Unless, that is, one resorts to cheap tricks like saying "let every valid wff be an axiom". This trick is "cheap" because there would be no mechanical procedure for telling what an axiom is.[53]) Moreover, the compactness theorem fails for second-order logic. Moreover, one can write down a single second-order sentence whose second-order semantic consequences are all and only the truths of arithmetic. (This is cold comfort given the incompleteness of second-order logic: there is no complete axiomatic system we can use to draw out the consequences of this arithmetic "axiom".)

Second-order logic also differs "expressively" from PC: the second-order variables let us, in a sense, say new things that we couldn't say using PC. For example, in second-order logic we can state the two principles that are sometimes collectively called "Leibniz's Law":

$$\forall x \forall y (x{=}y \rightarrow \forall X(Xx \leftrightarrow Xy)) \qquad \text{(indiscernibility of identicals)}$$
$$\forall x \forall y (\forall X(Xx \leftrightarrow Xy) \rightarrow x{=}y) \qquad \text{(identity of indiscernibles)}$$

The indiscernibility of identicals says, intuitively, that identical objects have exactly the same properties; the identity of indiscernibles says that objects with exactly the

---

[53]For a rigorous statement and proof of this and other metalogical results about second-order logic, see, e.g., Boolos *et al.* (2007, chapter 18).

same properties are identical. Given our definitions, each is a logical truth (exercise 5.11).[54]

This might seem like an unwanted result. The identity of indiscernibles isn't necessarily true, it might be thought: there could exist two distinct objects that are nevertheless exactly alike—perfectly alike marbles, say, made by the same factory. But in fact nothing is amiss here. The identity of indiscernibles *is* necessarily true, provided we construe 'property' very broadly, so that "being a member of such-and-such set" counts as a property. Under this construal, there just couldn't be two marbles, A and B, with exactly the same properties, since if $A \neq B$, then A would have the property of being a member of the set $\{A\}$ whereas B would not. If we want to say that two marbles *could* have the same properties, we must construe 'property' more restrictively—perhaps as meaning *qualitative* property.[55] It was the broad conception of property that I had in mind when I wrote above that "the identity of indiscernibles says that objects with exactly the same properties are identical", since the second-order variable X ranges over all the subsets of the domain (in the semantics I gave above, anyway), not just those picked out by some qualitative property.

The increased expressive power of second-order logic can be illustrated by the "Geach–Kaplan sentence":[56]

> Some critics admire only one another (GK)

On one reading, anyway, this sentence says that there is a (nonempty) *group* of critics in which members admire only other members. Suppose we want to symbolize (GK) as some formal sentence ϕ. What must ϕ be like? First, ϕ must contain a one-place predicate symbolizing 'critic' and a two-place predicate symbolizing 'admires'. Let these be C and A, respectively. Second, ϕ must have the right truth condition; ϕ must be true in an arbitrary model $\langle \mathscr{D}, \mathscr{I} \rangle$ iff:

> $\mathscr{I}(C)$ has some nonempty subset E, such that whenever $\langle u, v \rangle \in \mathscr{I}(A)$ and $u \in E$, then $v \in E$ and $v \neq u$ (*)

Now, it can be shown that no sentence of PC (with identity) has this truth condition. That is, for no sentence ϕ of first-order logic containing A and C is (*) true of every model $\langle \mathscr{D}, \mathscr{I} \rangle$. However, there is a sentence of second-order logic with this truth-condition; namely:

$$\exists X[\exists x Xx \wedge \forall x(Xx \rightarrow Cx) \wedge \forall x \forall y([Xx \wedge Axy] \rightarrow [Xy \wedge x \neq y])] \quad (\text{GK}^2)$$

So in a sense, you need to use second-order logic if you want to symbolize the Geach–Kaplan sentence. But we have to be careful with this talk of symbolizing, since there is another sense of 'symbolize' on which the Geach–Kaplan sentence can

---

[54] Relatedly, one can now define "$\alpha = \beta$" as $\forall X(X\alpha \leftrightarrow X\beta)$.

[55] See Lewis (1986, section 1.5) on different conceptions of properties.

[56] The sentence and its significance were discovered by Peter Geach and David Kaplan. See Boolos (1984).

be symbolized in first-order logic after all. Suppose we use a two-place predicate M for set-membership:[57]

$$\exists z[\exists x Mxz \wedge \forall x(Mxz \rightarrow Cx) \wedge \forall x \forall y([Mxz \wedge Axy] \rightarrow [Myz \wedge x \neq y])] \qquad (\text{GK}^1)$$

(GK^1) doesn't symbolize (GK) in the sense of being true in exactly those models that satisfy (*); correspondingly, it isn't true in exactly the same models as (GK^2). For even though we said that M is to be a predicate "for" set-membership, there's nothing in the definition of a model that reflects this, and so there are models in which M doesn't mean set-membership; and in such models, (GK^1) and (GK^2) needn't have the same truth value. But if we restrict our attention to models $\langle \mathscr{D}, \mathscr{I} \rangle$ in which M *does* mean set-membership (restricted to the model's domain, of course—that is, $\mathscr{I}(M) = \{\langle u, v \rangle : u, v \in \mathscr{D} \text{ and } u \in v\}$), and in which each subset of $\mathscr{I}(C)$ is a member of $\mathscr{D}$, then (GK^1) will indeed be true iff (GK^2) is (and iff the model satisfies (*)). In essence, the difference between (GK^1) and (GK^2) is that it is hard-wired into the definition of truth in a model that second-order predications $X\alpha$ express set-membership, whereas this is not hard-wired into the definition of the first-order predication $M\alpha\beta$.[58]

> **Exercise 5.11** Show that the indiscernibility of identicals and the identity of indiscernibles are both true under every variable assignment in every model.

5.5 Complex predicates

In section 5.3 we introduced the ι symbol, which allowed us to create complex terms from sentences. In this section we'll introduce something analogous: complex predicates. In particular, we'll introduce the means for taking a sentence, ϕ, and creating a corresponding complex predicate that means "is such that ϕ".

The means is a new symbol, λ, with the following grammar:

- if α is a variable and ϕ is a wff then $\lambda\alpha\phi$ is a one-place predicate

Think of $\lambda\alpha\phi$ as meaning "is an α such that ϕ". Such predicates are often called "λ-abstracts" ("lambda-abstracts").

We now have two kinds of predicates, simple predicates (like F, G, R, and so on) which are part of the primitive vocabulary, and complex predicates formed by λ-abstraction. As a result, the class of atomic wffs now includes wffs like the following (in addition to wffs like Fa, Gy, and Ryb):

---

[57] One can in the same sense symbolize the identity of indiscernibles and the indiscernibility of identicals using first-order sentences and the predicate M.

[58] For more on second-order logic, see Boolos (1975; 1984; 1985).

$\lambda x F x(a)$ "a is such that: it is F"
$\lambda x \sim G x(y)$ "y is such that: it is not G"
$\lambda x \forall y R y x(b)$ "b is such that: everyone respects her/him"

(Officially these wffs do not contain parentheses; I added them for readability.) I call these atomic, even though the latter two contain $\sim$ and $\forall$, because each is formed by attaching a predicate (albeit a complex one) to a term.

As for semantics, in any model $\mathcal{M}$ ($= \langle \mathcal{D}, \mathcal{I} \rangle$), what should the meaning of $\lambda \alpha \phi$ be? Since it's a one-place predicate, its meaning should be the same kind of animal as the meaning of a simple one-place predicate like F: a set of members of $\mathcal{D}$. Which set? Roughly: the set of members of $\mathcal{D}$ for which ϕ is true. More precisely (using the notation of section 5.4.1): the set $\phi^{\mathcal{M},g,\alpha}$ (i.e., $\{u : u \in \mathcal{D}$ and $V_{\mathcal{M},g_u^{\alpha}}(\phi) = 1\}$). So the meaning of $\lambda x \sim F x$, for example, will be the set of members of the domain that are not in the extension of F. This talk of "the meaning" of λ-abstracts is incorporated into the semantics officially as a new clause in the definition of the valuation function governing atomic sentences containing λ-abstracts:

- For any wff ϕ, variable α, and term β, $V_{\mathcal{M},g}(\lambda \alpha \phi \, \beta) = 1$ iff $[\beta]_{\mathcal{M},g} \in \phi^{\mathcal{M},g,\alpha}$

The λ-abstracts are semantically superfluous (given our current setup, anyway). For example, $\lambda x(Fx \wedge Gx)(a)$ is true in a model iff $Fa \wedge Ga$ is true in that model, $\lambda x R x x(y)$ is true in a model under a variable assignment iff Ryy is true in that model under that assignment, and so on. So what is their point?

For one thing, even though $\lambda x(Fx \wedge Gx)(a)$ and $Fa \wedge Ga$ are semantically equivalent, they are grammatically different. The former has a subject–predicate form, whereas the latter is a conjunction. Likewise, $\lambda x R x x(y)$ is a one-place predication, whereas Ryy is a two-place predication. Such grammatical differences are important in some theoretical contexts, such as in empirical linguistics when semantics must be integrated with natural-language syntax. We might prefer $\lambda x(Fx \wedge Gx)(a)$ as the symbolization of "John is cold and hungry", for example, since it treats 'is cold and hungry' as a single predicate. And we might prefer to symbolize 'No self-respecting Philadelphian is a Yankees fan' as $\sim \exists x(\lambda y(Ryy \wedge Py)(x) \wedge Yx)$ since this treats 'self-respecting Philadelphian' as a single one-place predicate.[59] For another case of this sort, consider the symbolization of natural-language definite descriptions.[60] The semantics of section 5.3 treated atomic sentences containing ι terms (terms of the form $\iota \alpha \phi$) as "existence-entailing"—as being true only if the contained ι terms are nonempty. But sometimes we want existence-entailing sentences containing ι terms even when those sentences aren't atomic. Suppose, for example, that we want to symbolize a reading of "The King of the USA is not bald" that is existence-entailing. (Imagine the sentence uttered by someone who believes that there *is* a King of the USA; intuitively, the person is trying to say that "the King of the USA is *nonbald*.") This reading of the sentence is false since the USA has no king. So it can't be symbolized as $\sim B\iota x K x u$: the atomic sentence $B\iota x K x u$ is false since $\iota x K x u$ is empty, and

---

[59] See Gamut (1991*b*, section 4.4.1).
[60] Compare Stalnaker (1977).

thus the whole sentence is true. We could always give up on using the ι, and use Russell's wide-scope symbolization instead:

$$\exists x(Kxu \wedge \forall y(Kyu \rightarrow y=x) \wedge \sim Bx)$$

This generates the right truth conditions. But 'The King of the USA' functions syntactically in English as a singular term, whereas the Russellian symbolization contains no corresponding syntactic unit. Lambda-abstraction lets us capture the correct truth conditions[61] while continuing to symbolize 'The King of the USA' with an ι term, thus treating it as a syntactic unit:

$$\lambda x \sim Bx(\iota x Kxu)$$

The difference between a sentence of the form $\lambda x \sim F(\alpha)$ ("α is non-F"), on the one hand, and the sentences $\sim \lambda x F(\alpha)$ and $\sim F\alpha$ ("it's not the case that α is F"), on the other, is often called the difference between "internal" and "external" negation.

The kind of λ-abstraction we have been discussing is a special case of a much more general and powerful tool, of particular interest in linguistics.[62] For just a taste of the possibilities, consider the sentences:

> John crossed the street without looking
> Crossing the street without looking is dangerous.

It's natural to regard 'crossed the street' and 'looking' in the first sentence as predicates, generating the symbolization: $Cj \wedge \sim Lj$. And it would be strange to treat 'crossing the street' and 'looking' as meaning something different in the second sentence. But the second sentence doesn't seem to be claiming that people who cross the street without looking are dangerous. Rather, it seems to be saying that *crossing the street without looking* in general—the activity (or feature, or property)—is dangerous. So how do we represent the second sentence? One possibility is to use λ-abstraction, together with a *second-order predicate*. A second-order predicate attaches to an ordinary (first-order) predicate to form a sentence. Thus, "walking is dangerous" might be symbolized by attaching a second-order predicate D^2 to the first-order predicate W: $D^2(W)$. So, we could symbolize the second displayed sentence above by attaching D^2 to a λ-abstract:

$$D^2(\lambda x(Cx \wedge \sim Lx))$$

As a final example, we might additionally bring in second-order variables to symbolize "If John crossed the street without looking, and crossing the street without looking is dangerous, then John did something dangerous":

$$(Cj \wedge \sim Lj \wedge D^2(\lambda x(Cx \wedge \sim Lx))) \rightarrow \exists X(D^2(X) \wedge Xj)$$

---

[61] Assuming we update the semantics of section 5.3.2 in the obvious way, treating atomic sentences with λ-abstract predicates as false when they contain terms with undefined denotations.

[62] See for example Dowty *et al.* (1981); Gamut (1991*b*); Heim and Kratzer (1998).

Exercise 5.12 Symbolize the following sentences, sticking as close to the English syntax as possible:

(a) Any friend of Barry is either insane or friends with everyone

(b) If a man is from Philadelphia, then insulting him is foolish

Exercise 5.13 Show that $\lambda x \forall y Ryx(a)$ and $\forall x Rxa$ are semantically equivalent (true in the same models).

5.6 Free logic

So far we have considered *extensions* of standard predicate logic. Let's finish this chapter with a brief discussion of a variation: free logic. In standard predicate logic, it is assumed that individual constants denote existing entities. In each model, the interpretation function assigns to each individual constant some member of the domain. But some natural-language names, for example 'Pegasus', 'Santa Claus', and 'Sherlock Holmes', seem not to denote existing entities. Call such names "empty names".

Standard predicate logic does not capture the logic of empty names, according to the advocates of free logic. Consider, for example, the sentence "Sherlock Holmes exists". This sentence seems false. But it's natural to symbolize it as $\exists x\, x{=}a$ (to say that something exists is to say that something is identical to it), and $\exists x\, x{=}a$ is a valid sentence of standard predicate logic. (In any model, the name a must denote some member u of the model's domain. But then, where g is any variable assignment for this model, the open sentence $x{=}a$ is true with respect to g_u^x. So, $\exists x\, x{=}a$ is true with respect to g, and so is true in the model.) In essence: standard predicate logic assumes that all names are nonempty.

How to respond to this apparent discrepancy? The free logicians propose to alter the semantics and proof theory of predicate logic so as to allow empty names.

In addition to assuming that names are nonempty, standard predicate logic also assumes that: *something exists*. The definition of a model in standard predicate logic requires the domain to be nonempty. (As a result, the sentence $\exists x(Fx \lor {\sim}Fx)$, for example, comes out valid.) This too might be regarded as objectionable. Other things being equal, it would be good to have a logic that recognizes the possibility of there existing nothing at all.

One could admit empty names without admitting the logical possibility of there existing nothing. Nevertheless, it's natural to follow up the former with the latter. There's a barrier to the latter: if nothing exists, then what do empty names denote? So if we're in the business of figuring out how to admit empty names anyway, why not simultaneously figure out how to recognize the possibility of nothing? Logics allowing the possibility of nothing existing are sometimes called "inclusive".

5.6.1 Semantics for free logic

There are various ways to implement a semantics for (inclusive) free logic. The most straightforward introduces, in addition to the normal domain over which quantifiers range, a further *outer* domain. Think of the normal domain—now called the "inner" domain—as containing the existent entities; think of the outer domain as containing the nonexistent ones, such as Pegasus, Santa Claus, and Sherlock Holmes. Here are the definitions (the language in question is assumed to be the language of predicate logic plus identity):

DEFINITION OF MODEL: An FPC-model ("F" for "free") is an ordered triple $\langle \mathscr{D}, \mathscr{D}', \mathscr{I} \rangle$ such that

- $\mathscr{D}$ is a set   ("inner domain")
- $\mathscr{D}'$ is a set   ("outer domain")
- $\mathscr{D}$ and $\mathscr{D}'$ have no member in common, and while either one of them may be empty, their union must be nonempty
- $\mathscr{I}$ is a function obeying the following constraints:
    - If α is a constant, then $\mathscr{I}(\alpha)$ is a member of $\mathscr{D} \cup \mathscr{D}'$
    - If Π is an n-place predicate, then $\mathscr{I}(\Pi)$ is an n-place relation over $\mathscr{D}$

DEFINITION OF VARIABLE ASSIGNMENT: A variable assignment for an FPC-model, $\langle \mathscr{D}, \mathscr{D}', \mathscr{I} \rangle$, is a function that assigns to each variable some member of $\mathscr{D} \cup \mathscr{D}'$.

DEFINITION OF VALUATION: The FPC-valuation function, $V_{\mathscr{M},g}$, for FPC-model $\mathscr{M}$ ($= \langle \mathscr{D}, \mathscr{D}', \mathscr{I} \rangle$) and variable assignment g, is defined as the function that assigns to each wff either 0 or 1 subject to the following constraints:

- For any n-place predicate Π and any terms $\alpha_1 \ldots \alpha_n$, $V_{\mathscr{M},g}(\Pi \alpha_1 \ldots \alpha_n) = 1$ iff $\langle [\alpha_1]_{\mathscr{M},g} \ldots [\alpha_n]_{\mathscr{M},g} \rangle \in \mathscr{I}(\Pi)$
- $V_{\mathscr{M},g}(\alpha = \beta) = 1$ iff $[\alpha]_{\mathscr{M},g} =$ (i.e., is the same object as) $[\beta]_{\mathscr{M},g}$
- For any wffs ϕ, ψ, and any variable α:

$$V_{\mathscr{M},g}(\sim\phi) = 1 \text{ iff } V_{\mathscr{M},g}(\phi) = 0$$
$$V_{\mathscr{M},g}(\phi \rightarrow \psi) = 1 \text{ iff either } V_{\mathscr{M},g}(\phi) = 0 \text{ or } V_{\mathscr{M},g}(\psi) = 1$$
$$V_{\mathscr{M},g}(\forall \alpha \phi) = 1 \text{ iff for every } u \in \mathscr{D}, V_{\mathscr{M},g_u^\alpha}(\phi) = 1$$

The definition of denotation, $[\alpha]_{\mathscr{M},g}$, is unchanged, as are the definitions of truth in a model, validity, and semantic consequence.

Let me make several comments about these definitions. First, few philosophers believe in such things as nonexistent objects. But using the FPC formalism doesn't commit one to real live nonexistent objects. We call $\mathscr{D}'$ the "outer domain" for the sake of vividness, and it is a convenient heuristic to call its members "nonexistent objects", but nowhere do the formal definitions require its members really to be nonexistent. Its members can be any sorts of existent entities one likes. There is, however, a genuine worry about the FPC-semantics in the neighborhood. If the philosophical opponents of nonexistent objects are right, then the structure of FPC-models doesn't match the structure of the real world; so why should FPC-validity and FPC-semantic-consequence shed any light on genuine validity and logical consequence? The question is legitimate and pressing. Nevertheless, let's stick to our inner/outer domain approach to the semantics of free logic. It's an approach that many free logicians have taken; and it's also the most straightforward.[63]

Second, the definition of the valuation function says that $\forall \alpha \phi$ is true if and only if ϕ is true for each object of the *inner* domain. (Similarly, the obvious derived clause for the $\exists$ says that $\exists \alpha \phi$ is true iff ϕ is true for some object in the inner domain.) The quantifiers range only over the inner domain, not the outer. As a result, since the inner domain is allowed to be empty, no sentence of the form $\exists \alpha \phi$ turns out valid (example 5.5). Thus, $\exists x(Fx \vee \sim Fx)$ turns out invalid. This is what we wanted: if it's logically possible that there be nothing, then it shouldn't be a logical truth that there is something that is either green or not green.

Third, notice that the definition of a model does not require the denotation of a constant to be a member of the inner domain (though it must be a member either of the inner or outer domain). This gives us another thing we wanted out of free logic: individual constants don't need to denote what one usually thinks of as existing objects—i.e., objects in the range of the quantifiers. Now, the fact noted in the previous paragraph already showed that $\exists x\, x=a$ is not valid (since it has the form $\exists \alpha \phi$). But something stronger is true: $\exists x\, x=a$ doesn't even follow from $\exists x\, x=x$, which says in effect that "something exists" (example 5.6). This too is what we wanted: it shouldn't follow (according to the defenders of free logic) from the fact that something exists that Sherlock Holmes exists.

Fourth, notice that the definition of a model requires the extension of a predicate to be an n-place relation over the *inner* domain.[64] As a result, formulas of the form $\Pi \alpha_1 \ldots \alpha_n$ are false (relative to a variable assignment) whenever any of the α_is fail to denote anything in the inner domain (relative to that variable assignment). Informally: atomic formulas containing "empty terms" are always false. Free logics with this feature are often called "negative" free logics. This is not the only alternative. *Positive* free logics allow some atomic formulas containing empty terms to be true. And *neutral* free logics say that all such formulas are neither true nor false.[65] We won't pursue these alternatives in detail, but note some possible strategies: for positive free logic, we might redefine predicate extensions as relations over all of $\mathscr{D} \cup \mathscr{D}'$; and for neutral free logic, we might use three-valued logic (section 3.4).

Some examples:

Example 5.5: Show that $\nvDash_{\text{FPC}} \exists \alpha \phi$, for any variable α and any wff ϕ. Consider any model in which the inner domain is empty, and let g be any variable assignment

---

[63] Another approach is to stick to a single domain, allow that domain to sometimes be empty, and allow the interpretation function to be partial, so that $\mathscr{I}(\alpha)$ is undefined for some names α. But a formal obstacle looms: no variable assignments will exist if the domain is empty; how then will truth in such models be defined? Williamson (1999*a*) discusses some of these issues.

[64] The identity predicate is a kind of exception. Though the interpretation function $\mathscr{I}$ does not assign values to the identity predicate, the valuation function counts $\alpha=\beta$ as being true whenever α and β denote the same thing—even if that thing is in the outer domain. Thus the identity sign is in effect treated as if its extension is $\{\langle u,u \rangle\}$, for all $u \in \mathscr{D} \cup \mathscr{D}'$.

[65] Exception: neutral free logics that treat 'exists' as a primitive predicate (rather than defining "α exists" as $\exists x\, x=\alpha$) sometimes allow 'α exists' to be false, rather than lacking in truth value, when α fails to denote an existing entity.

in this model. (Since the inner domain is empty, g assigns only members of the outer domain.) The derived truth condition for the $\exists$ then says that $V_g(\exists\alpha\phi)=1$ iff there is some u in the inner domain such that $V_{g_u^\alpha}(\phi)=1$. But there is no such u since the inner domain is empty. So $V_g(\exists\alpha\phi)=0$ for this model; and so $\exists\alpha\phi$ is invalid.

Example 5.6: Show that $\exists x\, x{=}x \nvDash_{FPC} \exists x\, x{=}a$. Consider a model with a nonempty inner domain, but in which the constant a denotes something in the outer domain. Where g is any variable assignment, note first that $V_g(\exists x\, x{=}x)=1$. For $V_g(\exists x\, x{=}x)=1$ iff for some $u\in\mathscr{D}$, $V_{g_u^x}(x{=}x)=1$. But $\mathscr{D}$ is nonempty, so we can let u be any member of $\mathscr{D}$. And note second that $V_g(\exists x\, x{=}a)=0$. For $V_g(\exists x\, x{=}a)=1$ iff for some $u\in\mathscr{D}$, $V_{g_u^x}(x{=}a)=1$, which holds iff for some $u\in\mathscr{D}$, $[x]_{g_u^x}=[a]_{g_u^x}$, i.e. iff for some $u\in\mathscr{D}$, $u=\mathscr{I}(a)$. But there is no such u, since $\mathscr{I}(a)\notin\mathscr{D}$.

> **Exercise 5.14** Show that $\nvDash_{FPC} \forall x Fx \rightarrow Fa$.
>
> **Exercise 5.15** Show $\vDash_{FPC} \forall x Fx \rightarrow (\exists y\, y{=}a \rightarrow Fa)$.

5.6.2 Proof theory for free logic

Here we will be brief. How would the free logician view the axioms and rules of PC from section 4.4?

$$\frac{\phi}{\forall\alpha\phi} \quad \text{UG}$$

$$\forall\alpha\phi \rightarrow \phi(\beta/\alpha) \tag{PC1}$$
$$\forall\alpha(\phi{\rightarrow}\psi) \rightarrow (\phi{\rightarrow}\forall\alpha\psi) \tag{PC2}$$

UG and PC2 seem unobjectionable, but the free logician will reject PC1. She will not accept that $\forall x Fx{\rightarrow}Fa$, for example, is a logical truth: if a is an empty name, then Fa will be false even if all *existing* things are F. (Compare exercise 5.14.) To make things even more vivid, consider another instance of PC1: $\forall x\exists y\, y{=}x \rightarrow \exists y\, y{=}a$ ("if everything exists, then a exists"). This the free logician will clearly reject. For, since she thinks that *both* the existential and the universal quantifier range only over the existent entities, she thinks that the antecedent $\forall x\exists y\, y{=}x$ is a logical truth. For every existent thing, there is some *existent* thing to which it is identical. But she thinks that the consequent might be false: there will be no existent thing identical to a, if a is an empty name.

If PC1 is to be rejected, what should be put in its place? One possibility is:

$$\forall\alpha\phi \rightarrow (\exists x\, x{=}\beta \rightarrow \phi(\beta/\alpha)) \tag{PC1$'$}$$

That is: if everything is ϕ, then if β exists, β must be ϕ as well. The principle of "universal instantiation" has been restricted to existing entities; the free logician will accept this restricted principle. (Compare exercise 5.15.)

6

MODAL PROPOSITIONAL LOGIC

Modal logic is the logic of necessity and possibility. In it we treat "modal" words like 'necessary', 'possible', 'can', and 'must' as logical constants. Our new symbols for these words are called "modal operators":

$\Box\phi$: "It is necessary that ϕ" (or: "Necessarily, ϕ", "It must be that ϕ")

$\Diamond\phi$: "It is possible that ϕ" (or: "Possibly, ϕ", "It could be that ϕ", "It can be that ϕ", "It might be that ϕ", "It might have been that ϕ")

It helps to think of modality in terms of *possible worlds*. A possible world is a *complete* and *possible* scenario. Calling a scenario "possible" means simply that it's possible in the broadest sense for the scenario to happen. This requirement disqualifies scenarios in which, for example, it is both raining and also not raining (at the same time and place)—such a thing couldn't happen, and so doesn't happen in any possible world. But within this limit, we can imagine all sorts of possible worlds: possible worlds with talking donkeys, possible worlds in which I am ten feet tall, and so on. "Complete" means simply that no detail is left out—possible worlds are completely *specific* scenarios. There is no possible world in which I am "somewhere between ten and eleven feet tall" without being some particular height.[66] Likewise, in any possible world in which I am exactly 10 feet, 6 inches tall (say), I must have some particular weight, must live in some particular place, and so on. One of these possible worlds is the actual world—this is the complete and possible scenario that in fact obtains. The rest of them are merely possible—they do not obtain, but would have obtained if things had gone differently. In terms of possible worlds, we can think of our modal operators thus:[67]

"$\Box\phi$" is true iff ϕ is true in *all* possible worlds

"$\Diamond\phi$" is true iff ϕ is true in *at least one* possible world

It is necessarily true that all bachelors are male; in every possible world, every bachelor is male. There might have existed a talking donkey; in some possible world there exists a talking donkey.

Possible worlds provide, at the very least, a vivid way to think about necessity and possibility. How much more they provide is an open philosophical question. Some maintain that possible worlds are the key to the metaphysics of modality, that *what it is* for a proposition to be necessarily true is for it to be true in all possible worlds.[68]

---

[66]This is not to say that possible worlds exclude vagueness.

[67]On one strength of the modal operators anyway—see below.

[68]Sider (2003) presents an overview of this topic.

Whether this view is defensible is a question beyond the scope of this book; what is important for present purposes is that we distinguish possible worlds as a vivid heuristic from possible worlds as a concern in serious metaphysics.

Natural-language modal words are semantically flexible in a systematic way. For example, suppose I say that I can't attend a certain conference in Cleveland. What is the force of "can't" here? Probably I'm saying that my attending the conference is inconsistent with honoring other commitments I've made at that time. But notice that another sentence I might utter is: "I *could* attend the conference; but I would have to cancel my class, and I don't want to do that." Now I've said that I *can* attend the conference; have I contradicted my earlier assertion that I cannot attend the conference? No—what I mean now is perhaps that I have the means to get to Cleveland on that date. I have shifted what I mean by "can".

In fact, there is quite a wide range of things one can mean by words for possibility:

> *I can come to the party, but I can't stay late.* ("can" = "is not inconvenient")

> *Humans can travel to the moon, but not to Mars.* ("can" = "is achievable with current technology")

> *It's possible to move almost as fast as the speed of light, but not to travel faster than light.* ("possible" = "is consistent with the laws of nature")

> *Objects could have traveled faster than the speed of light (if the laws of nature had been different), but no matter what the laws had been, nothing could have traveled faster than itself.* ("could" = "metaphysical possibility")

> *You may borrow but you may not steal.* ("may" = "morally acceptable")

> *It might rain tomorrow* ("might" = "epistemic possibility")

Think of these as different "strengths" of possibility. For any strength of possibility, there is a corresponding strength of necessity, since "necessarily ϕ" is equivalent to "not-possibly-not-ϕ". (Similarly, "possibly ϕ" is equivalent to "not-necessarily-not-ϕ".) So we have a range of strengths of necessity as well: natural necessity (guaranteed by the laws of nature), moral or "deontic" necessity (required by morality), epistemic necessity ("known to be true"), and so on.

Some strengths of necessity imply truth; those that do are called "alethic" necessities. For example, if P is known, then P is true; if it is naturally necessary that massive particles attract one another, then massive particles do in fact attract one another. Epistemic and natural necessity are alethic. Deontic necessity, on the other hand, is not alethic: we do not always do what is morally required.

As we saw, we can think of the $\Box$ and the $\Diamond$ as quantifiers over possible worlds (the former a universal quantifier, the latter an existential quantifier). This idea can accommodate the fact that necessity and possibility come in different strengths: those different strengths result from different restrictions on the quantifiers over possible worlds. Thus natural possibility is truth in some possible world that obeys the actual world's laws; deontic possibility is truth in some possible world in which nothing morally forbidden occurs; and so on.[69]

6.1 Grammar of MPL

Our first topic in modal logic is the addition of the □ and the ◇ to propositional logic; the result is *modal propositional logic* ("MPL"). A further step will be modal predicate logic (Chapter 9).

We need a new language: the language of MPL. The grammar of this language is just like the grammar of propositional logic, except that we add the □ as a new one-place sentence connective:

PRIMITIVE VOCABULARY:

- Sentence letters: $P, Q, R \ldots$, with or without numerical subscripts
- Connectives: →, ∼, □
- Parentheses: (,)

DEFINITION OF WFF:

- Sentence letters are wffs
- If ϕ and ψ are wffs, then $(\phi \rightarrow \psi)$, $\sim\phi$, and $\Box\phi$ are also wffs
- Only strings that can be shown to be wffs using the preceding clauses are wffs

The □ is the only new primitive connective. But just as we were able to define ∧, ∨, and ↔, we can define new nonprimitive modal connectives:

- "$\Diamond\phi$" ("Possibly ϕ") is short for "$\sim\Box\sim\phi$"
- "$\phi \rightarrow\!\!\!3\, \psi$" is short for "$\Box(\phi \rightarrow \psi)$"

⫝3 is called the strict conditional. With some violence to grammar, $\phi\rightarrow\!\!\!3\,\psi$ can be read as "ϕ strictly implies ψ".

6.2 Symbolizations in MPL

Modal logic lets us symbolize many sentences we couldn't adequately symbolize before. Most obviously there are sentences that overtly involve "necessarily", "possibly", or equivalent expressions:

> Necessarily, if snow is white, then snow is white or grass is green
> $\Box[S \rightarrow (S \lor G)]$

> I'll go if I must
> $\Box G \rightarrow G$

> It is possible that Bush will lose the election
> $\Diamond L$

---

[69]This raises a question, though: to what strength of 'necessary' and 'possible' does the notion of possible world itself correspond? Is there some special, strictest notion of necessity, which can be thought of as truth in absolutely all possible worlds? Or do we simply have different notions of possible world corresponding to different strengths of necessity?

Snow might have been either green or blue
$\Diamond(G \lor B)$

If snow could have been green, then grass could have been white
$\Diamond G \rightarrow \Diamond W$

'Impossible' and related expressions signify the lack of possibility:

It is impossible for snow to be both white and not white
$\sim\Diamond(W \land \sim W)$

If grass cannot be clever, then snow cannot be furry
$\sim\Diamond C \rightarrow \sim\Diamond F$

God's being merciful is inconsistent with your imperfection being incompatible with your going to heaven
$\sim\Diamond(M \land \sim\Diamond(I \land H))$

As for the strict conditional, it arguably does a decent job of representing certain English conditional constructions:

Snow is a necessary condition for skiing
$\sim W \dashv\!\!3 \sim K$

Food and water are required for survival
$\sim(F \land W) \dashv\!\!3 \sim S$

Thunder implies lightning
$T \dashv\!\!3 L$

With modal operators we can make an important distinction involving modal conditionals in natural language. Consider the sentence "If Jones is a bachelor, then he must be unmarried". The surface grammar misleadingly suggests the symbolization:

$$B \rightarrow \Box U$$

But suppose that Jones is in fact a bachelor. It would then follow from this symbolization that the proposition that Jones is unmarried is necessarily true. But nothing we have said suggests that Jones is *necessarily* a bachelor. Surely Jones *could* have been married! In fact, one would normally *not* use the sentence "If Jones is a bachelor, then he must be unmarried" to mean that if Jones is in fact a bachelor, then the following is a necessary truth: Jones is unmarried. Rather, one would mean: necessarily, if Jones is a bachelor, then Jones is unmarried:

$$\Box(B \rightarrow U)$$

It is the *relationship* between Jones's being a bachelor and his being unmarried that is necessary. Think of this in terms of possible worlds: the first symbolization says that if Jones is a bachelor in the actual world, then Jones is unmarried in every possible world (which is absurd); whereas the second one says that in each possible world,

w, if Jones is a bachelor *in w*, then Jones is unmarried *in w* (which is quite sensible). The distinction between $\phi\rightarrow\Box\psi$ and $\Box(\phi\rightarrow\psi)$ is called the distinction between the "necessity of the consequent" (first sentence) and the "necessity of the consequence" (second sentence).

One final point: when representing English sentences using the $\Box$ and the $\Diamond$, keep in mind that these expressions can be used to express different strengths of necessity and possibility. (One could introduce different symbols for the different strengths; we'll do a bit of this in Chapter 7.)

6.3 Semantics for MPL

As usual, we'll consider semantics first. We'll show how to construct mathematical configurations in a way that's appropriate to modal logic, and how to define truth for formulas of MPL within these configurations. Ideally, we'd like the assignment of truth values to wffs to mirror the way that natural-language modal statements are made true by the real world, so that we can shed light on the meanings of natural-language modal words, and in order to provide plausible semantic models of the notions of logical truth and logical consequence.

In constructing a semantics for MPL, we face two main challenges, one philosophical, the other technical. The philosophical challenge is simply that it isn't wholly clear which formulas of MPL are indeed logical truths. It's hard to construct an engine to spit out logical truths if you don't know which logical truths you want it to spit out. With a few exceptions, there is widespread agreement over which formulas of nonmodal propositional and predicate logic are logical truths. But for modal logic this is less clear, especially for sentences that contain iterations of modal operators. Is $\Box P\rightarrow\Box\Box P$ a logical truth? It's hard to say.

A quick peek at the history of modal logic is in order. Modal logic arose from dissatisfaction with the material conditional $\rightarrow$ of standard propositional logic. In standard logic, $\phi\rightarrow\psi$ is true whenever ϕ is false or ψ is true; but in expressing the conditionality of ψ on ϕ, we sometimes require a tighter relationship: that it not be a mere *accident* that either ϕ is false or ψ is true. To express this tighter relationship, C. I. Lewis introduced the strict conditional $\phi\rightarrow\psi$, which he defined, as above, as $\Box(\phi\rightarrow\psi)$.[70] Thus defined, $\phi\rightarrow\psi$ isn't automatically true just because ϕ is false or ψ is true. It must be *necessarily true* that either ϕ is false or ψ is true.

Lewis then asked: what principles govern this new symbol $\Box$? Certain principles seemed clearly appropriate, for instance: $\Box(\phi\rightarrow\psi)\rightarrow(\Box\phi\rightarrow\Box\psi)$. Others were less clear. Is $\Box\phi\rightarrow\Box\Box\phi$ a logical truth? What about $\Diamond\Box\phi\rightarrow\phi$?

Lewis's solution to this problem was not to choose. Instead, he formulated several different *modal systems*. He did this axiomatically, by formulating different systems that differed from one another by containing different axioms and hence different theorems.

We will follow Lewis's approach, and construct several different modal systems. Unlike Lewis, we'll do this semantically at first (the semantics for modal logic we

---

[70]See Lewis (1918); Lewis and Langford (1932).

will study was published by Saul Kripke in the 1950s, long after Lewis was writing), by constructing different definitions of a model for modal logic. The definitions will differ from one another in ways that result in different sets of valid formulas. In section 6.4 we'll study Lewis's axiomatic systems, and in sections 6.5 and 6.6 we'll discuss the relationship between the semantics and the axiom systems.

Formulating multiple systems does not answer the philosophical question of which formulas of modal logic are logically true; it merely postpones it. The question re-arises when we want to *apply* Lewis's systems; when we ask which system is the *correct* system—i.e., which one correctly mirrors the logical properties of the *English* words 'possibly' and 'necessarily'. (Note that since there are different strengths of necessity and possibility, different systems might correctly represent different strengths.) But I'll mostly ignore such philosophical questions here.

The technical challenge to constructing a semantics for MPL is that the modal operators $\Box$ and $\Diamond$ are not truth-functional. A sentential connective is truth-functional iff whenever it combines with sentences to form a new sentence, the truth value of the resulting sentence is determined by the truth values of the component sentences. For example, 'it is not the case that' is truth-functional because the truth value of "it is not the case that ϕ" is determined by the truth value of ϕ. But 'necessarily' is not truth-functional. If I tell you that ϕ is true, you won't yet have enough information to determine whether "Necessarily ϕ" is true or false, since you won't know whether ϕ is necessarily true or merely contingently true. Here's another way to put the point: even though the sentences "If Ted is a philosopher, then Ted is a philosopher" and "Ted is a philosopher" have the same truth value, if you prefix each with 'Necessarily' (intended to mean metaphysical necessity, say), you get sentences with different truth values. Hence the truth value of "Necessarily ϕ" is not a function of the truth value of ϕ. Similarly, 'possibly' isn't truth-functional either: 'I might have been six feet tall' is true, whereas 'I might have been a round square' is false, despite the sad fact that 'I am six feet tall' and 'I am a round square' have the same truth value.

Since the $\Box$ and the $\Diamond$ are supposed to represent 'necessarily' and 'possibly', and since the latter aren't truth-functional, we can't do modal semantics with truth tables. For the method of truth tables assumes truth functionality. Truth tables are just pictures of truth functions: they specify what truth value a complex sentence has as a function of what truth values its parts have. Our challenge is clear: we need a semantics for the $\Box$ and the $\Diamond$ other than the method of truth tables.

6.3.1 *Kripke models*

Our approach will be that of *possible-worlds semantics*, which is based on the intuitive idea that necessity is truth in all possible worlds. Formally, we will develop models for MPL containing objects that we will call "possible worlds". Formulas are going to be true or false "in" these worlds. That is, our interpretation and valuation functions will assign truth values to formulas relative to possible worlds, rather than absolutely. Truth values of propositional-logic compound formulas—that is, negations and conditionals—will be determined by truth tables within each world; $\sim\phi$, for example, will be true in a world iff ϕ is false in that world. But the truth value of $\Box\phi$ in a world won't be determined by the truth value of ϕ in that world; the truth value of ϕ in *other* worlds will also be relevant.

Specifically, $\Box\phi$ will count as true in a world iff ϕ is true in every world that is "accessible" from the first world. What does "accessible" mean? Each model will come equipped with a binary relation, $\mathscr{R}$, over the set of possible worlds; we will say that world v is "accessible from" world w when $\mathscr{R}wv$. The intuitive idea is that $\mathscr{R}wv$ if and only if v is *possible relative to* w. That is, if you live in world w, then from your perspective, the events in world v are possible.

The idea that what is possible might vary depending on what possible world you live in might at first seem strange, but it isn't really. "It is physically impossible to travel faster than the speed of light" is true in the actual world, but false in worlds where the laws of nature allow faster-than-light travel.

On to the semantics. We first define a generic notion of an MPL-model, which we'll then use to give a semantics for different modal systems:

DEFINITION OF MODEL: An MPL-model is an ordered triple, $\langle \mathscr{W}, \mathscr{R}, \mathscr{I} \rangle$, where:

- $\mathscr{W}$ is a non-empty set of objects   ("possible worlds")
- $\mathscr{R}$ is a binary relation over $\mathscr{W}$ ("accessibility relation")
- $\mathscr{I}$ is a two-place function that assigns 0 or 1 to each sentence letter, relative to ("in") each world—that is, for any sentence letter α, and any $w \in \mathscr{W}$, $\mathscr{I}(\alpha, w)$ is either 0 or 1.   ("interpretation function")

Each MPL-model contains a set $\mathscr{W}$ of possible worlds, and an accessibility relation $\mathscr{R}$ over $\mathscr{W}$. $\langle \mathscr{W}, \mathscr{R} \rangle$ is sometimes called the model's *frame*. Think of the frame as giving the "structure" of the model's space of possible worlds: it says how many worlds there are, and which worlds are accessible from which. In addition to a frame, each model also contains an interpretation function $\mathscr{I}$, which assigns truth values to sentence letters in worlds.

MPL-models are the configurations for modal propositional logic (recall section 2.2). A configuration is supposed to represent both a way for the world to be, and also the meanings of nonlogical expressions. In MPL-models, the former is represented by the frame. (When we say that a configuration represents "the world", we don't just mean the actual world. "The world" signifies, rather, *reality*, which is here thought of as including the entire space of possible worlds.) The latter is represented by the interpretation function. (Recall that in propositional logic, the meaning of a sentence letter was a mere truth value. The meaning is now richer: a truth value for each possible world.)

A model's interpretation function assigns truth values only to sentence letters. But the sum total of all the truth values of sentence letters in worlds, together with the frame, determines the truth values of all complex wffs, again relative to worlds. It is the job of the model's valuation function to specify exactly how these truth values get determined:

DEFINITION OF VALUATION: Where $\mathscr{M}$ $(= \langle \mathscr{W}, \mathscr{R}, \mathscr{I} \rangle)$ is any MPL-model, the *valuation* for $\mathscr{M}$, $V_{\mathscr{M}}$, is defined as the two-place function that assigns either 0 or 1 to each wff relative to each member of $\mathscr{W}$, subject to the following constraints, where α is any sentence letter, ϕ and ψ are any wffs, and w is any member of $\mathscr{W}$:

$$V_{\mathscr{M}}(\alpha, w) = \mathscr{I}(\alpha, w)$$
$$V_{\mathscr{M}}(\sim\phi, w) = 1 \text{ iff } V_{\mathscr{M}}(\phi, w) = 0$$
$$V_{\mathscr{M}}(\phi{\rightarrow}\psi, w) = 1 \text{ iff either } V_{\mathscr{M}}(\phi, w) = 0 \text{ or } V_{\mathscr{M}}(\psi, w) = 1$$
$$V_{\mathscr{M}}(\Box\phi, w) = 1 \text{ iff for each } v \in \mathscr{W}, \text{if } \mathscr{R}wv, \text{then } V_{\mathscr{M}}(\phi, v) = 1$$

What about truth values for complex formulas containing $\wedge, \vee, \leftrightarrow, \Diamond$, and ⥽? Given the definitions of these defined connectives in terms of the primitive connectives, it is easy to prove that the following derived conditions hold:

$$V_{\mathscr{M}}(\phi\wedge\psi, w) = 1 \text{ iff } V_{\mathscr{M}}(\phi, w) = 1 \text{ and } V_{\mathscr{M}}(\psi, w) = 1$$
$$V_{\mathscr{M}}(\phi\vee\psi, w) = 1 \text{ iff } V_{\mathscr{M}}(\phi, w) = 1 \text{ or } V_{\mathscr{M}}(\psi, w) = 1$$
$$V_{\mathscr{M}}(\phi\leftrightarrow\psi, w) = 1 \text{ iff } V_{\mathscr{M}}(\phi, w) = V_{\mathscr{M}}(\psi, w)$$
$$V_{\mathscr{M}}(\Diamond\phi, w) = 1 \text{ iff for some } v \in \mathscr{W}, \mathscr{R}wv \text{ and } V_{\mathscr{M}}(\phi, v) = 1$$
$$V_{\mathscr{M}}(\phi{⥽}\psi, w) = 1 \text{ iff for each } v \in \mathscr{W}, \text{ if } \mathscr{R}wv \text{ then either } V_{\mathscr{M}}(\phi, v) = 0 \text{ or }$$
$$V_{\mathscr{M}}(\psi, v) = 1$$

So far, we have introduced a generic notion of an MPL-model, and have defined the notion of a wff's being true in a world in an MPL-model. But remember C. I. Lewis's plight: it wasn't clear which modal formulas ought to count as logical truths. His response, and our response, is to construct different modal systems, in which different formulas count as logical truths. The systems we will discuss are named: K, D, T, B, S4, S5. Here in our discussion of semantics, we will come up with different definitions of what counts as a model, one for each system: K, D, T, B, S4, S5. As a result, different formulas will come out valid in the different systems. For example, the formula $\Box P{\rightarrow}\Box\Box P$ is going to come out valid in S4 and S5, but not in the other systems.

The models for the different systems differ according to the formal properties of their accessibility relations. (Formal properties of relations were discussed in section 1.8.) For example, we will define a model for system T ("T-model") as any MPL-model whose accessibility relation is reflexive (in $\mathscr{W}$, the set of worlds in that model). Here is the definition:

DEFINITION OF MODEL FOR MODAL SYSTEMS: An "S-model", for any of our systems S, is defined as an MPL-model $\langle \mathscr{W}, \mathscr{R}, \mathscr{I} \rangle$ whose accessibility relation $\mathscr{R}$ has the formal feature given for system S in the following chart:

System	accessibility relation must be
K	no requirement
D	serial (in $\mathscr{W}$)
T	reflexive (in $\mathscr{W}$)
B	reflexive (in $\mathscr{W}$) and symmetric
S4	reflexive (in $\mathscr{W}$) and transitive
S5	reflexive (in $\mathscr{W}$), symmetric, and transitive

Thus, *any* MPL-model counts as a K-model, whereas the requirements for the other systems are more stringent.

Our next task is to define validity and semantic consequence for the various systems. A slight wrinkle arises: we can't just define validity as "truth in all models", since formulas aren't simply true or false in MPL-models; they're true or false in various worlds in these models. Instead, we first define a notion of being valid in an MPL-model:

DEFINITION OF VALIDITY IN AN MPL-MODEL: An MPL-wff ϕ is valid in MPL-model $\mathcal{M}$ $(= \langle \mathcal{W}, \mathcal{R}, \mathcal{I} \rangle$ iff for every $w \in \mathcal{W}$, $V_{\mathcal{M}}(\phi, w) = 1$.

Finally we can give the desired definitions:

DEFINITION OF VALIDITY AND SEMANTIC CONSEQUENCE:

- An MPL-wff is valid in system S (where S is either K, D, T, B, S4, or S5) iff it is valid in every S-model
- MPL-wff ϕ is a semantic consequence in system S of set of MPL-wffs Γ iff for every S-model $\langle \mathcal{W}, \mathcal{R}, \mathcal{I} \rangle$ and each $w \in \mathcal{W}$, if $V_{\mathcal{M}}(\gamma, w) = 1$ for each $\gamma \in \Gamma$, then $V_{\mathcal{M}}(\phi, w) = 1$

As before, we'll use the $\vDash$ notation for validity and semantic consequence. But since we have many modal systems, if we claim that a formula is valid, we'll need to indicate which system we're talking about. Let's do that by subscripting $\vDash$ with the name of the system; e.g., "$\vDash_T \phi$" means that ϕ is T-valid.

It's important to get clear on the status of possible-worlds lingo here. Where $\langle \mathcal{W}, \mathcal{R}, \mathcal{I} \rangle$ is an MPL-model, we call the members of $\mathcal{W}$ "worlds", and we call $\mathcal{R}$ the "accessibility" relation. This is certainly a vivid way to talk about these models. But officially, $\mathcal{W}$ is nothing but a nonempty set, any old nonempty set. Its members needn't be the kinds of things metaphysicians call possible worlds. They can be numbers, people, bananas—whatever you like. Similarly for $\mathcal{R}$ and $\mathcal{I}$. The former is just defined to be any old binary relation on $\mathcal{W}$; the latter is just defined to be any old function mapping each pair of a sentence letter and a member of $\mathcal{W}$ to either 1 or 0. Neither needs to have anything to do with the metaphysics of modality. Officially, then, the possible-worlds talk we use to describe our models is just talk, not heavy-duty metaphysics.

Still, models are usually intended to depict some aspect of the real world. The usual intention is that wffs get their truth values within models in a parallel fashion to how natural-language sentences are made true by the real world. So if natural-language modal sentences aren't made true by anything like possible worlds, then possible-worlds semantics would be less valuable than, say, the usual semantics for nonmodal propositional and predicate logic. To be sure, possible-worlds semantics would still be useful for various purely formal purposes. For example, given the soundness proofs we will give in section 6.5, the semantics could still be used to establish facts about unprovability in the axiomatic systems to be introduced in section 6.4. But it would be hard to see why possible-worlds models would shed any light on the meanings of English modal words, or why truth-in-all-possible-worlds-models would be a good way of modeling (genuine) logical truth for modal statements.

On the other hand, if English modal sentences *are* made true by facts about possible worlds, then the semantics takes on a greater importance. Perhaps then we can, for example, decide what the right logic is, for a given strength of necessity, by reflecting on the formal properties of the accessibility relation—the real accessibility relation, over real possible worlds, not the relation $\mathcal{R}$ over the members of $\mathcal{W}$ in our models. Suppose we're considering some strength, M, of modality. A (real) possible world v is M-accessible from another world, w, iff what happens in v counts as being M-possible, from the point of view of w. Perhaps we can figure out the logic of M-necessity and M-possibility by investigating the formal properties of M-accessibility.

Consider deontic necessity and possibility, for example: a proposition is deontically necessary iff it ought to be the case; a proposition is deontically possible iff it is morally acceptable that it be the case. The relation of deontic accessibility seems not to be reflexive: in an imperfect world like our own, many things that ought not to be true are nevertheless true. Thus a world can fail to be deontically accessible relative to itself. (As we will see, this corresponds to the fact that deontic necessity is non-alethic: it does not imply truth.) On the other hand, one might argue, deontic accessibility *is* serial, since surely there must always be *some* deontically accessible world—some world in which what occurs is morally acceptable. (To deny this would be to admit that everything could be forbidden.) So perhaps system D gives the logic of deontic necessity and possibility (see also section 7.1).

To take one other example: some have argued that the relation of *metaphysical* accessibility (the relation relevant to metaphysical necessity and possibility) is a total relation: every world is metaphysically possible relative to every other.[71] What modal logic would result from requiring $\mathcal{R}$ to be a total (in $\mathcal{W}$) relation? The answer is: S5. In S5-models, $\mathcal{R}$ must be reflexive, symmetric, and transitive—i.e., an equivalence relation; and you get the same valid formulas whether you require $\mathcal{R}$ to be a total relation or an equivalence relation (see exercise 6.1). So, if the (real) metaphysical accessibility relation is a total relation, the correct logic for metaphysical necessity is S5. But others have argued that metaphysical accessibility is intransitive.[72] Perhaps one possible world is metaphysically accessible from another only if the individuals in the latter world aren't too different from how they are in the former world—only if such differences are below a certain threshold. In that case, it might be argued, a world in which I'm a frog is not metaphysically accessible from the actual world: any world in which I'm that drastically different from my actual, human, self just isn't metaphysically possible, relative to actuality. But perhaps a world, w, in which I'm a human–frog hybrid *is* accessible from the actual world (the difference between a human and a human–frog hybrid is below the threshold); and perhaps the frog world is accessible from w (since the difference between a human–frog hybrid and a

---

[71]See Lewis (1986, 246).
[72]Compare Salmon (1986).

frog is also below the threshold). If so, then metaphysical accessibility is intransitive. Metaphysical accessibility is clearly reflexive. So perhaps the logic of metaphysical possibility is given by system B or system T.

> **Exercise 6.1**** Let O be the modal system given by the requirement that $\mathscr{R}$ must be total (in $\mathscr{W}$). Show that $\vDash_O \phi$ iff $\vDash_{S_5} \phi$.

6.3.2 Establishing validity in MPL

Given our definitions, we can now show particular formulas to be valid in various systems.

Example 6.1: Show that the wff $\square(P \lor {\sim}P)$ is K-valid. K-validity is validity-in-all-MPL-models; and validity in a model is truth-in-every-world-of-the-model. So, consider any MPL-model $\langle \mathscr{W}, \mathscr{R}, \mathscr{I} \rangle$, and let w be any world in $\mathscr{W}$; we must show that $V_{\mathscr{M}}(\square(P \lor {\sim}P), w) = 1$. (As before, I'll start to omit the subscript $\mathscr{M}$ on $V_{\mathscr{M}}$ when it's clear which model we're talking about.)

(i) Suppose for reductio that $V(\square(P \lor {\sim}P), w) = 0$. Then, by the truth condition for $\square$ in the definition of the valuation function, there is some world, v, such that $\mathscr{R}wv$ and $V(P \lor {\sim}P, v) = 0$. And so, given the (derived) truth condition for $\lor$, $V(P, v) = 0$ and ...

(ii) ... $V({\sim}P, v) = 0$. Thus $V(P, v) = 1$ (truth condition for $\sim$), contradicting (i).

Thus $\vDash_K \square(P \lor {\sim}P)$.

Note that similar reasoning would establish $\vDash_K \square\phi$, for any tautology ϕ. For within any world, the truth values of complex statements of propositional logic are determined by the truth values of their constituents in that world by the usual truth tables. So if ϕ is a tautology, it will be true in any world in any model; hence $\square\phi$ will turn out true in any world in any model.

Example 6.2: Show that $\vDash_T (\Diamond\square(P{\rightarrow}Q) \land \square P) \rightarrow \Diamond Q$. Let w be any world in any T-model $\mathscr{M}$; we must show that $V_{\mathscr{M}}((\Diamond\square(P{\rightarrow}Q) \land \square P) \rightarrow \Diamond Q, w) = 1$:

(i) Suppose for reductio that $V((\Diamond\square(P{\rightarrow}Q) \land \square P) \rightarrow \Diamond Q, w) = 0$.

(ii) So $V(\Diamond\square(P{\rightarrow}Q) \land \square P, w) = 1$ and ...

(iii) ... $V(\Diamond Q, w) = 0$. So Q is false in every world accessible from w.

(iv) From (ii), $\Diamond\square(P{\rightarrow}Q)$ is true in w, and so $V(\square(P{\rightarrow}Q), v) = 1$, for some world, call it v, such that $\mathscr{R}wv$.

(v) From (ii), $V(\square P, w) = 1$. So, by the truth condition for the $\square$, P is true in every world accessible from w; since $\mathscr{R}wv$, it follows that $V(P, v) = 1$. $V(Q, v) = 0$ given (iii). So $V(P{\rightarrow}Q, v) = 0$.

(vi) From (iv), $P{\rightarrow}Q$ is true in every world accessible from v; since $\mathscr{M}$ is a T-model, $\mathscr{R}$ is reflexive; so $\mathscr{R}vv$; so $V(P{\rightarrow}Q, v) = 1$, contradicting (v).

The last example showed that the formula $(\Diamond\Box(P{\to}Q)\wedge\Box P) \to \Diamond Q$ is valid in T. Suppose we wanted to show that it is also valid in S4. What more would we have to do? Nothing! To be S4-valid is to be valid in every S4-model. But a quick look at the definitions shows that every S4-model is a T-model. So, since we already know that the formula is valid in all T-models, we may conclude that it must be valid in all S4-models without doing a separate proof:

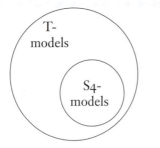

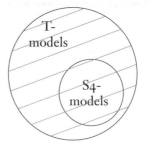

The S4-models are a subset of the T-models.

So if a formula is valid in all T-models, it's automatically valid in all S4-models

Think of it another way. A proof that a wff is S4-valid *may* use the information that the accessibility relation is both transitive and reflexive. But it doesn't need to. So the T-validity proof in example 6.2 also counts as an S4-validity proof. (It also counts as a B-validity proof and an S5-validity proof.) But it doesn't count as a K-validity proof, since it assumes in line (vi) that $\mathscr{R}$ is reflexive, and a model for system K needn't be reflexive. (In fact $(\Diamond\Box(P{\to}Q)\wedge\Box P) \to \Diamond Q$ isn't K-valid, as we'll be able to demonstrate shortly.)

Consider the following diagram of systems:

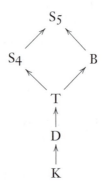

An arrow from one system to another indicates that validity in the first system implies validity in the second system. For example, all D-valid wffs are also T-valid. For if a wff is valid in all D-models, then, since every T-model is also a D-model (reflexivity implies seriality), it must be valid in all T-models as well.

S5 is the strongest system, since it has the most valid formulas. That's because it has the fewest models: it's easy to be S5-valid since there are so few potentially falsifying models. K is the weakest system—fewest validities—since it has the most potentially falsifying models. The other systems are intermediate.

Notice that the diagram isn't linear. Both B and S4 are stronger than T: each contains all the T-valid formulas and more besides. And S5 is stronger than both B and S4. But (as we will see below) neither B nor S4 is stronger than the other (nor are they equally strong): some B-valid wffs aren't S4-valid, and some S4-valid wffs aren't B-valid. (The definitions of B and S4 hint at this. B requires symmetry but not transitivity, whereas S4 requires transitivity but not symmetry, so some B-models aren't S4-models, and some S4-models aren't B-models.)

Suppose you're given a formula, and for each system in which it is valid, you want to give a semantic proof of its validity. This needn't require multiple semantic proofs. As we saw with example 6.2, to prove that a wff is valid in a number of systems, it suffices to give a validity proof in the weakest of those systems, since that very proof will automatically be a proof that it is valid in all stronger systems. For example, a K-validity proof is itself a validity proof for D, T, B, S4, and S5. But there is an exception. Suppose a wff is *not* valid in T, but you've given a semantic proof of its validity in B. This proof also shows that the wff is S5-valid, since every S5-model is a B-model. But you can't yet conclude that the wff is S4-valid, since not every S4-model is a B-model. Another semantic proof may be needed: of the formula's S4-validity. (Of course, the formula may not be S4-valid.) So: when a wff is valid in both B and S4, but not in T, two semantic proofs of its validity are needed.

We are now in a position to do validity proofs. But as we'll see in the next section, it's often easier to do proofs of validity when one has failed to construct a countermodel for a formula.

Exercise 6.2 Use validity proofs to demonstrate the following:

(a) $\vDash_D [\Box P \wedge \Box(\sim P \vee Q)] \rightarrow \Diamond Q$

(b) $\vDash_{S4} \Diamond\Diamond(P \wedge Q) \rightarrow \Diamond Q$

6.3.3 *Establishing invalidity in MPL*

We have a definition of validity for the various systems, and we've shown how to establish validity of particular formulas. (We have also defined semantic consequence for these systems, but our focus will be on validity.) Now we'll see how to establish *in*validity. We establish that a formula is invalid by constructing a countermodel for it—a model containing a world in which the formula is false. (Since validity means truth in every world in every model, the existence of a single countermodel establishes invalidity.)

I'm going to describe a helpful graphical procedure, introduced by Hughes and Cresswell (1996), for constructing countermodels. Now, it's always an option to bypass the graphical procedure and directly intuit what a countermodel might look like. But the graphical procedure makes things a lot easier, especially with more complicated formulas.

I'll illustrate the procedure by using it to show that the wff $\Diamond P \rightarrow \Box P$ is *not* K-valid. To be K-valid, a wff must be valid in all MPL-models, so all we must do is find one MPL-model in which $\Diamond P \rightarrow \Box P$ is false in some world.

Place the formula in a box   We begin by drawing a box, which represents some chosen world in the model we're in the process of pictorially constructing. The goal is to make the formula false in this world. In these examples I'll always call this first world "r":

$$\text{r}\ \boxed{\ \Diamond P \rightarrow \Box P\ }$$

Now, since the box represents a world, we should have some way of representing the accessibility relation. What worlds are accessible from r; what worlds does r "see"? Well, to represent one world (box) seeing another, we'll draw an arrow from the first to the second. But in this case we don't need to draw any arrows. All we're trying to show is that $\Diamond P \rightarrow \Box P$ is K-invalid, and the accessibility relation for system K doesn't even need to be serial—no world needs to see any worlds at all. So we'll forget about other worlds and arrows for the time being.

Make the formula false in the world   We'll indicate a formula's truth value by writing that truth value above the formula's major connective. (The "major connective" of a wff is the last connective that was added when the wff was formed via the rules of grammar.[73] Thus the major connective of $P \rightarrow \Box Q$ is the $\rightarrow$, and the major connective of $\Box(P \rightarrow \Box Q)$ is the leftmost $\Box$.) So to indicate that $\Diamond P \rightarrow \Box P$ is to be false in this model, we'll put a 0 above its arrow:

$$\text{r}\ \boxed{\begin{array}{c} 0 \\ \Diamond P \rightarrow \Box P \end{array}}$$

Enter forced truth values   Assigning a truth value to a formula sometimes forces us to assign truth values to other formulas in the same world. For example, if we make a conjunction true in a world, then we must make each of its conjuncts true in that world; and if we make a conditional false in a world, we must make its antecedent true and its consequent false in that world. In the current example, since we've made $\Diamond P \rightarrow \Box P$ false in r, we've got to make $\Diamond P$ true in r (indicated on the diagram by a 1 over its major connective, the $\Diamond$), and we've got to make its consequent $\Box P$ false in r:

$$\text{r}\ \boxed{\begin{array}{c} 1\quad\ \ 0\ 0 \\ \Diamond P \rightarrow \Box P \end{array}}$$

---

[73] In talking about major connectives, let's treat nonprimitive connectives as if they were primitive. Thus the major connective of $\Box P \wedge \sim Q$ is the $\wedge$.

Enter asterisks When we assign a truth value to a modal formula, we thereby commit ourselves to assigning certain other truth values to various formulas at various worlds. For example, when we make $\Diamond P$ true at r, we commit ourselves to making P true in some world that r sees. To remind ourselves of this commitment, we'll put an asterisk (∗) below $\Diamond P$. An asterisk *below* indicates a commitment to there being *some* world of a certain sort. Similarly, since $\Box P$ is false in r, this means that P must be false in some world P sees (if it were true in all such worlds, then $\Box P$ would be true in r). We again have a commitment to there being some world of a certain sort, so we enter an asterisk below $\Box P$ as well:

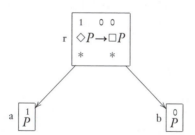

Discharge bottom asterisks The next step is to fulfill the commitments we incurred when we added the bottom asterisks. For each, we need to add a world to the diagram. The first asterisk requires us to add a world in which P is true; the second requires us to add a world in which P is false. We do this as follows:

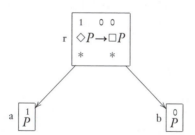

The official model We now have a diagram of a K-model containing a world in which $\Diamond P \rightarrow \Box P$ is false. But we need to produce an official model, according to the official definition of a model. A model is an ordered triple $\langle \mathscr{W}, \mathscr{R}, \mathscr{I} \rangle$, so we must specify the model's three members.

$\mathscr{W}$ is simply the set of worlds I depicted with the boxes:

$$\mathscr{W} = \{r, a, b\}$$

What *are* r, a, and b? Let's just take them to be the letters 'r', 'a', and 'b'. No reason not to—the members of $\mathscr{W}$, recall, can be any things whatsoever.

Next, the accessibility relation. This is represented on the diagram by the arrows. In our model, there is an arrow from r to a, an arrow from r to b, and no other arrows. Thus the diagram represents that r sees a, that r sees b, and that there are no further cases of seeing. Now, remember that the accessibility relation, like all relations, is a set of ordered pairs. So, we simply write:

$$\mathscr{R} = \{\langle r, a \rangle, \langle r, b \rangle\}$$

That is, we write out the set of all ordered pairs $\langle w_1, w_2 \rangle$ such that w_1 "sees" w_2.

Finally, we need to specify the interpretation function, $\mathscr{I}$, which assigns truth values to sentence letters at worlds. In our model, $\mathscr{I}$ must assign 1 to P at world a, and 0 to P at world b. Now, our official definition requires an interpretation to assign a truth value to each of the infinitely many sentence letters at each world; but so long as P is true in world a and false in world b, it doesn't matter what other truth values $\mathscr{I}$ assigns. So let's just (arbitrarily) choose to make all other sentence letters false in all worlds in the model. We have, then:

$$\mathscr{I}(P, a) = 1$$
$$\mathscr{I}(P, b) = 0$$
$$\mathscr{I}(\alpha, w) = 0 \text{ for all other sentence letters } \alpha \text{ and worlds } w$$

That's it—we're done. We have produced a model in which $\diamond P \rightarrow \square P$ is false in some world; hence this formula is not valid in all models; and hence it's not K-valid: $\not\models_K \diamond P \rightarrow \square P$.

Check the model   At the end of this process, it's a good idea to double-check that your model is correct. This involves various things. First, make sure that you've succeeded in producing the correct kind of model. For example, if you're trying to produce a T-model, make sure that the accessibility relation you've written down is reflexive. (In our case, we were trying only to construct a K-model, and so for us this step is trivial.) Second, make sure that the formula in question really does come out false in one of the worlds in your model.

Simplifying models   Sometimes a model can be simplified. In the countermodel for $\diamond P \rightarrow \square P$, we needn't have used three worlds. We added world a because the truth of $\diamond P$ called for a world that r sees in which P is true. But we needn't have made that a *new* world—we could have made P true in r and made r see itself. (We couldn't have done that for both asterisks; that would have made P both true and false in r.) So, we could make this one simplification:

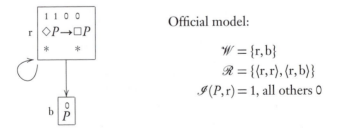

Official model:

$$\mathscr{W} = \{r, b\}$$
$$\mathscr{R} = \{\langle r, r \rangle, \langle r, b \rangle\}$$
$$\mathscr{I}(P, r) = 1, \text{ all others } 0$$

Adapting models to different systems   We have shown that $\diamond P \rightarrow \square P$ is not K-valid. Next let's show that this formula isn't D-valid—that it is false in some world of some model with a serial accessibility relation. The model we just constructed won't do, since its accessibility relation isn't serial: world b doesn't see any world. But we can easily change that:

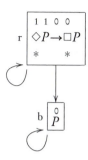

Official model:

$$\mathscr{W} = \{r, b\}$$
$$\mathscr{R} = \{\langle r, r \rangle, \langle r, b \rangle, \langle b, b \rangle\}$$
$$\mathscr{I}(P, r) = 1, \text{ all others } 0$$

Suppose we want now to show that $\Diamond P \rightarrow \Box P$ isn't T-valid. What more must we do? Nothing! The model we just displayed is a T-model, in addition to being a D-model, since its accessibility relation is reflexive. In fact, its accessibility relation is also transitive, so it's also an S4-model. What about B? It's easy to make the accessibility relation symmetric:

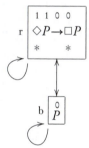

Official model:

$$\mathscr{W} = \{r, b\}$$
$$\mathscr{R} = \{\langle r, r \rangle, \langle r, b \rangle, \langle b, b \rangle, \langle b, r \rangle\}$$
$$\mathscr{I}(P, r) = 1, \text{ all others } 0$$

So we've established B-invalidity as well. In fact, the model just displayed is also an S5-model since its accessibility relation is an equivalence relation. And so, since any S5-model is also a K-, D-, T-, B-, and S4-model, this one model shows that $\Diamond P \rightarrow \Box P$ is not valid in *any* of our systems. So we have established that: $\nvDash_{K,D,T,B,S4,S5} \Diamond P \rightarrow \Box P$.

In this case it wouldn't have been hard to move straight to the final S5-model, right from the start. But in more difficult cases, it's best to proceed slowly, as I did here. Try first for a countermodel in K. Then build the model up gradually, trying to make its accessibility relation satisfy the requirements of stronger systems. When you get a countermodel in a stronger system (a system with more requirements on its models), that very countermodel will establish invalidity in all weaker systems. Keep in mind the diagram of systems:

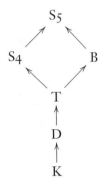

An arrow from one system to another, recall, indicates that validity in the first system implies validity in the second. The arrows also indicate facts about *invalidity*, but in reverse: when an arrow points from one system to another, then invalidity in the *second* system implies invalidity in the *first*. For example, if a wff is invalid in T, then it is invalid in D. (That's because every T-model is a D-model; a countermodel in T is therefore a countermodel in D.)

When our task is to discover the systems in which a given formula is invalid, usually only one countermodel will be needed—a countermodel in the strongest system in which the formula is invalid. But there is an exception involving B and S4. Suppose a given formula is valid in S5, but we discover a model showing that it isn't valid in B. That model is automatically a T-, D-, and K-model, so we know that the formula isn't T-, D-, or K-valid. But we don't yet know about S4-validity. If the formula is S4-invalid, then we will need to produce a second countermodel, an S4-countermodel. (Notice that the B-model couldn't *already* be an S4-model. If it were, then its accessibility relation would be reflexive, symmetric, and transitive, and so it would be an S5-model, contradicting the fact that the formula was S5-valid.)

So far we have the following steps for constructing countermodels:

1. Place the formula in a box and make it false

2. Enter forced truth values

3. Enter asterisks

4. Discharge bottom asterisks

5. The official model

We need to add to this list.

Top asterisks   Let's try to get a countermodel for $\Diamond\Box P \to \Box\Diamond P$ in all the systems in which it is invalid. A cautious beginning would be to try for a K-model. After the first few steps, we have:

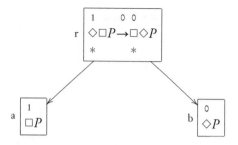

At this point we have a true □ (in world a) and a false ◇ (in world b). Like true ◇s and false □s, these generate commitments pertaining to other worlds. But unlike true ◇s and false □s, they don't commit us to the existence of *some* accessible world of a certain type; they carry commitments for *every* accessible world. The true □P in world a, for example, requires us to make P true in every world accessible from a. Similarly, the falsity of ◇P in world b commits us to making P false in every world accessible from b. We indicate such commitments—universal rather than existential commitments—by putting asterisks *above* the relevant modal operators:

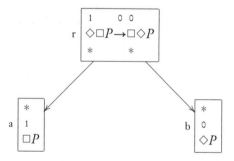

Now, how can we honor these commitments; how must we "discharge" these asterisks? In this case, when trying to construct a K-model, we don't need to do anything. Since world a, for example, doesn't see any world, P is automatically true in every world that world a sees; the statement "for every world, w, if $\mathscr{R}aw$, then $V(P, w) = 1$" is vacuously true. Same goes for b—P is automatically false in all worlds that b sees. So we've got a K-model in which ◇□P→□◇P is false.

Now let's turn the model into a D-model. Every world must now see at least one world. Let's try:

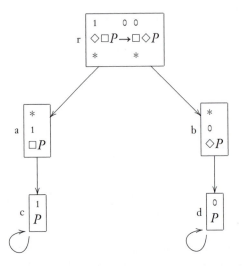

I added worlds c and d, so that a and b would each see at least one world. (Further, worlds c and d each had to see a world, to keep the relation serial. I could have added new worlds e and f seen by c and d, but e and f would have needed to see some worlds. So I just let c and d see themselves.) But once c and d were added, discharging the upper asterisks in worlds a and b required making P true in c and false in d (since a sees c and b sees d).

Let's now try for a T-model. Worlds a and b must now see themselves. But then we no longer need worlds c and d, since they were added just to make the relation serial. So we can simplify:

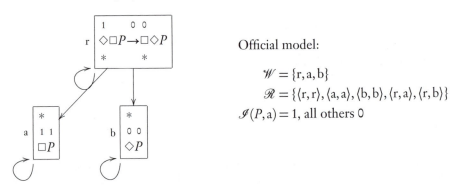

Official model:

$$\mathcal{W} = \{r, a, b\}$$
$$\mathcal{R} = \{\langle r, r \rangle, \langle a, a \rangle, \langle b, b \rangle, \langle r, a \rangle, \langle r, b \rangle\}$$
$$\mathcal{I}(P, a) = 1, \text{ all others } 0$$

When you add arrows, you need to make sure that all top asterisks are discharged. In this case this required nothing of world r, since there were no top asterisks there. There were top asterisks in worlds a and b; these I discharged by making P be true in a and false in b.

Notice that I could have moved straight to this T-model—which is itself a D-model—rather than first going through the earlier mere D-model. However, this won't always be possible—sometimes you'll be able to get a D-model, but no T-model.

At this point let's verify that our model does indeed assign the value 0 to our formula $\Diamond\Box P\to\Box\Diamond P$. First notice that $\Box P$ is true in a (since a sees only one world—itself—and P is true there). But r sees a. So $\Diamond\Box P$ is true in r. Now, consider b. b sees only one world, itself; and P is false there. So $\Diamond P$ must also be false there. But r sees b. So $\Box\Diamond P$ is false in r. But now, the antecedent of $\Diamond\Box P\to\Box\Diamond P$ is true, while its consequent is false, at r. So that conditional is false in r. Which is what we wanted.

Onward. Our model is not a B-model since r sees a and b but they don't see r back. Suppose we try to make a and b see r:

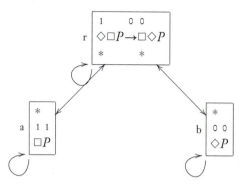

We must now make sure that all top asterisks are discharged. Since a now sees r, P must be true in r. But b sees r too, so P must be false in r. Since P can't be both true and false in r, we're stuck. We have failed to construct a B-model in which this formula is false.

Our failure to construct a B-countermodel suggests that it may be impossible to do so. We can *prove* that this is impossible by showing that the formula is true in every world of every B-model—that is, that the formula is B-valid. Let $\mathcal{M}=\langle\mathcal{W},\mathcal{R},\mathcal{I}\rangle$ be any model in which $\mathcal{R}$ is reflexive and symmetric, and consider any $w\in\mathcal{W}$; we must show that $V_{\mathcal{M}}(\Diamond\Box P\to\Box\Diamond P,w)=1$:

(i) Suppose for reductio that $V(\Diamond\Box P\to\Box\Diamond P,w)=0$. Then $V(\Diamond\Box P,w)=1$ and $V(\Box\Diamond P,w)=0$.

(ii) Given the former, for some v, $\mathcal{R}wv$ and $V(\Box P,v)=1$.

(iii) Given the latter, for some u, $\mathcal{R}wu$ and $V(\Diamond P,u)=0$.

(iv) From (ii), P is true in every world accessible from v; by symmetry, $\mathcal{R}vw$; so $V(P,w)=1$.

(v) From (iii), P is false in every world accessible from u; by symmetry, $\mathcal{R}uw$; so $V(P,w)=0$, contradicting (iv).

Just as we suspected: the formula is indeed B-valid; no wonder we failed to come up with a B-countermodel!

Might there be an S_5-countermodel? No: the B-validity proof we just constructed also shows that the formula is S_5-valid. What about an S_4-countermodel? The existence of the B-validity proof doesn't tell us one way or the other. Remember the diagram: validity in S4 doesn't imply validity in B, nor does validity in B imply validity in S4. So we must either try to come up with an S4-model, or try to construct an S4-semantic-validity proof. Usually it's best to try for a model. In the present case this is easy: the T-model we gave earlier is itself an S4-model. Thus, on the basis of that model, we can conclude that $\nvDash_{K,D,T,S4} \Diamond\Box P \to \Box\Diamond P$.

We have accomplished our task. We gave an S4-countermodel, which is a countermodel for each system in which $\Diamond\Box P \to \Box\Diamond P$ is invalid. And we gave a validity proof in B, which is a validity proof for each system in which the formula is valid.

Example 6.3: Determine in which systems $\Diamond\Box P \to \Diamond\Box\Diamond\Box P$ is valid and in which systems it is invalid. We can get a T-model as follows:

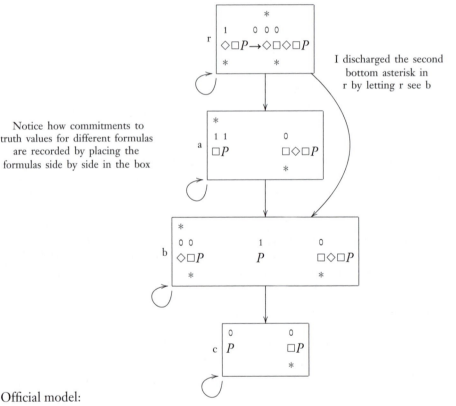

I discharged the second bottom asterisk in r by letting r see b

Notice how commitments to truth values for different formulas are recorded by placing the formulas side by side in the box

Official model:

$$\mathcal{W} = \{r,a,b,c\}$$
$$\mathcal{R} = \{\langle r,r\rangle, \langle a,a\rangle, \langle b,b\rangle, \langle c,c\rangle, \langle r,a\rangle, \langle r,b\rangle, \langle a,b\rangle, \langle b,c\rangle\}$$
$$\mathcal{I}(P,a) = \mathcal{I}(P,b) = 1, \text{ all others } 0$$

Now consider what happens when we try to turn this model into a B-model. World b must see back to world a. But then the false $\Diamond\Box P$ in b conflicts with the true $\Box P$

in a. So it's time for a validity proof. In constructing this validity proof, we can be guided by our failed attempt to construct a countermodel (assuming all the choices leading to the failure were forced). In the following proof that the formula is B-valid, I use variables for worlds that match up with the attempted countermodel:

(i) Suppose for reductio that $V(\Diamond\Box P \rightarrow \Diamond\Box\Diamond\Box P, r) = 0$, in some world r in some B-model $\langle \mathscr{W}, \mathscr{R}, \mathscr{I} \rangle$. So $V(\Diamond\Box P, r) = 1$ and $V(\Diamond\Box\Diamond\Box P, r) = 0$.

(ii) Given the former, for some world a, $\mathscr{R}ra$ and $V(\Box P, a) = 1$.

(iii) Given the latter, since $\mathscr{R}ra$, $V(\Box\Diamond\Box P, a) = 0$. So for some b, $\mathscr{R}ab$ and $V(\Diamond\Box P, b) = 0$. By symmetry, $\mathscr{R}ba$; so $V(\Box P, a) = 0$, contradicting (ii).

We now have a T-model for the formula, and a proof that it is B-valid. The B-validity proof shows the formula to be S5-valid; the T-model shows it to be K- and D-invalid. We don't yet know about S4. So let's return to the T-model above and try to make its accessibility relation transitive. World a must then see world c, which is impossible since $\Box P$ is true in a and P is false in c. So we're ready for a S4-validity proof (the proof looks like the B-validity proof at first, but then diverges):

(i) Suppose for reductio that $V(\Diamond\Box P \rightarrow \Diamond\Box\Diamond\Box P, r) = 0$, in some world r in some B-model $\langle \mathscr{W}, \mathscr{R}, \mathscr{I} \rangle$. So $V(\Diamond\Box P, r) = 1$ and $V(\Diamond\Box\Diamond\Box P, r) = 0$.

(ii) Given the former, for some world a, $\mathscr{R}ra$ and $V(\Box P, a) = 1$.

(iii) Given the latter, since $\mathscr{R}ra$, $V(\Box\Diamond\Box P, a) = 0$. So for some b, $\mathscr{R}ab$ and $V(\Diamond\Box P, b) = 0$. By reflexivity, $\mathscr{R}bb$, so $V(\Box P, b) = 0$. So for some world c, $\mathscr{R}bc$ and $V(P, c) = 0$.

(iv) Since $\mathscr{R}ab$ and $\mathscr{R}bc$, by transitivity we have $\mathscr{R}ac$. So, given (ii), $V(P, c) = 1$, contradicting (iii).

Daggers   If we make a conditional false, we're forced to enter certain truth values for its components: 1 for the antecedent, 0 for the consequent. Similarly, making a conjunction true forces us to make its conjuncts true, making a disjunction false forces us to make its disjuncts false, and making a negation either true or false forces us to give the negated formula the opposite truth value. But consider making a disjunction true. Here we have a choice: we can make either disjunct true. We similarly have a choice for how to make a conditional true, or a conjunction false, or a biconditional either true or false.

When facing choices like these, it's best to delay making the choice as long as possible. After all, some other part of the model might force you to make one choice rather than the other. If you investigate the rest of the countermodel, and nothing has forced your hand, you may need then to make a guess: try one of the truth-value combinations open to you, and see whether you can finish the countermodel. If not, go back and try another combination.

To remind ourselves of these choices, we will place a dagger (†) underneath the major connective of the formula in question. Consider, as an example, constructing a countermodel for the formula $\Diamond(\Diamond P \vee \Box Q) \rightarrow (\Diamond P \vee Q)$. Throwing caution to the wind and going straight for a T-model, we have after a few steps:

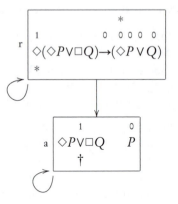

We still have to decide how to make $\diamond P \lor \Box Q$ true in world a: which disjunct to make true? Well, making $\Box Q$ true won't require adding another world to the model, so let's try that first. We have, then, a T-model:

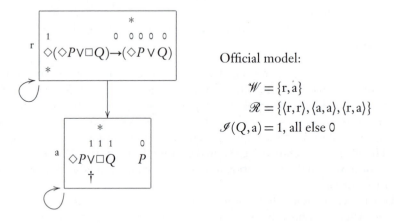

Official model:

$$\mathcal{W} = \{r, a\}$$
$$\mathcal{R} = \{\langle r, r \rangle, \langle a, a \rangle, \langle r, a \rangle\}$$
$$\mathcal{I}(Q, a) = 1, \text{ all else } 0$$

Next let's try to upgrade this to a B-model. We can't simply leave everything as is while letting world a see back to world r, since $\Box Q$ is true in a and Q is false in r. But there's another possibility. We weren't forced to discharge the dagger in world a by making $\Box Q$ true. So let's explore the other possibility; let's make $\diamond P$ true:

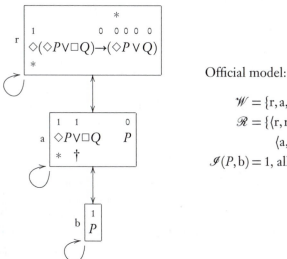

Official model:

$$\mathcal{W} = \{r, a, b\}$$
$$\mathcal{R} = \{\langle r,r\rangle, \langle a,a\rangle, \langle b,b\rangle, \langle r,a\rangle, \langle a,r\rangle,$$
$$\langle a,b\rangle, \langle b,a\rangle\}$$
$$\mathcal{I}(P, b) = 1, \text{ all else } 0$$

What about an S4-model? We can't just add the arrows demanded by transitivity to our B-model, since $\Diamond P$ is false in world r and P is true in world b. What we can do instead is revisit the choice of which disjunct of $\Diamond P \vee \Box Q$ to make true. Instead of making $\Diamond P$ true, we can make $\Box Q$ true, as we did when we constructed our T-model. In fact, that T-model is already an S4-model.

So, we have countermodels in both S4 and B. The first resulted from one choice for discharging the dagger in world a, the second from the other choice. An S5-model, though, looks impossible. When we made the left disjunct of $\Diamond P \vee \Box Q$ true we couldn't make the accessibility relation transitive, and when we made the right disjunct true we couldn't make the accessibility relation symmetric. So apparently we can't make the accessibility relation both transitive and symmetric. Here is an S5-validity proof, based on this line of thought. Note the "separation of cases" reasoning:

(i) Suppose for reductio that $V(\Diamond(\Diamond P \vee \Box Q) \rightarrow (\Diamond P \vee Q), r) = 0$, for some world r in some S5-model. Then $V(\Diamond(\Diamond P \vee \Box Q), r) = 1$ and ...

(ii) ...$V(\Diamond P \vee Q, r) = 0$. So $V(\Diamond P, r) = 0$ and $V(Q, r) = 0$.

(iii) Given (i), for some world a, $\mathcal{R} ra$ and $V(\Diamond P \vee \Box Q, a) = 1$. So, either $V(\Diamond P, a) = 1$ or $V(\Box Q, a) = 1$.

(iv) The first possibility leads to a contradiction. For if $V(\Diamond P, a) = 1$, then for some b, $\mathcal{R} ab$ and $V(P, b) = 1$. But then given transitivity, $\mathcal{R} r b$, and so, given $V(\Diamond P, r) = 0$ (line (ii)), $V(P, b) = 0$.

(v) So does the second. For symmetry yields $\mathcal{R} ar$, so if $V(\Box Q, a) = 1$ then $V(Q, r) = 1$, contradicting (ii).

(vi) Either way we have a contradiction.

So we have demonstrated that $\vDash_{S_5} \Diamond(\Diamond P \vee \Box Q) \rightarrow (\Diamond P \vee Q)$.

Summary of steps Here, then, is a final list of the steps for constructing countermodels:

1. Place the formula in a box and make it false
2. Enter forced truth values
3. Enter daggers, and after all forced moves are over…
4. …enter asterisks
5. Discharge asterisks (hint: do bottom asterisks first)
6. Back to step 2 if not finished
7. The official model

Exercise 6.3 For each of the following wffs, give a countermodel for every system in which it is not valid, and give a semantic validity proof for every system in which it is valid. When you use a single countermodel or validity proof for multiple systems, indicate which systems it is good for.

(a)* $\Box[P\rightarrow\Diamond(Q\rightarrow R)]\rightarrow\Diamond[Q\rightarrow(\Box P\rightarrow\Diamond R)]$

(b) $\Diamond(P\wedge\Diamond Q)\rightarrow(\Box\Diamond P\rightarrow\Diamond\Box Q)$

(c) $\Box(P\vee\Diamond Q)\rightarrow(\Box P\vee\Diamond Q)$

(d)* $\Box(P\leftrightarrow Q)\rightarrow\Box(\Box P\leftrightarrow\Box Q)$

(e) $\Box(P\wedge Q)\rightarrow\Box\Box(\Diamond P\rightarrow\Diamond Q)$

(f) $\Box(\Box P\rightarrow Q)\rightarrow\Box(\Box P\rightarrow\Box Q)$

(g)* $\Diamond\Diamond\Box P\leftrightarrow\Box P$

(h) $\Diamond\Diamond P\rightarrow\Box\Diamond P$

(i) $\Box[\Box(P\rightarrow\Box P)\rightarrow\Box P]\rightarrow(\Diamond\Box P\rightarrow\Box P)$

6.4 Axiomatic systems of MPL

Let's turn next to proof theory. In one respect the proof-theoretic approach to logic is particularly attractive in the case of modal logic. Model-theoretic approaches are most attractive when they are "realistic"—when truth-in-a-model parallels real truth in the real world. But possible-worlds models are realistic only if a possible-worlds metaphysics of modality is correct. Proof theory, on the other hand, has the virtue of caution, since its attraction does not rely on assumptions about semantics. Opponents of possible-worlds metaphysics can always retreat to proof theory and characterize the inferential roles of modal expressions directly.

Our approach to proof theory will be axiomatic: we'll write down axioms, which are sentences of modal propositional logic that seem clearly to be logical truths, and we'll write down rules of inference, which say which sentences can be logically inferred from which other sentences.

We'll continue to follow C. I. Lewis in constructing multiple modal systems, since it's so unclear which sentences of MPL are logical truths. We'll formulate multiple axiomatic systems, which differ from one another by containing different axioms (and so, different theorems). In fact, we'll give these systems the same names as the systems we investigated semantically: K, D, T, B, S4, and S5. (Thus we will subscript the symbol for theoremhood with the names of systems; $\vdash_K \phi$, for example, will mean that ϕ is a theorem of system K.) Our re-use of the system names will be justified in sections 6.5 and 6.6, where we will establish soundness and completeness for each system, thereby showing that, in each system, exactly the same formulas are provable as are valid.

6.4.1 System K

Our first system, K, is the weakest system—the system with the fewest theorems.

AXIOMATIC SYSTEM K:

- *Rules*: MP plus *necessitation*:

$$\frac{\phi}{\Box\phi} \quad \text{NEC}$$

- *Axioms*: all instances (with MPL-wffs) of PL1–PL3, plus:

$$\Box(\phi\rightarrow\psi) \rightarrow (\Box\phi\rightarrow\Box\psi) \tag{K}$$

System K (like all the modal systems we'll study) is an *extension* of propositional logic, in the sense that it includes all of the theorems of propositional logic, but then adds more theorems. It includes all of propositional logic because it contains all of the propositional logic rules and axioms; it adds theorems by adding a new rule of inference (NEC), and a new axiom schema (the K-schema) (as well as adding new wffs—wffs containing the $\Box$—to the stock of wffs that can occur in the PL-axioms.)

If you've been paying attention, the rule of necessitation ought to strike you as being, well, *wrong*. It says that if you have a formula ϕ on a line, then you may infer the formula $\Box\phi$. But can't a sentence be true without being necessarily true? Yes; but so long as we're careful how we use our axiomatic system, this fact won't get us into trouble. Recall the distinction from section 2.6 between a proof (simpliciter) and a proof *from* a set Γ. In a proof, each line must be either (i) an axiom or (ii) a wff that follows from earlier lines in the proof by a rule; in a proof from Γ a line may also be (iii) a member of Γ (i.e., a "premise"). A theorem is defined as the last line of any proof (any proof simpliciter, that is). So every line of every proof (simpliciter) is a theorem. So whenever one uses necessitation in a proof (simpliciter), one is applying it to a theorem. And necessitation *does* seem appropriate when applied to theorems: if ϕ is a theorem, then $\Box\phi$ ought also to be a theorem. Think of it another way. The worry about necessitation is that it doesn't preserve truth: its premise can be true when its conclusion is false. But necessitation does preserve *logical truth*. So if we're thinking of our axiomatic definition of theoremhood as being a (proof-theoretic) way to represent logical truth, there seems to be no trouble with its use of necessitation.

So we don't get into trouble with NEC in proofs of theorems. But we do get into trouble in proofs from premises. Consider the following:

1. P premise
2. $\Box P$ 1, NEC

This is a proof of $\Box P$ *from* $\{P\}$. Thus $P \vdash_K \Box P$ (given the way our definitions are set up). But it's easy to construct a model showing that $P \nvDash_K \Box P$. Thus we have a failure of the generalized version of soundness, according to which $\Gamma \vDash_K \phi$ whenever $\Gamma \vdash_K \phi$. What's more, even though $P \vdash_K \Box P$, it's *not* the case that $\vdash_K P \rightarrow \Box P$. (We'll be able to demonstrate this once we've proved soundness for K.) So the deduction theorem (section 2.9) fails for our axiomatic system K—and indeed, for all the axiomatic modal systems we will consider. As a result, we cannot "do conditional proof" in these systems: we cannot show that a conditional is a theorem by assuming its antecedent and proving its consequent on that basis.[74]

These problems aren't insurmountable. One can develop more complex definitions of provability from premises that lack these negative consequences.[75] But for our purposes, it will be simpler to sidestep rather than solve the problems. We'll just stay away from proofs from premises. Our axiomatic system delivers bad results when it comes to proofs from premises, so we won't think of that aspect of the system as representing logical consequence.

Let's investigate some proof techniques. The simplest consists of first proving something from the PL-axioms, and then necessitating it.

Example 6.4: Proof of $\Box((P \rightarrow Q) \rightarrow (P \rightarrow P))$:

1. $P \rightarrow (Q \rightarrow P)$ PL1
2. $P \rightarrow (Q \rightarrow P)) \rightarrow ((P \rightarrow Q) \rightarrow (P \rightarrow P))$ PL2
3. $(P \rightarrow Q) \rightarrow (P \rightarrow P)$ 1, 2, MP
4. $\Box((P \rightarrow Q) \rightarrow (P \rightarrow P))$ 3, NEC

To save on sweat, tears, and ink, let's reinstate the time-saving shortcuts introduced in sections 2.8 and 4.4. Whenever ϕ is an "MPL-tautology"—i.e., results from some tautology (PL-valid wff) by uniform substitution of MPL-wffs for sentence letters—we allow ourselves to simply write down ϕ in an axiomatic proof, with the annotation "PL". (Since our PL-axioms and rule are complete, and are included here in K, we know we could always insert an official K-proof of ϕ.) Thus the previous proof could be shortened to:[76]

---

[74]Compare the shortcomings connected with free variables of our section 4.4 proof system for PC, and also the discussion of conditional proof given a supervaluational semantics for $\triangle$ at the end of section 3.4.5.

[75]See, for example, Garson (2006).

[76]Here the formula annotated "PL" is in fact a genuine tautology, but in other cases it won't be. The MPL-tautology $\Box P \rightarrow \Box P$ comes from the tautology $P \rightarrow P$ by uniformly substituting $\Box P$ for P, but it isn't itself a tautology because it isn't a PL-wff—the $\Box$ isn't part of the primitive vocabulary of propositional logic.

1. $(P{\to}Q){\to}(P{\to}P)$ ⠀⠀⠀⠀⠀PL
2. $\Box((P{\to}Q){\to}(P{\to}P))$ ⠀1, NEC

And we allow ourselves to move directly from some wffs $\phi_1 \dots \phi_n$ to any "MPL-tautological consequence" of those wffs. That is, if we already have $\phi_1 \dots \phi_n$, then we may write ψ, annotating the line numbers of $\phi_1 \dots \phi_n$ and "PL", if the conditional $\phi_1{\to}(\phi_2{\to}\cdots(\phi_n{\to}\psi))$ is an MPL-tautology. (As in section 4.4, after writing "PL" I will sometimes cite one of the tautologies from table 4.1 to clarify what I've done.) And we allow ourselves to perform multiple steps at once, if it's obvious what's going on.

Back to investigating what we can do in K. In K, tautologies are necessary: the strategy of example 6.4 can be used to prove $\Box\phi$ whenever ϕ is a MPL-tautology. The next example illustrates a related fact about K: in it, contradictions are impossible.

Example 6.5: Proof of $\sim\Diamond(P{\land}{\sim}P)$—i.e., of $\sim\sim\Box\sim(P{\land}{\sim}P)$

1. $\sim(P{\land}{\sim}P)$ ⠀⠀⠀⠀⠀PL
2. $\Box\sim(P{\land}{\sim}P)$ ⠀⠀⠀1, NEC
3. $\sim\sim\Box\sim(P{\land}{\sim}P)$ ⠀2, PL

So far we have used only necessitation and the PL-axioms. What about the K-axioms $\Box(\phi{\to}\psi){\to}(\Box\phi{\to}\Box\psi)$? Their point is to enable "distribution of the $\Box$ over the $\to$". That is, if you ever have the formula $\Box(\phi{\to}\psi)$, then you can always move to $\Box\phi{\to}\Box\psi$ as follows:

$i.$ ⠀$\Box(\phi{\to}\psi)$
$i+1.$ ⠀$\Box(\phi{\to}\psi){\to}(\Box\phi{\to}\Box\psi)$ ⠀K
$i+2.$ ⠀$\Box\phi{\to}\Box\psi$ ⠀⠀⠀⠀⠀⠀⠀$i, i+1$, MP

Distribution of the $\Box$ over the $\to$, plus the rule of necessitation, combine to give us a powerful technique for proving wffs of the form $\Box\phi{\to}\Box\psi$. First prove $\phi{\to}\psi$ (the technique works only if you can do this); then necessitate it to get $\Box(\phi{\to}\psi)$; then distribute the $\Box$ over the arrow to get $\Box\phi{\to}\Box\psi$. This is one of the core K-techniques, and is featured in the next example.

Example 6.6: Proof of $\Box(P{\land}Q){\to}(\Box P{\land}\Box Q)$:

1. $(P{\land}Q){\to}P$ ⠀⠀⠀⠀⠀⠀⠀⠀⠀⠀⠀⠀PL
2. $\Box[(P{\land}Q){\to}P]$ ⠀⠀⠀⠀⠀⠀⠀⠀⠀1, NEC
3. $\Box[(P{\land}Q){\to}P] \to [\Box(P{\land}Q){\to}\Box P]$ ⠀K
4. $\Box(P{\land}Q){\to}\Box P$ ⠀⠀⠀⠀⠀⠀⠀⠀2, 3, MP
5. $\Box(P{\land}Q){\to}\Box Q$ ⠀⠀⠀⠀⠀⠀⠀⠀Insert steps similar to 1–4
6. $\Box(P{\land}Q){\to}(\Box P{\land}\Box Q)$ ⠀⠀⠀4, 5, PL (composition)

Next, let's consider how to prove $(\Box P{\lor}\Box Q){\to}\Box(P{\lor}Q)$. Here we run into problems. We must prove a conditional whose antecedent is a disjunction of two $\Box$s. But the modal techniques we've developed so far don't deliver results of this form. They show us only how to put $\Box$s in front of theorems, and how to distribute $\Box$s over $\to$s, and so deliver only results of the form $\Box\phi$ and $\Box\phi{\to}\Box\psi$. And since we're working in an axiomatic system, we cannot use proof strategies like conditional proof and reductio ad absurdum. To overcome these problems, I'll use our modal techniques to prove two conditionals, $\Box P{\to}\Box(P{\lor}Q)$ and $\Box Q{\to}\Box(P{\lor}Q)$, from which the desired result follows by PL.

Example 6.7: Proof of $(\Box P{\lor}\Box Q){\to}\Box(P{\lor}Q)$:

1. $P{\to}(P{\lor}Q)$ PL
2. $\Box(P{\to}(P{\lor}Q))$ 1, NEC
3. $\Box P{\to}\Box(P{\lor}Q)$ K, 2, MP
4. $Q{\to}(P{\lor}Q)$ PL
5. $\Box Q{\to}\Box(P{\lor}Q)$ 4, NEC, K, MP
6. $(\Box P{\lor}\Box Q){\to}\Box(P{\lor}Q)$ 3, 5, PL (dilemma)

In general: if the modal techniques don't deliver the result you're after, look for one or more modal formulas that they *do* deliver which, by PL, imply the desired result. (Again, remember to consult table 4.1.) Assemble the modal formulas using the modal techniques, and then write down your desired result, annotating "PL".

The next example illustrates our next modal technique: combining two $\Box$s to get a single $\Box$.

Example 6.8: Proof of $(\Box P{\land}\Box Q){\to}\Box(P{\land}Q)$:

1. $P \to (Q{\to}(P{\land}Q))$ PL
2. $\Box P \to \Box(Q{\to}(P{\land}Q))$ 1, NEC, K, MP
3. $\Box(Q{\to}(P{\land}Q)) \to (\Box Q{\to}\Box(P{\land}Q))$ K
4. $\Box P{\to}(\Box Q{\to}\Box(P{\land}Q))$ 2, 3, PL (syllogism)
5. $(\Box P{\land}\Box Q){\to}\Box(P{\land}Q)$ 4, PL (import/export)

(Step 4 is unnecessary since you could go straight from 2 and 3 to 5 by propositional logic; I put it in for perspicuity.)

In general, whenever $\phi_1{\to}(\phi_2{\to}\cdots(\phi_n{\to}\psi))$ is provable you can use the technique of example 6.8 to prove $\Box\phi_1{\to}(\Box\phi_2{\to}\cdots(\Box\phi_n{\to}\Box\psi))$. Thus you can move from $\Box\phi_1\ldots\Box\phi_n$ to $\Box\psi$ in any such case. Roughly speaking: you can combine several $\Box$s to get a further $\Box$, provided you can prove the inside of the further $\Box$ from the insides of the former $\Box$s. First prove the conditional $\phi_1{\to}(\phi_2{\to}\cdots(\phi_n{\to}\psi))$; then necessitate it to get $\Box[\phi_1{\to}(\phi_2{\to}\cdots(\phi_n{\to}\psi))]$; then distribute the $\Box$ over the arrows repeatedly using K-axioms and PL to get $\Box\phi_1{\to}(\Box\phi_2{\to}\cdots(\Box\phi_n{\to}\Box\psi))$.

Onward. The next example illustrates one way to prove formulas with "nested" modal operators:

Example 6.9: Proof of $\Box\Box(P{\land}Q){\to}\Box\Box P$:

1. $(P\wedge Q)\rightarrow P$ PL
2. $\square(P\wedge Q)\rightarrow\square P$ 1, NEC, K, MP
3. $\square[\square(P\wedge Q)\rightarrow\square P]$ 2, NEC
4. $\square\square(P\wedge Q)\rightarrow\square\square P$ K, 3, MP

Notice in line 3 that we necessitated something that was not a PL-theorem. That's allowed; the rule of necessitation applies to all K-theorems, even those whose proofs were distinctively modal. Notice also how this proof contains two instances of the technique of example 6.6. This technique involves obtaining a conditional, necessitating it, and then distributing the $\square$ over the $\rightarrow$. We did this first using the conditional $(P\wedge Q)\rightarrow P$; that led us to a conditional, $\square(P\wedge Q)\rightarrow\square P$. Then we started the technique over again, using the latter as our initial conditional.

So far we have no techniques for dealing with the $\Diamond$, other than eliminating it by definition. It will be convenient to derive some shortcuts involving the $\Diamond$—some theorems that we may subsequently cite in proofs. The most important is an analog of the K-axiom:

$$\square(\phi\rightarrow\psi)\rightarrow(\Diamond\phi\rightarrow\Diamond\psi) \tag{K$\Diamond$}$$

By definition of the $\Diamond$, this is an abbreviation of $\square(\phi\rightarrow\psi)\rightarrow(\sim\square\sim\phi\rightarrow\sim\square\sim\psi)$. How to prove it? None of our modal techniques delivers a wff of this form. But notice that this wff follows by PL from $\square(\phi\rightarrow\psi)\rightarrow(\square\sim\psi\rightarrow\square\sim\phi)$. And this latter wff looks like the result of necessitating an MPL-tautology and then distributing the $\square$ over the $\rightarrow$ a couple of times—just the kind of thing we know how to do in K. So, any instance of K$\Diamond$ may be proved as follows:

1. $(\phi\rightarrow\psi)\rightarrow(\sim\psi\rightarrow\sim\phi)$ PL (contraposition)
2. $\square(\phi\rightarrow\psi)\rightarrow\square(\sim\psi\rightarrow\sim\phi)$ 1, NEC, K, MP
3. $\square(\sim\psi\rightarrow\sim\phi)\rightarrow(\square\sim\psi\rightarrow\square\sim\phi)$ K
4. $\square(\phi\rightarrow\psi)\rightarrow(\square\sim\psi\rightarrow\square\sim\phi)$ 2, 3, PL (syllogism)
5. $\square(\phi\rightarrow\psi)\rightarrow(\sim\square\sim\phi\rightarrow\sim\square\sim\psi)$ 4, PL (contraposition)

The next example illustrates the importance of K$\Diamond$:

Example 6.10: Proof of $\square P\rightarrow(\Diamond Q\rightarrow\Diamond(P\wedge Q))$:

1. $P\rightarrow[Q\rightarrow(P\wedge Q)]$ PL
2. $\square P\rightarrow\square[Q\rightarrow(P\wedge Q)]$ 1, NEC, K, MP
3. $\square[Q\rightarrow(P\wedge Q)]\rightarrow[\Diamond Q\rightarrow\Diamond(P\wedge Q)]$ K$\Diamond$
4. $\square P\rightarrow[\Diamond Q\rightarrow\Diamond(P\wedge Q)]$ 2, 3, PL (syllogism)

In general, K$\Diamond$ lets us construct proofs of the following sort. Suppose we wish to prove a formula of the form:

$$\mathcal{O}_1\phi_1\rightarrow(\mathcal{O}_2\phi_2\rightarrow\cdots(\mathcal{O}_n\phi_n\rightarrow\Diamond\psi))$$

where the $\mathcal{O}_i$s are modal operators, *all but one of which are* $\square$s. (Thus the remaining $\mathcal{O}_i$ is $\Diamond$.) The technique is like that of example 6.8. First prove a nested conditional, the antecedents of which are the ϕ_is, and the consequent of which is ψ (the technique works only when this can be done); then necessitate it; then repeatedly distribute the $\Box$ over the $\to$s, once using K$\Diamond$, the rest of the times using K. But there is one catch. We need to use K$\Diamond$ *last*, after all the uses of K. This in turn requires that the final antecedent in the initial nested conditional must be whichever of the ϕ_is that we want to end up underneath the $\Diamond$. For instance, suppose that $\mathcal{O}_2$ is $\Diamond$. Thus, what we are trying to prove is:

$$\Box\phi_1\to(\Diamond\phi_2\to(\Box\phi_3\to\cdots(\Box\phi_n\to\Diamond\psi)))$$

In this case, the conditional to use would be:

$$\phi_1\to(\phi_n\to(\phi_3\to\cdots(\phi_{n-1}\to(\phi_2\to\psi))))$$

In other words, one must swap ϕ_n with ϕ_2. The end result will therefore have the modal statements out of order:

$$\Box\phi_1\to(\Box\phi_n\to(\Box\phi_3\to\cdots(\Box\phi_{n-1}\to(\Diamond\phi_2\to\Diamond\psi))))$$

But that's not a problem since this implies our desired result by PL. (Recall permutation from table 4.1.)

Why do we need to save K$\Diamond$ for last? The strategy of successively distributing the box over all the nested conditionals comes to a halt as soon as the K$\Diamond$-theorem is used. Suppose, for example, that we attempted to prove $\Diamond P\to(\Box Q\to\Diamond(P\wedge Q))$ as follows:

1. $P\to(Q\to(P\wedge Q))$ PL
2. $\Box[P\to(Q\to(P\wedge Q))]$ 1, NEC
3. $\Diamond P\to\Diamond(Q\to(P\wedge Q))$ K$\Diamond$, 2, MP
4. ?

Now we're stuck. We need $\Diamond(Q\to(P\wedge Q))\to(\Box Q\to\Diamond(P\wedge Q))$ to finish the proof; but neither K nor K$\Diamond$ gets us this. We must start over, beginning with a different conditional:

Example 6.11: Proof of $\Diamond P\to(\Box Q\to\Diamond(P\wedge Q))$:

1. $Q\to(P\to(P\wedge Q))$ PL
2. $\Box(Q\to(P\to(P\wedge Q)))$ 1, NEC
3. $\Box Q\to\Box(P\to(P\wedge Q))$ K, 2, MP
4. $\Box(P\to(P\wedge Q))\to(\Diamond P\to\Diamond(P\wedge Q))$ K$\Diamond$
5. $\Box Q\to(\Diamond P\to\Diamond(P\wedge Q))$ 3, 4, PL (syllogism)
6. $\Diamond P\to(\Box Q\to\Diamond(P\wedge Q))$ 5, PL (permutation)

Let's derive another helpful shortcut involving the $\Diamond$, the following "modal negation" (MN) theorem schemas:

$$\vdash_K \sim\Box\phi\to\Diamond\sim\phi \qquad\qquad \vdash_K \Diamond\sim\phi\to\sim\Box\phi \qquad\qquad \text{(MN)}$$
$$\vdash_K \sim\Diamond\phi\to\Box\sim\phi \qquad\qquad \vdash_K \Box\sim\phi\to\sim\Diamond\phi$$

I'll prove one of these; the rest can be proved as exercises.

Example 6.12: Proof of $\sim\Box\phi\rightarrow\Diamond\sim\phi$, i.e. $\sim\Box\phi\rightarrow\sim\Box\sim\sim\phi$ (for any ϕ):

1. $\sim\sim\phi\rightarrow\phi$ PL
2. $\Box\sim\sim\phi\rightarrow\Box\phi$ 1, NEC, K, MP
3. $\sim\Box\phi\rightarrow\sim\Box\sim\sim\phi$ 2, PL (contraposition)

The MN theorems let us "move" $\sim$s through strings of $\Box$s and $\Diamond$s.

Example 6.13: Show that $\vdash_K \Box\Diamond\Box\sim P\rightarrow\sim\Diamond\Box\Diamond P$:

1. $\Box\sim P\rightarrow\sim\Diamond P$ MN
2. $\Diamond\Box\sim P\rightarrow\Diamond\sim\Diamond P$ 1, NEC, K$\Diamond$, MP
3. $\Diamond\sim\Diamond P\rightarrow\sim\Box\Diamond P$ MN
4. $\Diamond\Box\sim P\rightarrow\sim\Box\Diamond P$ 2, 3, PL (syllogism)
5. $\Box\Diamond\Box\sim P\rightarrow\Box\sim\Box\Diamond P$ 4, NEC, K, MP
6. $\Box\sim\Box\Diamond P\rightarrow\sim\Diamond\Box\Diamond P$ MN
7. $\Box\Diamond\Box\sim P\rightarrow\sim\Diamond\Box\Diamond P$ 5, 6, PL (syllogism)

It's important to note, by the way, that this proof can't be shortened as follows:

1. $\Box\Diamond\Box\sim P\rightarrow\Box\Diamond\sim\Diamond P$ MN
2. $\Box\Diamond\sim\Diamond P\rightarrow\Box\sim\Box\Diamond P$ MN
3. $\Box\sim\Box\Diamond P\rightarrow\sim\Diamond\Box\Diamond P$ MN
4. $\Box\Diamond\Box\sim P\rightarrow\sim\Diamond\Box\Diamond P$ 1, 2, 3, PL

Steps 1 and 2 of the latter proof are mistaken. The MN-theorems say only that particular wffs are provable, whereas steps 1 and 2 attempt to apply MN to the *insides* of complex wffs.

K is a very weak system. In it you can't prove anything interesting about iterated modalities—sentences with strings of multiple modal operators. You can't even prove that necessity implies possibility. (We'll be able to establish facts of unprovability after section 6.5.) So it's unclear whether K represents any sort of necessity. Still, there's a point to K. K gives a *minimal* proof theory for the $\Box$: if $\Box$ is to represent any sort of necessity at all, it must obey *at least* K's axioms and rules. For on any sense of necessity, surely logical truths must be necessary; and surely, if both a conditional and its antecedent are necessary, then its consequent must be necessary as well. (Think of the latter in terms of possible worlds: if $\phi\rightarrow\psi$ is true in all accessible worlds, and ϕ is true in all accessible worlds, then by modus ponens within each accessible world, ψ must be true in all accessible worlds.)

So even if K doesn't itself represent any sort of necessity, K is well suited to be the proof-theoretic basis for all the other systems we'll study. Each of those other systems will result from adding appropriate axioms to K. For example, to get system T we'll add each instance of $\Box\phi\rightarrow\phi$; and to get S4 we'll additionally add each instance of $\Box\phi\rightarrow\Box\Box\phi$. Thus each of our systems will be extensions of K: every theorem of K is also a theorem of all the other systems (since each system differs from K only by containing additional axioms).

Exercise 6.4 Prove the remaining MN-theorems.

Exercise 6.5 Give axiomatic proofs in K of the following wffs:

(a)* $\Diamond(P \wedge Q) \rightarrow (\Diamond P \wedge \Diamond Q)$

(b) $\Box{\sim}P \rightarrow \Box(P \rightarrow Q)$

(c)* ${\sim}\Diamond(Q \wedge R) \leftrightarrow \Box(Q \rightarrow {\sim}R)$

(d)** $\Box(P \leftrightarrow Q) \rightarrow (\Box P \leftrightarrow \Box Q)$

(e) $[\Box(P \rightarrow Q) \wedge \Box(P \rightarrow {\sim}Q)] \rightarrow {\sim}\Diamond P$

(f) $(\Box P \wedge \Box Q) \rightarrow \Box(P \leftrightarrow Q)$

(g)* $\Diamond(P \rightarrow Q) \leftrightarrow (\Box P \rightarrow \Diamond Q)$

(h) $\Diamond P \rightarrow (\Box Q \rightarrow \Diamond Q)$

(i) ${\sim}\Diamond\Diamond\Box(P \vee Q) \rightarrow \Box\Box\Diamond{\sim}P$

6.4.2 *System D*

To get D we add to K a new axiom saying that "what's necessary is possible":

AXIOMATIC SYSTEM D:

- Rules: MP, NEC
- Axioms: the PL1-, PL2-, PL3-, and K-schemas, plus the D-schema:

$$\Box\phi \rightarrow \Diamond\phi \qquad\qquad (D)$$

In D it can be proved that tautologies are possible and contradictions are not necessary, as the next example and exercise 6.6a illustrate.

Example 6.14: Show that $\vdash_D \Diamond(P \vee {\sim}P)$

1.	$P \vee {\sim}P$	PL
2.	$\Box(P \vee {\sim}P)$	1, NEC
3.	$\Box(P \vee {\sim}P) \rightarrow \Diamond(P \vee {\sim}P)$	D
4.	$\Diamond(P \vee {\sim}P)$	2, 3, MP

One more example:

Example 6.15: Show that $\vdash_D \Box\Box P \rightarrow \Box\Diamond P$.

1.	$\Box P \rightarrow \Diamond P$	D
2.	$\Box(\Box P \rightarrow \Diamond P)$	1, NEC
3.	$\Box\Box P \rightarrow \Box\Diamond P$	2, K, MP

Like K, system D is very weak. As we will see later, $\Box P \rightarrow P$ isn't a D-theorem. This is not a problem if the $\Box$ is to be given a deontic sense, since as we noted earlier, some things that ought to be, aren't. But anything that is metaphysically, naturally, or technologically necessary, for example, must be true. (If something is true in all metaphysically possible worlds, or all naturally possible worlds, or all technologically possible worlds, then surely it must be true in the actual world, and so must be plain old true.) So any system aspiring to represent these further sorts of necessity will need new axioms.

> **Exercise 6.6** Give axiomatic proofs in D of the following wffs:
>
> (a) $\sim\Box(P\wedge\sim P)$
>
> (b) $\sim(\Box P\wedge\Box\sim P)$
>
> (c) $\sim\Box[\Box(P\wedge Q)\wedge\Box(P\rightarrow\sim Q)]$

6.4.3 System T

Here we drop the D-schema, and add all instances of the T-schema:

AXIOMATIC SYSTEM T:

- Rules: MP, NEC
- Axioms: the PL1-, PL2-, PL3-, and K-schemas, plus the T-schema:

$$\Box\phi\rightarrow\phi \tag{T}$$

In section 6.4.1 we proved a theorem schema, K$\diamond$, which was the analog for the $\diamond$ of the K-axiom schema. Let's do the same thing here; let's prove a theorem schema T$\diamond$, which is the analog for the $\diamond$ of the T-axiom schema:

$$\phi\rightarrow\diamond\phi \tag{T$\diamond$}$$

For any wff ϕ, the following is a proof of $\phi\rightarrow\sim\Box\sim\phi$, i.e., $\phi\rightarrow\diamond\phi$.

1. $\Box\sim\phi\rightarrow\sim\phi$ T
2. $\phi\rightarrow\sim\Box\sim\phi$ 1, PL

So let's allow ourselves to write down instances of T$\diamond$ in proofs.

Notice that instances of the D-axioms are now theorems ($\Box\phi\rightarrow\phi$ is a T-axiom; $\phi\rightarrow\diamond\phi$ is an instance of T$\diamond$; $\Box\phi\rightarrow\diamond\phi$ then follows by PL). Thus T is an extension of D: every theorem of D remains a theorem of T.

> **Exercise 6.7** Give axiomatic proofs in T of the following wffs:
>
> (a) $\diamond\Box P\rightarrow\diamond(P\vee Q)$
>
> (b)** $[\Box P\wedge\diamond\Box(P\rightarrow Q)]\rightarrow\diamond Q$
>
> (c) $\diamond(P\rightarrow\Box Q)\rightarrow(\Box P\rightarrow\diamond Q)$

6.4.4 System B

We turn now to systems that say something distinctive about iterated modalities.

AXIOMATIC SYSTEM B:

- Rules: MP, NEC
- Axioms: the PL1-, PL2-, PL3-, K-, and T-schemas, plus the B-schema:

$$\Diamond\Box\phi\rightarrow\phi \tag{B}$$

Since we retain the T-axiom schema, B is an extension of T (and hence of D—and K, of course—as well).

As with K and T, we can establish a theorem schema that is the analog for the $\Diamond$ of B's characteristic axiom schema.

$$\phi\rightarrow\Box\Diamond\phi \tag{B$\Diamond$}$$

For any ϕ, we can prove $\phi\rightarrow\Box\Diamond\phi$ (i.e., $\phi\rightarrow\Box{\sim}\Box{\sim}\phi$, given the definition of the $\Diamond$) as follows:

1. ${\sim}\Box{\sim}\Box{\sim}\phi\rightarrow{\sim}\phi$ B (given the def of $\Diamond$)
2. $\phi\rightarrow\Box{\sim}\Box{\sim}\phi$ 1, PL

Example 6.16: Show that $\vdash_B [\Box P\wedge\Box\Diamond\Box(P\rightarrow Q)]\rightarrow\Box Q$.

1. $\Diamond\Box(P\rightarrow Q)\rightarrow(P\rightarrow Q)$ B
2. $\Box\Diamond\Box(P\rightarrow Q)\rightarrow\Box(P\rightarrow Q)$ 1, NEC, K, MP
3. $\Box(P\rightarrow Q)\rightarrow(\Box P\rightarrow\Box Q)$ K
4. $\Box\Diamond\Box(P\rightarrow Q)\rightarrow(\Box P\rightarrow\Box Q)$ 2, 3, PL (syllogism)
5. $[\Box P\wedge\Box\Diamond\Box(P\rightarrow Q)]\rightarrow\Box Q$ 4, PL (import/export)

Exercise 6.8 Give axiomatic proofs in B of the following wffs:

(a) $\Diamond\Box P\leftrightarrow\Diamond\Box\Diamond\Box P$

(b)** $\Box\Box(P\rightarrow\Box P)\rightarrow\Box({\sim}P\rightarrow\Box{\sim}P)$

6.4.5 System S4

S4 takes a different stand from B on iterated modalities:

AXIOMATIC SYSTEM S4:

- Rules: MP, NEC
- Axioms: the PL1-, PL2-, PL3-, K-, and T-schemas, plus the S4-schema:

$$\Box\phi\rightarrow\Box\Box\phi \tag{S4}$$

Both B and S4 are extensions of T; but neither is an extension of the other. (The nonlinearity here mirrors the nonlinearity of the diagram of semantic systems in section 6.3.2.) S4 contains the S4-schema but not the B-schema, whereas B contains the B-schema but not the S4-schema. As a result, some B-theorems are unprovable in S4, and some S4-theorems are unprovable in B.

As before, we have a theorem schema that is the analog for the $\Diamond$ of the S4-axiom schema:

$$\Diamond\Diamond\phi\rightarrow\Diamond\phi \qquad\qquad (S4\Diamond)$$

I'll prove it by proving its definitional equivalent, $\sim\Box\sim\sim\Box\sim\phi\rightarrow\sim\Box\sim\phi$:

1. $\Box\sim\phi\rightarrow\Box\Box\sim\phi$ S4
2. $\Box\sim\phi\rightarrow\sim\sim\Box\sim\phi$ PL
3. $\Box\Box\sim\phi\rightarrow\Box\sim\sim\Box\sim\phi$ 2, NEC, K, MP
4. $\Box\sim\phi\rightarrow\Box\sim\sim\Box\sim\phi$ 1, 3, PL (syllogism)
5. $\sim\Box\sim\sim\Box\sim\phi\rightarrow\sim\Box\sim\phi$ 4, PL (contraposition)

Example 6.17: Show that $\vdash_{S4} (\Diamond P\wedge\Box Q)\rightarrow\Diamond(P\wedge\Box Q)$. This problem is reasonably difficult. Here's my approach. We know from example 6.10 how to prove things of the form $\Box\phi\rightarrow(\Diamond\psi\rightarrow\Diamond\chi)$, provided we can prove the conditional $\phi\rightarrow(\psi\rightarrow\chi)$. Now, this technique won't help directly with the formula we're after, since we can't prove the conditional $Q\rightarrow(P\rightarrow(P\wedge\Box Q))$. But we can use this technique to prove something related to the formula we're after: $\Box\Box Q\rightarrow(\Diamond P\rightarrow\Diamond(P\wedge\Box Q))$ (since the conditional $\Box Q\rightarrow(P\rightarrow(P\wedge\Box Q))$ is an MPL-tautology). This thought inspires the following proof:

1. $\Box Q\rightarrow(P\rightarrow(P\wedge\Box Q))$ PL
2. $\Box\Box Q\rightarrow\Box(P\rightarrow(P\wedge\Box Q))$ 1, NEC, K, MP
3. $\Box(P\rightarrow(P\wedge\Box Q))\rightarrow(\Diamond P\rightarrow\Diamond(P\wedge\Box Q))$ K$\Diamond$
4. $\Box\Box Q\rightarrow(\Diamond P\rightarrow\Diamond(P\wedge\Box Q))$ 2, 3, PL (syllogism)
5. $\Box Q\rightarrow\Box\Box Q$ S4
6. $(\Diamond P\wedge\Box Q)\rightarrow\Diamond(P\wedge\Box Q)$ 4, 5, PL (syll., import/export)

Exercise 6.9 Give axiomatic proofs in S4 of the following wffs:

    (a) $\Box P\rightarrow\Box\Diamond\Box P$

    (b) $\Box\Diamond\Box\Diamond P\rightarrow\Box\Diamond P$

    (c) $\Diamond\Box P\rightarrow\Diamond\Box\Diamond\Box P$

6.4.6 *System S5*

Our final system, S5, takes the strongest stand on iterated modalities. It results from adding to T the S5-schema:

AXIOMATIC SYSTEM S5:

- Rules: MP, NEC
- Axioms: the PL1-, PL2-, PL3-, K-, and T-schemas, plus the S5-schema:

$$\Diamond\Box\phi\rightarrow\Box\phi \qquad\qquad (S5)$$

The analog of the S5-schema for the $\Diamond$ is:

$$\Diamond\phi\rightarrow\Box\Diamond\phi \qquad\qquad (S5\Diamond)$$

We can prove $\Diamond\phi\rightarrow\Box\Diamond\phi$, i.e., $\sim\Box\sim\phi\rightarrow\Box\sim\Box\sim\phi$, as follows:

1. $\sim\Box\sim\Box\sim\phi\rightarrow\Box\sim\phi$ S5 (def of $\Diamond$)
2. $\sim\Box\sim\phi\rightarrow\Box\sim\Box\sim\phi$ 1, PL

Notice that we didn't include the B- and S4-schemas as axiom schemas of S5. Nevertheless, all their instances are theorems of S5 (so we can still appeal to them in proofs). Any instance of the B-schema, $\Diamond\Box\phi\rightarrow\phi$, follows immediately via PL from an S5-axiom $\Diamond\Box\phi\rightarrow\Box\phi$ and a T-axiom $\Box\phi\rightarrow\phi$. As for the S4-schema, the following proof uses B$\Diamond$, which is a theorem of B and hence of S5.

1. $\Box\phi\rightarrow\Box\Diamond\Box\phi$ B$\Diamond$
2. $\Diamond\Box\phi\rightarrow\Box\phi$ S5
3. $\Box\Diamond\Box\phi\rightarrow\Box\Box\phi$ 2, NEC, K, MP
4. $\Box\phi\rightarrow\Box\Box\phi$ 1, 3, PL (syllogism)

Exercise 6.10 Give axiomatic proofs in S5 of the following wffs:

(a) $(\Box P\vee\Diamond Q)\leftrightarrow\Box(P\vee\Diamond Q)$

(b) $\Diamond(P\wedge\Diamond Q)\leftrightarrow(\Diamond P\wedge\Diamond Q)$

(c)** $\Box(\Box P\rightarrow\Box Q)\vee\Box(\Box Q\rightarrow\Box P)$

(d) $\Box[\Box(\Diamond P\rightarrow Q)\leftrightarrow\Box(P\rightarrow\Box Q)]$

6.4.7 *Substitution of equivalents and modal reduction*

Let's conclude our discussion of provability in modal logic by proving two simple metatheorems. The first, substitution of equivalents, says roughly that you can substitute provably equivalent wffs within complex wffs. More carefully: call two wffs "α/β variants" iff they differ only in that in zero or more places, wff α occurs in one where wff β occurs in the other. Thus you can turn one into the other by changing (zero or more) αs to βs or βs to αs. (For example, $P\rightarrow(Q\rightarrow P)$ and $\sim S\rightarrow(Q\rightarrow\sim S)$ are $P/\sim S$ variants, as are $P\rightarrow(Q\rightarrow P)$ and $\sim S\rightarrow(Q\rightarrow P)$.)

Substitution of equivalents: Where S is any of our modal systems, if $\vdash_S \alpha\leftrightarrow\beta$, then $\vdash_S \chi\leftrightarrow\chi'$ for any α/β variants χ and χ'.

Proof. Suppose $\vdash_S \alpha \leftrightarrow \beta$. I'll argue by induction that the following holds for any wff, χ:

$$\vdash_S \chi \leftrightarrow \chi', \text{ for any } \alpha/\beta \text{ variant } \chi' \text{ of } \chi$$

Base case: here χ is a sentence letter. Let χ' be any α/β variant of χ. If χ is neither α nor β, then χ' is just χ itself. If, on the other hand, χ is either α or β, then χ' is either α or β. Either way, we have one of the following cases: $\chi' = \chi$, or $\chi = \alpha$ and $\chi' = \beta$, or $\chi = \beta$ and $\chi' = \alpha$. Since $\vdash_S \alpha \leftrightarrow \beta$ and S includes PL, $\vdash_S (\chi \leftrightarrow \chi')$ in each case.

Inductive step: Now we assume the inductive hypothesis, that wffs χ_1 and χ_2 obey the theorem:

$$\vdash_S \chi_1 \leftrightarrow \chi_1', \text{ for any } \alpha/\beta \text{ variant } \chi_1' \text{ of } \chi_1$$
$$\vdash_S \chi_2 \leftrightarrow \chi_2', \text{ for any } \alpha/\beta \text{ variant } \chi_2' \text{ of } \chi_2$$

We must show that the theorem holds for $\sim\chi_1$, $\chi_1 \rightarrow \chi_2$, and $\Box\chi_1$.

Take the first case. We must show that the theorem holds for $\sim\chi_1$—i.e., that $\vdash_S \sim\chi_1 \leftrightarrow \phi$, for any α/β variant ϕ of $\sim\chi_1$. Suppose first that ϕ has the form $\sim\chi_1'$, where χ_1' is an α/β variant of χ_1. By the inductive hypothesis, $\vdash_S \chi_1 \leftrightarrow \chi_1'$; since S includes PL, $\vdash_S \sim\chi_1 \leftrightarrow \sim\chi_1'$, i.e., $\vdash_S \sim\chi_1 \leftrightarrow \phi$. If, on the other hand, ϕ does not have the form $\sim\chi_1'$ for some α/β variant χ_1' of χ_1, then ϕ must result from changing the whole of $\sim\chi_1$ from α to β or from β to α. Thus each of $\sim\chi_1$ and ϕ must be either α or β. But then, as in the base case, $\vdash_S \sim\chi_1 \leftrightarrow \phi$.

I leave the remaining cases as an exercise. □

The following examples illustrate the power of substitution of equivalents. First, in our discussion of K we proved the following two theorems:

$$\Box(P \wedge Q) \rightarrow (\Box P \wedge \Box Q)$$
$$(\Box P \wedge \Box Q) \rightarrow \Box(P \wedge Q)$$

Hence (by PL), $\Box(P \wedge Q) \leftrightarrow (\Box P \wedge \Box Q)$ is a K-theorem. Given substitution of equivalents, whenever we prove a theorem in which the formula $\Box(P \wedge Q)$ occurs as a subformula, we can infer that the result of changing $\Box(P \wedge Q)$ to $\Box P \wedge \Box Q$ is also a K-theorem—without having to do a separate proof.

Second, given the modal negation theorems, we know that all instances of the following schemas are theorems of K (and hence of every other system):

$$\Box\sim\phi \leftrightarrow \sim\Diamond\phi \qquad \Diamond\sim\phi \leftrightarrow \sim\Box\phi$$

Call these "the duals equivalences".[77] Given the duals equivalences, we can swap $\sim\Diamond\phi$ and $\Box\sim\phi$, or $\sim\Box\phi$ and $\Diamond\sim\phi$, within any theorem, and the result will also be

---

[77] Given the duals equivalences, $\Box$ is to $\Diamond$ as $\forall$ is to $\exists$ ($\forall x \sim\phi \leftrightarrow \sim\exists x\phi$ and $\exists x \sim\phi \leftrightarrow \sim\forall x\phi$ are logical truths). This shared relationship is called "duality": $\Box$ and $\Diamond$ are said to be duals, as are $\forall$ and $\exists$. The duality of $\Box$ and $\Diamond$ would be neatly explained by a metaphysics according to which necessity just is truth in *all* worlds and possibility just is truth in *some* worlds!

a theorem. So we can easily "move" a ∼ through a series of modal operators. For example, it's easy to show that each of the following is a theorem of each system S:

$$\Diamond\Diamond\Box{\sim}\phi \leftrightarrow \Diamond\Diamond\Box{\sim}\phi \tag{1}$$

$$\Diamond\Diamond{\sim}\Diamond\phi \leftrightarrow \Diamond\Diamond\Box{\sim}\phi \tag{2}$$

$$\Diamond{\sim}\Box\Diamond\phi \leftrightarrow \Diamond\Diamond\Box{\sim}\phi \tag{3}$$

$${\sim}\Box\Box\Diamond\phi \leftrightarrow \Diamond\Diamond\Box{\sim}\phi \tag{4}$$

(1) is a theorem of S, since it has the form $\psi{\rightarrow}\psi$. (2) is the result of changing $\Box{\sim}\phi$ on the left of (1) to ${\sim}\Diamond\phi$. Since (1) is a theorem of S, (2) is also a theorem of S, by substitution of equivalents via a duals equivalence. We then obtain (3) by changing $\Diamond{\sim}\Diamond\phi$ in (2) to ${\sim}\Box\Diamond\phi$; by substitution of equivalents via a duals equivalence, this too is a theorem of S. Finally, (4) follows from (3) and a duals equivalence by PL, so it too is a theorem of S. (Note how much easier this is than example 6.13!)

Our second metatheorem concerns only system S5:[78]

Modal reduction theorem for S5: Where $\mathcal{O}_1 \ldots \mathcal{O}_n$ are modal operators and ϕ is a wff:

$$\vdash_{S5} \mathcal{O}_1 \ldots \mathcal{O}_n\phi \leftrightarrow \mathcal{O}_n\phi$$

Intuitively: a string of modal operators always boils down to the innermost operator. For example, $\Box\Box\Diamond\Box\Diamond\Box\Box\Diamond\Box\Diamond\Box\Diamond\Diamond\phi$ boils down to $\Diamond\phi$; that is, the following is a theorem of S5: $\Box\Box\Diamond\Box\Diamond\Box\Box\Diamond\Box\Diamond\Box\Diamond\Diamond\phi \leftrightarrow \Diamond\phi$.

Proof. The following equivalences are all theorems of S5:

$$\Diamond\Box\phi \leftrightarrow \Box\phi \tag{a}$$

$$\Box\Box\phi \leftrightarrow \Box\phi \tag{b}$$

$$\Box\Diamond\phi \leftrightarrow \Diamond\phi \tag{c}$$

$$\Diamond\Diamond\phi \leftrightarrow \Diamond\phi \tag{d}$$

The left-to-right direction of (a) is just S5; the right-to-left is T◇; (b) is T and S4; (c) is T and S5◇; and (d) is S4◇ and T◇. Now consider $\mathcal{O}_1\mathcal{O}_2\ldots\mathcal{O}_n\phi$. Depending on which two modal operators $\mathcal{O}_1$ and $\mathcal{O}_2$ are, one of (a)–(d) tells us that $\vdash_{S5} \mathcal{O}_1\mathcal{O}_2\ldots\mathcal{O}_n\phi\leftrightarrow\mathcal{O}_2\ldots\mathcal{O}_n\phi$. By repeating this process $n-1$ times we get $\vdash_{S5} \mathcal{O}_1\ldots\mathcal{O}_n\phi\leftrightarrow\mathcal{O}_n\phi$. (It is straightforward to convert this argument into a more rigorous inductive proof.) □

Exercise 6.11 Finish the proof of substitution of equivalents.

---

[78] The modal reduction formula, the duals equivalences, and substitution of equivalents together let us reduce strings of operators that include ∼s as well as modal operators. Simply use the duals equivalences to drive any ∼s in the string to the far right-hand side, then use the modal reduction theorem to eliminate all but the innermost modal operator.

6.5 Soundness in MPL

We have defined twelve logical systems: six semantic systems and six axiomatic systems. But each semantic system was paired with an axiomatic system of the same name. The time has come to justify this nomenclature. In this section and the next, we'll show that for each semantic system, exactly the same wffs are counted valid in that system as are counted theorems by the axiomatic system of the same name. That is, for each of our systems, S (for S = K, D, T, B, S4, and S5), we will prove soundness and completeness:

S-soundness: every S-theorem is S-valid.

S-completeness: every S-valid formula is a S-theorem.

Our study of modal logic has been in reverse historical order. We began with semantics, because that is the more intuitive approach. Historically (as we noted earlier), the axiomatic systems came first, in the work of C. I. Lewis. Given the uncertainty over which axioms to choose, modal logic was in disarray. The discovery by the teenaged Saul Kripke in the late 1950s of the possible-worlds semantics we studied in section 6.3, and of the correspondence between simple constraints (reflexivity, transitivity, and so on) on the accessibility relation in his models and Lewis's axiomatic systems, transformed modal logic.

The soundness and completeness theorems have practical as well as theoretical value. First, once we've proved soundness, we'll have a method for showing that formulas are *not* theorems. We already know from section 6.3.3 how to establish invalidity (by constructing countermodels), and the soundness theorem tells us that an invalid wff is not a theorem. Second, once we've proved completeness, if we want to know that a given formula is a theorem, rather than constructing an axiomatic proof we can instead construct a semantic validity proof, which is much easier.

Let's begin with soundness. We're going to prove a general theorem, which we'll use in several soundness proofs. First we'll need a piece of terminology. Where Γ is any set of modal wffs, let's call "$K + \Gamma$" the axiomatic system that consists of the same rules of inference as K (MP and NEC), and which has as axioms the axioms of K (instances of the K- and PL-schemas), plus the members of Γ. Here, then, is the theorem:

Theorem 6.1 If Γ is any set of modal wffs and $\mathcal{M}$ is an MPL-model in which each wff in Γ is valid, then every theorem of $K + \Gamma$ is valid in $\mathcal{M}$.

Modal systems of the form $K + \Gamma$ are commonly called *normal*. Normal modal systems contain all the K-theorems, plus possibly more. What theorem 6.1 gives us is a method for constructing a soundness proof for any normal system. Since all the systems we have studied here (K, D, etc.) are normal, this method is sufficiently general for us. Here's how the method works for system T. System T has the same rules of inference as K, and its axioms are all the axioms of K, plus the instances of the T-schema. In the "$K + \Gamma$" notation, therefore, $T = K + T$, where T is the set of instances of the T-schema. To establish soundness for T, all we need to do is show that every instance of the T-schema is valid in all reflexive models; for we may then conclude by theorem 6.1 that every theorem of T is valid in all reflexive models. This method can be applied to each of our systems: for each system, S, to establish S's soundness it will suffice to show that S's "extra-K" axioms are valid in all S-models.

Theorem 6.1 follows from two lemmas we will need to prove:

Lemma 6.2 All instances of the PL- and K-axiom schemas are valid in all MPL-models

Lemma 6.3 For every MPL-model, $\mathcal{M}$, MP and NEC preserve validity in $\mathcal{M}$

Proof of theorem 6.1 from the lemmas. Assume that every wff in Γ is valid in a given MPL-model $\mathcal{M}$. Any $K+\Gamma$-proof is a series of wffs in which each line is either an axiom of $K+\Gamma$, or follows from earlier lines in the proof by MP or NEC. Now, axioms of $K+\Gamma$ are either PL-axioms, K-axioms, or members of Γ. By lemma 6.2, PL- and K-axioms are valid in all MPL-models, and so are valid in $\mathcal{M}$; and members of Γ are valid in $\mathcal{M}$ by hypothesis. So all axioms in the proof are valid in $\mathcal{M}$. Moreover, by lemma 6.3, MP and NEC preserve validity in $\mathcal{M}$. Therefore, by induction, every line in every $K+\Gamma$-proof is valid in $\mathcal{M}$. Hence every theorem of $K+\Gamma$ is valid in $\mathcal{M}$.   □

We now need to prove the lemmas. I'll prove half of lemma 6.2, and leave the rest for exercises.

Proof that PL-axioms are valid in all MPL-models. From our proof of soundness for PL (section 2.7), we know that the PL truth tables generate the value 1 for each PL-axiom, no matter what truth value its immediate constituents have. But here in MPL, the truth values of conditionals and negations are determined at a given world by the truth values at that world of its immediate constituents via the truth tables. So any PL-axiom must have truth value 1 at any world, regardless of what truth values its immediate constituents have. PL-axioms, therefore, are true in every world in every model, and so are valid in every model.   □

Exercise 6.12 Show that every K-axiom is valid in every MPL-model.

Exercise 6.13 Prove lemma 6.3—i.e., that for any MPL-model $\mathcal{M}$, if the inputs to either MP or NEC are valid in $\mathcal{M}$, then that rule's output is also valid in $\mathcal{M}$.

6.5.1 *Soundness of K*

We can now construct soundness proofs for the individual systems. I'll do this for some of the systems, and leave the verification of soundness for the other systems as exercises.

First, K. In the "$K+\Gamma$" notation, K is just $K+\varnothing$, and so it follows immediately from theorem 6.1 that every theorem of K is valid in every MPL-model. So K is sound.

6.5.2 *Soundness of T*

T is $K + T$, where T is the set of all instances of the T-schema. So, given theorem 6.1, to show that every theorem of T is valid in all T-models, it suffices to show that all instances of the T-schema are valid in all T-models. Assume for reductio that $V(\Box\phi \rightarrow \phi, w) = 0$ for some world w in some T-model (i.e., some model with a reflexive accessibility relation). So $V(\Box\phi, w) = 1$ and $V(\phi, w) = 0$. By reflexivity, $\mathscr{R}ww$, and so $V(\phi, w) = 1$; contradiction.

6.5.3 *Soundness of B*

B is $K + B$, where B is the set of all instances of the T- and B-schemas. Given theorem 6.1, it suffices to show that every instance of the B-schema and every instance of the T-schema is valid in every B-model. Let $\mathscr{M}$ be any B-model and w be any world in that model; we must show that all instances of the T- and B-schemas are true in w in $\mathscr{M}$. The proof of the previous section shows that the T-axioms are true in w (since $\mathscr{M}$'s accessibility relation is reflexive). Now for the B-axioms. Assume for reductio that $V(\Diamond\Box\phi \rightarrow \phi, w) = 0$. So $V(\Diamond\Box\phi, w) = 1$ and $V(\phi, w) = 0$. Given the former, $V(\Box\phi, v) = 1$, for some v such that $\mathscr{R}wv$; by symmetry, $\mathscr{R}vw$; so $V(\phi, w) = 1$, contradicting the latter.

Exercise 6.14 Prove soundness for systems D, S4, and S5.

Exercise 6.15 Consider the system $K5$ that results from adding to K all instances of the S5-schema (thus $K5$ is S5 minus the T-schema). Let $K5$-models be understood as MPL-models whose accessibility relation is *Euclidean*: for any worlds w, u, v, if $\mathscr{R}wu$ and $\mathscr{R}wv$ then $\mathscr{R}uv$. Establish soundness for $K5$.

6.6 Completeness in MPL

Next, completeness: for each system, we'll show that every valid formula is a theorem. As with soundness, most of the work will go into developing some general-purpose machinery. At the end we'll use the machinery to construct completeness proofs for each system. (As in section 2.9, we'll be constructing a proof of the Henkin variety.)

For each of our systems, we're going to show how to construct a certain special model, the *canonical model* for that system. The canonical model for a system, S, will be shown to have the following feature:

If a formula is valid in the canonical model for S, then it is a theorem of S

This sufficient condition for theoremhood can then be used to give completeness proofs, as the following example brings out. Suppose we can demonstrate that the accessibility relation in the canonical model for T is reflexive. Then, since T-valid formulas are by definition true in every world in every model with a reflexive accessibility relation, we know that every T-valid formula is valid in the canonical model for T. But then the italicized statement tells us that every T-valid formula is a theorem of T. So we would have established completeness for T.

The trick for constructing canonical models will be to let the worlds in these models be *sets of formulas* (remember, worlds are allowed to be anything we like), and to let a formula be true at a world iff it is a member of that world. Working out this idea will occupy us for some time.

6.6.1 Definition of canonical models

If we want to use sets of wffs as the worlds in canonical models, and if wffs are to be true at worlds iff they're members of those worlds, then we can't use just any old sets of wffs. It's part of the definition of a valuation function that for any wff ϕ and any world w, either ϕ or $\sim\phi$ is true in w. That means that any set of wffs that we're going to call a world had better contain either ϕ or $\sim\phi$. Moreover, we'd better not let such a set contain both ϕ and $\sim\phi$, since a wff can't be both true and false in a world. This suggests that we might try using the maximal consistent sets of wffs introduced in section 2.9.1.

As before, a maximal set is defined as one that contains, for each wff (now: each MPL-wff), either it or its negation. But the definition of consistency needs to be modified a bit. Consistency was defined in section 2.9.1 in terms of provability in PL; here we will define a notion of S-consistency, in terms of provability in system S, for each of our modal systems. Further, the section 2.9.1 definition made use of the notion of provability from a set of premises; but we've been avoiding speaking of provability from premise sets in modal logic since the rule of necessitation is appropriate only when applied to theorems. What I'll do is introduce a new notion of provability from a set, and in terms of this new notion retain the earlier definition of consistency:

NEW DEFINITION OF S-PROVABILITY-FROM: A wff ϕ is provable in system S from a set Γ ("$\Gamma \vdash_S \phi$") iff for some $\gamma_1 \ldots \gamma_n \in \Gamma$, $\vdash_S (\gamma_1 \wedge \cdots \wedge \gamma_n) \to \phi$ (or else $\Gamma = \varnothing$ and $\vdash_S \phi$)

DEFINITION OF S-CONSISTENCY: A set of wffs Γ is S-inconsistent iff $\Gamma \vdash_S \bot$. Γ is S-consistent iff it is not S-inconsistent.

In the definition of S-provability-from, understand "$(\gamma_1 \wedge \cdots \wedge \gamma_n) \to \phi$" to be $\gamma_1 \to \phi$ if $n = 1$. $\bot$, remember, is defined as the wff $\sim(P \to P)$.

Given these definitions, we can now define canonical models. It may not be fully clear at this point why the definition is phrased as it is. For now, take it on faith that the definition will get us where we want to go.

DEFINITION OF CANONICAL MODEL: The canonical model for system S is the MPL-model $\langle \mathscr{W}, \mathscr{R}, \mathscr{I} \rangle$ where:

- $\mathscr{W}$ is the set of all maximal S-consistent sets of wffs
- $\mathscr{R} w w'$ iff $\Box^-(w) \subseteq w'$
- $\mathscr{I}(\alpha, w) = 1$ iff $\alpha \in w$, for each sentence letter α and each $w \in \mathscr{W}$
- $\Box^-(\Delta)$ is defined as the set of wffs ϕ such that $\Box\phi$ is a member of Δ

Let's think for a bit about this definition. As promised, we have defined the members of $\mathscr{W}$ to be maximal S-consistent sets of wffs. And note that *all* maximal S-consistent sets of wffs are included in $\mathscr{W}$.

Accessibility is defined using the "$\Box^-$" notation. Think of this operation as "stripping off the boxes": to arrive at $\Box^-(\Delta)$ ("the box-strip of set Δ"), begin with set Δ, discard any formula that doesn't begin with a $\Box$, line up the remaining formulas, and then strip one $\Box$ off of the front of each. For example, the box-strip of set $\{P{\rightarrow}Q, \Box{\sim}R, {\sim}\Box Q, \Box\Box(P{\rightarrow}\Box P)\}$, is the set $\{{\sim}R, \Box(P{\rightarrow}\Box P)\}$. The definition of accessibility, therefore, says that $\mathscr{R}ww'$ iff for each wff $\Box\phi$ that is a member of w, the wff ϕ is a member of w'.

The definition of accessibility in the canonical model says nothing about formal properties like transitivity, reflexivity, and so on. As a result, it is not true by definition that the canonical model for S is an S-model. T-models, for example, must have reflexive accessibility relations, whereas the definition of the accessibility relation in the canonical model for T says nothing about reflexivity. As we will soon see, for each of the systems S that we have introduced in this book, the canonical model for S turns out to be an S-model. But this fact must be proven; it's not built into the definition of a canonical model.

An atomic wff (sentence letter) is defined to be true in a world in the canonical model iff it is a member of that world. Thus, for atomic wffs, truth and membership coincide. What we really need to know, however, is that truth and membership coincide for *all* wffs, including complex wffs. Proving this is the biggest part of establishing completeness, and will take a while.

6.6.2 *Facts about maximal consistent sets*

In section 2.9 we proved various results about maximal consistent sets of PL-wffs, where "consistency" was defined in terms of provability in PL. Here, we're going to need to know, among other things, that analogous results hold for maximal S-consistent sets of MPL-wffs:

Theorem 6.4 If Δ is an S-consistent set of MPL-wffs, then there exists some maximal S-consistent set of MPL-wffs, Γ, such that $\Delta \subseteq \Gamma$.

Lemma 6.5 Where Γ is any maximal S-consistent set of MPL-wffs:

6.5a for any MPL-wff ϕ, exactly one of ϕ, $\sim\phi$ is a member of Γ

6.5b $\phi{\rightarrow}\psi \in \Gamma$ iff either $\phi \notin \Gamma$ or $\psi \in \Gamma$

Proof. A look back at the proofs of theorem 2.3 and lemma 2.4 reveals that the only features of the relation of provability-in-PL-from-a-set on which they depend are the following:

- If $\Gamma \vdash_{PL} \phi$, then $\gamma_1 \ldots \gamma_n \vdash_{PL} \phi$, for some $\gamma_1 \ldots \gamma_n \in \Gamma$ (or else $\vdash_{PL} \phi$) (lemma 2.1)
- "Excluded middle MP": $\phi{\rightarrow}\psi, \sim\phi{\rightarrow}\psi \vdash_{PL} \psi$
- "Ex falso quodlibet": $\phi, \sim\phi \vdash_{PL} \psi$
- Modus ponens: $\phi, \phi{\rightarrow}\psi \vdash_{PL} \psi$

- "Negated conditional": $\sim(\phi \rightarrow \psi) \vdash_{PL} \phi$ and $\sim(\phi \rightarrow \psi) \vdash_{PL} \sim\psi$
- If $\phi \in \Gamma$, then $\Gamma \vdash_{PL} \phi$
- Cut for PL
- The deduction theorem for PL

(I invite the reader to go back and verify this.) So if the relation of provability-from-a-set in modal system S also has these features, then one can give exactly analogous proofs of theorem 6.4 and lemma 6.5. And this is indeed the case, as may easily be verified, since each modal system is an axiomatic proof system whose axioms include the PL-axiom schemas and whose rules include MP. The one sticking point is the deduction theorem. As we pointed out in section 6.4.1, the deduction theorem fails for our modal systems if provability-from-a-set is understood in the usual way. But we are not understanding provability-from-a-set in the usual way; and given our new definition of provability-from-a-set, the deduction theorem holds:

Deduction theorem for MPL: For each of our modal systems S (and given our new definition of provability from a set), if $\Gamma \cup \{\phi\} \vdash_S \psi$, then $\Gamma \vdash_S \phi \rightarrow \psi$.

Proof. Suppose $\Gamma \cup \{\phi\} \vdash_S \psi$. So for some $\alpha_1 \ldots \alpha_n$, $\vdash_S (\alpha_1 \wedge \cdots \wedge \alpha_n) \rightarrow \psi$, where perhaps one of the α_is is ϕ and the others are members of Γ. If ϕ is one of the α_is, say α_k, then $(\alpha_1 \wedge \cdots \wedge \alpha_{k-1} \wedge \alpha_{k+1} \wedge \cdots \wedge \alpha_n) \rightarrow (\phi \rightarrow \psi)$ is an MPL-tautological consequence of $(\alpha_1 \wedge \cdots \wedge \alpha_n) \rightarrow \psi$, and so is a theorem of S, whence $\Gamma \vdash_S \phi \rightarrow \psi$. And if none of the α_is is ϕ, then each is in Γ; but $(\alpha_1 \wedge \cdots \wedge \alpha_n) \rightarrow (\phi \rightarrow \psi)$ is an MPL-tautological consequence of $(\alpha_1 \wedge \cdots \wedge \alpha_n) \rightarrow \psi$, whence again $\Gamma \vdash_S \phi \rightarrow \psi$. □

Given the deduction theorem for MPL, then, the proof of theorem 6.4 and lemma 6.5 is complete.   □

Before we end this section, it will be convenient to establish two further sub-lemmas of lemma 6.5:

6.5c if $\vdash_S \phi$, then $\phi \in \Gamma$

6.5d if $\vdash_S \phi \rightarrow \psi$ and $\phi \in \Gamma$, then $\psi \in \Gamma$

Proof. For 6.5c, if $\vdash_S \phi$, then $\vdash_S (\sim\phi \rightarrow \bot)$, since S includes PL. Since Γ is S-consistent, $\sim\phi \notin \Gamma$; and so, since Γ is maximal, $\phi \in \Gamma$. For 6.5d, use lemmas 6.5c and 6.5b.   □

> **Exercise 6.16** (Long.) Show that the relation of provability-from-a-set defined in this section does indeed have the listed features. (As elsewhere in this chapter, you may simply assume the completeness of the PL-axioms, and hence that any MPL-tautology is a theorem of each system S.)

6.6.3 "Mesh"

In addition to theorem 6.4 and lemma 6.5, we'll also need one further fact about maximal S-consistent sets that is specific to modal systems. Our ultimate goal, remember, is to show that in canonical models, a wff is true in a world iff it is a member of that world. If we're going to be able to show this, we'd better be sure that each of the following is true of canonical models:

($\Box$) If $\Box\phi$ is a member of world w, then ϕ is a member of every world accessible from w

($\Diamond$) If $\Diamond\phi$ is a member of world w, then ϕ is a member of some world accessible from w

($\Box$) and ($\Diamond$) had better be true because it's part of the definition of truth in *any* MPL-model (whether canonical or not) that $\Box\phi$ is *true* at w iff ϕ is *true* at each world accessible from w, and that $\Diamond\phi$ is *true* at w iff ϕ is *true* at some world accessible from w. Think of it this way: ($\Box$) and ($\Diamond$) say that the modal statements that are members of a world w in a canonical model "mesh" with the members of accessible worlds. This sort of mesh had better hold if truth and membership are going to coincide.

($\Box$) we know to be true straightaway, since it follows from the definition of the accessibility relation in canonical models. The definition of the canonical model for S, recall, stipulated that w' is accessible from w iff for each wff $\Box\phi$ in w, the wff ϕ is a member of w'. ($\Diamond$), on the other hand, doesn't follow immediately from our definitions; we'll need to prove it. Actually, it will be convenient to prove something slightly different which involves only the $\Box$:

Lemma 6.6 If Δ is a maximal S-consistent set of wffs containing $\sim\Box\phi$, then there exists a maximal S-consistent set of wffs Γ such that $\Box^-(\Delta) \subseteq \Gamma$ and $\sim\phi \in \Gamma$

(Given the definition of accessibility in the canonical model and the definition of the $\Diamond$ in terms of the $\Box$, lemma 6.6 basically amounts to ($\Diamond$).)

Proof of lemma 6.6. Let Δ be as described. The first step is to show that the set $\Box^-(\Delta) \cup \{\sim\phi\}$ is S-consistent. Suppose for reductio that it isn't, and hence that $\Box^-(\Delta) \cup \{\sim\phi\} \vdash_S \bot$. By the deduction theorem for MPL, $\Box^-(\Delta) \vdash_S \sim\phi \rightarrow \bot$. So for some $\psi_1 \ldots \psi_n \in \Box^-(\Delta)$, we have: $\vdash_S (\psi_1 \wedge \cdots \wedge \psi_n) \rightarrow (\sim\phi \rightarrow \bot)$.[79] Next, begin a proof in S with a proof of this wff, and then continue as follows:

i. $(\psi_1 \wedge \cdots \wedge \psi_n) \rightarrow (\sim\phi \rightarrow \bot)$

$i+1$. $\psi_1 \rightarrow (\psi_2 \rightarrow \cdots (\psi_n \rightarrow \phi))$ i, PL (recall the definition of $\bot$)

$i+2$. $\Box(\psi_1 \rightarrow (\psi_2 \rightarrow \cdots (\psi_n \rightarrow \phi)))$ $i+1$, NEC

$i+3$. $\Box\psi_1 \rightarrow (\Box\psi_2 \rightarrow \cdots (\Box\psi_n \rightarrow \Box\phi))$ $i+2$, K, PL ($\times n$)

$i+4$. $(\Box\psi_1 \wedge \cdots \wedge \Box\psi_n \wedge \sim\Box\phi) \rightarrow \bot$ $i+3$, PL

---

[79] If $\Box^-(\Delta)$ is empty, we have instead $\vdash_S \sim\phi \rightarrow \bot$, and the argument runs much as in the text: by PL, $\vdash_S \phi$, so by NEC, $\vdash_S \Box\phi$, so by PL, $\vdash_S \sim\Box\phi \rightarrow \bot$, contradicting Δ's S-consistency.

Given this proof, $\vdash_S (\Box\psi_1 \wedge \cdots \wedge \Box\psi_n \wedge \sim\Box\phi) \to \bot$. But since $\Box\psi_1 \ldots \Box\psi_n$, and $\sim\Box\phi$ are all in Δ, this contradicts Δ's S-consistency ($\Box\psi_1 \ldots \Box\psi_n$ are members of Δ because $\psi_1 \ldots \psi_n$ are members of $\Box^-(\Delta)$).

We've shown that $\Box^-(\Delta) \cup \{\sim\phi\}$ is S-consistent. It therefore has a maximal S-consistent extension, Γ, by theorem 6.4. Since $\Box^-(\Delta) \cup \{\sim\phi\} \subseteq \Gamma$, we know that $\Box^-(\Delta) \subseteq \Gamma$ and that $\sim\phi \in \Gamma$. Γ is therefore our desired set. $\qquad\square$

> **Exercise 6.17** Where S is any of our modal systems, show that if Δ is an S-consistent set of wffs containing the formula $\Diamond\phi$, then $\Box^-(\Delta) \cup \phi$ is also S-consistent. You may appeal to lemmas and theorems proved so far.

6.6.4 Truth and membership in canonical models

We're now in a position to put all of our lemmas to work, and prove that canonical models have the property that I promised they would have: a wff is true in a world iff it is a member of that world:

Theorem 6.7 Where $\mathcal{M}$ ($= \langle \mathcal{W}, \mathcal{R}, \mathcal{I} \rangle$) is the canonical model for any normal modal system, S, for any wff ϕ and any $w \in \mathcal{W}$, $V_{\mathcal{M}}(\phi, w) = 1$ iff $\phi \in w$.

Proof of theorem 6.7. We'll use induction. The base case is when ϕ has zero connectives. That is, ϕ is a sentence letter. Here the result is immediate: by the definition of the canonical model, $\mathcal{I}(\phi, w) = 1$ iff $\phi \in w$; but by the definition of the valuation function, $V_{\mathcal{M}}(\phi, w) = 1$ iff $\mathcal{I}(\phi, w) = 1$.

Now the inductive step. We assume the inductive hypothesis (ih), that the result holds for ϕ and ψ, and show that it must then hold for $\sim\phi$, $\phi \to \psi$, and $\Box\phi$ as well. The proofs of the first two facts make use of lemmas 6.5a and 6.5b, and are parallel to the proofs of the analogous facts in section 2.9.4. Finally, $\Box$: we must show that $\Box\phi$ is true in w iff $\Box\phi \in w$. First the forwards direction. Assume $\Box\phi$ is true in w; then ϕ is true in every $w' \in \mathcal{W}$ such that $\mathcal{R}ww'$. By the (ih), we have (+) ϕ is a member of every such w'. Now suppose for reductio that $\Box\phi \notin w$; since w is maximal, $\sim\Box\phi \in w$. Since w is maximal S-consistent, by lemma 6.6, we know that there exists some maximal S-consistent set Γ such that $\Box^-(w) \subseteq \Gamma$ and $\sim\phi \in \Gamma$. By definition of $\mathcal{W}$, $\Gamma \in \mathcal{W}$; by definition of $\mathcal{R}$, $\mathcal{R}w\Gamma$; and so by (+) Γ contains ϕ. But Γ also contains $\sim\phi$, which contradicts its S-consistency given 6.5a.

Now the backwards direction. Assume $\Box\phi \in w$. Then by definition of $\mathcal{R}$, for every w' such that $\mathcal{R}ww'$, $\phi \in w'$. By the (ih), ϕ is true in every such world; hence by the truth condition for $\Box$, $\Box\phi$ is true in w. $\qquad\square$

What is the point of theorem 6.7? The overall idea of canonical models was that validity in the canonical model for S would imply being a theorem of S. And we can show that this fact (actually a slightly stronger fact) follows fairly immediately from theorem 6.7:

Corollary 6.8 ϕ is valid in the canonical model for S iff $\vdash_S \phi$.

Proof of corollary 6.8. Let $\langle \mathcal{W}, \mathcal{R}, \mathcal{I} \rangle$ be the canonical model for S. Suppose $\vdash_S \phi$. Then, by lemma 6.5c, ϕ is a member of every maximal S-consistent set, and hence $\phi \in w$, for every $w \in \mathcal{W}$. By theorem 6.7, ϕ is true in every $w \in \mathcal{W}$, and so is valid in this model. Now for the other direction: suppose $\nvdash_S \phi$. Then $\{\sim\phi\}$ is S-consistent (if it weren't, then $\sim\phi \vdash_S \bot$, and hence $\vdash_S \sim\phi{\rightarrow}\bot$, and hence, given the definition of $\bot$, $\vdash_S \phi$). So, by theorem 6.4, $\{\sim\phi\}$ has a maximal consistent extension; thus $\sim\phi \in w$ for some $w \in \mathcal{W}$; by theorem 6.7, $\sim\phi$ is therefore true in w, and so ϕ is not true in w, and hence ϕ is not valid in this model. $\square$

So we've gotten where we wanted to go: we've shown that every system has a canonical model, and that a wff is valid in the canonical model iff it is a theorem of the system. In the next section we'll use this fact to prove completeness for our various systems.

6.6.5 *Completeness of systems of MPL*

I'll run through the completeness proofs for K, D, and B, leaving the remainder as exercises.

First, K. Any K-valid wff is valid in all MPL-models, and so is valid in the canonical model for K, and so, by corollary 6.8, is a theorem of K.

For any other system, S, all we need to do to prove S-completeness is to show that the canonical model for S is an S-model. That is, we must show that the accessibility relation in the canonical model for S satisfies the formal constraint for system S (seriality for D, reflexivity for T and so on).

For D, first let's show that in the canonical model for D, the accessibility relation, $\mathcal{R}$, is serial. Let w be any world in that model. Example 6.14 showed that $\diamond(P{\rightarrow}P)$ is a theorem of D, so it's a member of w by lemma 6.5c, and so is true in w by theorem 6.7. Thus, by the truth condition for $\diamond$, there must be some world accessible to w in which $P{\rightarrow}P$ is true; and hence there must be some world accessible to w.

Now for D's completeness. Let ϕ be D-valid. ϕ is then valid in all D-models, i.e., all models with a serial accessibility relation. But we just showed that the canonical model for D has a serial accessibility relation. ϕ is therefore valid in that model, and hence, by corollary 6.8, $\vdash_D \phi$.

Next, B. We must show that the accessibility relation in the canonical model for B is reflexive and symmetric (as with D, B's completeness then follows from corollary 6.8). Reflexivity may be proved just as it is proved in the proof of T's completeness (exercise 6.18). As for symmetry: in the canonical model for B, suppose that $\mathcal{R}wv$. We must show that $\mathcal{R}vw$—that is, that for any ψ, if $\Box\psi \in v$, then $\psi \in w$. Suppose $\Box\psi \in v$. By theorem 6.7, $\Box\psi$ is true in v; since $\mathcal{R}wv$, by the truth condition for $\diamond$, $\diamond\Box\psi$ is true in w, and hence is a member of w by theorem 6.7. Since $\vdash_B \diamond\Box\psi{\rightarrow}\psi$, by lemma 6.5d, $\psi \in w$.

Exercise 6.18 Prove completeness for T, S4, and S5.

Exercise 6.19 Prove completeness for K5 (see exercise 6.15).

Exercise 6.20 Consider the system that results from adding to K every axiom of the form $\Diamond\phi\rightarrow\Box\phi$. Let the models for this system be defined as those whose accessibility relation meets the following condition: *every world can see at most one world*. Prove completeness for this (strange) system.

7

BEYOND STANDARD MODAL PROPOSITIONAL LOGIC

Kᴿɪᴘᴋᴇ'ꜱ ᴘᴏꜱꜱɪʙʟᴇ-ᴡᴏʀʟᴅꜱ semantics has proved itself useful in many areas. In this chapter we will briefly examine its use in deontic, epistemic, tense, and intuitionistic logic.

7.1 Deontic logic

Deontic logic is the study of the logic of normative notions. Let's introduce operators O and M, for, roughly speaking, "ought" and "may". Grammatically, these are one-place sentence operators (like □ and ~): each combines with a single wff to form another wff. Thus we can write OP, $\sim MQ \rightarrow OR$, and so on.

One can read $O\phi$ and $M\phi$ as saying "Agent S ought to see to it that ϕ" and "Agent S may see to it that ϕ", respectively, for some fixed agent S. Or, one can read them as saying "it ought to be the case that ϕ" and "it is acceptable for it to be the case that ϕ". Either way, the formalism is the same.

It's plausible to define M as $\sim O\sim$, thus enabling us to take O as the sole new bit of primitive vocabulary. The definition of a wff for deontic logic is thus like that of nonmodal propositional logic, with the following added clause:

- If ϕ is a wff, then so is $O\phi$

For semantics, we use possible worlds. In fact, we'll use the very same apparatus as for modal logic: MPL-models, truth relative to worlds in these models, and so on. O replaces the □, and behaves exactly analogously: $O\phi$ says that ϕ is true in all accessible possible worlds. Thus its truth condition is:

- $V(O\phi, w) = 1$ iff $V(\phi, v) = 1$ for each $v \in \mathcal{W}$ such that $\mathcal{R}wv$

The derived condition for M is then:

- $V(M\phi, w) = 1$ iff $V(\phi, v) = 1$ for some $v \in \mathcal{W}$ such that $\mathcal{R}wv$

The clauses for atomics, $\sim$ and $\rightarrow$, and the definitions of validity and semantic consequence, remain unchanged.

Indeed, this just *is* modal logic. Nothing in the formalism has changed. The only difference is that we now think of accessibility deontically. We now think of v as being accessible from w if the goings-on in v are *permitted*, given the operative norms in w (or: given the norms binding agent S in w). That is, $\mathcal{R}wv$ iff everything that, in w, ought to be true is in fact true in v (thus v violates nothing that in w is mandatory). We think of $\mathcal{R}$ as being a relation of "deontic accessibility". When we conceptualize modal logic in this way, we write O instead of □ and M instead of ◇.

If we're thinking of $\mathcal{R}$ in this way, what formal properties should it be required to have? One simple and common answer is that the only required property is seriality. Seriality does seem right to require: there must always be *some* possibility that morality permits; from every world there is at least one deontically accessible world. Note that reflexivity would be inappropriate to impose. Things that morally ought to be nevertheless sometimes are not.

If seriality is the sole constraint on $\mathscr{R}$, the resulting logic for O is the modal logic D. Logic D, recall, builds on the modal system K by validating in addition all instances of $\Box\phi\rightarrow\Diamond\phi$, or $O\phi\rightarrow M\phi$ in the present context. These do indeed seem like logical truths: whatever is obligatory is permissible. The characteristic features of K also seem welcome: if ϕ is valid, so is $O\phi$ (recall the rule NEC); and every instance of the K-schema is valid (O distributes over $\rightarrow$). Further, since accessibility need not be reflexive, some instances of the T-schema $O\phi\rightarrow\phi$ turn out invalid, which is what we want (deontic necessity isn't alethic).

Formally speaking, there is no difference whatsoever between this semantics for deontic logic and the semantics for the modal system D. "Reconceptualizing" the accessibility relation has no effect on the definition of a model or the valuation function. But suppose you took possible-worlds semantics seriously, as being more than a mere formal semantics for formal languages—suppose you took it to give real truth conditions in terms of real possible worlds and real accessibility for natural-language modal and deontic talk. Then you would take the truth conditions for 'necessarily' and 'possibly' (understood in some nondeontic sense) to differ from the truth conditions for 'ought' and 'may', since their accessibility relations would be different relations. The accessibility relation in the semantics of 'ought' and 'may' would be a real relation of deontic accessibility (we wouldn't just be "thinking of it" as being such a relation), whereas the accessibility relation for 'necessarily' and 'possibly' would have nothing to do with normativity.

This is a mere beginning for deontic logic. Should we impose further constraints on the models? For example, is the principle (U) (for "utopia") $O(O\phi\rightarrow\phi)$ a valid principle of deontic logic? (This principle says that it *ought* to be the case that everything that ought to be true is true.) If so, we should find a corresponding condition to impose on the deontic accessibility relation, and impose it. And is our operator O adequate to represent all deontic reasoning? For example, how can we represent the apparently true sentence "if you kill the victim, you ought to kill him quickly" using O? The obvious candidates are:

$$K\rightarrow OQ$$
$$O(K\rightarrow Q)$$

But neither seems right. Against the first: suppose that you do in fact kill the victim. Then it would follow from the first that one of your obligations is to do the following: kill the victim quickly. But surely that's wrong; you ought not to kill the victim at all! Against the second: if it's the right representation of "if you kill the victim, you ought to kill him quickly", then the right representation of "if you kill the victim, you ought to kill him slowly" should be $O(K\rightarrow S)$. But $O(K\rightarrow S)$ follows from $O{\sim}K$ (given just a K modal logic for O), and "you ought not to kill the victim" certainly does not imply "if you kill the victim, you ought to kill him slowly".[80]

> **Exercise 7.1*** Find a condition on accessibility that validates every instance of (U).
>
> **Exercise 7.2*** Let X be the axiomatic system that results from modal system D by adding as additional axioms all instances of (U). Show that X is sound and complete with respect to a Kripke semantics in which the accessibility relation is required to be serial and also to obey the condition you came up with in exercise 7.1.

7.2 Epistemic logic

In deontic logic we took the $\Box$ of modal logic and gave it a deontic reading. In epistemic logic we give it an epistemic reading: we treat it as meaning "it is known (perhaps by a fixed agent S) to be the case that". On this reading, we write it: K. Thus $K\phi$ means that ϕ is known. ($\sim K\sim\phi$ can be thought of as a kind of epistemic possibility: "as far as what is known is concerned, ϕ might be true".)

As with deontic logic, we do semantics with Kripke models, conceptualized in a certain way. Formally, this is just modal logic: we still treat $K\phi$ as true at w iff ϕ is true at every accessible world. But now we think of the accessibility relation as "epistemic accessibility": $\mathcal{R}wv$ iff everything known in w is true in v.

The constraints on the formal properties of epistemic accessibility must clearly be different from those on deontic accessibility. For one thing, epistemic accessibility should be required to be reflexive: since knowledge implies truth, we want $K\phi\to\phi$ to be a valid principle of epistemic logic. Whether further constraints are appropriate is debatable. Do we want K to obey an S5 modal logic? The analogs for K of the characteristic axioms of S4 and S5 are controversial, but do have some plausibility. The S4-axiom for K is also known as the "KK" principle, or the principle of "positive introspection": $K\phi\to KK\phi$. From the S5-axiom schema we get the so-called principle of "negative introspection": $\sim K\phi\to K\sim K\phi$. These schemas (as well as the T-axiom schema) are all validated if we require the relation of epistemic accessibility to be an equivalence relation.

Whether the introspection principles are correct is a disputed question among epistemologists. It goes without saying that epistemic logic cannot hope to resolve this question on its own. The question is a philosophical one, about the nature of knowledge. One can develop formal systems in which these principles are valid, and formal systems in which they are not; it is up to the epistemologists to tell us which of these formal systems best models the actual logic of knowledge.

Regardless of what constraints we place on accessibility, the mere use of Kripke semantics gives K at least the features from system K. Some of these features are apparently objectionable. For example, if ϕ in fact logically implies ψ, then our

---

[80] See Feldman (1986) for more on this last issue.

system says that Kϕ logically implies Kψ (see exercise 7.3). That is, we know all the logical consequences of our knowledge. That seems wrong; can't I be unaware of subtle or complex consequences of what I know? But perhaps epistemic logic can be regarded as a useful idealization.

In addition to a logic of knowledge, we can develop a logic of belief, based on a new one-place sentence operator B. As before, the models are Kripke models, only now we think of $\mathcal{R}$ as a relation of "doxastic accessibility": $\mathcal{R}wv$ iff everything *believed* in w is true in v. Unlike epistemic accessibility, doxastic accessibility shouldn't be required to be reflexive (since belief is not factive); we don't want the T-principle B$P{\rightarrow}P$ to be valid. Nor do we want the B-principle ${\sim}$B${\sim}$B$P{\rightarrow}P$ to be valid: just because I don't believe that I don't believe P, it doesn't follow that P is true. As before, there is controversy over introspection—over whether B$\phi{\rightarrow}$BBϕ and ${\sim}$B$\phi{\rightarrow}$B${\sim}$Bϕ should be validated. If they should, then doxastic accessibility must be required to be transitive and also *Euclidean*: if $\mathcal{R}wv$ and $\mathcal{R}wu$, then $\mathcal{R}vu$. (We know from Chapter 6 that transitivity validates the S4 schema, and if you did exercise 6.15 you showed that Euclideanness validates the S5-schema.) This generates the modal logic K45, in which the K-, S4-, and S5-axioms are valid, but not the T- or B-axioms.

Exercise 7.3 Show that knowledge is closed under entailment in our epistemic logic. That is, show that if $\phi \vDash \psi$ then K$\phi \vDash$ Kψ. (For this problem it does not matter which constraints on accessibility are assumed.)

7.3 Propositional tense logic

7.3.1 *The metaphysics of time*

A logical treatment of the full range of things we say and think must cover temporal discourse. Some philosophers, however, think that this demands nothing beyond standard predicate logic. This was the view of many early logicians, notably Quine.[81] Here are some examples of how Quine would regiment temporal sentences in predicate logic:

Everyone who is now an adult was once a child
$\forall x(Axn \rightarrow \exists t[Etn \wedge Cxt])$

A dinosaur once trampled a mammal
$\exists x \exists y \exists t(Etn \wedge Dx \wedge My \wedge Txyt)$

Here, n (for "now") is a name of the present time (Quine treats moments of time as entities). E is a predicate for the *earlier-than* relation over moments of time. Thus Etn means that moment t is earlier than the present moment; $\exists t(Etn \wedge \phi(t))$ means that $\phi(t)$ is true at some moment t in the past, and so on. Quine adds an argument

---

[81]See, for example, Quine (1953*a*).

place for a moment of time to every predicate that can hold temporarily. Thus, instead of saying Cx—"x is a child"—he says Cxt: "x is a child at t". Finally, the quantifier $\exists x$ is *atemporal*, ranging over all objects at all times. Thus Quine is willing to say that *there is* a thing, x, that is a dinosaur, and which, at some previous time, trampled a mammal.

So: we can use Quine's strategy to represent temporal notions using standard predicate logic. But Quine's strategy presupposes a metaphysics of time that some philosophers reject. First, Quine assumes that there exist past objects. His symbolization of the presumably true sentence "A dinosaur once trampled a mammal" says that *there is* such a thing as a dinosaur. Quine's view is that time is "space-like". Past objects are as real as present ones; they're just temporally distant, just as spatially distant objects are just as real as the ones around here. (Defenders of this metaphysics usually say that future objects exist as well.) Second, Quine presupposes a distinctive metaphysics of change. Quine would describe my change from childhood to adulthood thus: $Cap \wedge Aan$, where a names me, n again names the present moment, and p names some past moment at which I was a child. Note the symmetry between the past state of my childhood, Cap, and the current state of my adulthood, Aan. Tenselessly speaking, the states are on a par: there's nothing metaphysically special about either. Some conclude that Quine's approach leaves no room for *genuine* change. His approach, they say, assimilates change too closely to variation across space: compare my being a child-at-p and an adult-at-n with the USA being mountainous-in-the-west and flat-in-the-middle.

Arthur Prior (1967; 1968) and others reject Quine's metaphysics of time. According to Prior, we must abandon Quine's approach to regimenting temporal discourse, and instead introduce *tense operators* into our most basic languages and develop an account of their logic. Thus he initiated the study of tense logic.

One of Prior's tense operators was P, symbolizing "it was the case that". Grammatically, P attaches to a complete sentence and forms another complete sentence. Thus, if R symbolizes "it is raining", then PR symbolizes "it was raining". If a sentence letter occurs by itself, outside of the scope of all temporal operators, then for Prior it is to be read as present-tensed. Thus it was appropriate to let R symbolize "it is raining"—i.e., it is *now* raining.

Suppose we symbolize "there exists a dinosaur" as $\exists x D x$. Prior would then symbolize "there once existed a dinosaur" as:

$$P \exists x D x$$

And according to Prior, $P \exists x D x$ is not to be analyzed as saying that there exist dinosaurs located in the past. For him, there is no further analysis of $P \exists x D x$. Prior's attitude toward P is like nearly everyone's attitude toward $\sim$. Nearly everyone agrees that $\sim$ is not further analyzable (for example, no one thinks that $\sim \exists x U x$, "there are no unicorns", is to be analyzed as saying that there exist unreal unicorns). Further, for Prior there is an asymmetry between past and present events that allows the possibility of genuine change. He represents the fact that I *was* a child thus: PCa, and the fact that I'm now an adult thus: Aa. Only statements about the present can be made unqualifiedly, without tense operators. Note also that Prior does away with Quine's relativization of temporary predicates to times. For Prior, the sentence *Aa* ("Ted is an adult") is a complete statement, but nevertheless can alter its truth value.

7.3.2 *Tense operators*

We will consider the result of adding tense operators to propositional logic. (One can also study predicate tense logic.) There are various tense operators one can add; here is one group:

> Gϕ : "it is, and is always going to be, the case that ϕ"
>
> Hϕ : "it is, and always has been, the case that ϕ"
>
> Fϕ : "it either is, or will at some point in the future be, the case that, ϕ"
>
> Pϕ : "it either is, or was at some point in the past, the case that ϕ"

Grammatically, we can take G and H as primitive, governed by the following clause in the definition of a wff:

- If ϕ is a wff, then so are Gϕ and Hϕ

Then we can define F and P:

- "Fϕ" is short for "$\sim$G$\sim\phi$"
- "Pϕ" is short for "$\sim$H$\sim\phi$"

One could also define further tense operators, for example A and S, for "always" and "sometimes", in terms of G and H:

- "Aϕ" is short for "H$\phi \wedge$ Gϕ"
- "Sϕ" is short for "P$\phi \vee$ Fϕ" (i.e., "$\sim$H$\sim\phi \vee \sim$G$\sim\phi$")

Other tense operators are not definable in terms of G and H. *Metrical* tense operators, for example, concern what happened or will happen at specific temporal distances in the past or future:

> P$^x \phi$: "it was the case x minutes ago that ϕ"
>
> F$^x \phi$: "it will be the case in x minutes that ϕ"

We will not consider metrical tense operators further.

The (nonmetrical) tense operators, as interpreted above, "include the present moment". For example, if Gϕ is now true, then ϕ must now be true. One could specify an alternate interpretation on which they do not include the present moment:

> Gϕ : "it is always going to be the case that ϕ"
>
> Hϕ : "it always has been the case that ϕ"
>
> Fϕ : "it will at some point in the future be the case that ϕ"
>
> Pϕ : "it was at some point in the past the case that ϕ"

Whether we take the tense operators as including the present moment will affect what kind of logic we develop. For example, Gϕ and Hϕ should imply ϕ if G and H are interpreted as including the present moment, but not otherwise.

7.3.3 Possible-worlds semantics for tense logic

As with deontic and epistemic logic, our semantic approach is to use Kripke models, conceived in a certain way. But our new conception is drastically different from our earlier conceptions. Now we think of the members of $\mathscr{W}$ as *times* rather than as possible worlds, we think of the accessibility relation as a temporal ordering relation, and we think of the interpretation function as assigning truth values to sentence letters at times.

(A Priorean faces hard philosophical questions about the use of such a semantics, since according to him, the semantics doesn't accurately model the metaphysics of time. The questions are like those questions that confront someone who uses possible-worlds semantics for modal logic but rejects a possible-worlds metaphysics of modality.)

This reconceptualization requires no change to the definition of an MPL-model. But to mark the change in thinking, let's change our notation. Since we're thinking of $\mathscr{W}$ as the set of times, let's rename it "$\mathscr{T}$", and let's use variables like t, t', etc., for its members. And since we're thinking of accessibility as a relation of temporal ordering— the *at-least-as-early-as* relation over times, in particular—let's rename it too: "$\leq$". (If we were interpreting the tense operators as not including the present moment, then we would think of the temporal ordering relation as the strictly-earlier-than relation, and would write it "$<$".) Thus, instead of writing "$\mathscr{R}ww'$", we write: $t \leq t'$.

We need to update the definition of the valuation function. The clauses for atomics, $\sim$, and $\rightarrow$ remain the same; but in place of the $\Box$ we now have two $\Box$-like operators, G and H, which look at different directions along the accessibility relation, so to speak. Here are their semantic clauses:

$$V_{\mathscr{M}}(G\phi, t) = 1 \text{ iff for every } t' \text{ such that } t \leq t', V_{\mathscr{M}}(\phi, t') = 1$$
$$V_{\mathscr{M}}(H\phi, t) = 1 \text{ iff for every } t' \text{ such that } t' \leq t, V_{\mathscr{M}}(\phi, t') = 1$$

F and P are then governed by the following derived clauses:

$$V_{\mathscr{M}}(F\phi, t) = 1 \text{ iff for some } t' \text{ such that } t \leq t', V_{\mathscr{M}}(\phi, t') = 1$$
$$V_{\mathscr{M}}(P\phi, t) = 1 \text{ iff for some } t' \text{ such that } t' \leq t, V_{\mathscr{M}}(\phi, t') = 1$$

Call an MPL-model, thought of in this way, a "PTL-model" (for "Priorean tense logic"). And say that a wff of tense logic is PTL-valid iff it is true in every time in every PTL-model. Given our discussion of system K from Chapter 6, we already know a lot about PTL-validity. The truth condition for the G is the same as the truth condition for the $\Box$ in MPL. So if you take a K-valid wff of MPL and change all the $\Box$s to Gs, you get a PTL-valid wff of tense logic. (For example, since $\Box(P{\wedge}Q){\rightarrow}\Box P$ is K-valid, $G(P{\wedge}Q){\rightarrow}GP$ is PTL-valid.) Similarly, replacing $\Box$s with Hs in a K-valid wff results in a PTL-valid wff (exercise 7.5). But in other cases, PTL-validity depends on the interaction between different tense operators; this has no direct analog in MPL. For example, $\phi{\rightarrow}GP\phi$ and $\phi{\rightarrow}HF\phi$ are both PTL-valid.

Exercise 7.4 Show that $\vDash_{\text{PTL}} \phi \rightarrow \text{GP}\phi$ and $\vDash_{\text{PTL}} \phi \rightarrow \text{HF}\phi$

Exercise 7.5* Show that replacing $\square$s with Hs in a K-valid formula of MPL results in a PTL-valid formula.

7.3.4 *Formal constraints on* $\leq$

PTL-validity is not a good model for logical truth in tense logic. We have so far placed no constraints on the formal properties of the relation $\leq$ in a PTL-model. That means that there are PTL-models in which the $\leq$ looks nothing like a temporal ordering. We don't normally think that time could consist of a number of temporally disconnected points, for example, or of many points each of which is at-least-as-early-as all of the rest, and so on, but there are PTL-models answering to these strange descriptions. PTL-validity, as I defined it, requires truth at every time in *every* PTL-model, even these strange models. This means that many tense-logical statements that ought, intuitively, to count as logical truths are in fact not PTL-valid.

The formula $\text{GP} \rightarrow \text{GGP}$ is an example. It is PTL-invalid, for consider a model with three times, t_1, t_2, and t_3, where $t_1 \leq t_2$, $t_2 \leq t_3$, and $t_1 \not\leq t_3$, and in which P is true at t_1 and t_2, but not at t_3:

In this model, $\text{GP} \rightarrow \text{GGP}$ is false at time t_1. But $\text{GP} \rightarrow \text{GGP}$ is, intuitively, a logical truth. If it is and will always be raining, then surely it must also be true that: it is and always will be the case that: it is and always will be raining. The problem, of course, is that the $\leq$ relation in the model we considered is intransitive, whereas one normally assumes that the at-least-as-early-as relation must be transitive.

More interesting notions of validity result from restricting the class of models in the definition of validity to those whose $\leq$ relations satisfy certain formal constraints. We might require $\leq$ to be transitive, for example. On this definition, every instance of the "S4"-schemas is valid:

$$\text{G}\phi \rightarrow \text{GG}\phi$$
$$\text{H}\phi \rightarrow \text{HH}\phi$$

It is also natural to require reflexivity, since doing so validates the "T"-schemas $\text{G}\phi \rightarrow \phi$ and $\text{H}\phi \rightarrow \phi$. (Assuming, that is, that we're construing the tense operators as including the present moment. If we construed them as not including the present moment, and thought of accessibility as meaning "strictly earlier than", then it would be natural to require that *no* time be accessible from itself.)

One might also require "connectivity" of some sort:

DEFINITION OF KINDS OF CONNECTIVITY: Let R be any binary relation over A.

- R is strongly connected in A iff for every $u, v \in A$, either Ruv or Rvu
- R is weakly connected iff for every u, v, v', IF: either Ruv and Ruv', or Rvu and $Rv'u$, THEN: either Rvv' or $Rv'v$

Thus we might require that the $\leq$ relation be strongly connected (in $\mathcal{T}$), or, alternatively, merely weakly connected. This would be to disallow "incomparable" pairs of times—pairs of times neither of which bears the $\leq$ relation to the other. The stronger requirement disallows *all* incomparable pairs; the weaker requirement merely disallows incomparable pairs when each member of the pair is after or before some one time. Thus the weaker requirement disallows "branches" in the temporal order but allows distinct timelines wholly disconnected from one another, whereas the stronger requirement insures that all times are part of a single non-branching structure. Each sort validates every instance of the following schemas (exercise 7.6):

$$\mathsf{G}(\mathsf{G}\phi \to \psi) \vee \mathsf{G}(\mathsf{G}\psi \to \phi)$$
$$\mathsf{H}(\mathsf{H}\phi \to \psi) \vee \mathsf{H}(\mathsf{H}\psi \to \phi)$$

There are other constraints one might impose, for example *anti-symmetry* (for no pair of distinct times does each time bear $\leq$ to the other), *density* (between any two times there is another time), or *eternality* (there exists neither a first nor a last time). Sometimes a constraint validates an interesting schema; sometimes it doesn't. Some constraints are more philosophically controversial than others.

Symmetry clearly should not be imposed. Obviously if one time is at least as early as another, then the second time needn't be at least as early as the first. Moreover, imposing symmetry would validate the "B"-schemas $\mathsf{FG}\phi \to \phi$ and $\mathsf{PH}\phi \to \phi$; but these clearly ought not to be validated. Take the first: it doesn't follow from *it will be the case that it is always going to be the case that I'm dead* that *I'm (now) dead*.

We have briefly examined Kripke semantics for deontic, epistemic and doxastic, and tense operators. Another interesting project in this vicinity is to explore connections between these and other operators. We might introduce a single language containing deontic, epistemic, and doxastic operators, as well as a $\square$ standing for some further sort of necessity—metaphysical necessity, say. A natural semantics for this language would be a Kripke semantics with multiple accessibility relations, one for each of the operators. This leads to interesting questions about how these operators logically relate to one another. Does knowledge logically imply belief? If so, $\mathsf{K}\phi \to \mathsf{B}\phi$ ought to come out valid, and so we should require that if one world is doxastically accessible from another, then it is epistemically accessible from it as well. Similarly, if metaphysical necessity implies knowledge, then we must validate $\square\phi \to \mathsf{K}\phi$, and so epistemic accessibility must be required to imply metaphysical accessibility (the kind of accessibility associated with the $\square$). Adding in tense operators generates a further dimension of complexity, since the models must now incorporate a set $\mathcal{T}$ of times in addition to the set $\mathcal{W}$ of worlds, and formulas must be evaluated for truth at world-time pairs.

We have considered only the semantic approach to deontic, epistemic and doxastic, and tense logic. What of a proof-theoretic approach? Since we have been treating these logics as modal logics, it should be no surprise that axiom systems similar to those of section 6.4 can be developed for them. Moreover, the techniques developed in sections 6.5–6.6 can be used to give soundness and completeness proofs for many of these axiomatic systems, relative to the possible-worlds semantics that we have developed.

> **Exercise 7.6** Show that all instances of $G(G\phi{\rightarrow}\psi)\vee G(G\psi{\rightarrow}\phi)$ and $H(H\phi{\rightarrow}\psi)\vee H(H\psi{\rightarrow}\phi)$ turn out valid if $\leq$ is required to be connected (either weakly or strongly).

7.4 Intuitionistic propositional logic: semantics

7.4.1 Proof stages

Intuitionistic propositional logic, recall, is a nonclassical logic developed by mathematical constructivists in which the law of the excluded middle and double-negation elimination fail. In section 3.5 we developed a proof theory for intuitionistic propositional logic by beginning with the classical sequent calculus and then dropping double-negation elimination while adding ex falso. In this section we will develop a semantics for intuitionistic logic due to Kripke.

The semantics is again of the possible-worlds variety. Formally speaking, the models will be just MPL-models, the only difference being a different definition of the valuation function. But informally, we think of these models differently. We no longer think of the members of $\mathcal{W}$ as possible worlds. Now we think of them as "stages" in an ongoing process of the construction of mathematical proofs. And now we think of the values 1 and 0 as "proof statuses" rather than as truth values: we think of $V(\phi, w) = 1$ as meaning that formula ϕ has been proved at stage w, and of $V(\phi, w) = 0$ as meaning that formula ϕ has not yet been proved at stage w.

Let's treat $\wedge$ and $\vee$, in addition to $\sim$ and $\rightarrow$, as primitive connectives. And to emphasize the different way we are regarding the "worlds", we rename $\mathcal{W}$ "$\mathscr{S}$", for proof *stages*, and we use the variables s, s', etc., for its members. Here is the semantics:

DEFINITION OF MODEL: An I-model is a triple $\langle \mathscr{S}, \mathscr{R}, \mathscr{I} \rangle$, such that:

- $\mathscr{S}$ is a non-empty set   ("proof stages")
- $\mathscr{R}$ is a reflexive and transitive binary relation over $\mathscr{S}$ ("accessibility")
- $\mathscr{I}$ is a two-place function that assigns 0 or 1 to each sentence letter, relative to each member of $\mathscr{S}$ ("interpretation function")
- for any sentence letter α, if $\mathscr{I}(\alpha, s) = 1$ and $\mathscr{R}ss'$, then $\mathscr{I}(\alpha, s') = 1$
                                                                    ("heredity condition")

DEFINITION OF VALUATION: Where $\mathscr{M}$ $(= \langle \mathscr{S}, \mathscr{R}, \mathscr{I} \rangle)$ is any I-model, the I-valuation for $\mathscr{M}$, $IV_{\mathscr{M}}$, is defined as the two-place function that assigns either 0 or 1 to each wff relative to each member of $\mathscr{S}$, subject to the following constraints, for any sentence letter α, any wffs ϕ and ψ, and any $s \in \mathscr{S}$:

$$\mathrm{IV}_{\mathscr{M}}(\alpha, s) = \mathscr{I}(\alpha, s)$$
$$\mathrm{IV}_{\mathscr{M}}(\phi \wedge \psi, s) = 1 \text{ iff } \mathrm{IV}_{\mathscr{M}}(\phi, s) = 1 \text{ and } \mathrm{IV}_{\mathscr{M}}(\psi, s) = 1$$
$$\mathrm{IV}_{\mathscr{M}}(\phi \vee \psi, s) = 1 \text{ iff } \mathrm{IV}_{\mathscr{M}}(\phi, s) = 1 \text{ or } \mathrm{IV}_{\mathscr{M}}(\psi, s) = 1$$
$$\mathrm{IV}_{\mathscr{M}}(\sim\phi, s) = 1 \text{ iff for every } s' \text{ such that } \mathscr{R}ss', \mathrm{IV}_{\mathscr{M}}(\phi, s') = 0$$
$$\mathrm{IV}_{\mathscr{M}}(\phi \to \psi, s) = 1 \text{ iff for every } s' \text{ such that } \mathscr{R}ss', \text{ either } \mathrm{IV}_{\mathscr{M}}(\phi, s') = 0$$
$$\text{or } \mathrm{IV}_{\mathscr{M}}(\psi, s') = 1$$

Note that the valuation conditions for the $\to$ and the $\sim$ at stage s no longer depend exclusively on what s is like: they are sensitive to what happens at stages accessible from s. Unlike the $\wedge$ and the $\vee$, $\to$ and $\sim$ are not "truth-functional" (relative to a stage); they behave like modal operators.

While it can be helpful to think informally of these models in terms of proof stages, this should be taken with more than the usual grain of salt. Intuitionists about mathematics would regard the real existence of a space of all possible future proof stages as clashing with their anti-platonistic philosophy of mathematics. Further, intuitionists don't regard mathematical statements (for example, those of arithmetic) as being *about* proofs. Finally, not everyone who employs intuitionistic logic is an intuitionist about mathematics. Officially, then, the semantics is nothing more than a formal tool, useful for establishing metalogical facts about section 3.5's proof theory (for example soundness and completeness—see below.)

Nevertheless, the proof-stage heuristic is vivid, so long as it isn't taken too seriously. In its terms, let's think a bit more about these models. Think of $\mathscr{S}$ as including all possible stages in the construction of mathematical proofs. Each stage s is associated with a certain collection Pr_s of proofs: those proofs you would have come up with if you were to arrive at that stage. When IV assigns 1 to a formula at stage s, that means that the formula is proved by some member of Pr_s—the formula is proven as of the stage. 0 means that none of the proofs in Pr_s proves the formula. (0 does *not* mean that the formula is *disproven*; perhaps it will be proven in some future stage.)

The holding of the accessibility relation represents which stages are left open, given what you know at your current stage. We can think of $\mathscr{R}ss'$ as meaning: if you're in stage s, then for all you know, you might subsequently be in stage s'. That is, if you know of the proofs in Pr_s, then for all you know, you might later come to possess $\mathrm{Pr}_{s'}$ as your set of proofs. At any point in time, various stages are accessible to you; the fewer proofs you've accumulated so far, the more accessible stages there are. As you accumulate more proofs, you move into one of these accessible stages.

Given this understanding of accessibility, reflexivity and transitivity are obviously correct to impose, as is the heredity condition, since (on the somewhat idealized conception of proof we are operating with) one does not *lose* proved information when constructing further proofs. But the accessibility relation will not in general be symmetric. Suppose that at stage s, you don't know whether you're going to be able to prove P. There is an accessible stage s' where you prove P (P is 1 there), and there are accessible stages (in addition to your own stage) where you don't prove P (P is 0 there). Now suppose you do in fact prove P, and so you reach stage s'. Stage s is then no longer accessible. For now you have a proof of P; and you know that you never *lose* proved information; so you know from your s' vantage point that you'll never again be in stage s.

Let's look at the conditions for the connectives $\wedge$, $\vee$, $\sim$, and $\rightarrow$, in the definition of IV. Remember that we are thinking of $IV(\phi, s) = 1$ intuitively as meaning that ϕ is proven at s. So the condition for the $\wedge$, for example, says that we've proved a conjunction $\phi \wedge \psi$, at some stage, if and only if we have proved ϕ at that stage and also have proved ψ at that stage. In fact, this is a very natural thing to say, since it is natural to take a proof of a conjunction $\phi \wedge \psi$ as consisting of two components, a proof of ϕ and a proof of ψ. Thus a natural conception of what a proof of a conjunction requires meshes with the clause for $\wedge$ in the definition of IV. The clauses for the other connectives also mesh with natural conceptions of the natures of proofs involving those connectives:

- a proof of $\phi \vee \psi$ is a proof of ϕ or a proof of ψ
- a proof of $\sim \phi$ is a construction for turning any proof of ϕ into a proof of a contradiction
- a proof of $\phi \rightarrow \psi$ is a construction for turning any proof of ϕ into a proof of ψ

Let's look more closely at the truth conditions for $\sim$ and $\rightarrow$. A proof of $\sim \phi$, according to the above conception, is a construction for turning a proof of ϕ into a proof of a contradiction. So if you've proved $\sim \phi$ at stage s ($IV(\sim \phi, s) = 1$), then at s you have such a construction, so you can rule out future stages in which you prove ϕ (provided you know that your methods of proof are consistent). And if you have *not* proved $\sim \phi$ at s ($IV(\sim \phi, s) = 0$), then you don't then have any such construction, and so for all you know, you will one day prove ϕ. So since $\mathscr{S}$ includes *all* possible stages in the development of proofs—and by these we'd better mean all epistemically possible stages, relative to any stage in $\mathscr{S}$—then there must be some $s' \in \mathscr{S}$ in which you prove ϕ, as the valuation condition for $\sim$ says. As for $\rightarrow$: if you have a method for converting any proof of ϕ into a proof of ψ, then at no stage in the future could you have a proof of ϕ without having a proof of ψ. Conversely, if you lack such a method, then for all you know, one day you will have a proof of ϕ but no proof of ψ.

We can now define intuitionistic validity and semantic consequence in the obvious way:

DEFINITIONS OF VALIDITY AND SEMANTIC CONSEQUENCE:

- ϕ is I-valid ($\vDash_I \phi$) iff $IV_{\mathscr{M}}(\phi, s) = 1$ for each stage s in each intuitionist model $\mathscr{M}$
- ϕ is an I-semantic-consequence of Γ ($\Gamma \vDash_I \phi$) iff for every intuitionist model $\mathscr{M}$ and every stage s in $\mathscr{M}$, if $IV_{\mathscr{M}}(\gamma, s) = 1$ for each $\gamma \in \Gamma$, then $IV_{\mathscr{M}}(\phi, s) = 1$

Exercise 7.7 Show that $\phi \vDash_I \psi$ iff $\vDash_I \phi \rightarrow \psi$.

Exercise 7.8* Show that intuitionist consequence implies classical consequence. That is, show that if $\Gamma \vDash_I \phi$, then $\Gamma \vDash_{PL} \phi$.

7.4.2 *Validity and semantic consequence*

Given the semantics just introduced, it's straightforward to demonstrate facts about validity and semantic consequence.

    Example 7.1: Show that $Q \vDash_I P \rightarrow Q$. (I'll omit the subscript "I" from now on.)

(i) Consider any model and any stage s; assume that $IV(Q, s) = 1$; and…

(ii) …suppose for reductio that $IV(P \rightarrow Q, s) = 0$. Thus, for some s', $\mathscr{R}ss'$ and $IV(P, s') = 1$ and $IV(Q, s') = 0$. Since $\mathscr{R}ss'$, the latter and (i) violate heredity.

    Example 7.2: Show that $P \rightarrow Q \vDash \sim Q \rightarrow \sim P$.

(i) Suppose $IV(P \rightarrow Q, s) = 1$; and…

(ii) …suppose for reductio that $IV(\sim Q \rightarrow \sim P, s) = 0$. So for some s', $\mathscr{R}ss'$ and $IV(\sim Q, s') = 1$ and…

(iii) …$IV(\sim P, s') = 0$. So for some s'', $\mathscr{R}s's''$ and $IV(P, s'') = 1$.

(iv) Given (ii), $IV(Q, s'') = 0$.

(v) By transitivity, $\mathscr{R}ss''$, and so given (i), either $IV(P, s'') = 0$ or $IV(Q, s'') = 1$. Contradiction with (iii) and (iv).

(Thus what I called "contraposition 2" in Chapter 2 is intuitionistically correct. But "contraposition 1" is not; see exercise 7.9d.)

    It's also straightforward to use the techniques of section 6.3.3 to construct countermodels.

    Example 7.3: Show that $\nvDash P \vee \sim P$. Here's a model in which $P \vee \sim P$ has the value 0 in stage r:

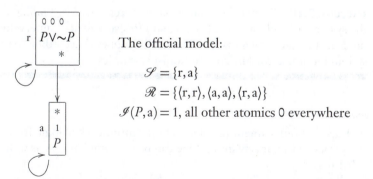

The official model:

$$\mathscr{S} = \{r, a\}$$
$$\mathscr{R} = \{\langle r, r \rangle, \langle a, a \rangle, \langle r, a \rangle\}$$
$$\mathscr{I}(P, a) = 1, \text{ all other atomics 0 everywhere}$$

(I'll skip the official models from now on.) As in section 6.3, we use asterisks to remind ourselves of commitments that concern other worlds/stages. The asterisk is under $\sim P$ in stage r because a negation with value 0 carries a commitment to including *some* stage at which the negated formula is 1. The asterisk is over the *P* in stage a because of the heredity condition: a sentence letter with value 1 commits us to making that letter 1 in *every* accessible stage. (Likewise, negations and conditionals that are 1 generate top-asterisks, and conditionals that are 0 generate bottom-asterisks.)

Example 7.4: Show that $\sim\sim P \nvDash P$. Here is a countermodel:

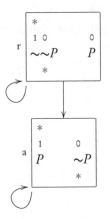

Note: since $\sim\sim P$ is 1 at r, that means that $\sim P$ must be 0 at every stage at which r sees. Now, $\mathscr{R}$rr, so $\sim P$ must be 0 at r. So r must see *some* stage in which P is 1. World a takes care of that.

Exercise 7.9 Establish the following facts.

   (a) $\sim(P{\wedge}Q) \nvDash_I \sim P \vee \sim Q$

   (b) $\sim P \vee \sim Q \vDash_I \sim(P{\wedge}Q)$

   (c) $P{\rightarrow}(Q{\vee}R) \nvDash_I (P{\rightarrow}Q)\vee(P{\rightarrow}R)$

   (d) $\sim P{\rightarrow}\sim Q \nvDash_I Q{\rightarrow}P$

Exercise 7.10* Bolster the conclusion of exercise 3.17 by finding, for the systems of Łukasiewicz, Kleene, and Priest, and also supervaluationism, a Γ and ϕ such that Γ semantically implies ϕ according to the system but not according to intuitionist semantics.

7.4.3 *Soundness*

Next let's show that our sequent proof system for intuitionistic logic from section 3.5 is sound, relative to our semantics. One can prove completeness as well, but we won't do that here.[82]

First we'll need to prove an intermediate theorem:

---

[82]See Kripke (1965); Priest (2001, section 6.7), although their proof systems are of the truth-tree variety.

Generalized heredity: The heredity condition holds for all formulas. That is, for any wff ϕ, whether atomic or no, and any stages s and s' in any I-model, if $IV(\phi, s) = 1$ and $\mathscr{R}ss'$, then $IV(\phi, s') = 1$.

Proof. The proof is by induction. The base case is just the official heredity condition. Next we make the inductive hypothesis (ih): heredity is true for formulas ϕ and ψ; we must now show that heredity also holds for $\sim\phi$, $\phi\rightarrow\psi$, $\phi\wedge\psi$, and $\phi\vee\psi$. I'll do this for $\phi\wedge\psi$, and leave the rest as exercises.

$\wedge$: Suppose for reductio that $IV(\phi\wedge\psi, s) = 1$, $\mathscr{R}ss'$, and $IV(\phi\wedge\psi, s') = 0$. Given the former, $IV(\phi, s) = 1$ and $IV(\psi, s) = 1$. By (ih), $IV(\phi, s') = 1$ and $IV(\psi, s') = 1$—contradiction. □

Now for soundness. What does soundness mean in the present context? The proof system in section 3.5 is a proof system for sequents, not individual formulas. So, first, we need a notion of intuitionist validity for sequents.

DEFINITION OF SEQUENT I-VALIDITY: Sequent $\Gamma \Rightarrow \phi$ is intuitionistically valid ("I-valid") iff $\Gamma \vDash_I \phi$.

We can now formulate soundness:

Soundness for intuitionism: Every intuitionistically provable sequent is I-valid.

Proof. This will be an inductive proof. Since a provable sequent is the last sequent in any proof, all we need to show is that every sequent in any proof is I-valid. And to do that, all we need to show is that the rule of assumptions generates I-valid sequents (base case), and that all the other rules allowed in intuitionist proofs preserve I-validity (induction step). For any set of wffs Γ, I-model $\mathcal{M}$, and stage s, let's write "$IV_{\mathcal{M}}(\Gamma, s) = 1$" to mean that $IV_{\mathcal{M}}(\gamma, s) = 1$ for each $\gamma \in \Gamma$.

Base case: the rule of assumptions generates sequents of the form $\phi \Rightarrow \phi$, which are clearly I-valid.

Inductive step: we show that the other sequent rules from section 3.5 preserve I-validity.

$\wedge$I: Here we assume that the inputs to $\wedge$I are I-valid, and show that its output is I-valid. That is, we assume that $\Gamma \Rightarrow \phi$ and $\Delta \Rightarrow \psi$ are I-valid sequents, and we must show that it follows that $\Gamma, \Delta \Rightarrow \phi\wedge\psi$ is also I-valid. So suppose otherwise for reductio. Then $IV(\Gamma\cup\Delta, s) = 1$ and $IV(\phi\wedge\psi, s) = 0$, for some stage s in some I-model. Since $\Gamma \Rightarrow \phi$ is I-valid, $IV(\phi, s) = 1$ (we know that $IV(\Gamma\cup\Delta, s) = 1$, i.e., all members of $\Gamma\cup\Delta$ are 1 at s in the model we're discussing; so all members of Γ are 1 at s in this model, so since $\Gamma \Rightarrow \phi$ is I-valid, ϕ is 1 at s in this model). Similarly, since $\Delta \Rightarrow \psi$ is I-valid, $IV(\psi, s) = 1$. Contradiction.

$\vee$E: Assume that (i) $\Gamma \Rightarrow \phi\vee\psi$, (ii) $\Delta_1, \phi \Rightarrow \chi$, and (iii) $\Delta_2, \psi \Rightarrow \chi$ are all I-valid, and suppose for reductio that $\Gamma, \Delta_1, \Delta_2 \Rightarrow \chi$ is I-invalid. So $IV(\Gamma\cup\Delta_1\cup\Delta_2, s) = 1$ but $IV(\chi, s) = 0$, for some stage s in some model. Since sequent (i) is I-valid, $IV(\phi\vee\psi, s) = 1$, so either ϕ or ψ is 1 at s. If the former, then by the I-validity of (ii), $IV(\chi, s) = 1$; if the latter, then by the I-validity of (iii), $IV(\chi, s) = 1$. Either way, we have a contradiction.

I leave the proof that the remaining rules preserve I-validity as an exercise.   □

I can now justify an assertion I made, but did not prove, in section 3.5. I asserted there that the sequent $\emptyset \Rightarrow P \lor {\sim}P$ is not intuitionistically provable. Given the soundness proof, to demonstrate that a sequent is not intuitionistically provable, it suffices to show that its premises do not I-semantically-imply its conclusion. But in example 7.3 we showed that $\nvDash P \lor {\sim}P$, which is equivalent to saying that $\emptyset \nvDash P \lor {\sim}P$.

Similarly, we showed in example 7.4 that ${\sim}{\sim}P \nvDash P$. Thus, by the soundness theorem, the sequent ${\sim}{\sim}P \Rightarrow P$ isn't provable. (Recall how, in constructing our proof system for intuitionism in section 3.5, we dropped the rule of double-negation elimination.)

Exercise 7.11 Of the PL-axiom schemas (section 2.6), which are intuitionistically acceptable (i.e., which have only I-valid instances)?

Exercise 7.12 Complete the proof of generalized heredity.

Exercise 7.13 Complete the soundness proof by showing that ∧E, ∨I, DNI, RAA, →I, →E, and EF preserve I-validity.

8

COUNTERFACTUALS

CERTAIN CONDITIONALS in natural language seem different both from propositional logic's material conditionals and from modal logic's strict conditionals.
In this chapter we consider "counterfactual" conditionals—conditionals that (loosely
speaking) have the form:

If it had been that ϕ, it would have been that ψ.

For instance:

If I had struck this match, it would have lit.

The counterfactuals that we typically utter have false antecedents (hence the
name), and are phrased in the subjunctive mood. It is common to distinguish counterfactuals from "indicative conditionals"—conditionals phrased in the indicative
mood. A famous example illustrates the apparent semantic difference: the counterfactual conditional 'If Oswald hadn't shot Kennedy, someone else would have' is false
(assuming that certain conspiracy theories are false and Oswald was acting alone);
but the indicative conditional 'If Oswald didn't shoot Kennedy, then someone else
did' is true (we know that *someone* shot Kennedy, so if it wasn't Oswald, it must have
been someone else). The semantics of indicative conditionals is an important topic
in its own right (they too seem to differ from material and strict conditionals), but
we won't take up that topic here.[83]

We symbolize the counterfactual with antecedent ϕ and consequent ψ thus:
$\phi \,\square\!\!\rightarrow \psi$. What should the logic of this new connective $\square\!\!\rightarrow$ be?

8.1 Natural-language counterfactuals

Well, let's have a look at how natural language counterfactuals behave. Our survey
will provide guidance for our main task: developing a semantics for $\square\!\!\rightarrow$. We will
attend in particular to the differences between counterfactual, material, and strict
conditionals.

8.1.1 Antecedents and consequents

Our system for counterfactuals should have the following features:

$$\sim\!P \nvDash P \,\square\!\!\rightarrow Q$$
$$Q \nvDash P \,\square\!\!\rightarrow Q$$

---

[83] For a good overview see Edgington (1995).

For suppose I did not in fact strike the match. It doesn't logically follow that if I had struck the match, it would have turned into a feather. So if $\square\!\!\rightarrow$ is to represent 'if it had been that…, it would have been that…', $\sim P$ should not semantically imply $P\square\!\!\rightarrow Q$. Similarly, George W. Bush (somehow) won the 2004 United States presidential election, but it doesn't follow that if the newspapers had discovered beforehand that Bush had an affair with Al Gore, he would still have won. So our semantics had better not count $P\square\!\!\rightarrow Q$ as a semantic consequence of Q either.

(Relatedly, counterfactuals aren't truth-functional. In the case where I did not in fact strike the match, the counterfactuals 'If I had struck the match, it would have turned into a feather' and 'If I had struck the match, it would have lit' both have false antecedents and false consequents; but they differ in truth value.)

Like counterfactuals, strict conditionals are not in general implied by the falsity of their antecedents or the truth of their consequents (in any modal system). The material conditional, however, *is* implied by the truth of its consequent or the falsity of its antecedent (and it's truth-functional). We have our first logical difference between counterfactual and material conditionals.

8.1.2 Can be contingent

In the actual world, since there was no conspiracy, it's not true that if Oswald hadn't shot Kennedy, someone else would have. But in a metaphysically possible world in which there is a conspiracy and Oswald has a backup (though shoots Kennedy himself), it presumably *is* true that if Oswald hadn't shot Kennedy, someone else would have. Thus our logic should allow counterfactuals to be contingent statements. Just because a counterfactual is true, it should not follow logically that it is metaphysically necessarily true; and just because a counterfactual is false, it should not follow logically that it is metaphysically necessarily false. That is, our semantics for $\square\!\!\rightarrow$ should have the following features:

$$P\square\!\!\rightarrow Q \nvDash \square(P\square\!\!\rightarrow Q)$$
$$\sim(P\square\!\!\rightarrow Q) \nvDash \square\sim(P\square\!\!\rightarrow Q)$$

where the $\square$ expresses metaphysical necessity.

Given the definition of $\phi\dashv\psi$ as $\square(\phi\rightarrow\psi)$, it's easy to check that $\phi\dashv\psi \vDash_{S4} \square(\phi\dashv\psi)$ and $\sim(\phi\dashv\psi)\vDash_{S5} \square\sim(\phi\dashv\psi)$. So if metaphysical necessity obeys S4 or S5, then $\square\!\!\rightarrow$ and $\dashv$ have different logics if the $\square$ in the definition of $\dashv$ expresses metaphysical necessity.

8.1.3 No augmentation

The $\rightarrow$ and the $\dashv$ (in all systems) obey the argument form *augmentation*:

$$\frac{\phi\rightarrow\psi}{(\phi\wedge\chi)\rightarrow\psi} \qquad \frac{\phi\dashv\psi}{(\phi\wedge\chi)\dashv\psi}$$

That is, $\phi\rightarrow\psi \vDash_{PL} (\phi\wedge\chi)\rightarrow\psi$ and $\phi\dashv\psi \vDash_K (\phi\wedge\chi)\dashv\psi$. However, natural-language counterfactuals famously appear *not* to obey augmentation. If I'm holding a dry match and am a competent match-striker, then the following sentence is true:

If I had struck the match, it would have lit.

But the following sentence—the result of applying augmentation—seems false:

If I had struck the match and had been in outer space, it would have lit.

So we have another desideratum for our semantics for counterfactuals: it should turn out that $P\square\rightarrow Q \nvDash (P\wedge R)\square\rightarrow Q$.

8.1.4 No contraposition

$\rightarrow$ and $\dashv3$ obey contraposition:

$$\frac{\phi\rightarrow\psi}{\sim\psi\rightarrow\sim\phi} \qquad \frac{\phi\dashv3\psi}{\sim\psi\dashv3\sim\phi}$$

But counterfactuals apparently do not. Suppose I'm on a firing squad that executes a victim. The only chance the victim had for survival was for all of our guns to jam; but unfortunately for him, none of the guns jammed. In this scenario, the following sentence seems true:

If my gun had jammed, the victim would (still) have died.

After all, there's no reason to suppose that the other guns would also have jammed if mine had. But since the only chance for survival was for all the guns to jam, the result of applying contraposition seems false:

If the victim had not died, my gun would not have jammed.

8.1.5 Some implications

Here is an argument form that intuitively *should* hold for the $\square\rightarrow$:

$$\frac{\phi\square\rightarrow\psi}{\phi\rightarrow\psi}$$

The counterfactual conditional should imply the material conditional.[84] We can argue for this contrapositively: if the material conditional $\phi\rightarrow\psi$ is false, then ϕ is true and ψ is false. But surely a counterfactual with a true antecedent and false consequent is false.

Also, when understood in terms of metaphysical necessity, the strict conditional arguably should imply the counterfactual:

$$\frac{\phi\dashv3\psi}{\phi\square\rightarrow\psi}$$

For if it's metaphysically necessary that ψ is true whenever ϕ is, then, it seems, if ϕ had been true, ψ would *have* to have been true as well.

---

[84] $\square\rightarrow$ will then obey modus ponens and modus tollens since $\rightarrow$ obeys both. That is, we'll have $\phi, \phi\square\rightarrow\psi \vDash \psi$ and $\sim\psi, \phi\square\rightarrow\psi \vDash \sim\phi$.

8.1.6 *Context dependence*

Years ago, a few of us were at a restaurant in NY—Red Smith, Frank Graham, Allie Reynolds, Yogi [Berra] and me. At about 11.30 p.m., Ted [Williams] walked in helped by a cane. Graham asked us what we thought Ted would hit if he were playing today. Allie said, "due to the better equipment probably about .350." Red Smith said, "About .385." I said, "due to the lack of really great pitching about .390." Yogi said, ".220." We all jumped up and I said, "You're nuts, Yogi! Ted's lifetime average is .344." "Yeah," said Yogi, "but he is 74 years old."

Buzzie Bavasi, baseball executive

Who was right? If Ted Williams had played at the time the story was told, would he or wouldn't he have hit over .300?

Clearly, there's no single correct answer. The first respondents were imagining Williams playing as a young man. Understood that way, the answer is, no doubt: yes, he would have hit over .300. But Berra took the question a different way: he was imagining Williams hitting as he was then: a 74-year-old man. Berra took the others off guard, by deliberately (?—this is Yogi Berra we're talking about) shifting how the question was construed, but he didn't make a semantic *mistake* in so doing. It's perfectly legitimate, in other circumstances anyway, to take the question in Berra's way. (Imagine Williams muttering to himself at the time: "These punks nowadays! If I were playing today, I'd *still* hit over .300!") Counterfactual sentences can be interpreted in different ways depending on the conversational context in which they are uttered.

Another example:

> If Syracuse had been located in Louisiana, Syracuse winters would have been warm.

True or false? It might seem true: Louisiana is in the south. But wait—perhaps Louisiana would have included Syracuse by having its borders extend north to Syracuse's actual latitude.

Would Syracuse have been warm in the winter? Would Williams have hit over .300? No single answer is correct, once and for all. Which answer is correct depends on the linguistic context. Whether a counterfactual is true or whether it is false depends in part on what the speaker means to say, and on what her audience takes her to be saying, when she utters the counterfactual. When we consider the counterfactual hypothesis that Syracuse is located in Louisiana, we imagine reality having been different in certain respects from actuality. In particular, we imagine Syracuse having been in Louisiana. But we don't imagine reality having been different in any old way—we don't imagine Syracuse and Louisiana both being located in China. We hold certain things constant (Syracuse and Louisiana not being in China) while varying others. The question then arises: what parts of reality, exactly, do we hold constant? In the Syracuse–Louisiana case, we seem to have at least two choices. Do we hold constant the location of Syracuse, or do we hold constant the borders of Louisiana? The truth value of the counterfactual depends on which choice we make.

What determines which things are to be held constant when we evaluate the truth value of a counterfactual? In large part: the context of utterance of the counterfactual.

Suppose I am in the middle of the following conversation: "Syracuse restaurants struggle to survive because the climate there is so bad: no one wants to go out to eat in the winter. If Syracuse had been located in Louisiana, its restaurants would have done much better." In such a context, an utterance of the counterfactual "If Syracuse had been located in Louisiana, Syracuse winters would have been warm" would be regarded as true. But if this counterfactual were uttered in the midst of the following conversation, it would be regarded as false: "You know, Louisiana is statistically the warmest state in the country. Good thing Syracuse isn't located in Louisiana, because that would have ruined the statistic."

Does just saying a sentence, intending it to be true, make it true? Well, sort of! When a sentence has a meaning that is partly determined by context, then when a person utters that sentence with the intention of saying something true, that tends to create a context in which the sentence *is* true. In ordinary circumstances, if you looked at your kitchen table and said "that table is flat", you would be saying something true. But suppose a scientist walked into your kitchen and said: "you know, macroscopic objects are far from being flat. Take that table, for instance. It isn't flat at all; when viewed under a microscope, it can be seen to have a very irregular surface." You'd take the scientist to be saying something true as well. Indeed, you'd go along with her and say yourself: "that table is not flat". (You wouldn't take this to contradict your earlier utterance of 'that table is flat'. You meant something different earlier.) The term 'flat' can mean different things depending on how strict the standards are for counting as "flat". What the standards are depends on the conversational context, and when the scientist made her speech, you and she adopted standards under which what she said came out true.[85]

8.2 The Lewis–Stalnaker theory

What do counterfactuals mean? What are their truth conditions? David Lewis (1973*a*) and Robert Stalnaker (1968) give versions of the following answer. To determine whether a counterfactual $P\square\!\!\rightarrow Q$ is true, we must consider all the possible worlds in which P is true, and find the one that is most similar to the actual world. $P\square\!\!\rightarrow Q$ is true in the actual world if and only if Q is true in that most similar world. Consider Lewis's example:

> If kangaroos had no tails, they would topple over.

This counterfactual seems true. Lewis explains this as follows. When we consider the possible world that would be actual if kangaroos had no tails, we do not depart gratuitously from actuality. We do not consider a world in which kangaroos have wings, or crutches. We do not consider a world with different laws of nature, in which there is no gravity. We keep the kangaroos and the laws of nature as similar as we can to how they actually are (while still removing the tails). In such a world, it seems, the kangaroos would topple over.

---

[85] See Lewis (1979).

In the previous section we saw how one and the same counterfactual sentence can have different truth values in different contexts. On the Lewis–Stalnaker view, this context dependence results from the fact that the similarity relation mentioned in the truth conditions for counterfactuals varies from context to context.

To clarify this point, let's think generally about similarity. Things can be similar in certain respects but not in others. A blue square is similar to a blue circle in respect of color, not in respect of shape. What happens when you compare objects that differ in multiple respects? Is a blue square more like a blue circle or a red square? There's clearly no once-and-for-all answer. If we grant more importance to similarity in color than to similarity in shape, then the blue square is more like the blue circle; if we grant more importance to shape, then the blue square is more like the red square. Put another way: a similarity relation that "weights" shape more heavily counts the red square as being more similar, whereas a similarity relation that weights color more heavily counts the blue circle as being more similar. The multiplicity of similarity relations only increases when we move to possible-worlds similarity. When comparing entire possible worlds, there is a vast number of respects of similarity, and so there is room for many, many similarity relations, differing from one another over the relative weights assigned to different respects of comparison.

Return, now, to the example of context dependence from the previous section:

> If Syracuse had been located in Louisiana, Syracuse winters would have been warm.

When we affirm this counterfactual, according to Lewis and Stalnaker we are using a similarity relation that weights heavily Louisiana's actual borders. Under this similarity relation, the possible world most similar to actuality is one in which Syracuse has moved south. When we reject the counterfactual, we are using a similarity relation that weights Syracuse's actual location more heavily; under this similarity relation, the most similar world is one in which Louisiana extends north.

8.3 Stalnaker's system

Lewis and Stalnaker give different semantic systems for counterfactuals. Each system is based on the intuitive idea described in the previous section, but the systems differ over details. I'll begin with Stalnaker's system (since it's simpler), and call it SC, for Stalnaker conditionals.[86]

8.3.1 Syntax of SC

The primitive vocabulary of SC is that of propositional modal logic, plus the connective $\Box\!\!\rightarrow$. Here's the grammar:

DEFINITION OF WFF:

- Sentence letters are wffs
- If ϕ, ψ are wffs, then $(\phi\!\rightarrow\!\psi)$, $\sim\!\phi$, $\Box\phi$, and $(\phi\,\Box\!\!\rightarrow\!\psi)$ are wffs

---

[86] See Stalnaker (1968). The version of the theory I present here is slightly different from Stalnaker's original version; see Lewis (1973*a*, p. 79).

- Nothing else is a wff

8.3.2 *Semantics of SC*

Where R is a three-place relation, let's abbreviate "$Rxyz$" as "R_zxy". And, where u is any object, let "R_u" be the *two*-place relation that holds between objects x and y iff R_uxy. (Think of R_u as the two-place relation that results from "plugging up" one place of the three-place relation R with object u.)

Here are the definitions of an SC-model and its valuation function (SC-validity and SC-semantic consequence are then defined in the usual way):

DEFINITION OF MODEL: An SC-model, $\mathcal{M}$, is an ordered triple $\langle \mathcal{W}, \preceq, \mathcal{I} \rangle$, where:

- $\mathcal{W}$ is a nonempty set ("worlds")
- $\mathcal{I}$ is a two-place function that assigns either 0 or 1 to each sentence letter relative to each $w \in \mathcal{W}$ ("interpretation function")
- $\preceq$ is a three-place relation over $\mathcal{W}$ ("nearness relation")
- The valuation function $V_{\mathcal{M}}$ for $\mathcal{M}$ (see below) and $\preceq$ satisfy the following conditions:
  - for any $w \in \mathcal{W}$: $\preceq_w$ is strongly connected in $\mathcal{W}$
  - for any $w \in \mathcal{W}$: $\preceq_w$ is transitive
  - for any $w \in \mathcal{W}$: $\preceq_w$ is anti-symmetric
  - for any $x, y \in \mathcal{W}$: $x \preceq_x y$ ("base")
  - for any SC-wff, ϕ, provided $V_{\mathcal{M}}(\phi, v) = 1$ for at least one $v \in \mathcal{W}$, then for every $z \in \mathcal{W}$, there's some $w \in \mathcal{W}$ such that $V_{\mathcal{M}}(\phi, w) = 1$, and such that for any $x \in \mathcal{W}$, if $V_{\mathcal{M}}(\phi, x) = 1$ then $w \preceq_z x$ ("limit")

(A binary relation R is strongly connected in set A iff for each $u, v \in A$, either Ruv or Rvu, and anti-symmetric iff $u = v$ whenever both Ruv and Rvu.)

DEFINITION OF VALUATION: Where $\mathcal{M}$ $(= \langle \mathcal{W}, \preceq, \mathcal{I} \rangle)$ is any SC-model, the SC-valuation for $\mathcal{M}$, $V_{\mathcal{M}}$ is defined as the two-place function that assigns either 0 or 1 to each SC-wff relative to each member of $\mathcal{W}$, subject to the following constraints, where α is any sentence letter, ϕ and ψ are any wffs, and w is any member of $\mathcal{W}$:

$$V_{\mathcal{M}}(\alpha, w) = \mathcal{I}(\alpha, w)$$
$$V_{\mathcal{M}}(\sim\phi, w) = 1 \text{ iff } V_{\mathcal{M}}(\phi, w) = 0$$
$$V_{\mathcal{M}}(\phi \rightarrow \psi, w) = 1 \text{ iff either } V_{\mathcal{M}}(\phi, w) = 0 \text{ or } V_{\mathcal{M}}(\psi, w) = 1$$
$$V_{\mathcal{M}}(\Box\phi, w) = 1 \text{ iff for any } v \in \mathcal{W}, V_{\mathcal{M}}(\phi, v) = 1$$
$$V_{\mathcal{M}}(\phi \Box\!\!\rightarrow \psi, w) = 1 \text{ iff for any } x \in \mathcal{W}, \text{ IF } [V_{\mathcal{M}}(\phi, x) = 1 \text{ and for any } y \in \mathcal{W} \text{ such that } V_{\mathcal{M}}(\phi, y) = 1, x \preceq_w y] \text{ THEN: } V_{\mathcal{M}}(\psi, x) = 1$$

Phew! Let's look into what this all means.

First, notice that much here is the same as with MPL. A model still has a set of worlds, and an interpretation function that assigns truth values to sentence letters relative to worlds. As before, a valuation function then assigns truth values to complex wffs relative to worlds. The propositional connectives → and ~ have their usual truth conditions (so the derived clauses for ∧, ∨, and ↔ remain the same).

What happened to the accessibility relation? I've dropped it for simplicity's sake. The truth condition for □ϕ is now just that ϕ is true in *all* worlds. (This is equivalent to including an accessibility relation but requiring it to be total, which generates an S5 modal logic for the □ as noted in exercise 6.1.) The derived truth condition for the ◇ is then:

$$\text{V}_{\mathcal{M}}(\Diamond\phi, w) = 1 \text{ iff for some } v \in \mathcal{W}, \text{V}_{\mathcal{M}}(\phi, v) = 1$$

Next, what about this nearness relation $\preceq$? Think of $x \preceq_z y$ as meaning that possible world x is at least as similar to ("near to") world z as is world y; thus, think of $\preceq$ as the similarity relation between possible worlds that we talked about before. To decide whether $x \preceq_w y$, place yourself in possible world w, and ask which possible world is more similar to yours, x or y.

(An option I won't pursue would be to represent context dependence by introducing a set $\mathcal{C}$ of "contexts of utterance" and multiple nearness relations $\preceq_1, \preceq_2 \ldots$ into the models. We could then relativize truth values to contexts (members of $\mathcal{C}$), allowing which nearness relation determines the truth conditions of □→ to depend on the context.)

I say "we can think of" $\preceq$ as a similarity relation, but take this with a grain of salt. As I keep emphasizing, model theory isn't metaphysics. Just as our definitions allow the members of $\mathcal{W}$ to be any old things, so $\preceq$ is allowed to be any old relation over $\mathcal{W}$. Just as the members of $\mathcal{W}$ could be numbers or people or bananas, so the $\preceq$ relation could be any old relation over those numbers or people or bananas. (But as before, if the truth conditions for natural-language counterfactuals have nothing to do with real possible worlds and similarity, then the interest of our semantics is diminished, since the models won't be *modeling* the semantics of natural-language counterfactuals.)

The constraints on the formal properties of $\preceq$—some of them, anyway—seem plausible if $\preceq$ is to be thought of as a similarity relation. Strong connectivity says that any two worlds can be compared for similarity to a given world. Transitivity has a transparent meaning. Anti-symmetry prohibits "ties"—it says that two distinct worlds cannot each be at least as close to a given world w as the other. The "base" constraint says that every world is at least as close to itself as is every other. (Given anti-symmetry, each world must then be *closer* to itself than any other world is, where "x is closer to w than y is" ($x \prec_w y$) means that $x \preceq_w y$ and $y \npreceq_w x$.) Finally, the "limit" assumption says that "there's always a closest ϕ-world". That is, no matter what world w you're in, for any wff ϕ there will always be some world x in which ϕ is true that is at least as close to your world as is any other ϕ-world (unless ϕ isn't true in any worlds at all). The limit assumption prohibits the following: there are no closest ϕ-worlds, only an infinite sequence of closer and closer ϕ-worlds. (Notice that the limit assumption automatically holds whenever there are only finitely many worlds. So when we start constructing countermodels, if they're finite then we won't need to separately verify that they satisfy the limit assumption.) Some of these assumptions have been challenged, especially anti-symmetry and limit. We will consider these challenges below.

Note how the limit assumption refers to the valuation function. (MPL-models, by contrast, are defined without reference to the valuation function.) The limit assumption is a constraint that relates the nearness relation to the truth values of *all* formulas, complex or otherwise: it says that *any* formula ϕ that is true somewhere is true in some closest-to-w-world. (See exercise 8.1.)

> **Exercise 8.1*** Could we have stated an official limit assumption just for atomics, and then proved a derived limit assumption for complex wffs (as with heredity in the semantics for intuitionistic logic)?

8.4 Establishing validity in SC

Here are some examples of semantic validity proofs in Stalnaker's system.

Example 8.1: Show that $\vDash_{SC} (P \wedge Q) \rightarrow (P \square\!\!\rightarrow Q)$. Where $\langle \mathcal{W}, \preceq, \mathscr{I} \rangle$ is any SC-model and r is any world in $\mathcal{W}$:

(i) Suppose for reductio that $V((P \wedge Q) \rightarrow (P \square\!\!\rightarrow Q), r) = 0$. Then $V(P \wedge Q, r) = 1$ and…

(ii) $V(P \square\!\!\rightarrow Q, r) = 0$. Now, the truth condition for $\square\!\!\rightarrow$ says that $P \square\!\!\rightarrow Q$ is true in r iff Q is true in every closest-to-r P-world. So since $P \square\!\!\rightarrow Q$ is false in r, there must be a closest-to-r P-world in which Q is false—that is, there is some world a such that:

    (a) $V(P, a) = 1$

    (b) for any x, if $V(P, x) = 1$ then $a \preceq_r x$

    (c) $V(Q, a) = 0$

(iii) From line (i), $V(P, r) = 1$. So given (b), $a \preceq_r r$. By base, $r \preceq_r a$. So, by anti-symmetry, $r = a$. Since $V(Q, r) = 1$ by (i), we have $V(Q, a) = 1$, contradicting (c).

Example 8.2: Show that $\vDash_{SC} [(P \square\!\!\rightarrow Q) \wedge ((P \wedge Q) \square\!\!\rightarrow R)] \rightarrow [P \square\!\!\rightarrow R]$. (This formula is worth taking note of, because it is valid despite its similarity to the invalid formula $[(P \square\!\!\rightarrow Q) \wedge (Q \square\!\!\rightarrow R)] \rightarrow [P \square\!\!\rightarrow R]$; see below.)

(i) Suppose for reductio that the formula is false in some world r in some SC-model. Then (given the truth conditions for $\rightarrow$ and $\wedge$) $V(P \square\!\!\rightarrow Q, r) = 1$ and…

(ii) $V((P \wedge Q) \square\!\!\rightarrow R, r) = 1$ but…

(iii) $V(P \square\!\!\rightarrow R, r) = 0$. So some a is a nearest-to-r P-world (i.e., $V(P, a) = 1$, and for any x, if $V(P, x) = 1$ then $a \preceq_r x$), and $V(R, a) = 0$.

(iv) By (i), Q is true in all nearest-to-r P-worlds, and so by (iii), $V(Q, a) = 1$.

(v) Note now that a is a nearest-to-r $P \wedge Q$-world. For:

    (a) By lines (iii) and (iv), $V(P \wedge Q, a) = 1$.

(b) For any world x, if $V(P \wedge Q, x) = 1$, then $a \preceq_r x$. For let $V(P \wedge Q, x) = 1$; then $V(P, x) = 1$; but then by (iii), $a \preceq_r x$.

(vi) So by (ii) and (v), $V(R, a) = 1$, contradicting (iii).

Exercise 8.2 Show that the counterfactual is intermediate in strength between the strict and material conditionals; i.e., that:

(a) $\phi \dashv 3 \psi \vDash_{SC} \phi \square\!\!\rightarrow \psi$

(b) $\phi \square\!\!\rightarrow \psi \vDash_{SC} \phi \rightarrow \psi$

8.5 Establishing invalidity in SC

In this section we'll learn how to construct countermodels in SC. Along the way we'll also look at how to decide whether a given formula is SC-valid or SC-invalid. As with plain old modal logic, the best strategy is to attempt to come up with a countermodel. If you fail, you can use your failed attempt to guide the construction of a validity proof.

We can use diagrams like those from section 6.3.3 to represent SC-countermodels. The diagrams will be a little different though. They will still contain boxes (rounded now, to distinguish them from the old countermodels) in which we put formulas; and we again indicate truth values of formulas with numbers above the formulas. But since there is no accessibility relation, we don't need the arrows between the boxes. And since we need to represent the nearness relation, we will arrange the boxes vertically. At the bottom goes a box for the world, r, of our model in which we're trying to make a given formula false. We string the other worlds in the diagram above this bottom world r: the further away a world is from r in the $\preceq_r$ ordering, the further above r we place it in the diagram. Thus a countermodel for the formula $\sim\!P \rightarrow (P \square\!\!\rightarrow Q)$ might look as follows:

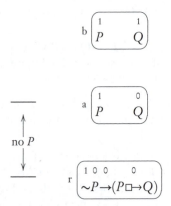

In this diagram, the world we're primarily focusing on is the bottom world, world r. The nearest world to r is world r itself. The next nearest world to r is the next world moving up from the bottom: world a. The furthest world from r is world b. Notice that P is false in world r, and true in worlds a and b. Thus a is the nearest world to r in which P is true. Since Q is false in world a, that makes the counterfactual $P\square\!\!\rightarrow Q$ false in world r. Since $\sim\!P$ is true and $P\square\!\!\rightarrow Q$ is false in r, the material conditional $\sim\!P\rightarrow(P\square\!\!\rightarrow Q)$ is false in r, as desired. (World b isn't needed in this countermodel; I included it merely for illustration.) The "no P" sign to the left of worlds a and r is a reminder to ourselves in case we want to add further worlds to the diagram later on. It reminds us not to put any P-worlds between a and r. Otherwise world a would no longer be the nearest P-world.

What strategy should one use for constructing SC-countermodels? As we saw in section 6.3.3, a good policy is to make "forced" moves first. For example, if you are committed to making a material conditional false in a world, go ahead and make its antecedent true and consequent false in that world, right away. A false counterfactual also forces certain moves. It follows from the truth condition for the $\square\!\!\rightarrow$ that if $\phi\square\!\!\rightarrow\psi$ is false in world w, then there exists a nearest-to-w ϕ-world in which ψ is false. So if you put a 0 above a counterfactual $\phi\square\!\!\rightarrow\psi$ in some world w, it's good to do the following two things right away. First, add a nearest-to-w world in which ϕ is true (if such a world isn't already present in your diagram). And second, make ψ false there.

True counterfactuals don't force your hand quite so much, since there are two ways for a counterfactual to be true. If $\phi\square\!\!\rightarrow\psi$ is true in w, then ψ must be true in every nearest-to-w ϕ-world. This could happen, not only if there exists a nearest-to-w ϕ-world in which ψ is true, but also if there are *no* nearest-to-w ϕ-worlds. In the latter case we say that $\phi\square\!\!\rightarrow\psi$ is "vacuously true" at w. A counterfactual can be vacuously true only when its antecedent is necessarily false, since the limit assumption guarantees that if there is at least one ϕ-world, then there is a nearest ϕ-world. So: if you want to make a counterfactual true in a world, it's a good idea to wait until you've been forced to make its antecedent true in at least one world. Only when this has happened, thus closing off the possibility of making the counterfactual vacuously true, should you add a nearest world in which its antecedent is true, and make its consequent true in that nearest antecedent-world. These strategies are illustrated by the following example.

Example 8.3: Show that $[(P\square\!\!\rightarrow Q)\wedge(Q\square\!\!\rightarrow R)]\rightarrow(P\square\!\!\rightarrow R)$ is SC-invalid. We begin as follows:

$$r \quad \overbrace{\underset{[(P\square\!\!\rightarrow Q)\wedge(Q\square\!\!\rightarrow R)]\rightarrow(P\square\!\!\rightarrow R)}{\overset{1\quad\ \ 1\quad\ \ 1\qquad 0\quad\ \ 0}{}}}$$

In keeping with the advice to make forced moves first, let's deal with the false counterfactual before dealing with the true counterfactual: let's make $P\square\!\!\rightarrow R$ false in r. This means adding a nearest-to-r P-world in which R is false. At this point, nothing prevents us from making this world r itself, but that might collide with other things we do later, so I'll make this nearest-to-r P-world a distinct world from r:

$$a \quad \boxed{\begin{matrix} 1 & 0 & 1 \\ P & R & Q \end{matrix}}$$

no P

$$r \quad \boxed{\begin{matrix} 0 & 1 & 1 & 1 & 0 & 0 \\ [(P\square\!\!\rightarrow Q)\wedge(Q\square\!\!\rightarrow R)]\rightarrow(P\square\!\!\rightarrow R) \end{matrix}}$$

"No P" reminds me not to add any P-worlds between a and r. Since world r is in the "no P zone", I made P false there.

Notice that I made Q true in a. I did this because $P\square\!\!\rightarrow Q$ is true in r. $P\square\!\!\rightarrow Q$ says that Q is true in every nearest-to-r P-world, and a is the nearest-to-r P-world. In general, whenever you add a new world to one of these diagrams, you should go back to all the counterfactuals in the bottom world and see whether they require their consequents to have certain truth values in the new world.

We now have to make the final counterfactual $Q\square\!\!\rightarrow R$ true. There are two ways this could happen: our model might contain no Q-worlds at all (the vacuous case), or it might contain a nearest-to-r Q-world in which R is true. Q is already true in at least one world (world a), so the vacuous case is ruled out. So we must include a nearest-to-r Q-world, call it "b", and make R true there. Where will we put this new world b? There are three possibilities. World b could be farther away from, identical to, or closer to r than a. (These are the only three possibilities, given anti-symmetry.) Let's try the first possibility:

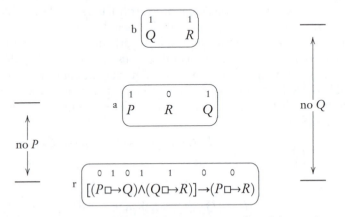

This doesn't work, because world a is in the no-Q zone, but Q is true in world a. Put another way: in this diagram, b isn't the nearest-to-r Q-world; world a is. And so, since R is false in world a, the counterfactual $Q\square\!\!\rightarrow R$ would come out false in world r, whereas we want it to be true.

Likewise, we can't make world b be identical to world a, since we need to make R true in b and R is already false in a.

But the final possibility works; we can let world b be closer to r than a:

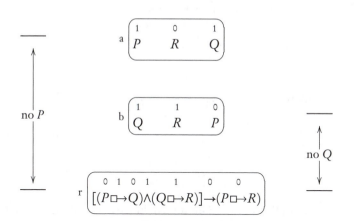

(I made *P* false in b since b is in the no *P* zone.) Here's the official model:

$$\mathscr{W} = \{r, a, b\}$$
$$\preceq_r = \{\langle b, a \rangle \ldots\}$$
$$\mathscr{I}(P, a) = \mathscr{I}(Q, a) = \mathscr{I}(Q, b) = \mathscr{I}(R, b) = 1, \text{ all others } 0$$

In this official model I left out a lot in the description of the similarity relation. First, I left out some of the elements of $\preceq_r$. Fully written out, it would be:

$$\preceq_r = \{\langle b, a \rangle, \langle r, b \rangle, \langle r, a \rangle, \langle r, r \rangle, \langle a, a \rangle, \langle b, b \rangle\}$$

My policy will be to leave out an ordered pair when you could work out from the definition of a model that the pair must be present. Thus I left out $\langle r, b \rangle$ and $\langle r, a \rangle$ because the base condition requires them ($\langle r, a \rangle$ is also required by transitivity given the presence of $\langle r, b \rangle$ and $\langle b, a \rangle$), and I left out $\langle r, r \rangle$, $\langle a, a \rangle$, and $\langle b, b \rangle$ because they're needed to make $\preceq_r$ reflexive. (Why must it be reflexive? Because reflexivity comes from strong connectivity. Let w and x be any members of $\mathscr{W}$; we get "$x \preceq_w x$ or $x \preceq_w x$" from strong connectivity of $\preceq_w$, and hence $x \preceq_w x$.) Second, to fully specify this model, strictly speaking it isn't enough to specify just $\preceq_r$. We'd need to specify the rest of $\preceq$ by writing out $\preceq_a$ and $\preceq_b$. But in this case, it doesn't matter what $\preceq_a$ and $\preceq_b$ are like, so I omitted them. (In some later problems we'll need to specify more of $\preceq$ than just $\preceq_r$.)

Example 8.4: Is $(P \square \rightarrow R) \rightarrow ((P \wedge Q) \square \rightarrow R)$ valid or invalid? (This formula corresponds to augmentation (section 8.1.3).) As always, we begin by trying for a countermodel. In this case we succeed:

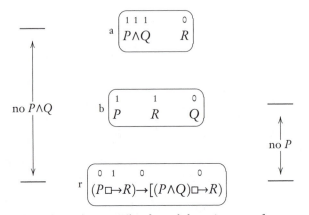

I began with the false: $(P \land Q) \square \rightarrow R$. This forced the existence of a nearest $P \land Q$-world (world a), in which R was false. But since $P \land Q$ was true there, P was true there; this ruled out the true $P \square \rightarrow R$ in r being vacuously true. So I was forced to include a nearest P-world, b, and make R true in it. It couldn't be farther out than a, since P is true in a. It couldn't *be* a, since R was already false there. So I had to put it nearer than a. Notice that I had to make Q false in b. Why? Well, it was in the "no-$P \land Q$ zone", and I had made P true in it. Here's the official model:

$$\mathcal{W} = \{r, a, b\}$$
$$\preceq_r = \{\langle b, a \rangle \dots\}$$
$$\mathcal{I}(P, a) = \mathcal{I}(Q, a) = \mathcal{I}(P, b) = \mathcal{I}(R, b) = 1, \text{ all else } 0$$

Example 8.5: Determine whether $\vDash_{SC} \Diamond P \rightarrow [(P \square \rightarrow Q) \rightarrow \sim (P \square \rightarrow \sim Q)]$. An attempt to find a countermodel fails at the following point:

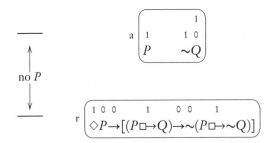

At world a, I've got Q being both true and false. A word about how I got to that point. I noticed that I had to make two counterfactuals true: $P \square \rightarrow Q$ and $P \square \rightarrow \sim Q$. Now, this isn't in itself impossible. Since counterfactuals are vacuously true if their antecedents are impossible, I could have made both counterfactuals true if I could have made P impossible. But this route was closed to me since $\Diamond P$ is true in r. The limit assumption forced me to include a closest P-world; and then the two true counterfactuals created the contradiction. This reasoning is embodied in the following semantic validity proof:

(i) Suppose for reductio that the formula is false in some world r in some model. Then $V(\Diamond P, r) = 1$ and…

(ii) $V(P \Box \!\!\to Q, r) = 1$ and…

(iii) …$V(\sim(P \Box \!\!\to \sim Q), r) = 0$. So $V(P \Box \!\!\to \sim Q, r) = 1$.

(iv) Given (i), P is true in some world, so by the limit assumption there is some closest-to-r P-world. Call one such world "a". Then by (ii), $V(Q, a) = 1$, but by (iii), $V(\sim Q, a) = 1$, and so $V(Q, a) = 0$; contradiction.

Note the use of the limit assumption. It's needed to establish that there is a nearest ϕ-world in cases where we couldn't infer this otherwise.

Example 8.6: Show that $[P \Box \!\!\to (Q \Box \!\!\to R)] \to [(P \wedge Q) \Box \!\!\to R]$ is SC-invalid. The antecedent contains a nested counterfactual, which, as we'll see, calls for something new.

We begin our countermodel by making the formula false in r, which means making the antecedent true and the consequent false. Since the consequent is a false counterfactual, we're forced to create a nearest $P \wedge Q$ world in which R is false:

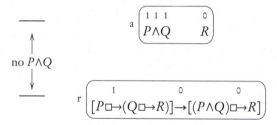

Next we must make $P \Box \!\!\to (Q \Box \!\!\to R)$ true. We can't make it vacuously true, because we've already got a P-world in the model: a. So we've got to create a nearest-to-r P-world. Could it be farther away than a? No, because a would be a closer P-world. Could it *be* a? No, because we've got to make $Q \Box \!\!\to R$ true in the closest P-world, and since Q is true but R is false in a, $Q \Box \!\!\to R$ is already false in a. So, we do it as follows:

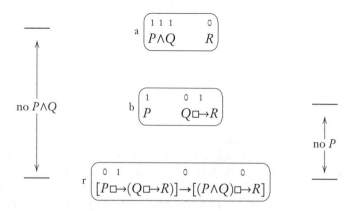

(I made Q false in b because b is in the no-$P \wedge Q$ zone and P is true in b.)

Now we must make $Q\square\rightarrow R$ true in b. This requires some thought. So far the diagram represents "the view from r". That is, it represents how near the worlds in the model are to r. That is, it represents the $\preceq_r$ relation. But the truth value of $Q\square\rightarrow R$ at b depends on "the view from b"—on the the the $\preceq_b$ relation. So we need to depict $\preceq_b$ with a *new* diagram, in which b is the bottom world:

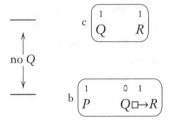

I created a nearest-to-b Q-world, c, and made R true there. Notice that I kept the old truth values of b from the other diagram. This is because this new diagram is a diagram of *the same worlds* as the old diagram; the difference is that the new diagram represents the $\preceq_b$ nearness relation, whereas the old one represented a different relation: $\preceq_r$. Now, this diagram isn't finished. The diagram is that of the $\preceq_b$ relation, and that relation relates all the worlds in the model (given strong connectivity). So worlds r and a have to show up somewhere here. The safest place to put them is far away from b, to avoid conflict with the no-Q zone. Thus the final appearance of this part of the diagram is as follows:

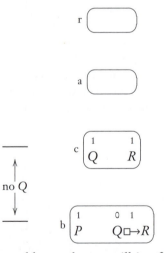

The old truth values from worlds r and a are still in effect (remember that this diagram represents the same worlds as the earlier diagram of the view from r), but I left them out since they're already specified in that earlier diagram.

The order of the worlds in the r-diagram does *not* in any way affect the order of the worlds in the b diagram. The nearness relations in the two diagrams are completely independent, because the definition of an SC-model does not constrain the relationship between $\preceq_i$ and $\preceq_j$ when $i \neq j$. This might seem unintuitive. The definition allows two halves of a model to look as follows:

The view from r	*The view from a*
c	r
b	b
a	c
r	a

It might, for example, seem odd that in the view from r, b is physically closer to a than c is, whereas in the view from a, c is closer to a than b is. But remember that in *any* diagram, only some of the features are intended to be genuinely representational. I've constructed these diagrams from ink, but I don't mean to be saying that the worlds in the model are made of ink. This feature of the diagram—that it's made of ink—isn't intended to convey information about the model. Analogously, the fact that b is physically closer to a than to c in the view from r is *not* intended to convey the information that, in the model, $b \prec_a c$. In fact, the diagram of the view from r is *only* intended to convey information about $\preceq_r$; it doesn't carry any information about $\preceq_a$, $\preceq_b$, or $\preceq_c$.

Back to the countermodel. The initial diagram, of the view from r, must be updated to include world c. It's safest to put c far from r to avoid collisions:

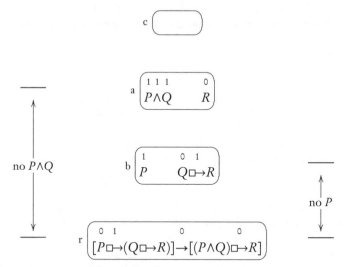

Again, I haven't rewritten the truth values in world c, because they're already in the other diagram. The official model:

$$\mathcal{W} = \{r, a, b, c\}$$
$$\preceq_r = \{\langle b, a \rangle, \langle a, c \rangle \dots\}$$
$$\preceq_b = \{\langle c, a \rangle, \langle a, r \rangle \dots\}$$
$$\mathcal{I}(P, a) = \mathcal{I}(Q, a) = \mathcal{I}(P, b) = \mathcal{I}(Q, c) = \mathcal{I}(R, c) = 1, \text{ all else } 0$$

As before, I didn't write out all of $\preceq$. I left out those bits that follow automatically (given the definition of a model) from what I wrote out, and I didn't specify $\preceq_a$ and $\preceq_c$ since they don't matter here. But I did specify both $\preceq_r$ and $\preceq_b$, since the falsity of the formula $[P\square\!\!\rightarrow(Q\square\!\!\rightarrow R)]\rightarrow[(P\wedge Q)\square\!\!\rightarrow R]$ at world r depended on $\preceq_r$ and $\preceq_b$ being as described.

Exercise 8.3 Establish each of the following facts.

(a) $Q\nvDash_{SC} P\square\!\!\rightarrow Q$

(b) $P\square\!\!\rightarrow Q\nvDash_{SC} {\sim}Q\square\!\!\rightarrow{\sim}P$

(c) $(P\vee Q)\square\!\!\rightarrow R\nvDash_{SC} P\rightarrow R$

(d) $(P\wedge Q)\square\!\!\rightarrow R\nvDash_{SC} P\square\!\!\rightarrow(Q\square\!\!\rightarrow R)$

(e)* $P\square\!\!\rightarrow(Q\square\!\!\rightarrow R)\nvDash_{SC} Q\square\!\!\rightarrow(P\square\!\!\rightarrow R)$

Exercise 8.4 Determine whether the following wffs are SC-valid or invalid. Give a falsifying model for every invalid wff, and a semantic validity proof for every valid wff.

(a) $\Diamond P\rightarrow[{\sim}(P\square\!\!\rightarrow{\sim}Q)\rightarrow(P\square\!\!\rightarrow Q)]$

(b) $[P\square\!\!\rightarrow(Q\rightarrow R)]\rightarrow[(P\wedge Q)\square\!\!\rightarrow R]$

(c) $(P\square\!\!\rightarrow{\sim}Q)\vee[((P\wedge Q)\square\!\!\rightarrow R)\leftrightarrow(P\square\!\!\rightarrow(Q\rightarrow R))]$

8.6 Logical features of SC

Does Stalnaker's semantics for $\square\!\!\rightarrow$ match the apparent logical features of natural-language counterfactuals that we discussed in section 8.1? Yes.

We wanted counterfactuals to differ from material conditionals by not following from the falsity of their antecedents or the truth of their consequents. The Stalnaker system delivers these results. In world r in the first model of section 8.5, ${\sim}P$ is true but $P\square\!\!\rightarrow Q$ is false; so ${\sim}P\nvDash_{SC} P\square\!\!\rightarrow Q$. And the second result is demonstrated in exercise 8.3a.

We wanted counterfactuals to differ from (metaphysical) strict conditionals by being capable of (metaphysical) contingency. The Stalnaker semantics also delivers this result, because different worlds can have different similarity metrics. For example: consider a model with worlds r and a, in which Q is true in the nearest-to-r P-world, but in which Q is false in the nearest-to-a P-world. $P\square\!\!\rightarrow Q$ is true in r and false in a, whence $\square(P\square\!\!\rightarrow Q)$ is false in r. So $P\square\!\!\rightarrow Q\nvDash_{SC} \square(P\square\!\!\rightarrow Q)$.

We noted that augmentation seems to fail for counterfactuals. Stalnaker delivers again: the model of example 8.4 shows that $P\square\!\!\rightarrow Q\nvDash_{SC} (P\wedge R)\square\!\!\rightarrow Q$.

We noted that contraposition seems to fail for counterfactuals. Exercise 8.3b shows that this result holds too.

We wanted the counterfactual conditional to be intermediate in strength between the (metaphysical) strict and material conditionals; see exercises 8.2a and 8.2b.

So: the SC-semantics reproduces the logical features of natural-language coun-terfactuals discussed in section 8.1. In the next few sections I'll discuss some further logical features of the SC-semantics, and compare them with the logical features of the →, the ⊰, and natural-language counterfactuals.

8.6.1 No exportation

The → obeys *exportation*:

$$\frac{(\phi \wedge \psi) \rightarrow \chi}{\phi \rightarrow (\psi \rightarrow \chi)}$$

But the ⊰ doesn't in any system; $(P \wedge Q) \!\!\dashrightarrow\!\! R \nvDash_{S_5} P \!\!\dashrightarrow\!\! (Q \!\!\dashrightarrow\!\! R)$. Nor does the □→ (exercise 8.3d).

Do natural-language counterfactuals obey exportation? Here is an argument that they do not. The following is true:

> If Bill had married Laura and Hillary, he would have been a bigamist.

But one can argue that the following is false:

> If Bill had married Laura, then it would have been the case that if he had married Hillary, he would have been a bigamist.

Suppose Bill had married Laura. Would it then have been true that: if he had married Hillary, he would have been a bigamist? Well, let's ask for comparison: what would the world have been like, had George W. Bush married Hillary Rodham Clinton? Would Bush have been a bigamist? Here the natural answer is *no*. George W. Bush is in fact married to Laura Bush; but when imagining him married to Hillary Rodham Clinton, we don't hold constant his actual marriage. We imagine him being married to Hillary *instead*. If this is true for Bush, then one might think it's also true for Bill in the counterfactual circumstance in which he's married to Laura: it would then have been true of him that, if he had married Hillary, he wouldn't have still been married to Laura, and hence would not have been a bigamist.

It's unclear whether this is a good argument, though, since it assumes that ordinary standards for evaluating *unembedded* counterfactuals ("If George had married Hillary, he would have been a bigamist") apply to counterfactuals embedded within other counterfactuals ("If Bill had married Hillary, he would have been a bigamist" as embedded within "If Bill had married Laura then..."). Contrary to the assumption, it seems most natural to evaluate the consequent of an embedded counterfactual by holding its antecedent constant.

So the argument is questionable. But a defender of the SC-semantics might argue that the second displayed counterfactual above has *a* reading on which it is false (recall the context-dependence of counterfactuals), and hence that we need a semantics that allows for the failure of exportation.

8.6.2 No importation

Importation holds for →, and for ⊰ in T and stronger systems:

$$\frac{\phi \to (\psi \to \chi)}{(\phi \land \psi) \to \chi} \qquad \frac{\phi \dashv (\psi \dashv \chi)}{(\phi \land \psi) \dashv \chi}$$

but not for the $\Box\!\!\to$ (see example 8.6).

The status of importation for natural-language counterfactuals is similar to that of exportation. One can argue that the following is true, at least on one reading:

> If Bill had married Laura, then it would have been the case that if he had married Hillary, he would have been happy.

without the result of importing being true:

> If Bill had married Laura and Hillary, he would have been happy.

(If he had married *both* he would have become a public spectacle.)

8.6.3 No permutation

Permutation governs the $\to$:

$$\frac{\phi \to (\psi \to \chi)}{\psi \to (\phi \to \chi)}$$

but not the $\dashv$ (in any of our modal systems); $P\dashv(Q\dashv R)\nvDash_{S_5} Q\dashv(P\dashv R)$. Nor does it govern the $\Box\!\!\to$ (see exercise 8.3e).

The status of permutation for natural-language counterfactuals is similar to that of importation and exportation. If we can ignore the effects of embedding on the evaluation of counterfactuals, then we have the following counterexample to permutation. It is true that:

> If Bill Clinton had married Laura Bush, then it would have been the case that: if he had married Hillary Rodham, he'd have been married to a Democrat.

But it is not true that:

> If Bill Clinton had married Hillary Rodham, then it would have been the case that: if he had married Laura Bush, he'd have been married to a Democrat.

8.6.4 No transitivity

Material and strict conditionals are *transitive*, in that the following implications hold (in all systems):

$$\frac{\phi \to \psi \quad \psi \to \chi}{\phi \to \chi} \qquad \frac{\phi \dashv \psi \quad \psi \dashv \chi}{\phi \dashv \chi}$$

But the model in example 8.3 shows that Stalnaker's $\Box\!\!\to$ is intransitive.

The following argument purports to show that natural-language counterfactuals are also intransitive. I am the oldest child in my family; my brother Mike is the second-oldest. So the following two counterfactuals seem true:

If I hadn't been born, Mike would have been my parent's oldest child.

If my parents had never met, I wouldn't have been born.

But the result of applying transitivity is false:

If my parents had never met, Mike would have been their oldest child.

8.7 Lewis's criticisms of Stalnaker's theory

As I mentioned earlier, David Lewis also defends a similarity-based theory of counterfactuals. Lewis's system is like Stalnaker's in many ways. But there are two points
of detail over which Lewis and Stalnaker disagree.[87]

First, Lewis challenges Stalnaker's assumption of anti-symmetry. Ties in similarity
are generally possible, so why couldn't two possible worlds be exactly similar to a
given world? The challenge is most straightforward if Stalnaker intends to be giving
truth conditions rather than merely doing model theory, for then Stalnaker would be
assuming anti-symmetry for a real similarity relation: the similarity relation used to
give the truth conditions for natural-language counterfactuals. But even if Stalnaker
is not doing this, the objection may yet have bite, to the extent that the semantics of
natural-language counterfactuals is *like* similarity-theoretic semantics.

The validity of certain wffs depends on whether you require anti-symmetry.
According to Stalnaker, all instances of the following two schemas are valid:

$$(\phi\square\!\!\rightarrow\psi)\vee(\phi\square\!\!\rightarrow\sim\psi) \qquad \text{(``conditional excluded middle'')}$$
$$[\phi\square\!\!\rightarrow(\psi\vee\chi)] \rightarrow [(\phi\square\!\!\rightarrow\psi)\vee(\phi\square\!\!\rightarrow\chi)] \qquad \text{(``distribution'')}$$

But Lewis challenges each verdict. Take the first one, for example. Suppose you gave
up anti-symmetry, thereby allowing ties. Then the following would be a countermodel for an instance of conditional excluded middle:

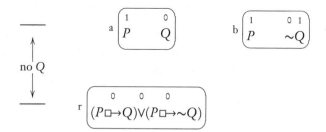

Here worlds a and b are tied for similarity to r. Remember that $\phi\square\!\!\rightarrow\psi$ is true only if
ψ is true in *all* the nearest ϕ-worlds. So since Q is not true in all the nearest-to-r
P-worlds (though it's true in one of them), $P\square\!\!\rightarrow Q$ is false in r. Similarly for $P\square\!\!\rightarrow\sim Q$.
A similar model shows that distribution fails if anti-symmetry is not required (see
exercise 8.5).

---

[87]See Lewis (1973*a*, section 3.4). For an interesting response see Stalnaker (1981).

So, should we give up conditional excluded middle? Lewis concedes that the principle is initially plausible. An equivalent formulation of conditional excluded middle is: $\sim(\phi\,\square\!\!\rightarrow\psi)\rightarrow(\phi\,\square\!\!\rightarrow\sim\psi)$. Now, whenever ϕ is possibly true, the converse of this conditional, namely $(\phi\,\square\!\!\rightarrow\sim\psi)\rightarrow\sim(\phi\,\square\!\!\rightarrow\psi)$, is agreed by everyone to be true. So if conditional excluded middle is valid, then whenever ϕ is possibly true, $\sim(\phi\,\square\!\!\rightarrow\psi)$ and $\phi\,\square\!\!\rightarrow\sim\psi$ are equivalent to each other. And we do normally treat them as being indistinguishable. We normally don't distinguish between "it's not true that if she had played, she would have won" and "if she had played, she would have failed to win" (which of these does "if she had played, she wouldn't have won" mean?).

And take distribution. If someone says: "if I had been a baseball player, I would have been either a third-baseman or a shortstop", it might seem natural to reply with a question: "well, which would you have been?" This reply presupposes that either "if you had been a baseball player, you would have been a third-baseman" or "if you had been a baseball player, you would have been a shortstop" must be true.

So there's some intuitive plausibility to both conditional excluded middle and distribution. But Lewis says two things. The first is metaphysical: if we're going to accept the similarity analysis, we've *got* to give them up, because ties in similarity just are possible. The second is purely semantic: the intuitions aren't completely compelling. About the baseball case, Lewis would deny both that if the person had been a baseball player, she *would* have been a third-baseman, and that if she had been a baseball player, she *would* have been a shortstop. What's true is that if she had been a baseball player, she *might* have been a third-baseman, and that if she had been a baseball player, she *might* have been a shortstop. Neither outcome would have resulted; each outcome might have. Against conditional excluded middle, Lewis says:

> It is not the case that if Bizet and Verdi were compatriots, Bizet would be Italian; and it is not the case that if Bizet and Verdi were compatriots, Bizet would not be Italian; nevertheless, if Bizet and Verdi were compatriots, Bizet either would or would not be Italian. (Lewis, 1973*a*, p. 80)

If Bizet and Verdi were compatriots, Bizet *might* be Italian, but it's not the case that if they were compatriots, he *would* be Italian.

Lewis has a related objection to Stalnaker's semantics. Consider English conditionals of the form "if it had been that ϕ, then it *might* have been that ψ" (I used such conditionals in the previous paragraph). Lewis calls these conditionals *might-counterfactuals* (to distinguish from the "would-counterfactuals" that we have mostly been discussing in this chapter). He symbolizes them as $\phi\,\Diamond\!\!\rightarrow\psi$, which he defines thus:

- "$\phi\,\Diamond\!\!\rightarrow\psi$" is short for "$\sim(\phi\,\square\!\!\rightarrow\sim\psi)$"

But, Lewis argues, this definition of $\Diamond\!\!\rightarrow$ doesn't work in Stalnaker's system. Since conditional excluded middle is valid in Stalnaker's system, $\phi\,\Diamond\!\!\rightarrow\psi$ would always imply $\phi\,\square\!\!\rightarrow\psi$. But we treat the might-counterfactual as being weaker than the would-counterfactual; we often use it when we're unwilling to utter the would-counterfactual. So Lewis's definition of $\Diamond\!\!\rightarrow$ doesn't work in Stalnaker's system. Moreover, Lewis argues, there isn't any other plausible definition.

Lewis also objects to Stalnaker's limit assumption. His example: the displayed line is less than one inch long.

Now, the following counterfactual is clearly false:

> If the line had been longer than one inch, it would have been one hundred miles long.

But if we use Stalnaker's truth conditions as truth conditions for natural-language counterfactuals, and take our intuitive judgments of similarity at face value, we seem to get the result that it is true! For there doesn't seem to be a *closest* world in which the line is more than one inch long. For every world in which the line is, say, $1 + k$ inches long, there seems to be a world that is more similar to the actual world: an otherwise similar world in which the line is $1 + \frac{k}{2}$ inches long.

8.8 Lewis's system

In light of the criticisms of the previous section, Lewis proposes a new similarity-based semantics for counterfactuals. I'll call it LC, for Lewis-conditionals.[88]

LEWIS'S SEMANTICS: LC-models and their valuation functions LV are defined as in Stalnaker's semantics except that:

- antisymmetry and limit are not assumed
- the base condition is changed to read: for any x, y, if $y \preceq_x x$, then $x = y$
- the truth condition for the $\square\!\!\rightarrow$ is changed to this: $LV_{\mathscr{M}}(\phi\square\!\!\rightarrow\psi, w) = 1$ iff EITHER ϕ is true in no worlds, OR: there is some world, x, such that $LV_{\mathscr{M}}(\phi, x) = 1$ and for all y, if $y \preceq_w x$, then $LV_{\mathscr{M}}(\phi\rightarrow\psi, y) = 1$

Note that the non-anti-symmetric model of the previous section counts as an LC-model in which $(P\square\!\!\rightarrow Q) \vee (P\square\!\!\rightarrow\sim Q)$ is false in world r. So Lewis's semantics invalidates conditional excluded middle. (It also invalidates distribution.)

Why the new base condition? Stalnaker's base condition said that each world is *at least as close* to itself as any other is; Lewis's makes the stronger claim that each world is *closer* to itself than any other is. Lewis needs the stronger claim in order to insure that $\phi, \psi \vDash_{LC} \phi\square\!\!\rightarrow\psi$. (Stalnaker could get by with the weaker claim since it plus anti-symmetry entails the stronger claim, but Lewis doesn't assume anti-symmetry.)

Why the new truth condition for the $\square\!\!\rightarrow$? The limit assumption is now allowed to fail; but as we saw with the nearly one-inch line, Stalnaker's truth condition yields unwanted vacuous truths when the limit assumption fails.[89] Lewis's new truth condition is designed to avoid this. Let's think about what it says. First, there's the vacuous case: if ϕ is necessarily false, then $\phi\square\!\!\rightarrow\psi$ comes out true. But if ϕ is possibly

---

[88] See Lewis (1973*a*, pp. 48–49). I have simplified Lewis's system.

[89] Actually, dropping the limit assumption doesn't affect which wffs are *valid* (Lewis, 1973*b*, p. 444). The issue of the limit assumption is an issue about the truth conditions of the counterfactual, not its logic.

true, then $\phi\square\!\!\rightarrow\!\psi$ is true in w iff there exists some ϕ-world with the following feature: no matter how much closer to w you go, you never find a ϕ-world where ψ is false. (*If there is a nearest-to-w ϕ-world, then $\phi\square\!\!\rightarrow\!\psi$ is true in w iff ψ is true in all the nearest-to-w ϕ-worlds.*) To see why this avoids vacuity, think for the moment of Lewis's semantics as providing truth conditions for natural-language counterfactuals, and recall the sentence:

> If the line had been longer than one inch, it would have been one hundred miles long.

There's no nearest world in which the line is longer than one inch, only an infinite series of worlds in which the line has lengths closer and closer to one inch. But this doesn't make the counterfactual true. Since its antecedent is possibly true, the only way for the counterfactual to be true, given Lewis's truth condition, is for there to be some world, x, in which the antecedent is true, and which is such that the material conditional (antecedent$\rightarrow$consequent) is true in every world at least as similar to the actual world as it is. Since the "at least as similar as" relation is reflexive, this can be rewritten thus:

- for some world, x, the antecedent and consequent are both true in x, and in all worlds that are at least as similar to the actual world as is x, the antecedent is never true while the consequent is false

So, is there any such world, x? No. For let x be any world in which the antecedent and consequent are both true. Since the line is one hundred miles long in x, we can find a world that is more similar to the actual world than x in which the antecedent is true but the consequent is false: just choose a world just like x but in which the line is only, say, two inches long.

Let's see how Lewis handles a true counterfactual when the limit assumption is false:

> If I had been taller than six feet, I would have been shorter than nine feet

(I am, in fact, shorter than six feet.) Again, there is no nearest world in which the antecedent is true. But now we *can* find our world x: simply take x to be a world just like the actual world but in which I am, say, six-feet-one. The antecedent and consequent are both true in x. And any world that is at least as similar to the actual world as x must surely be one in which I'm less than nine feet tall. So in no such world will the antecedent ("I'm taller than six feet") be true while the consequent ("I'm shorter than nine feet") is false.

Recall Lewis's definition of the might-counterfactual:

- "$\phi\diamond\!\!\rightarrow\!\psi$" is short for "$\sim\!(\phi\square\!\!\rightarrow\!\sim\!\psi)$"

From this we may obtain a derived clause for the truth conditions of $\phi\diamond\!\!\rightarrow\!\psi$:

- $LV_{\mathcal{M}}(\phi\diamond\!\!\rightarrow\!\psi, w) = 1$ iff for some world x, $LV_{\mathcal{M}}(\phi, x) = 1$; and for any world x, if $LV_{\mathcal{M}}(\phi, x) = 1$, then for some world y, $y \preceq_w x$ and $LV_{\mathcal{M}}(\phi\wedge\psi, y) = 1$)

That is, $\phi \diamond \rightarrow \psi$ is true in w iff ϕ is possible, and for any ϕ-world, there's a world as close or closer to w in which ϕ and ψ are both true. (In cases where there is a nearest ϕ-world, this means that ψ must be true in *at least one* of the nearest ϕ-worlds.)

Exercise 8.5 Show that $\nvDash_{LC} [\phi\Box\rightarrow(\psi\vee\chi)]\rightarrow[(\phi\Box\rightarrow\psi)\vee(\phi\Box\rightarrow\chi)]$

Exercise 8.6** Show that every LC-valid wff is SC-valid.

8.9 The problem of disjunctive antecedents

The following criticism has been raised against both Lewis's and Stalnaker's systems.[90] In neither system does $(P\vee Q)\Box\rightarrow R$ semantically imply $P\Box\rightarrow R$ (exercises 8.3c, 8.6). But in natural language, we normally do make this inference; we normally conclude from "If P or Q had been the case, then R would have been the case" that "If P had been the case, R would have been the case" (and also that "If Q had been the case, R would have been the case"). Imagine, for example, a conversation between Butch Cassidy and the Sundance Kid in heaven, after having been surrounded and killed by the Bolivian army. They say:

If we had surrendered or tried to run away, we would have been shot.

Intuitively, by saying this they are expressing their belief that *both* surrendering and running away would have led to getting shot. Thus, they take the counterfactual to entail:

If we had surrendered, we would have been shot.

If they thought the latter sentence was false (if, say, they thought they could have survived by surrendering), they wouldn't have uttered the former sentence.

Is this a problem for Lewis and Stalnaker? Some say that it is not, for the following reason. One must take great care in translating from natural language into logic. For example, no one would criticize the law of double-negation elimination on the grounds that "There ain't no cake" doesn't imply that there is some cake.[91] And 'or' behaves in notoriously peculiar ways in similar contexts.[92] Consider:

You are permitted to stay or go.

One can argue that this does *not* have the form:

You are permitted to do the action: (Stay ∨ Go)

After all, suppose that you are permitted to stay, but not to go. If you stay, you can't help doing the following act: staying-or-going. So, surely, you're permitted to do that. So the second sentence is true. But the first isn't: if someone uttered it to you

---

[90]For references, see the bibliography of Lewis (1977).

[91]The example is adapted from Loewer (1976).

[92]This behavior is sometimes thought to threaten the deontic logic of section 7.1.

when you were in jail, they'd be lying to you! It really means: "You are permitted to stay *and* you are permitted to go", one might argue. Similarly, "If either *P* or *Q* were true, then *R* would be true" seems usually to mean "If *P* were true, then *R* would be true, *and* if *Q* were true, then *R* would be true". We can't just expect natural language to translate directly into our logical language—sometimes the surface structure of natural language is misleading. Or so the reply goes. But it would be nice to have an explanation of why 'or' functions in this way.

8.10 Counterfactuals as strict conditionals

We have been considering the Lewis–Stalnaker approach to counterfactuals. I'll end this chapter with a brief discussion of one alternative approach, which treats counterfactuals as highly context-sensitive strict conditionals.[93]

Treating counterfactuals as strict conditionals might seem like a nonstarter. Consider:

(1) If I had struck the match, it would have lit

i.e., $M\,\square\!\!\rightarrow L$. The strict conditional approach takes this to mean $M\dashv 3L$, i.e., $\square(M\rightarrow L)$. Now, we normally take (1) to be true. But there are *some* possible worlds in which I strike the match and it doesn't light: worlds in which I strike the match in outer space, for example. So how can (1) mean $\square(M\rightarrow L)$?

Remember that necessity comes in different strengths. The strict conditionalist won't take the $\square$ in $\square(M\rightarrow L)$ to express truth in absolutely all possible worlds. She will instead take it to express truth in all *accessible* worlds (i.e., all worlds accessible from the actual world), given some notion of accessibility appropriate to counterfactuals. If worlds in which I strike the match in outer space aren't accessible (nor are worlds in which I'm under water or am too weak to strike matches with sufficient force or ...), then (1) can be true even if it means $\square(M\rightarrow L)$.

One important element of the strict conditional approach, then, is the use of a restricted notion of necessity. There is an important further element, which we can bring out by reconsidering the issues discussed in section 8.1.3. In that section we pointed out that counterfactuals seem not to obey augmentation. For example, (1) seems true whereas (2) seems false:

(2) If I had struck the match and had been in outer space, it would have lit

But the strict conditional obeys augmentation, even if its $\square$ expresses a restricted sort of necessity. No matter what accessibility relation the strict conditionalist uses, if all accessible match-striking worlds are match-lighting worlds, then all accessible match-striking-in-outer-space worlds are match-lighting worlds. And so, the strict conditionalist seems to be stuck with saying that (1) implies (2).

The further element deals with this problem: strict conditionalists don't always use the same accessibility relation. Rather, which accessibility relation they use depends on the conversational context in which the counterfactual is uttered. Thus

---

[93] See for example Lycan (2001); von Fintel (2001).

they interpret the counterfactual "If it had been the case that ϕ, then it would have been the case that ψ", as uttered in a context c, as meaning that all accessible$_c$ ϕ-worlds are ψ-worlds, where the accessibility$_c$ relation is picked out by the context c, and frequently changes as conversations progress. Different strict conditionalists take different views about how the accessibility relation gets changed, but one common idea is that the very utterance of a counterfactual causes at least some worlds in which its antecedent is true to become accessible.

Given this approach, (1) and (2) are represented as follows:

(1′) Every accessible$_{c_1}$ match-striking world is a match-lighting world

(2′) Every accessible$_{c_2}$ match-striking-in-outer-space world is a match-lighting world

where c_1 and c_2 are the contexts of utterance of (1) and (2), respectively. Now, if accessibility$_{c_1}$ and accessibility$_{c_2}$ were the same relation then (1′) would indeed imply (2′), and hence (1) would indeed imply (2). But in typical conversations in which (1) and then (2) are uttered, these relations are different; and moreover, worlds in which I strike the match in outer space are not accessible$_{c_1}$ but *are* accessible$_{c_2}$. So in such cases, (1) is true while (2) is false. Why this difference between the accessibility relations? "Strange" worlds such as those in which I strike the match in outer space are normally not accessible, and so they're not accessible$_{c_1}$. But recall that uttering a counterfactual causes some worlds in which its antecedent is true to become accessible. So the utterance of (2) causes some worlds in which I strike the match in outer space to become accessible$_{c_2}$.

But suppose we consider (1) and (2) in reverse order. That is, suppose we *first* utter (2) and ask whether it's true, and then ask whether (1) is true. (2) still seems false; but curiously, (1) no longer seems true. After having considered what would have happened if I had struck the match in outer space, we can no longer confidently say that the match would have lit if I had struck it—what if I had been in outer space? But how can the truth value of (1) depend on whether we consider it before or after (2)? The strict conditionalist has a ready answer. As we saw, uttering (2) causes some worlds in which I strike the match in outer space to become accessible. And further, according to strict conditionalists, once a world becomes accessible, it generally stays accessible for the rest of the conversation. So worlds in which I strike the match in outer space are still accessible when we consider (1); and so (1) is then false.

The strict conditional approach's ability to predict sensitivity to order of utterance is a major reason why its defenders like it. (For another example of order-sensitivity, go back and re-read the first two counterfactuals discussed in section 8.6.4 in reverse order.) The context-sensitivity of accessibility can also explain why it is so difficult to hear the alleged readings of embedded counterfactuals discussed in sections 8.6.1–8.6.3, and can explain away other apparent discrepancies between the logical behavior of counterfactual and strict conditionals.[94] Of course, Lewis and Stalnaker can also

---

[94] The strict conditional approach also predicts that $(P \vee Q) \,\square\!\!\rightarrow R$ implies $P \,\square\!\!\rightarrow R$ (section 8.3c).

appeal to context, by saying that their similarity orderings change with context. Which approach is ultimately best is a matter of current debate.

9

QUANTIFIED MODAL LOGIC

QUANTIFIED MODAL LOGIC is what you get when you combine modal logic with predicate logic. With it we can represent natural-language sentences such as:

"Necessarily, all bachelors are male": $\Box\forall x(Bx{\rightarrow}Mx)$
"Some male could have been female": $\exists x(Mx{\wedge}\Diamond Fx)$
"Ferris could have been a walrus": $\Diamond Wb$

9.1 Grammar of QML

The language of quantified modal logic, or "QML", is exactly what you'd expect: that of plain old predicate logic, but with the $\Box$ added. Thus the one new clause in the definition of a wff says that if ϕ is a wff, then so is $\Box\phi$. (We retain the old definitions of $\Diamond$, -3, $\exists$, $\wedge$, $\vee$, and $\leftrightarrow$.) You get a different grammar for QML depending on what version of predicate logic grammar you begin with. To keep things simple, let's consider a stripped-down version of predicate logic: no function symbols, and no definite description operator. But let's include the identity sign $=$.

9.2 De re and de dicto

Like any logical extension, QML increases our powers of analysis. Way back in propositional logic, we were able to analyze a certain level of structure, structure in terms of 'and', 'or', 'not', and so on. The move to predicate logic then let us analyze quantificational structure; and the move to modal propositional logic let us analyze modal structure. Moving to QML lets us do all three at once, as with:

It's not possible for something to create itself

whose tripartite propositional, predicate, and modal structure is revealed in its QML symbolization:

$$\sim\Diamond\exists x Cxx$$

This deeper level of analysis illuminates further logical phenomena. One example is the famous distinction between de re and de dicto modal statements. Consider:

Some rich person might have been poor
$\exists x(Rx{\wedge}\Diamond Px)$

It might have been the case that some rich person is poor
$\Diamond\exists x(Rx{\wedge}Px)$

The first sentence asserts the existence of someone who is in fact rich, but who might have been poor. This seems true, in contrast to the absurd second sentence, which says that the following state of affairs is possible: someone is both rich and poor. The second sentence is called "de dicto" because the modality is attributed to a sentence (dictum): the modal operator $\Diamond$ attaches to the closed sentence $\exists x(Rx \wedge Px)$. The first sentence is called "de re" because the modality is attributed to an object (res): the $\Diamond$ attaches to a sentence with a free variable, Px, and thus can be thought of as attributing a modal property, the property of *possibly being poor*, to an object u when x is assigned the value u.

Modal propositional logic alone does not adequately represent this distinction. Given only a Q to stand for "some rich person is poor", we can write only $\Diamond Q$, which represents only the absurd second sentence. To represent the first sentence we need to put the $\Diamond$ inside the Q, so to speak, as we can when we further analyze Q as $\exists x(Rx \wedge Px)$ using predicate logic.

A further example of the de re/de dicto distinction:

> Every bachelor is such that he is necessarily unmarried
> $\forall x(Bx \rightarrow \Box Ux)$

> It is necessary that every bachelor is unmarried
> $\Box \forall x(Bx \rightarrow Ux)$

It's helpful to think about the difference between these two statements in terms of possible worlds. The second, de dicto, sentence makes the true claim that in any possible world, anything that is in that world a bachelor is, in that world, unmarried. The first, de re, sentence makes the false claim that if any object, u, is a bachelor in the actual world, then that object u is necessarily unmarried—i.e., the object u is unmarried in all possible worlds.

What do the following English sentences mean?

> All bachelors are necessarily unmarried
> Bachelors must necessarily be unmarried

Surface grammar suggests that they would mean the de re claim that each bachelor is such that he is necessarily unmarried. But in fact, it's very natural to hear these sentences as making the de dicto claim that it's necessary that all bachelors are unmarried.

The de re/de dicto distinction also emerges with definite descriptions. This may be illustrated by using Russell's theory of descriptions (section 5.3.3). Recall how Russell's method generated two possible symbolizations for sentences containing definite descriptions and negations, depending on whether the definite description is given wide or narrow scope relative to the negation operator. A similar phenomenon arises with sentences containing definite descriptions and modal operators. There are two symbolizations of "The number of the planets is necessarily odd" (letting "Nx" mean that x "numbers the planets"—i.e., x is a number that corresponds to how many planets there are):

$$\Box \exists x(Nx \land \forall y(Ny \rightarrow x=y) \land Ox)$$
$$\exists x(Nx \land \forall y(Ny \rightarrow x=y) \land \Box Ox)$$

The first, in which the description has narrower scope than the $\Box$, is de dicto; it says that it's necessary that: one and only one thing numbers the planets, and that thing is odd. This claim is false, since there could have been two planets, or four planets, or six, etc. The second, in which the description takes wider scope, is de re; it says that (in fact) there is one and only one thing that numbers the planets, and that that thing is necessarily odd. That's true, I suppose: the number nine (the thing that in fact numbers the planets—let's count Pluto as a planet) is necessarily odd.

Natural-language sentences containing both definite descriptions and modal operators can perhaps be heard as expressing either de re or de dicto claims. "The number of the planets is necessarily odd" sounds (or can sound) de re; "The American president is necessarily an American citizen" sounds (or can sound) de dicto.

The de re/de dicto distinction is often extended in the following way: a sentence is said to be de re if it contains some formula of the form $\Box \phi$ or $\Diamond \phi$ in which ϕ contains a name or a free variable (free in ϕ, that is); otherwise the sentence is de dicto. For example, $\Diamond Wb$ and $\exists x \Box Fx$ are de re, whereas $\Box \forall x(Bx \rightarrow Ux)$ and $\Diamond \exists x(Fx \land Gx)$ are de dicto.

De re modality is sometimes thought to be especially philosophically problematic. Consider again the de re sentence "Each bachelor is such that: necessarily, he is unmarried"—$\forall x(Bx \rightarrow \Box Ux)$. To evaluate whether this sentence is true, we must go through each object, x, that is a bachelor in the actual world, and decide whether $\Box Ux$ is true. Take some particular bachelor, John, who is, let us say, the only child of certain parents. We must go through all the possible worlds and ask whether John is unmarried in all those worlds. But how do we *locate* John in other possible worlds? In worlds in which John is not too different from the way he is in the actual world, it will be easy. But consider a world in which his parents' only son is physically and psychologically very different. Is this son John? If his parents have two sons, which (if either) is John? What if their only child is female? And anyway, how are we figuring out who his parents are? This is the so-called "problem of trans-world identification". (It is analogous in some ways to the problem of how to re-identify individuals over time.) What to say about it (and even, whether there really is a problem) is up for grabs in the philosophy of modality.[95]

The problem (if it is a problem) is thought not to arise with de dicto modal sentences, for the evaluation of such sentences does not require taking an individual from one possible world and reidentifying it in another world. Return to the de dicto sentence "necessarily, all bachelors are unmarried"—$\Box \forall x(Bx \rightarrow Ux)$. Here, we take the sentence 'all bachelors are unmarried' around to the different worlds, rather than an individual like John. All we need to do, in any world w, is find all the people that in w are bachelors, and see whether they are all unmarried. We have the descriptive

---

[95] See, for starters: Quine (1953b); Kripke (1972, pp. 39–47); Lewis (1986, chapter 4).

predicate "bachelor" to help us find the relevant individuals in w; we don't need to do anything like identify which individual in w is John.

9.3 A simple semantics for QML

Let's begin with a very simple semantics, SQML (for "simple QML"). It's simple in two ways. First, there is no accessibility relation. $\Box\phi$ will be said to be true iff ϕ is true in *all* worlds in the model. In effect, each world is accessible from every other (and hence the underlying propositional modal logic is S5). Second, it will be a "constant domain" semantics. (We'll discuss what this means, and more complex semantical treatments of QML, below.)

DEFINITION OF MODEL: An SQML-model is an ordered triple $\langle \mathcal{W}, \mathcal{D}, \mathcal{I} \rangle$ where:

- $\mathcal{W}$ is a nonempty set   ("possible worlds")
- $\mathcal{D}$ is a nonempty set   ("domain")
- $\mathcal{I}$ is a function such that: ("interpretation function")
    - if α is a constant, then $\mathcal{I}(\alpha) \in \mathcal{D}$
    - if Π^n is an n-place predicate, then $\mathcal{I}(\Pi^n)$ is a set of $n+1$-tuples of the form $\langle u_1, \ldots, u_n, w \rangle$, where $u_1, \ldots, u_n$ are members of $\mathcal{D}$, and $w \in \mathcal{W}$

Recall that modal propositional logic models took the interpretations from *non-modal* propositional logic (functions assigning truth values to sentence letters) and relativized them to possible worlds. We have something similar here: we relativize the interpretation of predicates to possible worlds. The interpretation of a two-place predicate, for example, was in *nonmodal* predicate logic a set of ordered pairs of members of the domain; now it is a set of ordered triples, two members of which are in the domain, and one member of which is a possible world. When $\langle u_1, u_2, w \rangle$ is in the interpretation of a two-place predicate R, that represents R's applying to u_1 and u_2 *in possible world* w. This relativization makes intuitive sense: a predicate can apply to some objects in one possible world but fail to apply to those same objects in some other possible world.

These predicate interpretations are known as "intensions". The name emphasizes the analogy with extensions, which are the interpretations of predicates in nonmodal predicate logic. The analogy is this: the intension $\mathcal{I}(\Pi)$ of an n-place predicate Π can be thought of as determining an extension *within each possible world*, as follows: the extension of Π in world w is the set of n-tuples $\langle u_1 \ldots u_n \rangle$ such that $\langle u_1 \ldots u_n, w \rangle \in \mathcal{I}(\Pi)$.

Unlike the interpretations of predicates, the interpretations of constants are not relativized in any way to possible worlds. The interpretation function $\mathcal{I}$ simply assigns a member of the domain to a name. This reflects the common belief that natural-language proper names—which constants are intended to represent—are *rigid designators*, i.e., terms that have the same denotation relative to every possible world (Kripke, 1972). We'll discuss the significance of this feature of our semantics below.

Recall from section 2.2 that a semantics for a formal language defines both a set of configurations, and truth-in-a-configuration. The configurations here are

SQML-models. A configuration must represent both a way for the world to be, and the meanings of nonlogical expressions. An SQML-model's set of worlds and domain represent the world (i.e., reality); and its interpretation function represents the meanings of nonlogical expressions (by assigning denotations to names and intensions to predicates. Notice that intensions are a richer sort of meaning than the extensions of nonmodal predicate logic).

As for truth-in-a-configuration, this is the job of the valuation function for an SQML-model. To define this, we begin by keeping the definition of a variable assignment from nonmodal predicate logic (section 4.2). Our variable assignments therefore assign members of the domain to variables absolutely, rather than relative to worlds. (This is an appropriate choice given our choice to assign constants absolute semantic values.) But the valuation function will now relativize truth values to possible worlds (as well as to variable assignments). After all, the sentence 'Fa', if it represents "Ted is tall", should vary in truth value from world to world.

DEFINITION OF VALUATION: The valuation function $V_{\mathcal{M},g}$, for SQML-model $\mathcal{M}$ ($= \langle \mathcal{W}, \mathcal{D}, \mathcal{I} \rangle$) and variable assignment g is defined as the function that assigns either 0 or 1 to each wff relative to each member of $\mathcal{W}$, subject to the following constraints:

- For any terms α, β, $V_{\mathcal{M},g}(\alpha{=}\beta, w) = 1$ iff $[\alpha]_{\mathcal{M},g} = [\beta]_{\mathcal{M},g}$
- For any n-place predicate, Π, and any terms $\alpha_1, \ldots, \alpha_n$,
  $V_{\mathcal{M},g}(\Pi\alpha_1 \ldots \alpha_n, w) = 1$ iff $\langle [\alpha_1]_{\mathcal{M},g}, \ldots, [\alpha_n]_{\mathcal{M},g}, w \rangle \in \mathcal{I}(\Pi)$
- For any wffs ϕ, ψ, and variable, α,

$$V_{\mathcal{M},g}(\sim\phi, w) = 1 \text{ iff } V_{\mathcal{M},g}(\phi, w) = 0$$

$$V_{\mathcal{M},g}(\phi \rightarrow \psi, w) = 1 \text{ iff either } V_{\mathcal{M},g}(\phi, w) = 0 \text{ or } V_{\mathcal{M},g}(\psi, w) = 1$$

$$V_{\mathcal{M},g}(\forall \alpha \phi, w) = 1 \text{ iff for every } u \in \mathcal{D}, V_{\mathcal{M},g_u^\alpha}(\phi, w) = 1$$

$$V_{\mathcal{M},g}(\Box \phi, w) = 1 \text{ iff for every } v \in \mathcal{W}, V_{\mathcal{M},g}(\phi, v) = 1$$

The derived clauses are what you'd expect, including the following one for $\Diamond$:

$$V_{\mathcal{M},g}(\Diamond \phi, w) = 1 \text{ iff for some } v \in \mathcal{W}, V_{\mathcal{M},g}(\phi, v) = 1$$

Finally, we have:

DEFINITIONS OF VALIDITY AND SEMANTIC CONSEQUENCE:

- ϕ is valid in $\mathcal{M}$ ($= \langle \mathcal{W}, \mathcal{D}, \mathcal{I} \rangle$) iff for every variable assignment, g, for $\mathcal{M}$ and every $w \in \mathcal{W}$, $V_{\mathcal{M},g}(\phi, w) = 1$.
- ϕ is SQML-valid ("$\vDash_{\text{SQML}} \phi$") iff ϕ is valid in all SQML-models.
- Γ SQML-semantically-implies ϕ ("$\Gamma \vDash_{\text{SQML}} \phi$") iff for every SQML-model $\mathcal{M}$ ($= \langle \mathcal{W}, \mathcal{D}, \mathcal{I} \rangle$), every $w \in \mathcal{W}$, and every variable assignment g for $\mathcal{M}$, if $V_{\mathcal{M},g}(\gamma, w) = 1$ for each $\gamma \in \Gamma$, then $V_{\mathcal{M},g}(\phi, w) = 1$.

9.4 Establishing validity and invalidity in SQML

As before, we want to come up with countermodels for invalid formulas, and validity proofs for valid ones. Validity proofs introduce nothing new.

Example 9.1: Show that $\vDash_{\mathrm{SQML}} \Diamond \exists x(x{=}a \wedge \Box Fx) \rightarrow Fa$:

(i) Suppose for reductio that the wff is false in some world r in model, under some variable assignment g. Then $V_g(\Diamond \exists x(x{=}a \wedge \Box Fx), r) = 1$ and ...

(ii) ...$V_g(Fa, r) = 0$. Thus $\langle \mathscr{I}(a), r \rangle \notin \mathscr{I}(F)$.

(iii) From (i), for some $w \in \mathscr{W}$, $V_g(\exists x(x{=}a \wedge \Box Fx), w) = 1$. So for some $u \in \mathscr{D}$, $V_{g_u^x}(x{=}a \wedge \Box Fx, w) = 1$). So $V_{g_u^x}(x{=}a, w) = 1$ and ...

(iv) ...$V_{g_u^x}(\Box Fx, w) = 1$. So $V_{g_u^x}(Fx, r) = 1$, and so $\langle [x]_{g_u^x}, r \rangle \in \mathscr{I}(F)$—that is, $\langle u, r \rangle \in \mathscr{I}(F)$.

(v) From (iii), $[x]_{g_u^x} = [a]_{g_u^x}$; so $u = \mathscr{I}(a)$. So by (iv), $\langle \mathscr{I}(a), r \rangle \in \mathscr{I}(F)$, contradicting line (ii).

As for countermodels, we can use the pictorial method of section 6.3.3, asterisks and all, with a few changes. First, we no longer need the arrows between worlds since we've dropped the accessibility relation. Second, we have predicates and names instead of sentence letters; how to deal with this? Let's take an example.

Example 9.2: Show that $\nvDash_{\mathrm{SQML}} (\Diamond Fa \wedge \Diamond Ga) \rightarrow \Diamond(Fa \wedge Ga)$. We begin as follows:

The bottom asterisks make us create two new worlds:

In each world we must then discharge the top asterisk from the false diamond in r:

(I had to make either Fa or Ga false in r—I chose Fa arbitrarily.)

So far I've placed 1s and 0s above atomic formulas to indicate the truth values I want them to have. But to get them to have these truth values, I need to construct the model's domain and interpretation function accordingly. Let's use letters like 'u' and 'v' as the members of the domain in our models. Now, if we let the name a refer to (the letter) u, and let the extension of the predicate F in world r be $\varnothing$ (the empty set), then the truth value of Fa in world r will be 0, since the denotation of a isn't in the extension of F at world r. Likewise, we need to put u in the extension of F (but not in the extension of G) in world a, and put u in the extension of G (but not in the extension of F) in world b. All this may be indicated on the diagram as follows:

Within each world I specified the extension of each predicate. But the specification of the referent of the name 'a' does not go within any world. This is because names, unlike predicates, get assigned semantic values absolutely in a model, not relative to worlds. (Likewise the specification of the domain doesn't go within any world.) Time for the official model:

$$\mathscr{W} = \{r, a, b\}$$
$$\mathscr{D} = \{u\}$$
$$\mathscr{I}(a) = u$$
$$\mathscr{I}(F) = \{\langle u, a\rangle\}$$

$$\mathscr{I}(G) = \{\langle u, b \rangle\}$$

What about formulas with quantifiers?

Example 9.3: Show that $\nvDash_{\text{SQML}} \Box \exists x F x \to \exists x \Box F x$. We begin thus:

$$
\begin{array}{c|l}
& \begin{array}{cc} * & + \\ 1\ 1 & 0\ 0 \end{array} \\
r & \Box \exists x F x \to \exists x \Box F x \\
& +
\end{array}
$$

The asterisk above the $\Box$ in the antecedent must be discharged in r itself (remember: no accessibility relation). That gives us a true existential. Now, a true existential is a bit like a true $\Diamond$—the true $\exists x F x$ means that there must be *some* object u from the domain that's in the extension of F in r. I'll put a $+$ under true $\exists$s and false $\forall$s, to indicate a commitment to *some* instance of some sort or other. Analogously, I'll indicate a commitment to *all* instances of a given type (which would arise from a true $\forall$ or a false $\exists$) with a $+$ above the connective in question.

OK, how do we make $\exists x F x$ true in r? By making $F x$ true for some value of x. Let's put the letter u in the domain, and make $F x$ true when u is assigned to x. We'll indicate this by writing "$F\frac{x}{u}$" in the diagram, and putting a 1 above it. ($F\frac{x}{u}$ isn't a formula of our language; I'm just using it and related expressions in these diagrams to indicate truth values for open sentences relative to variable assignments.) And to make $F x$ true when u is assigned to x, we put u in the extension of F at r:

$$
\begin{array}{c|l}
& \begin{array}{ccc} * & + & \\ 1\ 1 & 0\ 0 & \qquad\qquad 1 \end{array} \\
r & \Box \exists x F x \to \exists x \Box F x \qquad F\frac{x}{u} \qquad\qquad \mathscr{D} : \{u\} \\
& + \\
& \qquad\quad F : \{u\}
\end{array}
$$

Good. Now to attend to the $+$ sign above the false $\exists x \Box F x$. It requires $\Box F x$ to be false for every object in the domain. So far there's only one object in our domain, u, so we've got to make $\Box F x$ false, when u is assigned to the variable 'x'. We'll indicate this on the diagram by putting a 0 above "$\Box F\frac{x}{u}$":

$$
\begin{array}{c|l}
& \begin{array}{cccc} * & + & & \\ 1\ 1 & 0\ 0 & \quad 1 & \quad 0 \end{array} \\
r & \Box \exists x F x \to \exists x \Box F x \qquad F\frac{x}{u} \qquad \Box F\frac{x}{u} \qquad \mathscr{D} : \{u\} \\
& + \qquad\qquad\qquad\qquad\qquad\quad * \\
& \qquad\quad F : \{u\}
\end{array}
$$

Now we have a bottom asterisk, so we need a new world. And we'll need then to discharge the top asterisk from the antecedent. We get:

$$
r\ \left|\ \begin{array}{}
* \qquad\qquad + \\
1\ 1 \qquad 0\ 0 \qquad\qquad 1 \qquad\qquad 0 \\
\Box\exists x F x \to \exists x\Box F x \qquad F\tfrac{x}{u} \qquad \Box F\tfrac{x}{u} \\
+ \qquad\qquad\qquad\qquad\qquad\qquad * \\[8pt]
\qquad\qquad F:\{u\}
\end{array}\right.
\qquad\qquad \mathscr{D}:\{u,v\}
$$

$$
a\ \left|\ \begin{array}{}
0 \qquad\quad 1 \qquad\qquad 1 \\
F\tfrac{x}{u} \qquad \exists x F x \qquad F\tfrac{x}{v} \\
\qquad + \\[8pt]
\qquad F:\{v\}
\end{array}\right.
$$

Why the v? Well, I had to make Fx false in a, with u assigned to x. That meant keeping u out of the extension of F at a. Easy enough, right—just make F's extension $\varnothing$? Well, no. Because of the true $\Box$ in r, I've got to make $\exists x F x$ true in a, and so *something* had to be in F's extension in a. It couldn't be u, so I added a new object, v, to the domain, and put it in F's extension in a.

But adding v to the domain of the model adds a complication, given the plus sign above r. Since $\exists x\Box F x$ is false in r, $\Box F x$ must be false in r for every member of the domain, and hence for v (as well as for u). That requires another bottom asterisk, and so a new world:

$$
r\ \left|\ \begin{array}{}
* \qquad\qquad + \\
1\ 1 \qquad 0\ 0 \qquad\quad 1 \qquad\quad 0 \qquad\quad 0 \\
\Box\exists x F x \to \exists x\Box F x \qquad F\tfrac{x}{u} \qquad \Box F\tfrac{x}{u} \qquad \Box F\tfrac{x}{v} \\
+ \qquad\qquad\qquad\qquad\qquad\qquad * \qquad\qquad * \\[8pt]
\qquad F:\{u\}
\end{array}\right.
\qquad \mathscr{D}:\{u,v\}
$$

$$
a\ \left|\ \begin{array}{}
0 \qquad\quad 1 \qquad\quad 1 \\
F\tfrac{x}{u} \quad \exists x F x \quad F\tfrac{x}{v} \\
\qquad + \\[8pt]
\qquad F:\{v\}
\end{array}\right.
\qquad\qquad
b\ \left|\ \begin{array}{}
0 \qquad\quad 1 \qquad\quad 1 \\
F\tfrac{x}{v} \quad \exists x F x \quad F\tfrac{x}{u} \\
\qquad + \\[8pt]
\qquad F:\{u\}
\end{array}\right.
$$

(Well, we didn't really need a new world; we could have discharged the bottom asterisk on r.) The official model:

$$\mathcal{W} = \{r, a, b\}$$
$$\mathcal{D} = \{u, v\}$$
$$\mathcal{I}(F) = \{\langle u, r \rangle, \langle u, b \rangle, \langle v, a \rangle\}$$

Exercise 9.1 For each formula, give a validity proof if the wff is SQML-valid, and a countermodel if it is invalid.

(a)* $(\Box \forall x (Fx \rightarrow Gx) \wedge \Diamond \exists x Fx) \rightarrow \Diamond \exists x Gx$

(b) $\Diamond \forall x Fx \rightarrow \exists x \Diamond Fx$

(c)* $\exists x \Diamond Rax \rightarrow \Diamond \Box \exists x \exists y Rxy$

(d) $\Box \forall x (Fx \rightarrow Gx) \rightarrow (\forall x \Box Fx \rightarrow \Box \forall x Gx)$

(e) $\exists x (Nx \wedge \forall y (Ny \rightarrow x=y) \wedge \Box Ox) \rightarrow$
$$\Box \exists x (Nx \wedge \forall y (Ny \rightarrow x=y) \wedge Ox)$$

9.5 Philosophical questions about SQML

Our semantics for quantified modal logic faces philosophical challenges. In each case we will be able to locate a particular feature of the SQML-semantics that gives rise to the alleged problem. In response, one can stick with SQML and give it a philosophical defense, or one can look for a new semantics.

9.5.1 *The necessity of identity*

Let's try to come up with a countermodel for the following formula:

$$\forall x \forall y (x=y \rightarrow \Box x=y)$$

When we try to make the formula false by putting a 0 over the initial $\forall$, we get an plus sign below it. So we've got to make the inside part, $\forall y(x=y \rightarrow \Box x=y)$, false for some value of x. We do this by putting some object u in the domain, and letting that be the value of x for which $\forall y(x=y \rightarrow \Box x=y)$ is false. We get:

r	$\overset{0}{\forall x \forall y(x=y \rightarrow \Box x=y)}$ $\overset{+}{}$	$\overset{0}{\forall y(\tfrac{x}{u}=y \rightarrow \Box(\tfrac{x}{u}=y))}$ $\overset{+}{}$	$\mathcal{D}:\{u\}$

Now we need to do the same thing for our new false universal: $\forall y(x=y \rightarrow \Box x=y)$. For some value of y, the inside conditional has to be false. But then the antecedent must be true, so the value for y has to be u again. We get:

	0	0	1 0 0	
r	$\forall x \forall y(x=y\rightarrow\Box x=y)$	$\forall y(\tfrac{x}{u}=y\rightarrow\Box(\tfrac{x}{u}=y))$	$\tfrac{x}{u}=\tfrac{y}{u}\rightarrow\Box(\tfrac{x}{u}=\tfrac{y}{u})$	$\mathscr{D}:\{u\}$
	+	+	*	

The bottom asterisk now calls for a new world in which $x=y$ is false, when both x and y are assigned u. But there can be no such world! An identity sentence is true (at any world) if the denotations of the terms are identical. Our attempt to find a countermodel has failed; time for a validity proof:

(i) suppose for reductio that $V_g(\forall x\forall y(x=y\rightarrow\Box x=y),r)=0$ (for some r and g in some SQML-model). Then $V_{g_u^x}(\forall y(x=y\rightarrow\Box x=y),r)=0$, for some $u\in\mathscr{D}$. So $V_{g_{uv}^{xy}}(x=y\rightarrow\Box x=y,r)=0$, for some $v\in\mathscr{D}$. So $V_{g_{uv}^{xy}}(x=y,r)=1$ (hence $[x]_{g_{uv}^{xy}}=[y]_{g_{uv}^{xy}}$) and ...

(ii) ...$V_{g_{uv}^{xy}}(\Box x=y,r)=0$. So $V_{g_{uv}^{xy}}(x=y,w)=0$ for some $w\in\mathscr{W}$. So $[x]_{g_{uv}^{xy}}\neq[y]_{g_{uv}^{xy}}$, contradicting (i).

Notice in this proof how the world at which an identity sentence is evaluated doesn't affect its truth condition. The truth condition for an identity sentence is simply that the terms (absolutely) denote the same thing.[96]

We can think of $\forall x\forall y(x=y\rightarrow\Box x=y)$ as expressing "the necessity of identity": it says that whenever objects are identical, they're necessarily identical. This claim is philosophically controversial. On the one hand it can seem obviously correct. If $x=y$, then x and y are one and the same thing, so a world in which x is distinct from y would have to be a world in which x was distinct from x; and how could that be? On the other hand, it was a great discovery that Hesperus = Phosphorus. Surely, it could have turned out the other way—surely, Hesperus might have turned out to be distinct from Phosphorus. Isn't this a counterexample to the necessity of identity? Kripke (1972) famously answered: no. According to Kripke, while it could indeed have "turned out the other way" in the sense that 'Hesperus' and Phosphorus' could have denoted distinct entities (while having their references fixed by the same procedure as in actuality), it is nevertheless necessarily true that Hesperus = Phosphorus, given that 'Hesperus' and 'Phosphorus' in fact denote the same entities.

It's worth noting *why* $\forall x\forall y(x=y\rightarrow\Box x=y)$ turns out SQML-valid. It was our definition of variable assignments. Our variable assignments assign members of the domain to variables absolutely, rather than relative to worlds. (Similarly: since the interpretation function $\mathscr{I}$ assigns referents to names absolutely, $a=b\rightarrow\Box a=b$

---

[96] A note about variables. In validity proofs, I'm using italicized 'u' and 'v' as variables to range over objects in the domain of the model I'm considering. So a sentence like '$u=v$' might be true, just as the sentence '$x=y$' of our object language can be true. But when I'm doing countermodels, I'm using upright roman letters 'u' and 'v' as themselves being members of the domain, not as variables ranging over members of the domain. Since 'u' and 'v' are different letters, they are different members of the domain. Thus, in a countermodel with letters in the domain, if the denotation of a name 'a' is the letter 'u', and the denotation of the name 'b' is the letter 'v', then the sentence '$a=b$' has got to be false, since 'u'≠'v'. This just goes to show that it's important to distinguish between the sentence $u=v$ and the sentence 'v'='v'.

turns out valid.) One could instead define variable assignments as functions that assign members of the domain to variables relative to worlds. Given appropriate adjustments to the valuation function, this would invalidate the necessity of identity.[97] (Similarly, one could make $\mathscr{I}$ assign denotations to names relative to worlds, thus invaliding $a{=}b{\rightarrow}\Box a{=}b$.)

9.5.2 The necessity of existence

Another (in)famous valid formula of SQML is the "Barcan formula", named after Ruth Barcan Marcus (1946):

$$\forall x\Box Fx\rightarrow\Box\forall xFx$$

(Call the *schema* $\forall\alpha\Box\phi\rightarrow\Box\forall\alpha\phi$ the "Barcan schema".) An attempt to produce a countermodel leads us to the following stage:

$$
r\left|\begin{array}{c} + \\ 1 \qquad 0\ 0 \\ \forall x\Box Fx\rightarrow\Box\forall xFx \\ * \end{array}\right.
\qquad
a\left|\begin{array}{c} 0 \qquad\qquad 0 \\ \forall xFx \qquad F\frac{x}{u} \\ + \\ \\ F:\varnothing \end{array}\right.
\qquad
\mathscr{D}:\{u\}
$$

Now, when working with these diagrams, if you have a choice between discharging top things or bottom things, whether plus signs or asterisks, always do the bottom things first. In this case, this means discharging the bottom asterisk and ignoring the top plus for the moment. Discharging the bottom asterisk gave us world a, in which we made a universal false. This gave a bottom plus, and forced us to make some instance false. So I put object u in our domain, and kept it out of the extension of F in a. This makes Fx false in a, when x is assigned u.

But now we must discharge the top plus in r; we must make $\Box Fx$ true for *every* member of the domain, including u, which is now in the domain. This requires Fx to be true, when u is assigned to x, in a:

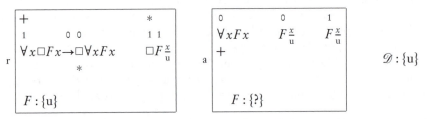

So, we failed to get a countermodel. Time for a validity proof. In fact, let's show that every instance of the Barcan schema is valid:

   (i) Suppose for reductio that $V_g(\forall\alpha\Box\phi\rightarrow\Box\forall\alpha\phi,r)=0$ (for any r and g in any model). Then $V_g(\forall\alpha\Box\phi,r)=1$ and ...

---

[97] See Gibbard (1975).

(ii) ...$V_g(\Box\forall\alpha\phi, r) = 0$. So for some world w, $V_g(\forall\alpha\phi, w) = 0$; and so for some u in the domain, $V_{g_u^\alpha}(\phi, w) = 0$.

(iii) Given (i), $V_{g_u^\alpha}(\Box\phi, r) = 1$; and so $V_{g_u^\alpha}(\phi, w) = 1$, contradicting (ii).

The fact that instances of the Barcan schema are SQML-valid is often regarded as a defect of SQML. To see why, we need to pause for a moment, and reflect on the intuitive significance of the relative order of quantifiers and modal operators. The point is perhaps clearest when we consider the following equivalent of the Barcan formula:

$$\Diamond\exists x F x \rightarrow \exists x \Diamond F x$$

The consequent of this conditional is existential in form. That is, its major connective is $\exists x$. Like any existential sentence, it says that *there exists* something of a certain sort, namely, something that could have been F. In contrast, the form of the antecedent is modal, not existential. Its major connective is $\Diamond$, not $\exists x$. What it says is that it would be *possible* for something to be the case (namely, for there to exist an F). It does *not* say that there exists something of a certain sort. (Of course, one might present a philosophical argument that it *implies* such a thing. But it doesn't *say* it.) This difference in what the antecedent and consequent say, in fact, suggests that in some cases the antecedent might be true and the consequent might be false. Perhaps, for example, it would be *possible* for there to exist a ghost, even though there in fact exists nothing that could have been a ghost. That is: if you go through all the things there are, $u_1, u_2 \ldots$, none of them is capable of having been a ghost; but nevertheless, there could have existed an *extra* thing, v, distinct from each u_i, which is a ghost.

(The contrast between $\exists x \Diamond F x$ and $\Diamond\exists x F x$ is analogous to the contrast between Quine's (1956) "there exists someone whom Ralph believes to be a spy" and "Ralph believes that someone is a spy". In the former, where the existential quantifier comes first, there is said to be someone of a certain sort—namely, someone who is believed-by-Ralph-to-be-a-spy. In the latter, where the existential quantifier occurs inside of "Ralph believes that", no existential statement is made; rather, the sentence attributes an existential belief to Ralph, to the effect that there are spies. On the face of it, Ralph might believe that there are spies, without there being any particular person whom Ralph believes to be a spy.)

With all this in mind, let's return to the Barcan formula, $\forall x \Box F x \rightarrow \Box \forall x F x$. Notice how the quantifier $\forall x$ comes before the modal operator $\Box$ in the antecedent, but after it in the consequent. Thus the antecedent is universal in form; it says that all entities have a certain feature: being-necessarily-F. The consequent, on the other hand, is modal in form; it says that a certain claim is necessarily true: the claim that *everything is F*. Apparently, this difference between what the antecedent and consequent say leads to the possibility that the antecedent could be true while the consequent is false. Let $u_1, u_2 \ldots$ again be all the entities there are; and suppose that each u_i is necessarily F, so that the antecedent is true. Mightn't it nevertheless be possible for there to exist an *extra* entity, v, distinct from each u_i, that fails to be F? In that case, the consequent would be false. Suppose, for instance, that each u_i is necessarily a material object. Then, letting F stand for "is a material object", $\forall x \Box F x$ is true. Nevertheless, $\Box \forall x F x$ seems false—it would presumably be *possible* for there to exist an immaterial object: a ghost, say. The ghost would simply need to be distinct from each u_i.

This objection to the validity of the Barcan formula is obviously based on the idea that it is contingent *which objects exist*, for it assumes that there could have existed an extra object distinct from each u_i. In terms of possible worlds, the objection assumes that what objects exist can vary from possible world to possible world. Anyone who thinks that the objection is correct will then point to a corresponding defect in the definition of an SQML-model. Each SQML-model contains a single domain, $\mathcal{D}$; and the truth condition for the quantified sentence $\forall \alpha \phi$, at a world w, is simply that ϕ is true at w of every member of $\mathcal{D}$. Thus the quantifier ranges over the same domain regardless of which possible world is being described—SQML does not represent it as being contingent which objects exist. That is why the Barcan formula turns out SQML-valid.

This feature of SQML-models is problematic for an even more direct reason: it makes the sentence $\forall x \Box \exists y\, y = x$ valid. To see this, suppose for reductio that $V_g(\forall x \Box \exists y\, y = x, w) = 0$. Then $V_{g_u^x}(\Box \exists y\, y = x, w) = 0$, for some $u \in \mathcal{D}$. So $V_{g_u^x}(\exists y\, y = x, w') = 0$, for some $w' \in \mathcal{W}$. So $V_{g_{uu}^{xy}}(y = x, w') = 0$, for every $u' \in \mathcal{D}$. So, since $u \in \mathcal{D}$, we have $V_{g_{uu}^{xy}}(y = x, w') = 0$. So $[y]_{g_{uu}^{xy}} \neq [x]_{g_{uu}^{xy}}$, i.e., $u \neq u$; contradiction. It's clear that the source of the validity here is the same as with the Barcan schema: SQML-models have a single domain common to each possible world. The validity of this formula is problematic because it seems to say that everything necessarily exists! It says that for each object x, it's necessary that *there is* something identical to x; but if there is something identical to x in a possible scenario, then, it would seem, x exists in that scenario.

The Barcan schema is just one of a number of interesting schemas concerning how quantifiers and modal operators interact (for each schema I also list an equivalent schema with $\Diamond$ in place of $\Box$):

$\forall \alpha \Box \phi \rightarrow \Box \forall \alpha \phi$	$\Diamond \exists \alpha \phi \rightarrow \exists \alpha \Diamond \phi$	(Barcan)
$\Box \forall \alpha \phi \rightarrow \forall \alpha \Box \phi$	$\exists \alpha \Diamond \phi \rightarrow \Diamond \exists \alpha \phi$	(converse Barcan)
$\exists \alpha \Box \phi \rightarrow \Box \exists \alpha \phi$	$\Diamond \forall \alpha \phi \rightarrow \forall \alpha \Diamond \phi$	
$\Box \exists \alpha \phi \rightarrow \exists \alpha \Box \phi$	$\forall \alpha \Diamond \phi \rightarrow \Diamond \forall \alpha \phi$	

We have already discussed the Barcan schema. The fourth schema raises no philosophical problems for SQML, since, quite properly, it has instances that turn out invalid (example 9.3). Let's look at the other two schemas.

First, the converse Barcan schema. Like the Barcan schema, each of its instances is SQML-valid (exercise 9.2), and like the Barcan schema, this verdict faces a philosophical challenge. Suppose the antecedent is true. So it's necessary that everything is ϕ: in every possible world, the statement "everything is ϕ" is true. But, the challenger says, this just means that in every world, all the things that exist in that world are

ϕ. So it permits things that *don't* exist in that world to fail to be ϕ in that world, in which case the consequent would be false. This talk of an object being ϕ in a world in which it doesn't exist may seem strange, but consider the following instance of the converse Barcan schema, substituting "$\exists y\, y=x$" (think: "x exists") for ϕ:

$$\Box\forall x\exists y\, y=x \rightarrow \forall x\Box\exists y\, y=x$$

This formula seems false. Its antecedent is clearly true; but its consequent seems to say that everything exists necessarily.

Each instance of the third schema, $\exists\alpha\Box\phi\rightarrow\Box\exists\alpha\phi$, is also SQML-valid (exercise 9.2); and again, this is philosophically questionable. Let's suppose that physical objects are necessarily physical. Then, $\exists x\Box Px$ seems true, letting P mean 'is physical'. But $\Box\exists x Px$ seems false—surely it would have been possible for there to have existed no physical objects. This counterexample (as well as the counterexample to the converse Barcan formula) requires that it be possible for some objects that in fact exist to go missing, whereas the counterexample to the Barcan formula required the possibility of *extra* objects.

> **Exercise 9.2** Show that all instances of the converse Barcan schema and the third schema are SQML-valid.

9.5.3 Necessary existence defended?

There are various ways to respond to the challenge of the previous section. From a logical point of view, the simplest is to stick to one's guns and defend the SQML-semantics. SQML-models accurately model the modal facts. Instances of the Barcan, converse Barcan, and third schemas, and the statement that everything necessarily exists, are all logical truths; the philosophical objections are mistaken. Contrary to appearances, it is *not* contingent what objects there are. Each possible world has exactly the same stock of individuals. Call this the doctrine of *constancy*.

One could uphold constancy either by taking a narrow view of what is possible, or by taking a broad view of what there is. On the former alternative, one would claim that it is just not possible for there to be any ghosts, and that it is just not possible in any sense for an actual object to have failed to exist. On the latter alternative, which I'll be discussing for the rest of this section, one accepts the possibility of ghosts, dragons, and so on, but claims, roughly, that there are possible ghosts and dragons in the actual world; and one accepts that actual objects could have failed to "exist" in a certain robust sense while denying that actual objects could have utterly failed to *be*.

The defender of constancy that I have in mind thinks that there are a great many more things than one would ordinarily suppose. In addition to *normal things*—what one would usually think of as the existing entities: people, tables and chairs, planets and electrons, and so on—our defender of constancy claims that there are also objects that, in other possible worlds, are ghosts, golden mountains, talking donkeys, and so forth. Call these further objects "extraordinary things". In order for the formula

"$\forall x\phi$" to be true, it's not enough for the normal things to be ϕ, for the normal things are not all of the things that there are. There are also all the extraordinary things, and each of these must be ϕ as well (must be ϕ here in the actual world, that is), in order for $\forall x\phi$ to be true. Hence the objection to the Barcan formula from the previous section fails. That objection assumed that $\forall x\Box Fx$, the antecedent of the Barcan formula, was true when F symbolizes "is a material object". But this neglects the extraordinary things. Even if all the *normal* objects are necessarily material objects, there are some further things—extraordinary things—that are not necessarily material objects.

Further: in ordinary language, when we say "everything" or "something", we typically don't mean to be talking about *absolutely all* objects; we're typically talking about just the normal objects. Otherwise we would be speaking falsely when we say, for example, "everything has mass": extraordinary things that might have been unicorns presumably have no mass (nor spatial location, nor any other physical feature). Ordinary quantification is restricted to normal things. So if we want to translate an ordinary claim into the language of QML, we must introduce a predicate for the normal things, "N", and use it to restrict quantifiers. But now, consider the following ordinary English statement:

> If everything is necessarily a material object, then necessarily: everything is a material object.

Mindlessly translating this into the language of QML gives us $\forall x\Box Fx\rightarrow\Box\forall xFx$—an instance of the Barcan schema. But since, in everyday usage, quantifiers are restricted to normal things, the thought in the mind of an ordinary speaker who utters this sentence is more likely the following:

$$\forall x(Nx\rightarrow\Box Fx)\rightarrow\Box\forall x(Nx\rightarrow Fx)$$

which says:

> If every normal thing is necessarily a material object, then necessarily: every normal thing is a material object.

And *this* formula is *not* an instance of the Barcan schema, nor is it valid, as may be shown by the following abbreviated countermodel:

Official model:

r $\boxed{N:\varnothing \qquad F:\varnothing}$ $\mathscr{D}:\{u\}$ $\mathscr{W}=\{r,a\}$

$\mathscr{D}=\{u\}$

$\mathscr{I}(N)=\{\langle u,a\rangle\}$

a $\boxed{N:\{u\} \qquad F:\varnothing}$ $\mathscr{I}(F)=\varnothing$

So in a sense, the ordinary intuitions that were alleged to undermine the Barcan schema are in fact consistent with constancy.

The defender of constancy can defend the converse Barcan schema and the third schema in similar fashion. The objection to the converse Barcan schema assumed the falsity of $\forall x \Box \exists y\, y = x$. "Sheer prejudice!", according to the friend of constancy. "And further, an ordinary utterance of 'Everything exists necessarily' expresses, not $\forall x \Box \exists y\, y = x$, but rather $\forall x (Nx \rightarrow \Box \exists y (Ny \land y = x))$, ($N$ for 'normal'), the falsity of which is is perfectly compatible with constancy. It's possible to fail to be normal; all that's impossible is to utterly fail to be. Likewise for the third schema."

The defender of constancy relies on a distinction between "normal" and "extraordinary" objects. This distinction is schematic; different defenders of constancy might understand this distinction in different ways. Some might say that the normal things are the *existent* things; extraordinary objects are things that do not exist, but nevertheless *are*. Others might say that the normal things are *actual*, and the extraordinary ones are nonactual—"merely possible"—objects. Still others might say that the extraordinary things are those that are not, but could have been, located in space and time.[98] However the distinction is understood, this defense of SQML has hefty metaphysical commitments. Some philosophers consider the postulation of nonexistent or nonactual entities as being anywhere from obviously false to conceptually incoherent, or subversive, or worse.[99] And even the postulation of contingently nonspatiotemporal entities will strike many as extravagant.

On the other hand, constancy's defenders can point to certain powerful arguments in its favor. Here's a quick sketch of one such argument. First, the following seems to be a logical truth:

$$\text{Ted} = \text{Ted}$$

But it follows from this that:[100]

$$\exists y\, y = \text{Ted}$$

This latter formula, too, is therefore a logical truth. But if ϕ is a logical truth, then so is $\Box \phi$ (recall the rule of necessitation from Chapter 6). So we may infer that the following is a logical truth:

$$\Box \exists y\, y = \text{Ted}$$

Now, nothing in this argument depended on any special features of me. We may therefore conclude that the reasoning holds good for every object; and so $\forall x \Box \exists y\, y = x$ is indeed a logical truth. Since, therefore, every object exists necessarily, it should come as no surprise that there are things that might have been ghosts, dragons, and so on—for if there had been a ghost, it would have necessarily existed, and thus must actually exist. This and other related arguments have apparently wild conclusions,

---

[98] Compare Williamson (1998), on whose defense of constancy this section is based.

[99] See Quine (1948); Lycan (1979).

[100] Free logicians will of course resist this step. See section 5.6.

but they cannot be lightly dismissed, for it is hard to say exactly where they go wrong (if they go wrong at all!).[101]

9.6 Variable domains

We now consider a way of dealing with the problems discussed in section 9.5.2 that does not require embracing constancy.

SQML-models contain a single domain, $\mathscr{D}$, over which the quantifiers range in each possible world. Since it was this feature that led to the problems of section 9.5.2, let's introduce a new semantics that instead provides different domains for different possible worlds. And let's also reinstate the accessibility relation, for reasons to be made clear below. The new semantics is called VDQML ("variable-domain quantified modal logic"):

DEFINITION OF MODEL: A VDQML-model is a 5-tuple $\langle \mathscr{W}, \mathscr{R}, \mathscr{D}, \mathscr{Q}, \mathscr{I} \rangle$ where:

- $\mathscr{W}$ is a nonempty set   ("possible worlds")
- $\mathscr{R}$ is a binary relation over $\mathscr{W}$ ("accessibility relation")
- $\mathscr{D}$ is a nonempty set   ("super-domain")
- $\mathscr{Q}$ is a function that assigns to any $w \in \mathscr{W}$ a subset of $\mathscr{D}$. Let us refer to $\mathscr{Q}(w)$ as "$\mathscr{D}_w$". Think of $\mathscr{D}_w$ as w's "subdomain"—the set of objects that exist at w.
- $\mathscr{I}$ is a function such that: ("interpretation function")
    - if α is a constant, then $\mathscr{I}(\alpha) \in \mathscr{D}$
    - if Π is an n-place predicate, then $\mathscr{I}(\Pi)$ is a set of ordered $n+1$-tuples $\langle u_1, \ldots, u_n, w \rangle$, where $u_1, \ldots, u_n$ are members of $\mathscr{D}$, and $w \in \mathscr{W}$.

DEFINITION OF VALUATION: The valuation function $V_{\mathscr{M},g}$, for VDQML-model $\mathscr{M}$ ($= \langle \mathscr{W}, \mathscr{R}, \mathscr{D}, \mathscr{Q}, \mathscr{I} \rangle$) and variable assignment g, is defined as the function that assigns either 0 or 1 to each wff relative to each member of $\mathscr{W}$, subject to the following constraints:

- for any terms α and β, $V_{\mathscr{M},g}(\alpha{=}\beta, w) = 1$ iff $[\alpha]_{\mathscr{M},g} = [\beta]_{\mathscr{M},g}$
- for any n-place predicate, Π, and any terms $\alpha_1, \ldots, \alpha_n$,
  $V_{\mathscr{M},g}(\Pi\alpha_1 \ldots \alpha_n, w) = 1$ iff $\langle [\alpha_1]_{\mathscr{M},g}, \ldots, [\alpha_n]_{\mathscr{M},g}, w \rangle \in \mathscr{I}(\Pi)$
- for any wffs ϕ and ψ, and variable, α,

$$V_{\mathscr{M},g}(\sim\phi, w) = 1 \text{ iff } V_{\mathscr{M},g}(\phi, w) = 0$$

$$V_{\mathscr{M},g}(\phi{\to}\psi, w) = 1 \text{ iff either } V_{\mathscr{M},g}(\phi, w) = 0 \text{ or } V_{\mathscr{M},g}(\psi, w) = 1$$

$$V_{\mathscr{M},g}(\forall\alpha\phi, w) = 1 \text{ iff for each } u \in \mathscr{D}_w, V_{\mathscr{M},g_u^\alpha}(\phi, w) = 1$$

$$V_{\mathscr{M},g}(\Box\phi, w) = 1 \text{ iff for each } v \in \mathscr{W}, \text{ if } \mathscr{R}wv \text{ then } V_{\mathscr{M},g}(\phi, v) = 1$$

---

[101]On this topic see Prior (1967, pp. 149–151); Plantinga (1983); Fine (1985); Linsky and Zalta (1994; 1996); Williamson (1998; 2002).

The definition of denotation remains unchanged. The obvious derived clauses for $\exists$ and $\diamond$ are as follows:

$$V_{\mathcal{M},g}(\exists\alpha\phi,w)=1 \text{ iff for some } u \in \mathcal{D}_w, V_{\mathcal{M},g_u^\alpha}(\phi,w)=1$$

$$V_{\mathcal{M},g}(\diamond\phi,w)=1 \text{ iff for some } v \in \mathcal{W}, \mathcal{R}wv \text{ and } V_{\mathcal{M},g}(\phi,v)=1$$

Thus, we have introduced *subdomains*. We still have $\mathcal{D}$, a set that contains all of the possible individuals. But for each possible world w, we introduce a subset of the domain, $\mathcal{D}_w$, to be the domain *for w*. When evaluating a quantified sentence at a world w, the quantifier ranges only over $\mathcal{D}_w$.

How should we define validity and semantic consequence here? There are some complications. Our earlier definitions were: a valid formula must be true at every world in every model under every variable assignment; and semantic consequence is truth-preservation at every world in every model under every variable assignment. Sticking to those definitions leads to some odd results. For example, the formula $\forall xFx \rightarrow Fy$ turns out to be invalid. For consider a model with a world w such that everything in $\mathcal{D}_w$ is F at w; suppose that some object u that is *not* a member of $\mathcal{D}_w$ is *not* F at w; and consider a variable assignment that assigns u to y. $\forall xFx$ is then true but Fy is false at w, relative to this model and variable assignment. This result is odd because $\forall xFx \rightarrow Fy$ is an instance of the principle of universal instantiation (axiom schema PC1 from section 4.4). For similar reasons, $\forall xFx \rightarrow Fa$ comes out invalid as well.

The example could be blocked by redefining validity. We could say that a formula is valid iff it is true for every *admissible* choice of a model $\mathcal{M}$, world w, and variable assignment g, where such a choice is admissible iff $[\alpha]_{\mathcal{M},g} \in \mathcal{D}_w$ for each term α (whether variable or constant). But this just relocates the oddity: now the rule of necessitation fails to preserve validity. $\forall xFx \rightarrow Fy$ now turns out valid, but $\square(\forall xFx \rightarrow Fy)$ does not (as a model like the one considered in the previous paragraph demonstrates). Alternatively, we could stick with the original definition, embrace the invalidity of $\forall xFx \rightarrow Fy$ (and of $\forall xFx \rightarrow Fa$), thus accepting a sort of free logic (section 5.6).

Note that if $\mathcal{M}$ is an SQML-model, then we can construct a corresponding VDQML-model with the same set of worlds, (super-) domain, and interpretation function, in which every world is accessible from every other, and in which $\mathcal{D}$ is a constant function assigning the whole super-domain to each world. It is intuitively clear that the same sentences are true in this corresponding model as are true in $\mathcal{M}$. Hence, whenever a sentence is SQML-invalid, it is VDQML-invalid. (The converse of course is not true.)

9.6.1 Contingent existence vindicated

What is the status in VDQML of the controversial SQML-valid formulas discussed in section 9.5.2? They all turn out invalid. Here is an abbreviated countermodel to the Barcan formula; for the others, see exercise 9.4.

Example 9.4: $\nvDash_{\text{VDQML}} \forall x\square Fx \rightarrow \square\forall xFx$:

Official model:

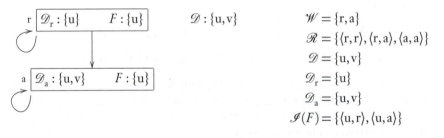

$$\mathcal{W} = \{r, a\}$$
$$\mathcal{R} = \{\langle r, r \rangle, \langle r, a \rangle, \langle a, a \rangle\}$$
$$\mathcal{D} = \{u, v\}$$
$$\mathcal{D}_r = \{u\}$$
$$\mathcal{D}_a = \{u, v\}$$
$$\mathcal{I}(F) = \{\langle u, r \rangle, \langle u, a \rangle\}$$

Exercise 9.3 Does the move to variable-domain semantics change whether any of the formulas in exercise set 9.1 are valid? Justify your answers.

Exercise 9.4 Demonstrate the VDQML-invalidity of the following formulas

(a) $\Box \forall x Fx \rightarrow \forall x \Box Fx$

(b) $\exists x \Box Fx \rightarrow \Box \exists x Fx$

(c) $\forall x \Box \exists y \ y = x$

9.6.2 Increasing, decreasing domains

If we made certain restrictions on the accessibility relation in variable-domain models, then the validity of the controversial formulas of section 9.5.2 would be reinstated. For example, the counterexample to the Barcan formula in the previous section required a model in which the domain expanded; world a was accessible from world r, and had a larger domain. But suppose we included the following constraint on $\mathcal{R}$ in any model:

$$\text{if } \mathcal{R}wv, \text{ then } \mathcal{D}_v \subseteq \mathcal{D}_w \qquad \text{(decreasing domains)}$$

The counterexample would then go away. Indeed, every instance of the Barcan schema would then become valid, which may be proved as follows:

(i) Suppose for reductio that $V_g(\forall \alpha \Box \phi \rightarrow \Box \forall \alpha \phi, w) = 0$. So $V_g(\forall \alpha \Box \phi, w) = 1$ and...

(ii) ...$V_g(\Box \forall \alpha \phi, w) = 0$. So for some v, $\mathcal{R}wv$ and $V_g(\forall \alpha \phi, v) = 0$; and so, for some $u \in \mathcal{D}_v$, $V_{g_u^\alpha}(\phi, v) = 0$.

(iii) Given decreasing domains, $\mathcal{D}_v \subseteq \mathcal{D}_w$, so $u \in \mathcal{D}_w$. So by (i), $V_{g_u^\alpha}(\Box \phi, w) = 1$; and so $V_{g_u^\alpha}(\phi, v) = 1$. This contradicts (ii).

Similarly, the following constraint would validate the converse Barcan schema as well as $\exists\alpha\Box\phi\rightarrow\Box\exists\alpha\phi$ (exercise 9.5):

$$\text{if } \mathscr{R}wv, \text{ then } \mathscr{D}_w \subseteq \mathscr{D}_v \qquad\qquad \text{(increasing domains)}$$

Even after imposing the increasing-domains constraint, the Barcan formula remains invalid; and after imposing the decreasing-domains constraint, the converse Barcan formula and also $\exists x\Box Fx\rightarrow\Box\exists xFx$ remain invalid. But when the accessibility relation is symmetric (as it is in B and S5) this collapses: imposing either constraint results in imposing both.

Exercise 9.5 Show that every instance of each of the following schemas is valid given the increasing-domains requirement.

(a) $\Box\forall\alpha\phi\rightarrow\forall\alpha\Box\phi$

(b) $\exists\alpha\Box\phi\rightarrow\Box\exists\alpha\phi$

9.6.3 Strong and weak necessity

In order for $\Box\phi$ to be true at a world, the VDQML-semantics requires that ϕ be true at every accessible world. This requirement might seem too strong. In order for $\Box Fa$, say, to be true, Fa must be true in all possible worlds. But what if a fails to exist in some worlds? In order for "Necessarily, I am human" to be true, must I be human in *every* possible world? Isn't it enough for me to be human in all the worlds in which I exist?

If the underlying worry here is that a must exist necessarily in order for $\Box Fa$ to be true—that I must exist necessarily in order to be necessarily human—then the worry is unfounded. The VDQML-semantics does require Fa to be true in every accessible world in order for $\Box Fa$ to be true; but it does not require a to exist in every world in which Fa is true. The clause in the definition of a VDQML-model for the interpretation of predicates was this:

- if Π is an n-place predicate, then $\mathscr{I}(\Pi)$ is a set of ordered $n+1$-tuples of the form $\langle u_1, \ldots, u_n, w\rangle$, where $u_1, \ldots, u_n$ are members <u>of $\mathscr{D}$</u>, and $w \in \mathscr{W}$.

(The underlined part mentions $\mathscr{D}$, not $\mathscr{D}_w$.) $\mathscr{I}(F)$ is allowed to contain pairs $\langle u, w\rangle$, where u is not a member of $\mathscr{D}_w$. So $\Box Fa$ is consistent with a's failing to necessarily exist; it's just that a has to be F even in worlds where it doesn't exist.

I doubt this really addresses the philosophical worry about the semantics, though, since it looks like bad metaphysics to say that a person could be human in a world where she doesn't exist. One could hard-wire a prohibition of this sort of bad metaphysics into VDQML-semantics by replacing the old clause with a new one:

- if Π is an n-place predicate then $\mathscr{I}(\Pi)$ is a set of ordered $n+1$-tuples of the form $\langle u_1, \ldots, u_n, w\rangle$, where $u_1, \ldots, u_n$ are members of <u>$\mathscr{D}_w$</u>, and $w \in \mathscr{W}$.

thus barring objects from having properties at worlds where they don't exist. But some would argue that this goes too far. The new clause validates $\forall x \Box (Fx \to \exists y\, y = x)$. "An object must exist in order to be F"—sounds clearly true if F stands for 'is human', but what if F stands for 'is famous'? If Baconians had been right and there had been no such person as Shakespeare, perhaps Shakespeare might still have been famous.

The issues here are complex.[102] But whether or not we should adopt the new clause, it looks as though there are *some* existence-entailing English predicates Π: predicates Π such that nothing can be a Π without existing. 'Is human' seems to be such a predicate. So we're back to our original worry about VDQML-semantics: its truth condition for $\Box \phi$ requires truth of ϕ at all worlds, which is allegedly too strong in at least some cases, for example the case where ϕ represents 'I am human'.

One could modify the clause for the $\Box$ in the definition of the valuation function, so that in order for $\Box Fa$ to be true, a only needs to be F in worlds in which it exists:

$$V_{\mathcal{M},g}(\Box \phi, w) = 1 \text{ iff for each } v \in \mathcal{W}, \text{ if } \mathcal{R}wv, \text{ and if } [\alpha]_{\mathcal{M},g} \in \mathcal{D}_w \text{ for each}$$
$$\text{name or free variable } \alpha \text{ occurring in } \phi, \text{ then } V_{\mathcal{M},g}(\phi, v) = 1$$

This would indeed have the result that $\Box Fa$ gets to be true provided a is F in every world in which it exists. But be careful what you wish for. Along with this result comes the following: even if a doesn't necessarily exist, the sentence $\Box \exists x\, x = a$ comes out true. For according to the new clause, in order for $\Box \exists x\, x = a$ to be true, it must merely be the case that $\exists x\, x = a$ is true *in every world in which a exists*, and of course this is indeed the case.

If $\Box \exists x\, x = a$ comes out true even if a doesn't necessarily exist, then $\Box \exists x\, x = a$ doesn't *say* that a necessarily exists. Indeed, it doesn't look like we have *any* way of saying that a necessarily exists if the $\Box$ has the meaning provided for it by the new clause.

A notion of necessity according to which "Necessarily ϕ" requires truth in *all* possible worlds is sometimes called a notion of *strong* necessity. In contrast, a notion of *weak* necessity is one according to which "Necessarily ϕ" requires merely that ϕ be true in all worlds in which objects referred to within ϕ exist. The new clause for the $\Box$ corresponds to weak necessity, whereas our original clause corresponds to strong necessity.

As we saw, if the $\Box$ expresses weak necessity, then one cannot even express the idea that a thing necessarily exists. That's because one needs strong necessity to say that a thing necessarily exists: in order to necessarily exist, you need to exist at *all* worlds, not just at all worlds at which you exist! So this is a deficiency of having the $\Box$ express weak necessity. But if we allow the $\Box$ to express strong necessity instead, there is no corresponding deficiency, for one can still express weak necessity using the strong $\Box$ and other connectives. For example, to say that a is weakly necessarily F (that is, that a is F in every world in which it exists), one can say: $\Box (\exists x\, x = a \to Fa)$.

So it would seem that we should stick with our original truth condition for the $\Box$, and live with the fact that statements like $\Box Fa$ turn out false if a fails to be F at

---

[102] The question is that of so-called "serious actualism" (Plantinga, 1983).

accessible worlds in which it doesn't exist. Those who think that "Necessarily, I am human" is true despite my possible nonexistence can always translate this natural-language sentence as $\Box(\exists x\, x{=}a{\to}Fa)$ (which requires a to be F only in accessible worlds in which it exists) rather than as $\Box Fa$.

9.6.4 *Actualist and possibilist quantification*

Suppose we kept the definition of a VDQML-model as is, but added a new expression $\forall_p$ to the language of QML, with a grammar just like $\forall$ (i.e., $\forall_p\alpha\phi$ is a wff for each variable α and wff ϕ), and with a semantics given by the following added clause to the definition of the valuation function:

$$V_{\mathscr{M},g}(\forall_p\alpha\phi) = 1 \text{ iff for each } \underline{u \in \mathscr{D}}, V_{\mathscr{M},g_u^\alpha}(\phi,w) = 1$$

Thus, in any world w, whereas $\forall$ ranges just over $\mathscr{D}_w$, $\forall_p$ ranges over all of $\mathscr{D}$.

$\forall_p$ is sometimes called a "possibilist" quantifier, since it ranges over all possible objects; $\forall$ is called an "actualist" quantifier since it ranges at world w only over the objects that are actual at w. In this setup, $\forall$ continues to behave as it does in VDQML, and hence the Barcan formula and company remain invalid. But the $\forall_p$ behaves just like $\forall$ did in SQML. For example, $\forall_p x\Box Fx{\to}\Box\forall_p xFx$ and $\forall_p x\Box\exists_p y\, y{=}x$ come out valid (where $\exists_p\alpha$ is defined as meaning $\sim\!\forall_p\alpha\sim$).

Formally speaking, this approach is very similar to the approach of section 9.5.3. For in effect, this section's $\forall_p$ is the sole quantifier of section 9.5.3; and this section's $\forall$ is the restricted quantifier "$\forall x(Nx{\to}$" of section 9.5.3, where N is a predicate symbolizing "is a normal object". On the face of it, the approaches are metaphysically similar as well. If there is a difference between introducing two quantifiers, one possibilist and one actualist, on the one hand, and introducing a single quantifier plus a predicate for normalcy/actuality, on the other, then it's a subtle one.[103]

9.7 Axiomatic proofs in SQML

So far our approach has been purely semantic. But one can also take a proof-theoretic approach to quantified modal logic. This is quite straightforward for SQML. (One can do it for VDQML as well, but we won't pursue that here.) To get an axiomatic system, for instance, one can simply combine the axioms for predicate logic introduced in section 4.4 with the axioms for S5 from section 6.4.6, plus axioms governing the identity sign:

AXIOMATIC SYSTEM SQML:

- Rules: MP, UG, NEC
- Axioms: all instances (with QML-wffs) of schemas PL1, PL2, PL3, PC1, PC2, K, T, and S5, plus:

$$\alpha = \alpha \tag{RX}$$
$$\alpha = \beta \to (\phi(\alpha){\to}\phi(\beta)) \tag{II}$$

---

[103] Although see McDaniel (2009); Turner (2010) for some related subtle metaphysics.

where α and β are terms, $\phi(\alpha)$ and $\phi(\beta)$ are wffs, and $\phi(\beta)$ is just like $\phi(\alpha)$ except with zero or more αs (free αs, if α is a variable) changed to βs (free βs, if β is a variable).

RX ("reflexivity") says that everything is self-identical. II ("indiscernibility of identicals") expresses the familiar principle of the indiscernibility of identicals: if objects are identical, then anything true of one is true of the other as well.[104]

As always, a theorem is defined as the last line of a proof in which each line is either an axiom or follows from earlier lines by a rule. As with MPL, we will be interested only in theoremhood, and will not consider proofs from premise sets. And we will use shortcuts as in sections 2.8, 4.4, and 6.4 to ease the pain of axiomatic proofs. Though we won't prove this here, our axiom system for SQML is sound and complete with respect to the SQML-semantics: a QML-wff is SQML-valid iff it is an SQML-theorem.[105]

Many theorems of SQML are just what you'd expect from the result of putting together axioms for predicate logic and axioms for S5 modal propositional logic. Examples include:

$$\Box\forall x(Fx \wedge Gx) \rightarrow \Box\forall x Fx$$
$$(\Box\forall x Fx \wedge \Box\forall x Gx) \rightarrow \Box\forall x(Fx \wedge Gx)$$
$$(\Box\forall x Fx \wedge \Diamond\exists x Gx) \rightarrow \Diamond\exists x(Fx \wedge Gx)$$

The first of these formulas, for example, is just an instance of a familiar sort of K-theorem, namely, a wff of the form $\Box\phi \rightarrow \Box\psi$ where $\phi \rightarrow \psi$ is provable on its own. The only difference in this case is that to prove $\phi \rightarrow \psi$ here, namely $\forall x(Fx \wedge Gx) \rightarrow \forall x Fx$, you need to use predicate logic techniques (see example 4.9). The other theorems are also unsurprising: each is, intuitively, an amalgam of a predicate logic theorem and an S5 MPL-theorem.

But other theorems of SQML are more surprising. In particular, all instances of the Barcan and converse Barcan schemas are theorems. An instance of the converse Barcan schema may be proved as follows:

1. $\forall x Fx \rightarrow Fx$ PC1
2. $\Box\forall x Fx \rightarrow \Box Fx$ 1, NEC, K, MP
3. $\forall x(\Box\forall x Fx \rightarrow \Box Fx)$ 2, UG
4. $\Box\forall x Fx \rightarrow \forall x \Box Fx$ PC2, 3, MP

Note that the only propositional modal logic required in this proof is K. The proof of the Barcan formula, on the other hand, requires B:

---

[104]II must be distinguished from section 5.4.3's "indiscernibility of identicals" (though each is based on the same idea). The former is an axiom schema—a claim in the metalanguage to the effect that any formula of a certain shape is an axiom; the axioms it generates have only first-order variables; and it is, intuitively, limited to "properties" that one can express in the language of QML. The latter is a single sentence of the object language (the language of second-order predicate logic); it contains second-order variables; and it is not limited to expressible properties (since the second-order variable X ranges over all subsets of the domain).

[105]See Hughes and Cresswell (1996, chapters 13–14).

1. $\forall x \Box Fx \rightarrow \Box Fx$ PC1
2. $\Diamond \forall x \Box Fx \rightarrow \Diamond \Box Fx$ 1, NEC, K$\Diamond$, MP
3. $\Diamond \Box Fx \rightarrow Fx$ B
4. $\Diamond \forall x \Box Fx \rightarrow Fx$ 2, 3, PL (syllogism)
5. $\Diamond \forall x \Box Fx \rightarrow \forall x Fx$ 4, UG, PC2, MP
6. $\Box \Diamond \forall x \Box Fx \rightarrow \Box \forall x Fx$ 5, NEC, K, MP
7. $\forall x \Box Fx \rightarrow \Box \Diamond \forall x \Box Fx$ B$\Diamond$
8. $\forall x \Box Fx \rightarrow \Box \forall x Fx$ 6, 7, PL (syllogism)

For one more example, the formula $\Box \exists x\, x{=}a$, which attributes necessary existence to a, may be proved as follows:

1. $a{=}a$ RX
2. $\forall x \sim x{=}a \rightarrow \sim a{=}a$ PC1
3. $\sim \forall x \sim x{=}a$ 1, 2, PL
4. $\Box \sim \forall x \sim x{=}a$ 3, NEC

The conclusion, $\Box \sim \forall x \sim x{=}a$, is the definitional equivalent of $\Box \exists x\, x{=}a$.

Given completeness, all the other controversial SQML-valid formulas are also SQML-theorems. Anyone who rejects these controversial formulas must therefore come up with some other proof-theoretic approach. There are indeed other proof-theoretic approaches. But these approaches are more complex. Though we won't go into this in detail, let's look quickly at one possibility.

Take the SQML-proof of $\Box \exists x\, x{=}a$. How might we revise the rules of our SQML axiomatic system to block it? The simplest method is to replace the standard predicate logic axioms with those from free predicate logic. Once we reach line 3 we have proved, purely by means of predicate logic, the sentence $\sim \forall x \sim x{=}a$—that is, $\exists x\, x{=}a$. This is just the kind of conclusion that the free logician wants to block; from her point of view, the name a might fail to denote any existing object. In section 5.6.2 we saw that the axiom of standard predicate logic that is objectionable to free logicians is PC1. PC1 expresses the principle of universal instantiation: if everything is ϕ, then β is ϕ. The free logical restriction of PC1 mentioned in section 5.6.2 was this:

$$\forall \alpha \phi \rightarrow (\exists x\, x{=}\beta \rightarrow \phi(\beta/\alpha)) \tag{PC1$'$}$$

which says: if everything is ϕ, then β is ϕ *provided β exists*. Replacing PC1 with PC1$'$ blocks the proof of $\Box \exists x\, x{=}a$ at step 2. It also blocks the proofs of the Barcan and converse Barcan formulas given above. Using this free-logical approach, one can develop various axiomatic systems for QML that are sound and complete with respect to variable-domain semantics.[106]

---

[106] See Garson (2006). An alternate approach is that originally taken by Kripke, who blocks the objectionable proofs by disallowing the style of reasoning using free variables on which those proofs are based. See Kripke (1963), and Hughes and Cresswell (1996, pp. 304–309).

Exercise 9.6 Construct axiomatic proofs in SQML for each of the following wffs.

(a)* $\Box(\Box\forall x(Fx{\rightarrow}Gx)\wedge\exists xFx)\rightarrow\Box\exists x\,Gx$

(b) $(\Box\forall xFx\wedge\Diamond\forall xGx)\rightarrow\Diamond\forall x(Fx\wedge Gx)$

(c) $(\forall x\Box(Fx{\rightarrow}Gx)\wedge\exists x\Diamond Fx)\rightarrow\exists x\Diamond Gx$

(d) $\forall y\Box\exists x\,x{=}y$

10

TWO-DIMENSIONAL MODAL LOGIC

I N THIS CHAPTER we consider a family of related extensions to modal logic that has considerable philosophical interest.

10.1 Actuality

The word 'actually', in one of its senses anyway, can be thought of as a one-place sentence operator: "Actually, ϕ".

'Actually' might at first seem redundant. "Actually, snow is white" just amounts to: "snow is white"; "actually, grass is blue" just amounts to: "grass is blue". But it's not redundant when it's embedded inside modal operators. The following two sentences, for example, have different meanings:

> Necessarily, if grass is blue then grass is blue
> Necessarily, if grass is blue then grass is actually blue

The first sentence makes the trivially true claim that grass is blue in any possible world in which grass is blue. But the second sentence makes the false claim that if grass is blue in any world, then grass is blue in the *actual* world. Intuitively, 'actual' lets us talk about what's going on in the actual world, even if we're inside the scope of a modal operator where normally we'd be talking about other possible worlds.

We symbolize "Actually, ϕ" as "@ϕ". (Grammar: whenever ϕ is a wff, so is @ϕ.) We can now symbolize the pair of sentences above as $\Box(B{\rightarrow}B)$ and $\Box(B{\rightarrow}@B)$, respectively. For some further examples of sentences we can symbolize using 'actually', consider:[107]

> It might have been that everyone who is actually rich is poor
> $\Diamond\forall x(@Rx{\rightarrow}Px)$

> There could have existed something that does not actually exist
> $\Diamond\exists x@{\sim}\exists y\, y{=}x$

10.1.1 Kripke models with designated worlds

Before doing semantics for @, let's return to the semantics of standard propositional modal logic. Here is a way of doing that semantics which differs slightly from that of section 6.3.1. First, instead of a triple $\langle \mathcal{W},\mathcal{R},\mathcal{I}\rangle$, let an MPL-model be a quadruple $\langle \mathcal{W},w_@,\mathcal{R},\mathcal{I}\rangle$, where $\mathcal{W}$, $\mathcal{R}$, and $\mathcal{I}$ are as before, and $w_@$ is some member of $\mathcal{W}$,

---

[107]In certain special cases, we could do without the new symbol @. For example, instead of symbolizing "Necessarily, if grass is blue then grass is actually blue" as $\Box(B{\rightarrow}@B)$, we could symbolize it as $\Diamond B{\rightarrow}B$. But the @ is not in general eliminable; see Hodes (1984*a*; *b*).

thought of as the *actual* or *designated* world of the model. Second, define the valuation function exactly as before (the designated world $w_@$ plays no role here). But third, use the designated worlds in the following new definitions (where S is any modal system):

DEFINITIONS OF TRUTH IN A MODEL, VALIDITY, AND SEMANTIC CONSEQUENCE:

- ϕ is true in model $\mathcal{M}$ $(= \langle \mathcal{W}, w_@, \mathcal{R}, \mathcal{I} \rangle)$ iff $V_{\mathcal{M}}(\phi, w_@) = 1$
- ϕ is S-valid iff ϕ is true in all S-models
- ϕ is an S-semantic consequence of Γ iff for any S-model $\mathcal{M}$, if each $\gamma \in \Gamma$ is true in $\mathcal{M}$ then ϕ is true in $\mathcal{M}$

One could add a designated world to models for quantified modal logic in a parallel way.

The old definitions of validity and semantic consequence, recall, never used any notion of truth in a model. (A valid formula, for example, was defined as a formula that is *valid* in all models.) But in model theory generally, one normally defines some notion of truth in a model, and then uses it to define validity as truth in all models, and semantic consequence as the preservation of truth in models. The nice thing about our new definitions is that they let us do the same for modal logic. But they don't differ in any substantive way from the old definitions; they yield exactly the same results (exercise 10.1).

> **Exercise 10.1*** Show that the new definitions of validity and semantic consequence are equivalent to the old ones.

10.1.2 Semantics for @

We can give @ a simple semantics using models with designated worlds. And now the designated worlds will play a role in the valuation function, not just in the definitions of validity and semantic consequence. We'll move straight to quantified modal logic, bypassing propositional logic. To keep things simple, let's go the SQML route: constant domain and no accessibility relation.

DEFINITION OF MODEL: A designated-world SQML-model is a 4-tuple $\langle \mathcal{W}, w_@, \mathcal{D}, \mathcal{I} \rangle$, where:

- $\mathcal{W}$ is a non-empty set ("worlds")
- $w_@$ is a member of $\mathcal{W}$ ("designated/actual world")
- $\mathcal{D}$ is a nonempty set ("domain")
- $\mathcal{I}$ is an "interpretation" function that assigns semantic values as before (members of $\mathcal{D}$ to names, intensions to predicates)

The valuation function is defined just as for SQML (section 9.3), with the following added clause for the new operator @:

- $V_{\mathcal{M},g}(@\phi, w) = 1$ iff $V_{\mathcal{M},g}(\phi, w_@) = 1$

Thus $@\phi$ is true in any world iff ϕ is true in the designated world.

10.1.3 Establishing validity and invalidity

The strategies for establishing the validity or invalidity of a given formula are similar to those from Chapter 9.

Example 10.1: Show that $\vDash \forall x(Fx \lor \Box Gx) \to \Box \forall x(Gx \lor @Fx)$:

(i) Suppose for reductio that this formula is not valid. Then for some model and variable assignment g, $V_g(\forall x(Fx \lor \Box Gx) \to \Box \forall x(Gx \lor @Fx), w_@) = 0$. So $V_g(\forall x(Fx \lor \Box Gx), w_@) = 1$ and...

(ii) ...$V_g(\Box \forall x(Gx \lor @Fx), w_@) = 0$. So $V_g(\forall x(Gx \lor @Fx), a) = 0$ for some $a \in \mathscr{W}$. So $V_{g_u^x}(Gx \lor @Fx, a) = 0$ for some $u \in \mathscr{D}$. So $V_{g_u^x}(Gx, a) = 0$ and...

(iii) ...$V_{g_u^x}(@Fx, a) = 0$. So $V_{g_u^x}(Fx, w_@) = 0$ (by the truth condition for @).

(iv) Given line (i), $V_{g_u^x}(Fx \lor \Box Gx, w_@) = 1$. So either $V_{g_u^x}(Fx, w_@) = 1$, or else $V_{g_u^x}(\Box Gx, w_@) = 1$. So, given (iii), $V_{g_u^x}(\Box Gx, w_@) = 1$, and so $V_{g_u^x}(Gx, a) = 1$, contradicting (ii).

Example 10.2: Show that $\nvDash \Box \forall x(Gx \lor @Fx) \to \Box \forall x(Gx \lor Fx)$:

$$\mathscr{W} = \{w_@, a\}$$
$$\mathscr{D} = \{u\}$$
$$\mathscr{I}(F) = \{\langle u, w_@ \rangle\}$$
$$\mathscr{I}(G) = \varnothing$$

The formula is false in world $w_@$ of this model. (The consequent is false in @ because at world a, something (namely, u) is neither G nor F; but the antecedent is true in @: since u is F at $w_@$, it's necessary that u is either G or *actually* F.) So the formula is false in the model; so it is invalid.

10.2 ×

Adding @ to the language of quantified modal logic lets us express certain kinds of comparisons between possible worlds that we couldn't express otherwise. But it doesn't go far enough; we need a further addition.[108] Consider this sentence:

> It might have been the case that, if all those then rich might all have been poor, then someone is happy

What it's saying, in possible-worlds terms, is this:

> For some world w, if there's a world v such that (everyone who is rich in w is poor in v), then someone is happy in w

This is a bit like "It might have been that everyone who is actually rich is poor"; in this new sentence the word 'then' plays a role a bit like the role played by 'actually'

---

[108] See Hodes (1984*a*) on the limitations of @; see Cresswell (1990) on × (his symbol is "Ref"), and further related additions.

in the earlier sentence. But the intention of the 'then' is not to take us back to the actual world; it is rather to take us back to the world, w, that was introduced by the first possibility operator, 'it might have been the case that'. We cannot, therefore, symbolize our new sentence this way:

$$\Diamond(\Diamond\forall x(@Rx{\rightarrow}Px){\rightarrow}\exists xHx)$$

For this says, in possible-worlds terms:

> For some world w, if there's a world v such that (everyone who is rich in $\underline{w_@}$
> is poor in v), then someone is happy in w

The problem is that @, as we've defined it, always takes us back to the designated world, whereas what we need to do is to "mark" the world w, and have @ take us back to the marked world:

$$\Diamond\times(\Diamond\forall x(@Rx{\rightarrow}Px){\rightarrow}\exists xHx)$$

$\times$ marks the spot: it is a point of reference for subsequent occurrences of @.

10.2.1 *Two-dimensional semantics for* $\times$

So let's add another one-place sentence operator, $\times$ (grammar: whenever ϕ is a wff, so is $\times\phi$). The idea is that $\times\phi$ means the same thing as ϕ, except that occurrences of @ in ϕ are to be interpreted as picking out the world that was the "current world of evaluation" when the $\times$ was encountered.

For semantics, let's return to the old SQML-models $\langle\mathcal{W},\mathcal{D},\mathcal{I}\rangle$ (without designated worlds). Denotation is defined as before. But let's change the valuation function: it will now assign truth values to formulas relative to *pairs* of possible worlds, rather than relative to single worlds (hence: "two-dimensional semantics"). So we'll write "$V^2_{\mathcal{M},g}(\phi,v,w)$" rather than "$V_{\mathcal{M},g}(\phi,w)$". The second world, w, plays the same role that the sole world w played before; call it the "world of evaluation". The first world, v, is new; call it the "reference world". Think of it as a "temporary actual world": it is the world that is picked out by @, and it can be changed by $\times$. Thus "$V^2_{\mathcal{M},g}(\phi,v,w)$" will mean that ϕ is true in world w, when v is treated as the actual world—when v is "considered as actual".

DEFINITION OF VALUATION: The two-dimensional valuation function, $V^2_{\mathcal{M},g}$, for an SQML-model $\mathcal{M}$ $(=\langle\mathcal{W},\mathcal{D},\mathcal{I}\rangle)$ is defined as the three-place function that assigns to each wff, relative to each pair of worlds, either 0 or 1 subject to the following constraints, for any n-place predicate Π, terms $\alpha_1\dots\alpha_n$, wffs ϕ and ψ, and variable β:

$$V^2_{\mathcal{M},g}(\Pi\alpha_1\ldots\alpha_n,v,w)=1 \text{ iff } \langle[\alpha_1]_{\mathcal{M},g},\ldots,[\alpha_n]_{\mathcal{M},g},w\rangle\in\mathscr{I}(\Pi)$$

$$V^2_{\mathcal{M},g}(\sim\phi,v,w)=1 \text{ iff } V^2_{\mathcal{M},g}(\phi,v,w)=0$$

$$V^2_{\mathcal{M},g}(\phi\to\psi,v,w)=1 \text{ iff } V^2_{\mathcal{M},g}(\phi,v,w)=0 \text{ or } V^2_{\mathcal{M},g}(\psi,v,w)=1$$

$$V^2_{\mathcal{M},g}(\forall\beta\phi,v,w)=1 \text{ iff for all } u\in\mathscr{D},V^2_{\mathcal{M},g^\beta_u}(\phi,v,w)=1$$

$$V^2_{\mathcal{M},g}(\Box\phi,v,w)=1 \text{ iff for all } w'\in\mathscr{W},V^2_{\mathcal{M},g}(\phi,v,w')=1$$

$$V^2_{\mathcal{M},g}(@\phi,v,w)=1 \text{ iff } V^2_{\mathcal{M},g}(\phi,v,v)=1$$

$$V^2_{\mathcal{M},g}(\times\phi,v,w)=1 \text{ iff } V^2_{\mathcal{M},g}(\phi,w,w)=1$$

Note the final two clauses. $@\phi$ says to forget the old world of evaluation and evaluate ϕ at the current reference world. $\times\phi$ says to forget about the old reference world, and let the new reference world be the current world of evaluation. As for validity and semantic consequence, our official definitions will be the following:

DEFINITIONS OF VALIDITY AND SEMANTIC CONSEQUENCE:

- ϕ is 2D-valid ("$\vDash_{2D}\phi$") iff for every model $\mathcal{M}$, every variable assignment g for $\mathcal{M}$, and every world w in $\mathcal{M}$, $V^2_{\mathcal{M},g}(\phi,w,w)=1$.
- ϕ is a 2D-semantic consequence of Γ ("$\Gamma\vDash_{2D}\phi$") iff for every model $\mathcal{M}$, every variable assignment g for $\mathcal{M}$, and every world w in $\mathcal{M}$, if $V^2_{\mathcal{M},g}(\gamma,w,w)=1$ for each $\gamma\in\Gamma$, then $V^2_{\mathcal{M},g}(\phi,w,w)=1$.

These define validity as truth in every pair of worlds of the form $\langle w,w\rangle$, and semantic consequence as truth-preservation at every such pair. But these aren't the only notions of validity and consequence that one could introduce. There are also the notions of truth and truth-preservation at *every* pair of worlds:[109]

DEFINITIONS OF GENERAL 2D-VALIDITY AND SEMANTIC CONSEQUENCE:

- ϕ is generally 2D-valid ("$\vDash_{G2D}\phi$") iff for every model $\mathcal{M}$, every variable assignment g for $\mathcal{M}$, and any worlds v and w in $\mathcal{M}$, $V^2_{\mathcal{M},g}(\phi,v,w)=1$.
- ϕ is a general 2D-semantic consequence of Γ ("$\Gamma\vDash_{G2D}\phi$") iff for every model $\mathcal{M}$, every variable assignment g for $\mathcal{M}$, and any worlds v and w in $\mathcal{M}$, if $V^2_{\mathcal{M},g}(\gamma,v,w)=1$ for each $\gamma\in\Gamma$, then $V^2_{\mathcal{M},g}(\phi,v,w)=1$.

Validity and general validity, and consequence and general consequence, come apart in various ways, as we'll see below.

As noted, we can now symbolize the sentence "It might have been the case that, if all those then rich might all have been poor, then someone is happy" as $\Diamond\times(\Diamond\forall x(@Rx\to Px)\to\exists xHx)$. Moreover, the change costs us nothing. For we can replace any sentence ϕ of the old language with $\times\phi$ in the new language (i.e. we

---

[109] The term 'general validity' is from Davies and Humberstone (1980); the first definition of validity corresponds to their "real-world validity".

just put the × operator at the front of the sentence).[110] For example, instead of symbolizing "It might have been that everyone who is actually rich is poor" as $\Diamond\forall x(@Rx{\rightarrow}Px)$ as we did before, we can symbolize it now as $\times\Diamond\forall x(@Rx{\rightarrow}Px)$.

Example 10.3: Show that if $\vDash_{2D} \phi$, then $\vDash_{2D} @\phi$. Suppose that $@\phi$ is not valid. Then in some model and some world, w (and some assignment g, but I'll suppress this when it isn't relevant), $V^2(@\phi, w, w) = 0$. Thus, given the truth condition for @, $V^2(\phi, w, w) = 0$, and so ϕ isn't valid.

Example 10.4: Show that every instance of $\phi{\leftrightarrow}@\phi$ is 2D-valid, but not every instance of $\Box(\phi{\leftrightarrow}@\phi)$ is. (Moral: any proof theory for this logic had better not include the rule of necessitation!) For the first, the truth condition for @ insures that for any world w in any model (and any variable assignment), $V^2(@\phi, w, w) = 1$ iff $V^2(\phi, w, w) = 1$, and so $V^2(\phi{\leftrightarrow}@\phi, w, w) = 1$. Thus $\vDash_{2D} \phi{\leftrightarrow}@\phi$. But here is a countermodel for $\Box(Fa{\leftrightarrow}@Fa)$:

$$\mathscr{W} = \{c, d\}$$
$$\mathscr{D} = \{u\}$$
$$\mathscr{I}(a) = u$$
$$\mathscr{I}(F) = \{\langle u, c\rangle\}$$

$V^2(\Box(Fa{\leftrightarrow}@Fa), c, c) = 0$ because $V^2(Fa{\leftrightarrow}@Fa, c, d) = 0$. For Fa is true at $\langle c, d\rangle$ iff the referent of a is in the extension of F at world d (it isn't) whereas $@Fa$ is true at $\langle c, d\rangle$ iff the referent of a is in the extension of F at world c (it is).

Note that this same model shows that $\phi{\leftrightarrow}@\phi$ is not *generally* valid. General validity is truth at all pairs of worlds, and the formula $Fa{\leftrightarrow}@Fa$, as we just showed, is false at the pair $\langle c, d\rangle$.

Exercise 10.2 Demonstrate the following facts:

(a) For any wff ϕ, $\vDash_{2D} \phi{\rightarrow}\Box@\phi$

(b) $\vDash_{2D} \Box\times\forall x\Diamond@Fx{\rightarrow}\Box\forall xFx$

10.3 Fixedly

The two-dimensional approach to possible-worlds semantics—evaluating formulas at pairs of worlds rather than single worlds—raises an intriguing possibility. The $\Box$ is a universal quantifier over the world of evaluation; we might, by analogy, follow Davies and Humberstone (1980) and introduce an operator that is a universal quantifier over the *reference* world. Davies and Humberstone call this operator "fixedly". We'll

---

[110]This amounts to the same thing as the old symbolization in the following sense. Let ϕ be any wff of the old language. Thus ϕ may have some occurrences of @, but it has no occurrences of ×. Then, for every SQML-model $\mathscr{M} = \langle\mathscr{W}, \mathscr{D}, \mathscr{I}\rangle$, and any $v, w \in \mathscr{W}$, $V^2_{\mathscr{M},g}(\times\phi, v, w) = V_{\mathscr{M}',g}(\phi, w)$, where $\mathscr{M}'$ is the designated-world model $\langle\mathscr{W}, w, \mathscr{D}, \mathscr{I}\rangle$.

symbolize "fixedly, ϕ" as $\mathsf{F}\phi$. Grammatically, $\mathsf{F}\phi$ is a wff whenever ϕ is; its semantic clause is this:[111]

$$V^2_{\mathcal{M},g}(\mathsf{F}\phi,v,w)=1 \text{ iff for every } v'\in\mathcal{W}, V^2_{\mathcal{M},g}(\phi,v',w)=1$$

The other two-dimensional semantic definitions, including the definitions of validity and semantic consequence, remain the same.

Humberstone and Davies point out that given F, @, and $\square$, we can introduce two new operators: F@ and $\mathsf{F}\square$. It's easy to show that:

$$V^2_{\mathcal{M},g}(\mathsf{F}@\phi,v,w)=1 \text{ iff for every } v'\in\mathcal{W}, V^2_{\mathcal{M},g}(\phi,v',v')=1$$
$$V^2_{\mathcal{M},g}(\mathsf{F}\square\phi,v,w)=1 \text{ iff for } v',w'\in\mathcal{W}, V^2_{\mathcal{M},g}(\phi,v',w')=1$$

Thus we can think of F@ and $\mathsf{F}\square$, as well as $\square$ and F themselves, as expressing "kinds of necessities", since their truth conditions introduce universal quantifiers over worlds of evaluation and reference worlds. (What about $\square\mathsf{F}$? It's easy to show that $\square\mathsf{F}$ is equivalent to $\mathsf{F}\square$.)

As with the semantics of the previous section, validity and general validity do not always coincide, as the following example shows.

Example 10.5: $\mathsf{F}@\phi\rightarrow\phi$ is 2D-valid for each wff ϕ (exercise 10.3). But some instances of this wff fail to be generally valid, for example:

$$\mathsf{F}@(@Ga\leftrightarrow Ga)\rightarrow(@Ga\leftrightarrow Ga)$$

General validity requires truth at all pairs $\langle v,w\rangle$ in all models. But in the following model, $V^2(\mathsf{F}@(@Ga\leftrightarrow Ga)\rightarrow(@Ga\leftrightarrow Ga),c,d)=0$:

$$\mathcal{W}=\{c,d\}$$
$$\mathcal{D}=\{u\}$$
$$\mathcal{I}(a)=u$$
$$\mathcal{I}(G)=\{\langle u,c\rangle\}$$

In this model, the referent of a is in the extension of G in world c, but not in world d. That means that $@Ga$ is true at $\langle c,d\rangle$ whereas Ga is false at $\langle c,d\rangle$, and so $@Ga\leftrightarrow Ga$ is false at $\langle c,d\rangle$. But $\mathsf{F}@\phi$ means that ϕ is true at all pairs of the form $\langle v,v\rangle$, and the formula $@Ga\leftrightarrow Ga$ is true at any such pair (in any model). Thus $\mathsf{F}@(@Ga\leftrightarrow Ga)$ is true at $\langle c,d\rangle$ in this model.

---

[111]Humberstone and Davies use designated-world QML models rather than two-dimensional semantics (and they don't include ×). Their truth condition for F is this: $V_{\mathcal{M},g}(\mathsf{F}\phi,w)=1$ iff $V_{\mathcal{M}',g}(\phi,w)=1$ for every model $\mathcal{M}'$ that is just like $\mathcal{M}$ except perhaps containing a different designated world. This approach isn't significantly different from the two-dimensional one.

Exercise 10.3 Show that $\vDash_{2D} F@\phi \rightarrow \phi$, for each wff ϕ.

Exercise 10.4 Show that for some ϕ, $\nvDash_{2D} \phi \rightarrow F\phi$.

Exercise 10.5** Show that if ϕ has no occurrences of @, then $\vDash_{2D}$ $\phi \rightarrow F\phi$.

10.4 Necessity and apriority

The two-dimensional modal framework has been applied to many philosophical issues during the past thirty or so years.[112] Here I will briefly present the two-dimensional approach to just one issue: the relationship between necessity and apriority.

In *Naming and Necessity*, Saul Kripke famously presented putative examples of necessary a posteriori statements and of contingent a priori statements:

Hesperus = Phosphorus
B [the standard meter bar] is one meter long

The first statement, Kripke argued, is necessary because whenever we try to imagine a possible world in which Hesperus is not Phosphorus, we find that we have merely imagined a world in which 'Hesperus' and 'Phosphorus' denote different objects than they in fact denote. Given that Hesperus and Phosphorus are in fact one and the same entity—namely, the planet Venus—there is no possible world in which Hesperus is distinct from Phosphorus, for such a world would have to be a world in which Venus is distinct from itself. Thus the statement is necessary. But it's a posteriori. It took astronomical investigation to learn that Hesperus and Phosphorus were identical; no amount of pure rational reflection would have sufficed. And the second sentence is a priori, according to Kripke, because it can be known to be true by anyone possessing the semantic knowledge that the description 'the length of bar *B*' fixes the reference of 'one meter'. Nevertheless, he argues, the sentence is contingent: bar *B* does not have its length essentially, and thus could have been longer or shorter than one meter.

But these conclusions are quite surprising. How can a statement that is true in all possible worlds be resistant to a priori investigation? Worse, how can a statement that *might have been false* be known a priori?

Some argue that the two-dimensional framework sheds light on all this. The idea in broad outline is as follows. In a superficial sense of 'necessary' and 'contingent', Kripke's examples are genuine but unproblematic. There is a deeper sense of those words in which necessary a posteriori or contingent a priori statements would indeed be problematic; but Kripke's examples are not statements of this sort. This position is due to Gareth Evans (1979); the two-dimensional formalization that we will be discussing is due to Martin Davies and Lloyd Humberstone (1980).

---

[112]For work in this tradition, see Stalnaker (1978; 2003; 2004); Evans (1979); Davies and Humberstone (1980); Hirsch (1986); Chalmers (1996; 2006); Jackson (1998); see Soames (2004) for a critique.

Kripke's examples employ two distinctions: necessity/contingency and apriority/aposteriority. We need to formalize both distinctions. But first let's get a little clearer about how the 2D formalism is to be applied. The formalism provides a notion of truth at pairs of worlds: ϕ is true at $\langle v, w \rangle$ iff ϕ truly describes w when v is "considered as actual". But there's also a more ordinary notion of truth: the notion of an utterance of a sentence being true full-stop. Utterance-truth is what we really care about; it is what reasonable people strive for. How are utterance-truth and truth at pairs of worlds connected? The two-dimensionalist's answer is that an utterance of ϕ in possible world w is true iff ϕ is true at the pair $\langle w, w \rangle$. For if the utterance takes place in w then of course the utterer is considering w as actual; but the utterance is *about* the world in which it takes place, and so w is the evaluation world as well as the reference world.

This leads to the following formalization of the a priori/a posteriori distinction: a sentence is a priori iff it is 2D-valid, and is a posteriori iff it is not 2D-valid. Since a 2D-valid sentence is true at every pair $\langle w, w \rangle$ of every model, any speaker who understands her language is in a position to know that an utterance of such a sentence would be true. A 2D-invalid sentence, on the other hand, needn't be true whenever uttered, and so a linguistically informed speaker needn't be in a position to know that an utterance of such a sentence would be true.

Next we need to formalize the necessary/contingent distinction. The two-dimensionalist wants to distinguish a "superficial" from a "deep" sense of these notions (we'll discuss what the superficiality and depth amount to below). These two senses correspond to two notions of necessity that can be distinguished in the 2D framework: $\Box$ and F@.[113] The basic idea is that ϕ is superficially necessary iff it would be true to utter $\Box\phi$, whereas ϕ is deeply necessary iff it would be true to utter F@ϕ. Officially:

DEFINITION OF SUPERFICIAL AND DEEP NECESSITY:

- ϕ is superficially necessary in model $\mathcal{M}$ at world w iff $V^2_{\mathcal{M},g}(\Box\phi, w, w) = 1$, for any variable assignment g for $\mathcal{M}$.
- ϕ is deeply necessary in $\mathcal{M}$ at w iff $V^2_{\mathcal{M},g}(F@\phi, w, w) = 1$, for any variable assignment g for $\mathcal{M}$.

For any sense of necessity there is a corresponding sense of contingency: a sentence is contingent iff neither it nor its negation is necessary. So we have a corresponding distinction between superficial and deep contingency as well.

$\Box\phi$ is true at $\langle w, w \rangle$ iff ϕ is true at $\langle w, v \rangle$ for all v; whereas F@ϕ is true at $\langle w, w \rangle$ iff ϕ is true at $\langle v, v \rangle$ for all v. So an utterance in w of a superficially necessary sentence is true iff the sentence is true in each world v when w is considered as actual; whereas an utterance in w of a deeply necessary sentence is true iff the sentence is true in each world v when $\underline{v}$ is considered as actual.

We're finally in a position to analyze Kripke's examples. First, the contingent a priori. Consider both Kripke's example and a related example from Evans:

Bar B is one meter long

---

[113] As noted in section 10.3 there are two others: F and F$\Box$.

Julius invented the zip

Bar B is the standard meter bar. 'One meter' and 'Julius' are supposed to be "descriptive names"—rigid designators whose references are fixed by the descriptions 'the length of bar B' and 'the inventor of the zip', respectively. Now, whether or not these English sentences are indeed contingent and a priori depends on delicate issues in the philosophy of language concerning descriptive names, rigid designation, and reference fixing. Rather than going into all that, let's construct some examples that are similar to Kripke's and Evans's. Let's *stipulate* that 'one meter' and 'Julius' are to abbreviate "actualized descriptions": 'the actual length of bar B' and 'the actual inventor of the zip'. With a little creative reconstruing in the first case, the sentences then have the form: "the actual G is G":

the actual length of bar B is a length of bar B
the actual inventor of the zip invented the zip

Now, these sentences are not quite a priori, since for all one knows, the G might not exist—there might exist no unique length of bar B, no unique inventor of the zip. So suppose we consider instead the following sentences:

If there is exactly one length of bar B, then the actual length of bar B is a length of bar B

If there is exactly one inventor of the zip, then the actual inventor of the zip invented the zip

Each has the form:

If there is exactly one G, then the actual G is G

Or, in symbols:

$$\exists x(Gx \wedge \forall y(Gy \to x=y)) \to \exists x(@Gx \wedge \forall y(@Gy \to x=y) \wedge Gx) \qquad (1)$$

(1) is 2D-valid (though not generally 2D-valid), and can be superficially contingent (exercise 10.6).

So if we formalize apriority as 2D validity and contingency as superficial contingency, (1) is an example of the contingent a priori. But according to the two-dimensionalist, this is unproblematic. Any utterance of (1) is guaranteed to be true, since (1) is true at all pairs $\langle w, w \rangle$ (it's 2D-valid, remember). So no utterance of (1) "makes any demand" on the world in which it's uttered (Evans's phrase). That's why (1) is knowable a priori. Corresponding to this, there is a sense in which (1) is necessary: (1) is deeply necessary. Yes, (1) is superficially contingent, but this means merely that the results of embedding it and its negation inside $\Box$ are both false; (1)'s superficial contingency is consistent with its utterance demanding nothing of the world (hence the epithet 'superficial').

Compare "Snow is white iff Snow is actually white"—$Fa \leftrightarrow @Fa$. This too is 2D-valid (example 10.4), and this too seems intuitively to "demand nothing of the world". (An utterance of this sentence demands no more of the world than an utterance of

"Snow is white iff Snow is white".) But $Fa \leftrightarrow @Fa$ is superficially contingent at any world of any model where Fa is true in some worlds and false in others.

As for the necessary a posteriori, the two-dimensionalist wants to concede that the examples are superficially necessary and fail to be 2D-valid (and then go on to say that this is unproblematic). But here we must take a bit more care. It's a trivial matter to construct models in which 2D-invalid sentences are necessarily true; and we don't need the two-dimensional framework to do it. We don't want to say that 'Everything is a lawyer' is an example of the necessary a posteriori. But let F symbolize 'is a lawyer'; we can construct a model in which the predicate F is true of every member of the domain at every world. $\forall x F x$ is superficially necessary at every world in this model, despite the fact that it is not 2D-valid. But this is too cheap. What's wrong is that this model isn't *realistic*. Relative to our choice to let F symbolize 'is a lawyer', the model doesn't accurately depict the modal fact that it's simply not necessarily true that everything is a lawyer.

To provide a nontrivial formalization of the necessary a posteriori, we will provide "realistic models" in which 2D-invalid sentences are necessarily true in the world corresponding to actuality. To do so, we will first think of nonlogical expressions of the language of QML as symbolizing certain particular expressions of natural language. And then we will choose a model that accurately depicts the real modal facts, given what the nonlogical expressions symbolize. (This notion of a "realistic model" is admittedly vague.)

Our example of the necessary a posteriori will be based on Kripke's Hesperus and Phosphorus example. To avoid controversies about the semantics of proper names in natural language, let's just stipulate that 'Hesperus' is to mean 'the actual first heavenly body visible in the evening' and that 'Phosphorus' is to mean 'the actual last heavenly body visible in the morning'. The example is then this:

If Hesperus and Phosphorus exist, then they are identical

i.e., letting F symbolize 'is a first heavenly body visible in the evening' and G symbolize 'is a last heavenly body visible in the morning':

If the actual F and the actual G exist, then they are identical

i.e.,

$$[\exists x (@Fx \wedge \forall y (@Fy \rightarrow x=y)) \wedge \exists z (@Gz \wedge \forall y (@Gy \rightarrow z=y))] \rightarrow$$
$$\exists x [@Fx \wedge \forall y (@Fy \rightarrow x=y) \wedge \exists z (@Gz \wedge \forall y (@Gy \rightarrow z=y) \wedge x=z)] \quad (2)$$

Sentence (2) isn't 2D-valid (exercise 10.7). But it is superficially necessary at the world corresponding to actuality in any realistic model. To see why, consider the facts. The planet Venus is in fact both the heavenly body last visible in the morning, and also the heavenly body first visible in the evening. (Or so we may pretend.) So any realistic model must have a part that looks as follows:

$$\mathcal{W} = \{c \dots\}$$
$$\mathcal{D} = \{u \dots\}$$

$$\mathscr{I}(F) = \{\langle u, c \rangle \dots\}$$
$$\mathscr{I}(G) = \{\langle u, c \rangle \dots\}$$

Object u corresponds to Venus, and world c corresponds to the actual world (note how u is both the unique F and the unique G in c). And in any such model, the necessitation of (2), i.e.:

$$\Box([\exists x(@Fx \land \forall y(@Fy \to x=y)) \land \exists z(@Gz \land \forall y(@Gy \to z=y)] \to$$
$$\exists x[@Fx \land \forall y(@Fy \to x=y) \land \exists z(@Gz \land \forall y(@Gy \to z=y) \land x=z)])$$

is true at $\langle c, c \rangle$ (since (2) is true at $\langle c, w \rangle$ for each world w). So (2) is superficially necessary at c in any such model.

But according to the two-dimensionalist, this is unproblematic. Even though (2) is superficially necessary, an utterance of that sentence does make a demand on the world; that is why (2) isn't knowable a priori. In order for an utterance of (2) in w to be true—i.e., in order for (2) to be true at the pair $\langle w, w \rangle$—the extensions of F and G in w need to satisfy the following condition: if each contains exactly one member then they must contain the same member. At worlds where this demand is not met, an utterance of the sentence is false. Correspondingly, (2) is capable of failing to be deeply necessary. Indeed, (2) isn't deeply necessary at the world corresponding to actuality in any realistic model. For consider again the facts. It could have been that Mars was the last heavenly body visible in the morning, while Venus remained the first heavenly body visible in the evening. So in addition to the part depicted above, any realistic model must also contain an object v corresponding to Mars, and a world, d, corresponding to the possibility just mentioned:

$$\mathscr{W} = \{c, d \dots\}$$
$$\mathscr{D} = \{u, v \dots\}$$
$$\mathscr{I}(F) = \{\langle u, c \rangle, \langle u, d \rangle \dots\}$$
$$\mathscr{I}(G) = \{\langle u, c \rangle, \langle v, d \rangle \dots\}$$

(Note that the unique G in d is v; u is the unique F there; as before, u is both the unique F and the unique G in c, which continues to correspond to the actual world.) In any such model, the result of prefixing (2) with F@:

$$F@\{[\exists x(@Fx \land \forall y(@Fy \to x=y)) \land \exists z(@Gz \land \forall y(@Gy \to z=y)] \to$$
$$\exists x[@Fx \land \forall y(@Fy \to x=y) \land \exists z(@Gz \land \forall y(@Gy \to z=y) \land x=z)]\}$$

is false at $\langle c, c \rangle$ (and indeed, at every pair of worlds), since (2) is false at $\langle d, d \rangle$. And so (2) is not deeply necessary at c in this model.

One might try to take this two-dimensional line further, and claim that in *every* case of the necessary a posteriori (or the contingent a priori), the necessity (contingency) is merely superficial. But defending this stronger line would require more than we have in place so far. To take one example, return again to 'Hesperus =

Phosphorus', but now, instead of thinking of 'Hesperus' and 'Phosphorus' as abbreviations for actualized descriptions, let us represent them by names in the logical sense (i.e., individual constants in our object language). Thus 'Hesperus = Phosphorus' becomes: $a=b$. Any realistic model will look in part as follows:

$$\mathscr{W} = \{c\ldots\}$$
$$\mathscr{D} = \{u\ldots\}$$
$$\mathscr{I}(a) = u$$
$$\mathscr{I}(b) = u$$

In any such model the sentence $a=b$ is deeply necessary (at any world in the model) (exercise 10.8). And yet it is a posteriori (2D-invalid), since some models assign different denotations to a and b (though these models won't be realistic).

Exercise 10.6 Show that sentence (1) is valid, though not generally valid, and is superficially contingent at some world in some model.

Exercise 10.7 Show that sentence (2) isn't 2D-valid.

Exercise 10.8 Show that $a = b$ is deeply necessary at any world of any model in which $\mathscr{I}(a) = \mathscr{I}(b)$.

Exercise 10.9 Show that a formula is capable of being superficially contingent (i.e., for some model and some world, it is superficially contingent at that world) iff it fails to be generally valid.

APPENDIX A

ANSWERS AND HINTS TO SELECTED EXERCISES

Exercise 1.1a "'$P \lor \sim P$' is a logical truth" is a sentence of the metalanguage, and (I would say) is false. '$P \lor \sim P$' contains the meaningless letter 'P', so it isn't a logical truth. Rather, it represents logical truths (assuming the law of the excluded middle is correct! See Chapter 3).

Exercise 1.1b '$(P \lor Q) \rightarrow (Q \lor P)$' is a sentence of the object language. Since it contains meaningless expressions ('P', 'Q'), it isn't true. (Not that it's false!)

Exercise 1.1c This is a bit of a trick question. "'Frank and Joe are brothers' logically implies 'Frank and Joe are siblings'" is a sentence of English, which is talking about further sentences of English. So English is functioning here both as the object language and as the metalanguage. As for whether the sentence is true, I would say no, since the implication is not "formal".

Exercise 1.2a 'Attorney and lawyer are synonyms' confuses use and mention; inserting quotation marks thus fixes the problem:

'Attorney' and 'lawyer' are synonyms.

Exercise 1.2b How can we insert quotation marks to remove the use–mention confusion in 'If S_1 is an English sentence and S_2 is another English sentence, then the string S_1 and S_2 is also an English sentence'? This is again a bit of a trick question. You might think to do it this way:

If S_1 is an English sentence and S_2 is another English sentence, then the string 'S_1 and S_2' is also an English sentence.

But this isn't quite right. It makes the (false) claim that the string of letters 'S_1 and S_2' (a string that contains the variables 'S_1' and 'S_2') is an English sentence, whereas the intention of the original sentence was to say that strings like 'Snow is white and grass is green' and 'Roses are red and violets are blue' are English sentences. Really, what we want is something like this:

If S_1 is an English sentence and S_2 is another English sentence, then the string consisting of S_1, followed by 'and', followed by S_2, is also an English sentence.

Quine (1940, p. 36) invented a device for saying such things more concisely. In his notation, we could write instead:

If S_1 is an English sentence and S_2 is another English sentence, then $\ulcorner S_1$ and $S_2 \urcorner$ is also an English sentence.

His "corner quotes", '$\ulcorner$' and '$\urcorner$', work like regular quotation marks, except when it comes to *variables of the metalanguage* such as 'S_1' and 'S_2'. Expressions other than such variables simply refer to themselves within corner quotes, just as all expressions do within regular quotation marks. But metalanguage variables refer to their values—i.e., the linguistic expressions they stand for—rather than themselves, within Quine's corner quotes. Thus,

$\ulcorner S_1$ and $S_2 \urcorner$

means the same as:

the string consisting of S_1, followed by 'and', followed by S_2

Exercise 1.3 Let sentence S_1 be 'There exists an x such that x and x are identical', and let S_2 be 'There exists an x such that there exists a y such that x and y are not identical'.

Does S_1 logically imply S_2 according to the modal criterion? Well, that depends. It depends on what is possible. You might think that there could have existed only a single thing, in which case S_1 would be true and S_2 would be false. If this is indeed possible, then S_1 doesn't logically imply S_2 (given the modal criterion). But some people think that numbers exist necessarily, and in particular that it's necessarily true that the numbers 0 and 1 exist and are not identical. If this is correct, then it wouldn't be possible for S_1 to be true while S_2 is false (since it wouldn't be possible for S_2 to be false). And so S_1 would logically imply S_2, given the modal criterion.

How about according to Quine's criterion? Again, it depends—in this case on which expressions are logical expressions. If (as is commonly supposed) 'there exists an x such that', 'there exists a y such that', 'not', and 'are identical' are all logical expressions, then *all* expressions in S_1 and S_2 are logical expressions. So, since each sentence is in fact true, there's no way to substitute *nonlogical* expressions to make S_1 true and S_2 false. So S_1 logically implies S_2 (according to Quine's criterion). But suppose 'are identical' is not a logical expression. Then S_1 would not logically imply S_2, according to Quine's criterion. For consider the result of substituting the predicate 'are both existent' for 'are identical'. S_1 then becomes true: 'There exists an x such that x and x are both existent', whereas S_2 becomes false: 'There exists an x such that there exists a y such that x and y are not both existent'.

Exercise 1.4 Here is the definition of the powerset of A: $\{u : u \subseteq A\}$. The powerset of $\{2, 4, 6\}$ is $\{\varnothing, \{2\}, \{4\}, \{6\}, \{2, 4\}, \{2, 6\}, \{4, 6\}, \{2, 4, 6\}\}$. Notice that the powerset of a set always contains both the null set and the set itself (look at the definition of 'subset' to see why this is so).

Exercise 1.5 $\mathbb{N}$ and $\mathbb{Z}$ are equinumerous, because of the following function f: $f(0) = 0, f(1) = 1, f(2) = -1, f(3) = 2, f(4) = -2, f(5) = 3, f(6) = -3, \ldots$. This function can be defined more rigorously as follows:

$$f(n) = \begin{cases} -\frac{n}{2} & \text{if } n \text{ is even} \\ \frac{n+1}{2} & \text{if } n \text{ is odd} \end{cases} \qquad \text{(for any } n \in \mathbb{N})$$

Exercise 2.8   Hint: instead of trying to show directly that every wff without repetition of sentence letters has the feature of PL-invalidity, find some feature F that is *stronger* than PL-invalidity (i.e., some feature F from which PL-invalidity follows), and show by induction that every wff without repeated sentence letters has this feature F; and then, finally, conclude that every wff without repeated sentence letters is PL-invalid.

Exercise 2.10   Hint: call a sequent $\Gamma \Rightarrow \phi$ *valid* iff $\Gamma \vDash \phi$; prove by induction that every provable sequent is a valid sequent.

Exercise 3.7   We're to show that there are no valid formulas in Kleene's system. Consider the trivalent interpretation $\mathscr{I}$ that assigns # to every sentence letter. If there existed any Kleene-valid formula ϕ, then $KV_{\mathscr{I}}(\phi)$ would need to be 1, whereas we can show by induction that $KV_{\mathscr{I}}(\psi) = \#$ for *every* wff ψ. Base case: all the sentence letters are obviously # in $\mathscr{I}$. Inductive step: assume that ϕ and ψ are both # in $\mathscr{I}$. We need now to show that $\phi \wedge \psi$, $\phi \vee \psi$, and $\phi \rightarrow \psi$ are all # in $\mathscr{I}$. But that's easy—just look at the truth tables for $\wedge$, $\vee$, and $\rightarrow$. #$\wedge$# is #, #$\vee$# is #, and #$\rightarrow$# is #.

Exercise 3.8   Hint: use induction.

Exercise 3.11   Hint: in each direction, prove the contrapositive. Exercise 3.8 might come in handy.

Exercise 3.15   Hint: this isn't hard, but it's a bit tricky. It might help to note that every classical (bivalent) interpretation also counts as a trivalent interpretation, with itself as its only precisification.

Exercise 3.16   We're to argue that contraposition and reductio should fail, given a supervaluational semantics for $\triangle$ (assuming the identification of truth with truth-on-all-sharpenings). Contraposition: as argued in the text, for all ϕ, ϕ logically implies "definitely, ϕ". So 'Middling Mary is rich' logically implies 'Middling Mary is definitely rich'. But 'not: definitely, middling Mary is rich' doesn't logically imply 'not: middling Mary is rich', since if Mary is a (definite) borderline case of being rich, the first is true on all sharpenings and hence is true, while the second is false on some sharpenings and so is not true. So to model these results, it should turn out under the supervaluationist semantics that $P \vDash \triangle P$ but $\sim\triangle P \nvDash \sim P$.

As for reductio, "Mary is rich and Mary is not definitely rich" cannot be true (on logical grounds), and so vacuously implies anything at all. (If it were true, then it would be true on all sharpenings; but then 'Mary is rich' would be true on all sharpenings; but then 'Mary is not definitely rich' would be false.) So, in particular, it logically implies 'Snow is white and Snow is not white' (say). But, contrary to reductio, 'not: Mary is rich and Mary is not definitely rich' is not a logical truth, since it isn't true. For there are sharpenings on which both 'Mary is rich' and 'Mary is not definitely rich' are true.

Exercise 3.17 For the systems of Łukasiewicz, Kleene, and Priest, we are to find intuitionistically provable sequents whose premises do not semantically imply their conclusions. Let's begin with Kleene's system. We showed in exercise 3.7 that there are no Kleene-valid wffs. Thus $\varnothing \nvDash_K P \rightarrow P$. But the following is an intuitionistically acceptable proof of the sequent $\varnothing \Rightarrow P \rightarrow P$:

1. $P \Rightarrow P$ RA   (for conditional proof)
2. $\varnothing \Rightarrow P \rightarrow P$ 1, $\rightarrow$I

Next, $ŁV_g(\sim(P \wedge \sim P)) = \#$ for any trivalent assignment $\mathscr{I}$ in which P is #, so $\sim(P \wedge \sim P)$ is Łukasiewicz-invalid. But $\varnothing \Rightarrow \sim(P \wedge \sim P)$ is intuitionistically provable:

1. $P \wedge \sim P \Rightarrow P \wedge \sim P$ RA   (for reductio)
2. $\varnothing \Rightarrow \sim(P \wedge \sim P)$ 1, RAA

(Since $\sim(P \wedge \sim P)$ is also Kleene-invalid, we could just as well have used this example for that system too.) Finally, $P, P \rightarrow Q \nvDash_{LP} Q$ (exercise 3.10d), whereas $P, P \rightarrow Q \Rightarrow Q$ is intuitionistically provable:

1. $P \Rightarrow P$ RA
2. $P \rightarrow Q \Rightarrow P \rightarrow Q$ RA
3. $P, P \rightarrow Q \Rightarrow Q$ 1, 2, $\rightarrow$E

Exercise 4.1 Hint: first prove by induction that for any wff ϕ and model $\mathscr{M}$, if variable assignments g and h agree on all variables with free occurrences in ϕ, then $V_{\mathscr{M},g}(\phi) = V_{\mathscr{M},h}(\phi)$; and then use this fact to establish the desired result.

Exercise 4.3d Hint: the premise has a free variable. Look carefully at the definition of semantic consequence to see how to accommodate this.

Exercise 4.5 We're to show that the set $\Gamma = \{\phi, F^2, F^3 \ldots\}$ would violate compactness, where by hypothesis, (i) for each $n \geq 2$, the sentence F^n is true in a model iff the extension of F in that model has at least n members; and (ii) the sentence ϕ is true in a given model iff the extension of F in that model is finite.

Γ is unsatisfiable. For suppose for reductio that each member of Γ were true in some model $\mathscr{M}$. Since $\phi \in \Gamma$, ϕ is true in $\mathscr{M}$, and so by (ii), $\mathscr{M}$'s domain has some finite number, k, of members. But F^{k+1} is also a member of Γ, and so by (i), $\mathscr{M}$'s domain would have to have at least $k + 1$ members. Contradiction.

But each finite subset Γ_0 of Γ is satisfiable. For since Γ_0 is finite, there's a limit to how many sentences of the form F^n are in it. Let k be the largest such n. So: every member of Γ_0 is either (a) ϕ, or is (b) F^n for some $n \leq k$. Now let $\mathcal{M}$ be some model in which the extension of F has k members. By (ii), ϕ is true in $\mathcal{M}$; and by (i), every sentence of type (b) is true in $\mathcal{M}$. So every member of Γ_0 is true in $\mathcal{M}$.

Exercise 5.5a   Hint: it's easy to get confused by the complexity of the antecedent here, "$\forall x L x \iota y F x y$". This just has the form: $\forall x L x \alpha$, where α is "$\iota y F x y$". L is a two-place predicate: it applies to the terms x and α. If you think of "Fxy" as meaning that x is a father of y, and "Lxy" as meaning that x loves y, then $\forall x L x \iota y F x y$ means "everyone x loves the y that he (x) is the father of".

Exercise 5.6   We must show that for any model $\langle \mathcal{D}, \mathcal{I} \rangle$, and any variable assignment g, $[\alpha]_g$ (relative to this model) is either undefined or a member of $\mathcal{D}$. We'll do this by induction on the grammar of α. So we'll show that the result holds when α is a variable, constant, or ι term (base cases), and then show that, assuming the result holds for simpler terms (inductive hypothesis), it also holds for complex terms made up of the simpler terms using a function symbol.

Base cases. If α is a variable, then $[\alpha]_g$ is $g(\alpha)$, which is a member of $\mathcal{D}$ given the definition of a variable assignment. If α is a constant, then $[\alpha]_g$ is $\mathcal{I}(\alpha)$, which is a member of $\mathcal{D}$ given the definition of a model's interpretation function. If α has the form $\iota \beta \phi$, then $[\alpha]_g$ is either the unique $u \in \mathcal{D}$ such that $V_{g_u^\beta}(\phi) = 1$ (if there is such a u) or undefined (if there isn't). So in all three cases, $[\alpha]_g$ is either undefined or a member of $\mathcal{D}$. (Note that even though ι terms are syntactically complex, we treated them here as a base case of our inductive proof. That's because we had no need for any inductive hypothesis; we could simply show directly that the result holds for all ι terms.)

Next we assume the inductive hypothesis (ih): the denotations of terms $\alpha_1 \ldots \alpha_n$ are either undefined or members of $\mathcal{D}$; and we must show that the same goes for the complex term $f(\alpha_1 \ldots \alpha_n)$. There are two cases; in each case we'll show that $[f(\alpha_1 \ldots \alpha_n)]_g$ is either undefined or a member of $\mathcal{D}$. Case 1: at least one of $[\alpha_1]_g \ldots [\alpha_n]_g$ is undefined. Then $[f(\alpha_1 \ldots \alpha_n)]_g$ is undefined. Case 2: all of $[\alpha_1]_g \ldots [\alpha_n]_g$ are defined. Then $[f(\alpha_1 \ldots \alpha_n)]_g$ is defined as $\mathcal{I}(f)([\alpha_1]_g \ldots [\alpha_n]_g)$. Moreover, the (ih) tells us that each of $[\alpha_1]_g \ldots [\alpha_n]_g$ is a member of $\mathcal{D}$. And we know from the definition of a model that $\mathcal{I}(f)$ is a total function over $\mathcal{D}$. So $\mathcal{I}(f)([\alpha_1]_g \ldots [\alpha_n]_g)$ is a member of $\mathcal{D}$.

Exercise 6.1   Hint: the only hard part is showing that if $\vDash_O \phi$, then $\vDash_{S5} \phi$. Suppose $\vDash_O \phi$ and let $\mathcal{M} = \langle \mathcal{W}, \mathcal{R}, \mathcal{I} \rangle$ be any S5-model; we must show that $V_{\mathcal{M}}(\phi, w) = 1$ for each $w \in \mathcal{W}$. Now, it's a fact from set theory that any equivalence relation R over set A "partitions" A—it divides A into non-overlapping subsets where: (i) each element of A is in exactly one of the subsets, and (ii) every member of every subset bears R to every member of that subset. So $\mathcal{R}$ partitions $\mathcal{W}$ in this way. Let $\mathcal{W}_w$ be the subset containing w, and consider the model $\mathcal{M}'$ that results from $\mathcal{M}$ by cutting away all worlds other than those in $\mathcal{W}_w$. $\mathcal{M}'$ is a total model, so ϕ is valid in it, so $V_{\mathcal{M}'}(\phi, w) = 1$. But then $V_{\mathcal{M}}(\phi, w) = 1$, as well. Why? You can prove by induction that the truth value of any wff at any world v in $\mathcal{M}$ is determined by the truth values of sentence letters within v's subset. (Intuitively: chains of modal operators take you to worlds seen by v, worlds seen by worlds seen by v, and so on; you'll never need to look at worlds outside of v's subset.)

Exercise 6.3a $\Box[P \rightarrow \Diamond(Q \rightarrow R)] \rightarrow \Diamond[Q \rightarrow (\Box P \rightarrow \Diamond R)]$:

D-countermodel:

$$\mathcal{W} = \{r, a, b\}$$
$$\mathcal{R} = \{\langle r, a\rangle, \langle a, b\rangle, \langle b, b\rangle\}$$
$$\mathcal{I}(Q, a) = \mathcal{I}(P, b) = 1, \text{ all else } 0$$

(also establishes K-invalidity)

T-validity proof (also establishes validity in B, S4, and S5):

(i) Suppose for reductio that the formula is false in some world r in some T-model $\langle \mathcal{W}, \mathcal{R}, \mathcal{I} \rangle$. Then $V(\Box[P \rightarrow \Diamond(Q \rightarrow R)], r) = 1$, and...

(ii) ...$V(\Diamond[Q \rightarrow (\Box P \rightarrow \Diamond R)], r) = 0$.

(iii) By reflexivity, $\mathcal{R} rr$, so by (ii), $V(Q \rightarrow (\Box P \rightarrow \Diamond R), r) = 0$. So $V(\Box P \rightarrow \Diamond R, r) = 0$. Thus $V(\Box P, r) = 1$ and so $V(P, r) = 1$; also...

(iv) ...$V(\Diamond R, r) = 0$

(v) From (i), given $\mathcal{R} rr$, $V(P \rightarrow \Diamond(Q \rightarrow R), r) = 1$, and so, given (iii), $V(\Diamond(Q \rightarrow R), r) = 1$. So for some world "$a$", $\mathcal{R} ra$ and $V(Q \rightarrow R, a) = 1$.

(vi) Since $\mathcal{R} ra$, from (ii) we have $V(Q \rightarrow (\Box P \rightarrow \Diamond R), a) = 0$, and so $V(Q, a) = 1$; and from (iv) we have $V(R, a) = 0$. These contradict line (v).

Exercise 6.3d $\Box(P \leftrightarrow Q) \rightarrow \Box(\Box P \leftrightarrow \Box Q)$:

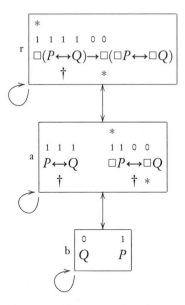

B-countermodel:

$$\mathscr{W} = \{r, a, b\}$$
$$\mathscr{R} = \{\langle r, r \rangle, \langle a, a \rangle, \langle b, b \rangle, \langle r, a \rangle, \langle a, r \rangle,$$
$$\langle a, b \rangle, \langle b, a \rangle\}$$
$$\mathscr{I}(P, r) = \mathscr{I}(Q, r) = \mathscr{I}(P, a) = \mathscr{I}(Q, a)$$
$$= \mathscr{I}(P, b) = 1, \text{ all else } 0$$

(also establishes K-, D-, and T-invalidity)

Validity proof for S4 (and so for S5 as well):

(i) Suppose for reductio that the formula is false in some world r of some S4-model. Then $V(\Box(P \leftrightarrow Q), r) = 1$ and...

(ii) ...$V(\Box(\Box P \leftrightarrow \Box Q), r) = 0$. So for some a, $\mathscr{R}ra$ and $V(\Box P \leftrightarrow \Box Q, a) = 0$, and so $\Box P$ and $\Box Q$ must have different truth values in a. Without loss of generality (given the symmetry between P and Q in the problem), let's suppose that $V(\Box P, a) = 1$ and ...

(iii) ...$V(\Box Q, a) = 0$. So for some world b, $\mathscr{R}ab$ and $V(Q, b) = 0$. Also, given (ii), $V(P, b) = 1$. So P and Q have different truth values in b.

(iv) By transitivity, $\mathscr{R}rb$, and so, given (i), $V(P \leftrightarrow Q, b) = 1$, contradicting (iii).

Exercise 6.3g $\Diamond\Diamond\Box P \leftrightarrow \Box P$:

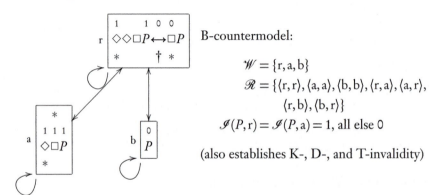

B-countermodel:

$$\mathscr{W} = \{r, a, b\}$$
$$\mathscr{R} = \{\langle r, r \rangle, \langle a, a \rangle, \langle b, b \rangle, \langle r, a \rangle, \langle a, r \rangle,$$
$$\langle r, b \rangle, \langle b, r \rangle\}$$
$$\mathscr{I}(P, r) = \mathscr{I}(P, a) = 1, \text{ all else } 0$$

(also establishes K-, D-, and T-invalidity)

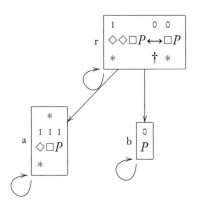

S4-countermodel:

$$\mathcal{W} = \{r, a, b\}$$
$$\mathcal{R} = \{\langle r, r \rangle, \langle a, a \rangle, \langle b, b \rangle, \langle r, a \rangle, \langle r, b \rangle\}$$
$$\mathcal{I}(P, a) = 1, \text{ all else } 0$$

S5-validity proof:

(i) Given the truth condition for the $\leftrightarrow$, it will suffice to show that $\Diamond\Diamond\Box P$ and $\Box P$ have the same truth value in every world of every S5-model. So let r be any world in any S5-model, and suppose first for reductio that $V(\Diamond\Diamond\Box P, r) = 1$ and ...

(ii) ...$V(\Box P, r) = 0$. So for some b, $\mathcal{R} r b$ and $V(P, b) = 0$

(iii) From (i), for some a, $\mathcal{R} r a$ and $V(\Diamond\Box P, a) = 1$, and so for some c, $\mathcal{R} a c$ and $V(\Box P, c) = 1$. By symmetry, $\mathcal{R} c a$ and $\mathcal{R} a r$, and so by transitivity, $\mathcal{R} c b$, and so $V(P, b) = 1$, contradicting (ii). So the first reductio assumption is false. Suppose next for reductio that $V(\Diamond\Diamond\Box P, r) = 0$ and ...

(iv) ...$V(\Box P, r) = 1$. By reflexivity, $\mathcal{R} r r$. So $V(\Diamond\Box P, r) = 1$; and so $V(\Diamond\Diamond\Box P, r) = 1$, contradicting (iii).

Exercise 6.5a $\vdash_K \Diamond(P \wedge Q) \rightarrow (\Diamond P \wedge \Diamond Q)$:

1. $(P \wedge Q) \rightarrow P$ PL
2. $\Box[(P \wedge Q) \rightarrow P]$ 1, NEC
3. $\Box[(P \wedge Q) \rightarrow P] \rightarrow [\Diamond(P \wedge Q) \rightarrow \Diamond P]$ K$\Diamond$
4. $\Diamond(P \wedge Q) \rightarrow \Diamond P$ 2, 3, MP
5. $\Diamond(P \wedge Q) \rightarrow \Diamond Q$ Similar to 1–4
6. $\Diamond(P \wedge Q) \rightarrow (\Diamond P \wedge \Diamond Q)$ 4, 5, PL (composition)

Exercise 6.5c $\vdash_K \sim\Diamond(Q \wedge R) \leftrightarrow \Box(Q \rightarrow \sim R)$:

1. $\sim\Diamond(Q\wedge R)\rightarrow\Box\sim(Q\wedge R)$ MN   (first one direction)
2. $\sim(Q\wedge R)\rightarrow(Q\rightarrow\sim R)$ PL
3. $\Box[\sim(Q\wedge R)\rightarrow(Q\rightarrow\sim R)]$ 2, NEC
4. $\Box\sim(Q\wedge R)\rightarrow\Box(Q\rightarrow\sim R)$ 3, K, MP
5. $\sim\Diamond(Q\wedge R)\rightarrow\Box(Q\rightarrow\sim R)$ 1, 4, PL (syllogism)
6. $(Q\rightarrow\sim R)\rightarrow\sim(Q\wedge R)$ PL (neg. conjunction)   (now the other)
7. $\Box(Q\rightarrow\sim R)\rightarrow\Box\sim(Q\wedge R)$ 6, NEC, K, MP
8. $\Box\sim(Q\wedge R)\rightarrow\sim\Diamond(Q\wedge R)$ MN
9. $\Box(Q\rightarrow\sim R)\rightarrow\sim\Diamond(Q\wedge R)$ 7, 8, PL (syllogism)
10. $\sim\Diamond(Q\wedge R)\leftrightarrow\Box(Q\rightarrow\sim R)$ 5, 9, PL (biconditional)

Exercise 6.5d Hint: you can move from $\phi\rightarrow(\psi\rightarrow\chi)$ and $\phi\rightarrow(\chi\rightarrow\psi)$ to $\phi\rightarrow(\psi\leftrightarrow\chi)$ using PL.

Exercise 6.5g We're to show that $\vdash_K \Diamond(P\rightarrow Q)\leftrightarrow(\Box P\rightarrow\Diamond Q)$. This one's a bit tough. The trick for the first half is choosing the right tautology, and for the second half, getting the right PL strategy.

1. $P\rightarrow[(P\rightarrow Q)\rightarrow Q]$ PL
2. $\Box P\rightarrow\Box[(P\rightarrow Q)\rightarrow Q]$ 1, NEC, K, MP
3. $\Box[(P\rightarrow Q)\rightarrow Q]\rightarrow[\Diamond(P\rightarrow Q)\rightarrow\Diamond Q]$ K$\Diamond$
4. $\Box P\rightarrow[\Diamond(P\rightarrow Q)\rightarrow\Diamond Q]$ 2, 3, PL (syllogism)
5. $\Diamond(P\rightarrow Q)\rightarrow(\Box P\rightarrow\Diamond Q)$ 4, PL (permutation)

I must now prove the right-to-left direction, namely, $(\Box P\rightarrow\Diamond Q)\rightarrow\Diamond(P\rightarrow Q)$. Note that the antecedent of this conditional is PL-equivalent to $\sim\Box P\vee\Diamond Q$ (disjunction from table 4.1), and that a conditional $(\phi\vee\psi)\rightarrow\chi$ follows in PL from the conditionals $\phi\rightarrow\chi$ and $\psi\rightarrow\chi$ (dilemma). So my goal will be to get two conditionals, $\sim\Box P\rightarrow\Diamond(P\rightarrow Q)$ and $\Diamond Q\rightarrow\Diamond(P\rightarrow Q)$, from which the desired conditional follows by PL (line 12 below).

6. $\sim\Box P\rightarrow\Diamond\sim P$ MN
7. $\sim P\rightarrow(P\rightarrow Q)$ PL
8. $\Diamond\sim P\rightarrow\Diamond(P\rightarrow Q)$ 7, NEC, K$\Diamond$, MP
9. $\sim\Box P\rightarrow\Diamond(P\rightarrow Q)$ 6, 8, PL (syllogism)
10. $Q\rightarrow(P\rightarrow Q)$ PL
11. $\Diamond Q\rightarrow\Diamond(P\rightarrow Q)$ 10, NEC, K$\Diamond$, MP
12. $(\Box P\rightarrow\Diamond Q)\rightarrow\Diamond(P\rightarrow Q)$ 9, 11, PL (dilemma, disjunction)
13. $\Diamond(P\rightarrow Q)\leftrightarrow(\Box P\rightarrow\Diamond Q)$ 5, 12, PL (biconditional)

Exercise 6.7b Hint: use the strategy of example 6.10.

Exercise 6.8b   Hint: first prove $\Box(P{\to}\Box P){\to}(\Diamond P{\to}P)$.

Exercise 6.10c   Hint: $\phi\vee\psi$ follows in PL from $\sim\!\phi{\to}\psi$; and remember MN.

Exercise 7.1   One condition on accessibility that validates every instance of (U) is the condition of *reflexivity at one remove*: if $\mathscr{R}wv$ for some w, then $\mathscr{R}vv$. Let w be any world in any MPL model obeying this condition, and suppose for reductio that $O(O\phi{\to}\phi)$ is false there. Then $O\phi{\to}\phi$ is false at some v accessible from w; and so $O\phi$ is true at v and ϕ is false there. By reflexivity at one remove, $\mathscr{R}vv$; so, since $O\phi$ is true at v, ϕ must be true at v; contradiction.

Exercise 7.2   To establish completeness for system X, we can employ the theorems and lemmas used to prove soundness and completeness for modal systems in Chapter 6 (strictly, those systems require the modal operator to be the $\Box$; so let's think of "O" as a kind of rounded way of writing "$\Box$"). For soundness, note that system X is K+$(D\cup U)$ in the notation of section 6.5, where D is the set of all instances of the D-schema and U is the set of all instances of the (U)-schema. So, given lemma 6.1, all we need to do is show that all members of $D\cup U$ are valid in every model whose accessibility relation is serial and reflexive at one remove. This follows, for the members of D, from the proof in exercise 6.14, and for the members of U, from the proof in exercise 7.1.

   As for completeness, first let's show that the accessibility relation in the canonical model for X is serial and reflexive at one remove. For seriality, the analogous part of the proof of D's completeness (section 6.6.5) may simply be repeated. As for reflexivity at one remove, suppose $\mathscr{R}wv$; we must show that $\mathscr{R}vv$. So let $\Box\phi$ be any member of v; we must show that $\phi\in v$. $\Box(\Box\phi{\to}\phi)$ is an axiom and hence a theorem of X, and so is a member of w (lemma 6.5c). So, by the definition of $\mathscr{R}$, $\Box\phi{\to}\phi\in v$; so, since $\Box\phi\in v$, $\phi\in v$ by 6.5b.

   Now for completeness. Suppose that $\vDash_X \phi$. That is, ϕ is valid in all serial-and-reflexive-at-one-remove MPL-models. Given the previous paragraph, ϕ is valid in the canonical model for X, and so by corollary 6.8, $\vdash_X \phi$.

Exercise 7.5   For any MPL-wff, δ, let δ^H be the result of replacing $\Box$s with Hs in δ. Now suppose χ is an MPL-wff and $\vDash_K \chi$; we must show that $\vDash_{PTL} \chi^H$. Intuitively, this holds because H works just like the $\Box$ except that it looks backward along the accessibility relation, and there's nothing special about either direction of the accessibility relation. But we need a proper argument.

   Let $\mathscr{M}=\langle\mathscr{T},\leq,\mathscr{I}\rangle$ be any PTL-model, and let t be any member of $\mathscr{T}$; we must show that χ^H is true at t in $\mathscr{M}$. Let $\geq$ be the converse of $\leq$ (that is, $t\geq t'$ iff $t'\leq t$); and let $\mathscr{M}'$ be the MPL-model just like $\mathscr{M}$ except that $\geq$ is its accessibility relation. Thus $\mathscr{M}'=\langle\mathscr{T},\geq,\mathscr{I}\rangle$. Now, since $\vDash_K \chi$, $V_{\mathscr{M}'}(\chi,t)=1$. And I'll show in a moment that:

$$\text{for any MPL-wff } \phi \text{ and any } s\in\mathscr{T}, V_{\mathscr{M}'}(\phi,s)=1 \text{ iff } V_{\mathscr{M}}(\phi^H,s)=1 \qquad (*)$$

Thus $V_{\mathcal{M}}(\chi^H, t) = 1$, which is what we wanted to show.

It remains to establish (*). I'll do this by induction. The base case, that $V_{\mathcal{M}'}(\alpha, s) = 1$ iff $V_{\mathcal{M}}(\alpha^H, s) = 1$ for any sentence letter α, is immediate since $\alpha = \alpha^H$ and $\mathcal{M}$ and $\mathcal{M}'$ share the same interpretation function $\mathcal{I}$. Now assume for induction that (*) holds for ϕ and ψ; we must show that it also holds for $\sim\phi$, $\phi\rightarrow\psi$, and $\Box\phi$. This is obvious in the first two cases; as for the latter:

$$V_{\mathcal{M}'}(\Box\phi, s) = 1 \text{ iff } V_{\mathcal{M}'}(\phi) = 1 \text{ for each } s' \text{ such that } s \geq s' \qquad \text{(t.c. for } \Box\text{)}$$
$$\text{iff } V_{\mathcal{M}'}(\phi) = 1 \text{ for each } s' \text{ such that } s' \leq s \qquad \text{(def of } \geq\text{)}$$
$$\text{iff } V_{\mathcal{M}}(\phi^H) = 1 \text{ for each } s' \text{ such that } s' \leq s \qquad \text{(ih)}$$
$$\text{iff } V_{\mathcal{M}}(H\phi^H) = 1 \qquad \text{(t.c. for H)}$$

Since $H\phi^H$ is the same wff as $(\Box\phi)^H$, we're done.

Exercise 7.8   We must show that if $\Gamma \vDash_I \phi$, then $\Gamma \vDash_{PL} \phi$. Suppose $\Gamma \vDash_I \phi$, and let $\mathcal{I}$ be a PL-interpretation in which every member of Γ is true; we must show that $V_{\mathcal{I}}(\phi) = 1$. ($V_{\mathcal{I}}$ is the classical valuation for $\mathcal{I}$.) Consider the intuitionist model $\mathcal{M}$ with just one stage, r, in which sentence letters have the same truth values in r as they have in $\mathcal{I}$—i.e., $\mathcal{M} = \langle\{r\}, \{\langle r, r\rangle\}, \mathcal{I}'\rangle$, where $\mathcal{I}'(\alpha, r) = \mathcal{I}(\alpha)$ for each sentence letter α. Since $\mathcal{M}$ has only one stage, the classical and intuitionist "truth" conditions collapse in this case—it would be easy to show by induction that for every wff ϕ, $IV_{\mathcal{M}}(\phi, r) = V_{\mathcal{I}}(\phi)$. So, since $V_{\mathcal{I}}(\gamma) = 1$ for each $\gamma \in \Gamma$, $IV_{\mathcal{M}}(\gamma, r) = 1$ for each $\gamma \in \Gamma$. Since $\Gamma \vDash_I \phi$, it follows that $IV_{\mathcal{M}}(\phi, r) = 1$; and so $V_{\mathcal{I}}(\phi) = 1$.

Exercise 7.10   We're to come up with cases of semantic consequence in the systems of Łukasiewicz, Kleene, Priest, and supervaluationism, that are not cases of intuitionist consequence. Actually a single case suffices. Exercise 7.9a shows that $\sim(P\wedge Q) \nvDash_I \sim P\vee\sim Q$. But $\sim(P\wedge Q) \vDash \sim P\vee\sim Q$ in each of these systems. Exercise 3.10c demonstrates this for LP. As for Łukasiewicz, suppose that $\text{ŁV}(\sim(P\wedge Q)) = 1$. Then $\text{ŁV}(P\wedge Q) = 0$, so either $\text{ŁV}(P) = 0$ or $\text{ŁV}(Q) = 0$. So either $\text{ŁV}(\sim P) = 1$ or $\text{ŁV}(\sim Q) = 1$. So $\text{ŁV}(\sim P\vee\sim Q) = 1$. Since the Kleene tables for the $\sim$, $\vee$, and $\wedge$ are the same as Łukasiewicz's, the implication holds in Kleene's system as well. Finally, supervaluationism: since $\sim(P\wedge Q)$ PL-implies $\sim P\vee\sim Q$, by exercise 3.13, $\sim(P\wedge Q) \vDash_S \sim P\vee\sim Q$.

Exercise 8.1   Could a general limit assumption be derived from a limit assumption for atomics? No. Consider the following model. (i) The model contains infinitely many worlds, including a certain world w in which P is true. (ii) P is false in all other worlds, and all other sentence letters are false in all worlds. (iii) There is no nearest-to-w world (other than w itself): for each world $x \neq w$, there is some $y \neq w$ such that $y \prec_w x$. (iv) w is always the nearest-to-x world (other than x itself), for any other world x: for any x and any $y \neq x$, $w \preceq_x y$. In this model the limit assumption for atomics holds (for any world x, w is the nearest-to-x P-world; and no other atomic is true in any world.) But the general limit assumption fails: although $\sim P$ is true in some worlds (indeed, infinitely many), there is no nearest-to-w $\sim P$-world.

Exercise 8.3e $P\square\!\!\rightarrow(Q\square\!\!\rightarrow R)\nvDash_{SC} Q\square\!\!\rightarrow(P\square\!\!\rightarrow R)$:

"view from r":

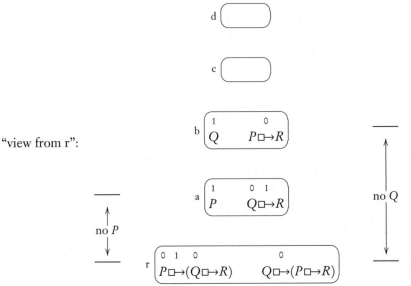

"view from a":   "view from b":

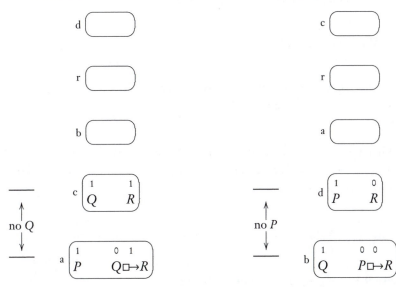

Official model:

$$\mathcal{W} = \{r, a, b, c, d\}$$
$$\preceq_r = \{\langle a, b \rangle, \langle b, c \rangle, \langle c, d \rangle \dots\}$$
$$\preceq_a = \{\langle c, b \rangle, \langle b, r \rangle, \langle r, d \rangle \dots\}$$
$$\preceq_b = \{\langle d, a \rangle, \langle a, r \rangle, \langle r, c \rangle \dots\}$$
$$\mathcal{I}(P, a) = \mathcal{I}(Q, b) = \mathcal{I}(Q, c) = \mathcal{I}(R, c) = \mathcal{I}(P, d) = 1, \text{ all else } 0$$

Exercise 8.6   Hint: say that an LC-model is "Stalnaker-acceptable" iff it obeys the limit and anti-symmetry assumptions. Show (by induction) that in Stalnaker-acceptable models, Lewis's truth conditions yield the same results as Stalnaker's. That is, in any such model, a wff counts as being true in a given world given Lewis's definition of truth in a model if and only if it counts as being true in that world given Stalnaker's definition.

Exercise 9.1a $\vDash_{\text{SQML}} (\Box\forall x(Fx{\rightarrow}Gx) \wedge \Diamond\exists xFx) \rightarrow \Diamond\exists xGx$:

(i)   Suppose for reductio that $V_g((\Box\forall x(Fx{\rightarrow}Gx) \wedge \Diamond\exists xFx) \rightarrow \Diamond\exists xGx, w) = 0$, for some world and variable assignment w and g in some model. Then $V_g(\Box\forall x(Fx{\rightarrow}Gx) \wedge \Diamond\exists xFx, w) = 1$ and...

(ii)   ...$V_g(\Diamond\exists xGx, w) = 0$.

(iii)   Given (i), $V_g(\Diamond\exists xFx, w) = 1$. So $V_g(\exists xFx, v) = 1$, for some $v \in \mathcal{W}$. So $V_{g_u^x}(Fx, v) = 1$, for some $u \in \mathcal{D}$.

(iv)   Given (i), $V_g(\Box\forall x(Fx{\rightarrow}Gx), w) = 1$. So $V_g(\forall x(Fx{\rightarrow}Gx), v) = 1$. So $V_{g_u^x}(Fx{\rightarrow}Gx, v) = 1$. So either $V_{g_u^x}(Fx, v) = 0$ or $V_{g_u^x}(Gx, v) = 1$; and so, given (iii), $V_{g_u^x}(Gx, v) = 1$.

(v)   Given (ii), $V_g(\exists xGx, v) = 0$. So $V_{g_u^x}(Gx, v) = 0$, contradicting (iv).

Exercise 9.1c $\nvDash_{\text{SQML}} \exists x\Diamond Rax \rightarrow \Diamond\Box\exists x\exists yRxy$:

$\mathscr{D} = \{u\}$
$\mathscr{I}(a) = u$

$$
\begin{array}{c}
* \\
1 0\ 0\ 0 1\ 1 \\
\exists x \Diamond Rax \rightarrow \Diamond \Box \exists x \exists y Rxy \Diamond Ra\frac{x}{u} \\
r\ + * * \\
\ \\
R : \{\langle u,u\rangle\}
\end{array}
$$

Official model:

$$\mathscr{W} = \{r, c\}$$
$$\mathscr{D} = \{u\}$$
$$\mathscr{I}(a) = u$$
$$\mathscr{I}(R) = \{\langle u,u,r\rangle\}$$

$$
\begin{array}{c}
+ + \\
0\ 0 0 0 \\
c\ \Box \exists x \exists y Rxy \exists y R\frac{x}{u} y R\frac{x}{u}\frac{y}{u} \\
* \\
R : \varnothing
\end{array}
$$

Exercise 9.6a $\vdash_{\mathrm{SQML}} \Box(\Box\forall x(Fx{\to}Gx) \wedge \exists x Fx) \to \Box\exists x Gx$:

1.	$\forall x(Fx{\to}Gx) \to (Fx{\to}Gx)$	PC1
2.	$\forall x(Fx{\to}Gx) \to ({\sim}Gx{\to}{\sim}Fx)$	1, PL (contr., syll.)
3.	$\forall x(\forall x(Fx{\to}Gx){\to}({\sim}Gx{\to}{\sim}Fx))$	2, UG
4.	$\forall x(Fx{\to}Gx) \to \forall x({\sim}Gx{\to}{\sim}Fx)$	PC2, 3, MP
5.	$\forall x({\sim}Gx{\to}{\sim}Fx) \to (\forall x{\sim}Gx{\to}\forall x{\sim}Fx)$	distribution
6.	$\forall x(Fx{\to}Gx) \to (\forall x{\sim}Gx{\to}\forall x{\sim}Fx)$	4, 5, PL (syllogism)
7.	$(\forall x(Fx{\to}Gx) \wedge {\sim}\forall x{\sim}Fx) \to {\sim}\forall x{\sim}Gx$	6, PL (contr., imp/exp.)
8.	$(\forall x(Fx{\to}Gx) \wedge \exists x Fx) \to \exists x Gx$	7, def of $\exists$
9.	$\Box\forall x(Fx{\to}Gx) \to \forall x(Fx{\to}Gx)$	T
10.	$(\Box\forall x(Fx{\to}Gx) \wedge \exists x Fx) \to \exists x Gx$	8, 9, PL (see below)
11.	$\Box(\Box\forall x(Fx{\to}Gx) \wedge \exists x Fx) \to \Box\exists x Gx$	10, NEC, K, MP

(Step 10 used the tautology: $((P{\wedge}Q){\to}R)\to((S{\to}P)\to((S{\wedge}Q){\to}R))$.) My approach: I set myself an ultimate goal of getting the conditional $(\Box\forall x(Fx{\to}Gx) \wedge \exists x Fx) \to \exists x Gx$ (since then I could use the usual K-technique for adding a $\Box$ to each side). Since SQML includes the T-axioms, it sufficed to establish $(\forall x(Fx{\to}Gx) \wedge \exists x Fx) \to \exists x Gx$, that is: $(\forall x(Fx{\to}Gx) \wedge {\sim}\forall x{\sim}Fx) \to {\sim}\forall x{\sim}Gx$. So this latter formula became my penultimate goal. But this follows via PL from $\forall x(Fx{\to}Gx) \to (\forall x{\sim}Gx{\to}\forall x{\sim}Fx)$. So this final formula became my first goal.

Exercise 10.1 I'll show that the designated-worlds definition of validity is equiva-lent to the old one; the proof for semantic consequence is parallel. First note that:

(*) For each new model $\mathscr{M} = \langle \mathscr{W}, w_{@}, \mathscr{R}, \mathscr{I}\rangle$, the corresponding old model $\mathscr{M}' = \langle \mathscr{W}, \mathscr{R}, \mathscr{I}\rangle$ has the same distribution of truth values—i.e., for every wff ϕ and every $w \in \mathcal{W}$, $V_{\mathcal{M}}(\phi, w) = V_{\mathcal{M}'}(\phi, w)$

(*) is true because the designated world plays no role in the definition of the valuation function.

Now, where S is any modal system, suppose first that ϕ is S-valid under the old definition. Then ϕ is valid in every old S-model. So by (*), ϕ is true in every world of every new S-model, and so is true in the designated world of every new S-model, and so is S-valid under the new definition.

For the other direction, suppose ϕ is S-invalid under the old definition. So ϕ is false at some world, w, in some old S-model $\mathcal{M}' = \langle \mathcal{W}, \mathcal{R}, \mathcal{I} \rangle$. Now consider the new S-model $\mathcal{M} = \langle \mathcal{W}, w, \mathcal{R}, \mathcal{I} \rangle$ (same worlds, accessibility, and interpretation function as $\mathcal{M}'$; w is the designated world). By (*), ϕ is false at w in $\mathcal{M}$, and so is false in $\mathcal{M}$, and so is S-invalid under the new definition.

Exercise 10.5   Hint: first prove by induction the stronger result that if ϕ has no occurrences of @, then $\phi \rightarrow F\phi$ is *generally valid*.

REFERENCES

Benacerraf, Paul and Putnam, Hilary (ed.) (1983). *Philosophy of Mathematics* (2nd edn). Cambridge University Press, Cambridge.

Bencivenga, Ermanno (1986). Free logics. In *Handbook of Philosophical Logic* (ed. D. Gabbay and F. Guenther), Volume 3, pp. 373–426. D. Reidel, Dordrecht.

Boolos, George (1975). On second-order logic. *Journal of Philosophy*, **72**, 509–27.

Boolos, George (1984). To be is to be the value of a variable (or to be some values of some variables). *Journal of Philosophy*, **81**, 430–49.

Boolos, George (1985). Nominalist platonism. *Philosophical Review*, **94**, 327–44.

Boolos, George S., Burgess, John P., and Jeffrey, Richard C. (2007). *Computability and Logic* (5th edn). Cambridge University Press, Cambridge.

Cartwright, Richard (1987). *Philosophical Essays*. MIT Press, Cambridge, MA.

Chalmers, David (1996). *The Conscious Mind*. Oxford University Press, Oxford.

Chalmers, David (2006). Two-dimensional semantics. In *Oxford Handbook of Philosophy of Language* (ed. E. Lepore and B. C. Smith), pp. 574–606. Oxford University Press, New York.

Cresswell, M. J. (1990). *Entities and Indices*. Kluwer, Dordrecht.

Davies, Martin and Humberstone, Lloyd (1980). Two notions of necessity. *Philosophical Studies*, **38**, 1–30.

Dowty, David R., Wall, Robert E., and Peters, Stanley (1981). *Introduction to Montague Semantics*. Kluwer, Dordrecht.

Edgington, Dorothy (1995). On conditionals. *Mind*, **104**, 235–329.

Etchemendy, John (1990). *The Concept of Logical Consequence*. Harvard University Press, Cambridge, MA.

Evans, Gareth (1979). Reference and contingency. *The Monist*, **62**, 161–89.

Feldman, Fred (1986). *Doing the Best We Can*. D. Reidel, Dordrecht.

Fine, Kit (1975). Vagueness, truth and logic. *Synthese*, **30**, 265–300.

Fine, Kit (1985). Plantinga on the reduction of possibilist discourse. In *Alvin Plantinga* (ed. J. Tomberlin and P. van Inwagen), pp. 145–86. D. Reidel, Dordrecht.

French, Peter, Theodore E. Uehling, Jr., and Wettstein, Howard K. (ed.) (1986). *Midwest Studies in Philosophy XI: Studies in Essentialism*. University of Minnesota Press, Minneapolis, MN.

Gamut, L. T. F. (1991*a*). *Logic, Language, and Meaning, Volume 1: Introduction to Logic*. University of Chicago Press, Chicago, IL.

Gamut, L. T. F. (1991*b*). *Logic, Language, and Meaning, Volume 2: Intensional Logic and Logical Grammar*. University of Chicago Press, Chicago, IL.

Garson, James W. (2006). *Modal Logic for Philosophers*. Cambridge University Press, New York.

Gentzen, Gerhard (1935). Investigations into logical deduction. *Mathematische Zeitschrift*, **39**, 176–210, 405–31. Originally entitled "Untersuchungen über das logische Schliessen".

Gibbard, Allan (1975). Contingent identity. *Journal of Philosophical Logic*, **4**, 187–221.

Goble, Lou (ed.) (2001). *The Blackwell Guide to Philosophical Logic*. Blackwell, Malden, MA.

Heim, Irene and Kratzer, Angelika (1998). *Semantics in Generative Grammar*. Blackwell, Malden, MA.

Hilpinen, Risto (2001). Deontic logic. In Goble (2001), pp. 159–82.

Hirsch, Eli (1986). Metaphysical necessity and conceptual truth. In French *et al.* (1986), pp. 243–56.

Hodes, Harold (1984*a*). On modal logics which enrich first-order S5. *Journal of Philosophical Logic*, **13**, 423–54.

Hodes, Harold (1984*b*). Some theorems on the expressive limitations of modal languages. *Journal of Philosophical Logic*, **13**, 13–26.

Hughes, G. E. and Cresswell, M. J. (1996). *A New Introduction to Modal Logic*. Routledge, London.

Jackson, Frank (1998). *From Metaphysics to Ethics: A Defence of Conceptual Analysis*. Oxford University Press, Oxford.

Kripke, Saul (1963). Semantical considerations on modal logic. *Acta Philosophica Fennica*, **16**, 83–94.

Kripke, Saul (1965). Semantical analysis of intuitionistic logic. In *Formal Systems and Recursive Functions* (ed. M. Dummett and J. Crossley), pp. 92–130. North-Holland, Amsterdam.

Kripke, Saul (1972). Naming and necessity. In *Semantics of Natural Language* (ed. D. Davidson and G. Harman), pp. 253–355, 763–9. D. Reidel, Dordrecht. Revised edition published in 1980 as *Naming and Necessity* (Cambridge, MA: Harvard University Press).

Lemmon, E. J. (1965). *Beginning Logic*. Chapman & Hall, London.

Lewis, C. I. (1918). *A Survey of Symbolic Logic*. University of California Press, Berkeley, CA.

Lewis, C. I. and Langford, C. H. (1932). *Symbolic Logic*. Century Company, New York.

Lewis, David (1973*a*). *Counterfactuals*. Blackwell, Oxford.

Lewis, David (1973*b*). Counterfactuals and comparative possibility. *Journal of Philosophical Logic*, **2**, 418–46.

Lewis, David (1977). Possible-world semantics for counterfactual logics: A rejoinder. *Journal of Philosophical Logic*, **6**, 359–63.

Lewis, David (1979). Scorekeeping in a language game. *Journal of Philosophical Logic*, **8**, 339–59.

Lewis, David (1986). *On the Plurality of Worlds*. Basil Blackwell, Oxford.

Linsky, Bernard and Zalta, Edward N. (1994). In defense of the simplest quantified modal logic. In *Philosophical Perspectives 8: Logic and Language* (ed. J. Tomberlin), pp. 431–58. Ridgeview, Atascadero, CA.

Linsky, Bernard and Zalta, Edward N. (1996). In defense of the contingently nonconcrete. *Philosophical Studies*, **84**, 283–94.

Loewer, Barry (1976). Counterfactuals with disjunctive antecedents. *Journal of Philosophy*, **73**, 531–37.

Lycan, William (1979). The trouble with possible worlds. In *The Possible and the Actual* (ed. M. J. Loux), pp. 274–316. Cornell University Press, Ithaca, NY.

Lycan, William (2001). *Real Conditionals*. Oxford University Press, Oxford.

MacFarlane, John (2005). Logical constants. *Stanford Encyclopedia of Philosophy*.

Marcus, Ruth Barcan (1946). A functional calculus of first order based on strict implication. *Journal of Symbolic Logic*, **11**, 1–16. Originally published under the name Ruth C. Barcan.

McDaniel, Kris (2009). Ways of being. In *Metametaphysics* (ed. D. Chalmers, D. Manley, and R. Wasserman), pp. 290–319. Oxford University Press, Oxford.

McGee, Vann and McLaughlin, Brian (1995). Distinctions without a difference. *Southern Journal of Philosophy*, **33 (Supp.)**, 203–51.

Mendelson, Elliott (1987). *Introduction to Mathematical Logic*. Wadsworth & Brooks, Belmont, CA.

Meyer, J.-J. Ch. (2001). Epistemic logic. In Goble (2001), pp. 183–202.

Plantinga, Alvin (1983). On existentialism. *Philosophical Studies*, **44**, 1–20.

Priest, Graham (1979). The logic of paradox. *Journal of Philosophical Logic*, **8**, 219–41.

Priest, Graham (2001). *An Introduction to Non-Classical Logic*. Cambridge University Press, Cambridge.

Prior, A. N. (1957). *Time and Modality*. Clarendon Press, Oxford.

Prior, A. N. (1967). *Past, Present, and Future*. Oxford University Press, Oxford.

Prior, A. N. (1968). *Papers on Time and Tense*. Oxford University Press, Oxford.

Quine, W. V. O. (1940). *Mathematical Logic*. Harvard University Press, Cambridge, MA.

Quine, W. V. O. (1948). On what there is. *Review of Metaphysics*, **2**, 21–38.

Quine, W. V. O. (1953a). Mr. Strawson on logical theory. *Mind*, **62**, 433–51.

Quine, W. V. O. (1953b). Reference and modality. In *From a Logical Point of View*, pp. 139–59. Harvard University Press, Cambridge, MA.

Quine, W. V. O. (1956). Quantifiers and propositional attitudes. *Journal of Philosophy*, **53**, 177–87.

Quine, W. V. O. (1960). Carnap and logical truth. *Synthese*, **12**, 350–74.

Quine, W. V. O. (1966). *The Ways of Paradox*. Random House, New York.

Restall, Greg (2000). *An Introduction to Substructural Logics*. Routledge, London.

Russell, Bertrand (1905). On denoting. *Mind*, 479–93.

Salmon, Nathan (1986). Modal paradox: Parts and counterparts, points and counterpoints. In French *et al.* (1986), pp. 75–120.

Sider, Theodore (2003). Reductive theories of modality. In *Oxford Handbook of Metaphysics* (ed. M. J. Loux and D. W. Zimmerman), pp. 180–208. Oxford University Press, Oxford.

Soames, Scott (2004). *Reference and Description: The Case against Two-Dimensionalism*. Princeton University Press, Princeton, NJ.

Stalnaker, Robert (1968). A theory of conditionals. In *Studies in Logical Theory:*

American Philosophical Quarterly Monograph Series, No. 2. Blackwell, Oxford.

Stalnaker, Robert (1977). Complex predicates. *The Monist*, **60**, 327–39.

Stalnaker, Robert (1978). Assertion. In *Syntax and Semantics, Volume 9: Pragmatics* (ed. P. Cole and J. Morgan), pp. 315–32. Academic Press, New York.

Stalnaker, Robert (1981). A defense of conditional excluded middle. In *Ifs: Conditionals, Belief, Decision, Chance, and Time* (ed. W. L. Harper, R. Stalnaker, and G. Pearce), pp. 87–104. D. Reidel, Dordrecht.

Stalnaker, Robert (2003). Conceptual truth and metaphysical necessity. In *Ways a World Might Be*, pp. 201–15. Oxford University Press, Oxford.

Stalnaker, Robert (2004). Assertion revisited: On the interpretation of two-dimensional modal semantics. *Philosophical Studies*, **118**, 299–322.

Turner, Jason (2010). Ontological pluralism. *Journal of Philosophy*. Forthcoming.

von Fintel, Kai (2001). Counterfactuals in a dynamic context. In *Ken Hale: A Life in Language*, pp. 123–52. MIT Press, Cambridge, MA.

Westerståhl, Dag (1989). Quantifiers in formal and natural languages. In *Handbook of Philosophical Logic* (ed. D. Gabbay and F. Guenther), Volume 4, pp. 1–131. Kluwer, Dordrecht.

Williamson, Timothy (1994). *Vagueness.* Routledge, London.

Williamson, Timothy (1998). Bare possibilia. *Erkenntnis*, **48**, 257–73.

Williamson, Timothy (1999*a*). A note on truth, satisfaction and the empty domain. *Analysis*, **59**, 3–8.

Williamson, Timothy (1999*b*). On the structure of higher-order vagueness. *Mind*, **108**, 127–144.

Williamson, Timothy (2002). Necessary existents. In *Logic, Thought and Language* (ed. A. O'Hear), pp. 233–51. Cambridge University Press, Cambridge.

Wright, Crispin (1992). *Truth and Objectivity.* Harvard University Press, Cambridge, MA.

INDEX